Private Fleming at
Chancellorsville

Shades of Blue and Gray Series

Edited by Herman Hattaway
and Jon L. Wakelyn

The Shades of Blue and Gray Series offers Civil War studies for the modern reader—Civil War buff and scholar alike. Military history today addresses the relationship between society and warfare. Thus biographies and thematic studies that deal with civilians, soldiers, and political leaders are increasingly important to a larger public. This series includes books that will appeal to Civil War Roundtable groups, individuals, libraries, and academics with a special interest in this era of American history.

Private Fleming at Chancellorsville

The Red Badge of Courage
and the Civil War

PERRY LENTZ

University of Missouri Press   Columbia and London

Library of Congress Cataloging-in-Publication Data

Lentz, Perry, 1943–
  Private Fleming at Chancellorsville : The red badge of courage and the
Civil War / Perry Lentz.
       p.   cm. — (Shades of blue and gray series)
  Includes bibliographical references and index.
  Summary: "Focusing on the exploits of Private Henry Fleming and his fellow
soldiers, Lentz's study of Stephen Crane's The Red Badge of Courage debunks
earlier criticism of the novel as impressionistic by proving, through a
close examination of war history, combat, and, specifically, the
Chancellorsville battle, its realistic founding"—Provided by publisher.
    ISBN-13: 978-0-8262-1654-0 (alk. paper)
    1. Crane, Stephen, 1871–1900. Red badge of courage. 2. War stories,
American—History and criticism. 3. United States—History—Civil War,
1861–1865—Literature and the war. 4. Chancellorsville, Battle of,
Chancellorsville, Va., 1863, in literature.   I. Title. II. Series.
  PS1449.C85R3955 2006
  813'.4—dc22
                                                                    2005036356

♾™ This paper meets the requirements of the
American National Standard for Permanence of Paper
for Printed Library Materials, Z39.48, 1984.

DESIGNER: KRISTIE LEE
TYPESETTER: CRANE COMPOSITION, INC.
PRINTER AND BINDER: THE MAPLE-VAIL BOOK MANUFACTURING GROUP
TYPEFACE: GOUDY OLDSTYLE

❧

The University of Missouri Press gratefully acknowledges the
support of Kenyon College in the publication of this book.

**Dedicated to the memory
of my parents**

Lucian Boyd Lentz
1920–1993

and

Carleton Sterne Lentz
1920–2001

Contents

Contents

Acknowledgments

**"He could perceive himself as
a very wee thing."**

My major indebtednesses are three. First, to Jack Finefrock: without his friendly, shrewd, generous, and persistent prodding, and without his astonishing expertise in all things having to do with publishing, this would yet remain in the electronic tomb in which it had been immured for a dozen years. Second, to my father, Lucian Lentz: a B-26 pilot in the Eighth Air Force, he spent twenty months as a prisoner of war in Stalag Luft III. Far from being alienated from the subject of war, he was fascinated. I grew up beneath *Lee's Lieutenants* and the green-bound histories of the operations of the U.S. Army during World War II. In the cool Alabama mornings of my childhood, while my father shaved and prepared to go to the mill, the two of us conversed about history. What was the derivation of the name "black and tans"? "The black of Irishmen's business suits," my father said, imaginatively, "and the tan of British soldiers' uniforms." Makes sense, doesn't it? Third, to those generations of Kenyon students who have studied American literature with me: their intelligence, their ability, their patience, their responsiveness, their papers, tests, and recitations—it was mostly through my long engagement with these students that I fully came to understand that the more deeply we trusted that Stephen Crane knew his history, the more deeply his novel repaid our attention.

I am further indebted to people who have contributed to the spirit, shape, reliability, and texture of this book. Tim Shutt gave it its first close reading, and

Will Scott gave me invaluable early encouragement. Hays Stone proofread its final version with unflagging good humor and unfailing professional precision. Chuck Leech proofread it with generous care and imagination. Barb Dupee with her legendary generosity of heart and spirit responded again and again to my numbskull questions and importunate requests.

Pippa Letsky's imaginative, intelligent, and indefatigable labors as copyeditor were of literally incalculable value. And of course my beloved wife, Jane, who patiently shared in the chore of verifying the accuracy of the book's rendition of Crane's prose, including its apple-knockers' eye-paralyzing dialect.

At a wider remove, there are my colleagues in the Department of English who have, for all the years of my professional life, embodied the American academy at its best. I hesitate to name any, for in truth I should name them all. But had it not been for the compassion and courage of David Lynn, Judy Smith, and Sergei Lobanov-Rostovksy, far more than this book would have been lost.

Private Fleming at
Chancellorsville

Introduction

The subtitle of Crane's famous novel is "An Episode of the American Civil War." Why? Why this subtitle in particular? Why not "An Episode of War"? According to eyewitnesses who in the scholarly world are unanimously considered reliable, Corwin Knapp Linson and R. G. Vosburgh, the only preparatory research Stephen Crane undertook for *The Red Badge of Courage* was to pore over old copies of the *Century Illustrated Magazine* containing articles from their series on "Battles and Leaders of the Civil War."[1] The September 1886 issue is devoted to the battle of Chancellorsville and contains five major articles and one speculative essay. All of this material is richly illustrated with steel engravings. There are portraits of commanders, line drawings of military equipment, scenes of soldiers either in camp (a Pennsylvania regiment aligned on parade) or on campaign (cavalrymen scouting, infantry columns crossing pontoon bridges at night). Holding pride of place in the magazine are the compelling pictures, steel engravings of defining moments in the battle—vital pictures, convincingly realistic down to the gleam of leather crossbelts and the texture of the uniforms. The primitive state of photography in the 1860s prevented cameramen from recording infantrymen in combat. These engravings are as convincing as photographs but they are even more vivid, because they are rendered by artists in tranquility

1. Stanley Wertheim and Paul Sorrentino, *The Crane Log: A Documentary Life of Stephen Crane, 1871–1900*, 89, 94.

1

rather than (as today) by cameramen themselves at hazard. One engraving shows the rout of the Eleventh Corps. Another shows one-armed General O. O. Howard, rallying his men, managing his horse with his left hand, an American flag pressed under the stump of his right arm. Another shows a twilight scene, with Federal artillery repulsing rebel infantry whose surge is just visible beyond the muzzle blasts of the cannon. Another engraving shows wounded men being rescued from brush fires in the Wilderness.

Let us consider the prose surrounding any one of these engravings—the prose surrounding, say, one that shows fleeing artillerymen, lashing their gun teams for more speed, and panicking infantrymen, one of them caparisoned in a Zouave's uniform, and an officer trying to arrest the rout with drawn saber and pistol. The prose? "The position of the army at Chancellorsville extended about three miles from east to west in the narrow clearings, which did not offer sufficient ground to maneuver an army of the size of the army of the Potomac. Besides this, we were ignorant of what might be going on outside the cordon of woods, and were giving the enemy every opportunity to take us at a disadvantage." The gap, the yawning chasm, between evocative, richly detailed picture and sterile generalizing prose is stunning—and inviting. The space of this gap was the space in which Crane's imagination formed his novel.[2]

The Red Badge of Courage is set firmly within the American Civil War. Its men are dressed, organized, arrayed, commanded, maneuvered, and above all armed as soldiers in the American Civil War were dressed, organized, arrayed, commanded, maneuvered, and armed. They are armed, to be specific, with muzzle-loading rifled muskets (see Chapter 2). This dictated a kind of combat particular to that time, the mid-1860s, and that place, the North American continent, where, for the first time in the history of warfare, two combatant nations were each able to outfit all their infantrymen with these weapons. The more readers know about the American Civil War, the more they can appreciate Crane's depiction of "An Episode" within it. Far more, indeed, is involved. The more readers know about the Civil War, the more powerfully Crane's novel will work upon their own perceptions of reality.

During the course of the long and rewarding career I have spent offering instruction in American literature to students at Kenyon College, each year when we turned our attention to The Red Badge of Courage, I would seek to explain these military circumstances. Over the span of thirty-five years, I found myself explaining more and more. Each year I reread the novel itself and frequently dis-

2. Alfred Pleasonton, "The Successes and Failures of the Chancellorsville Campaign."

covered something new. For example, about twenty years ago on about my fif-teenth rereading, I realized that the entire battle on the second day had been ac-complished by the noon hour. Each year I rewrote my lectures, reconceived my approach to discussions, and reconsidered my attitudes in light of student re-sponses. I discovered that the more extensive my research, in order to better ex-plain the military realities in which the novel is set, the more the novel proved capable of sustaining even the most detailed historical scrutiny, the richer and more expansive became the experience of rereading it, and the richer and more expansive became (I think—it is always possible for a professor to delude himself about this) my students' responses. I have read over two thousand student pro-lusions concerning *The Red Badge of Courage*, from research papers to single-page recitations, which prove a resource that is endlessly revivifying and informing.

During these decades I also continued to read the secondary literature on Crane. *The Red Badge of Courage* is as accessible as any of the works in our na-tional literature canon. Yet critical response has been extraordinarily uncer-tain—and particularly so on the seemingly self-evident issue of its hero's (repeatedly proclaimed) development into "manhood" during the course of his battlefield experiences (see Chapter 9). Several pieces of criticism were informa-tive and stimulating, others less so, but their persuasiveness did not at all divide along the lines of the various scholars' commitment to or repudiation of the theory that Crane's hero became a "man" because of his initiation into combat. Rather, the more the scholar knew about the Civil War the more persuasive the book or article and the more able its treatment of Crane's text.

This book presents a reading of *The Red Badge of Courage* that incorporates the facts of its historical setting into a close literary consideration of how the novel works upon a reader's imagination. Crane's novel, read accurately and imaginatively, can genuinely enrich a reader's understanding of human reality in general and of historical reality in particular. In Matthew Arnold's famous formulation, the proper function of criticism is "to see the object as in itself it really is."[3] I believe that bringing together the fields of historical and literary in-quiry will enable readers to see Crane's great novel as in itself it really is.

The central endeavor of this book is to see the *Red Badge of Courage* accu-rately, and to display its qualities through a close reading. The study relies upon the edition of *The Red Badge* that Crane himself shepherded through galley

3. Matthew Arnold, "The Function of Criticism at the Present Time," 1.

proofs into print, and which he himself would have taken pride in seeing in a bookseller's shop. This is the Appleton edition of 1895. In 1983, Henry Binder published a version of *The Red Badge of Courage* in which he reinstated some portions of the 1894 manuscript that Crane himself had deleted. Binder's supposition, powerfully supported by Hershel Parker, was that editorial prudishness at Appleton had compelled Crane to make these deletions. For about a decade the Binder edition held pride of place, and although it has since taken a critical and scholarly drubbing, it still remains in print. There is no need to add to the magisterial arguments against the Binder edition and the suppositions upon which it is based, but it is worth recalling the matter, because it focuses attention upon Crane's genuinely extraordinary literary achievement.[4] Through editing his initial materials with shrewd intelligence and imaginative insight, a process that clearly (and appropriately) involved consultation with his editors, Crane published a novel of surprising, almost underhanded, effectiveness: a flamboyant, immature, impressionistic style rests upon a subtle, sophisticated, mature structure. The book works upon us in unexpected and rewarding ways through which we may come to understand some things about ourselves as in ourselves we really are. But we can experience and appreciate these ways only by reading the book as in itself it really is.

The style of the current work warrants a word of explanation. Following the practice in the overwhelming majority of works of fiction, Crane wrote *The Red Badge of Courage* in the past tense: "The cold passed reluctantly from the earth and the retiring fogs revealed an army stretched out on the hills, resting."[5] The overwhelming majority of historical documents and works are, likewise, written in the past tense: "Three color-bearers were here shot down in succession, but the colors never touched the ground."[6] The ironclad convention in literary criticism, however, is to use the present tense: for example, "In the autumn of 1862, Henry Fleming had withdrawn from school and, defying his widowed mother's arguments, left their New York dairy farm to enlist in the company forming in a nearby town. On the morning of May 2, 1863, he finds himself in a line of battle advancing through the part of northern Virginia known as the Wilderness of

---

4. See especially James Colvert, "Crane, Hitchcock, and the Binder Edition of *The Red Badge of Courage*." This magisterial study closes the matter.

5. Stephen Crane, *The Red Badge of Courage: An Episode of the American Civil War*, 1. All quotations are taken from the Appleton 1895 edition. Subsequent references will given parenthetically in the text as *RBC*.

6. U.S. Department of War, *The War of the Rebellion: Official Records of the Union and Confederate Armies*, vol. 25, part 1, no. 163. All subsequent references to this volume will be given parenthetically in the text, as *OR* with report number (not page number).

Spotsylvania. Alongside him on this May morning are two other fictional enlisted men from that company, John Wilson and Jim Conklin, with whom he has shared a hut during the army's winter encampment." In this book, I will use the past tense in offering historical material. In dealing with Crane's fiction, I will use the present tense, working forward and backward (as in the example above) from the moment at hand.

Chapter 1 sets out in detail the historical framework within which Crane, with precision, placed his fictional characters and formations. It presents facts and conjectures about the historical research he undertook to accomplish this precision. First the chapter locates exactly where, in the landscape of the American Civil War, his fictional characters are placed, explaining why Crane would have researched this framework and considering the materials available to his research. The next section of the chapter is intended to be of particular use to anyone teaching the novel. It provides historical information about Civil War soldiers and about the basic formations—of company, regiment, and brigade—in which they were organized, before moving on to consider higher levels of military organization, the division and the corps, and explaining why I believe Crane's soldiers are set in the Third Division of the Second Corps of the Army of the Potomac during the Chancellorsville campaign. The chapter next explains, at some length, how details in the novel and in the historical record strongly suggest that Crane undertook research in the great multivolume work generally known as *The Official Records of the War of Rebellion,* which is the mother lode for Civil War research. The chapter concludes with a reiteration of points stressed throughout this book: that Crane's fictional characters are facing a particular kind of infantry combat, and that it is critically necessary to know something about this particular kind of combat in order to understand their experience and to judge their conduct.

Chapter 2 expands the historical focus, to explain how infantry combat of the particular kind depicted in *The Red Badge of Courage* actually came about. For much of the century before the American Civil War, the ordinary infantryman's weapon was the flintlock smoothbore, and because of the virtues and limitations of that weapon, the attacking side most often ruled the field of battle. Napoleon Bonaparte's ascendancy was based upon his capacity to seize the initiative at every level of war-making, from the swiftness of his strategic maneuvering to the swarms of skirmishers preceding his advancing infantry. In the decades immediately preceding the Civil War, however, progress in metalworking enabled Western nations to reequip their infantrymen with percussion rifles, and the superior range of these weapons changed the face of battle. Commanders schooled in Napoleonic doctrines struggled to readjust to a murderous new reality, and the tactical advantage on the field passed, dramatically, to the side that could deploy in a defensive array.

Chapter 3 places Private Henry Fleming and his fellow soldiers of the 304th New York Volunteer Infantry Regiment in the historical realities of Civil War infantry combat on the afternoon of May 2, 1863. The chapter focuses upon Private Fleming's unusual qualities of character, as he approaches his first experience of combat. It shows how fully his actions and those of his comrades can be envisioned and how clearly (and perhaps surprisingly) they can be assessed, once a reader understands the historical realities of battle in the Civil War in general, and the battle on this portion of the Chancellorsville field in particular.

The focus of the book changes in Chapter 4, which studies Crane's evocation of Civil War battle in literary rather than historical terms. The first three chapters were essentially concerned with establishing an awareness of historical realities in order to enhance a reader's response to Crane's novel. The intention in Chapter 4 is to set about establishing an equivalent literary awareness. This chapter develops around a close stylistic examination of the paragraphs in the novel that evoke Private Fleming's first experience of combat on the afternoon of May 2, 1863, and it uses other fictions, rather than historical records, to understand what Crane has accomplished and how his style works upon a reader's mind and imagination.

If readers are to understand the rest of Private Fleming's career during these two days of battle, one severe and almost ubiquitous misreading must be addressed directly. This is the subject of Chapter 5. Private Henry Fleming is a very unusual soldier, but over the last half century, he has come to be regarded as entirely, even wearisomely typical. This chapter shows that significant aspects of Crane's novel vanish if this conception is imposed upon it. The chapter argues that this misreading is the result of the effect of World War I upon modern literary theory on the one hand, and upon the portrayal of war in modern fiction, film, and drama on the other.[7]

Chapter 6 returns to the close reading of Private Henry Fleming's story, following him through his desertion on the afternoon of May 2, 1863, and his wanderings and experiences thereafter, and using the historical record to explain exactly what he is witnessing. This chapter continues to examine the novel's

---

7. Throughout this book, the titles of novels will be given in italics, whereas the titles of films and plays will be given in quotation marks: *All Quiet on the Western Front* is the novel, for example, and "All Quiet on the Western Front" is the movie.

unusual literary power, studying the way Crane uses readers' expectations to entangle them in the crucial issue of how, and whether, Fleming develops during his ordeal. The question of the hero's development is central in the critical response to *The Red Badge of Courage*, and the chapter surveys this critical response, illustrating that—in both the published criticism and a reader's individual response—the novel repeatedly evokes a set of very familiar expectations and yet almost simultaneously challenges or baffles them.

Chapter 7 studies Private Fleming's perceptions of himself and his situation after his return to the 304th New York. The chapter explains the strategic situation facing the combatant armies in the early morning hours of May 3, 1863, and argues that Private Fleming's solipsistic cast of mind makes the battle of Chancellorsville a particularly evocative historical setting for his story. The chapter shows how studying Fleming's mentality may reflect some light upon the crucial decision taken by General Joe Hooker himself during those early hours.

Chapter 8 continues the close examination of Private Fleming, this time in terms of the tactical situation in the center-right sector of the Union army following Hooker's decision to withdraw his forces from the Wilderness. It presents the historical reality of combat in that sector and demonstrates how precisely the experience of Crane's fictional regiment corresponds to that reality. The chapter shows how an awareness of that historical reality and an alertness to the subtleties of Crane's fiction enable a reader to evaluate, with some sophistication, the conduct of Fleming and his regiment during this morning's action.

The Red Badge of Courage concludes with Private Fleming's assessment of himself as having become a "man." Chapter 9 of this book places that assessment in the context of our close, historically informed reading of the novel. Its first substantial portion examines the similar self-assessment that the 304th New York had earlier rendered upon itself; its second portion examines Private Fleming's own self-assessment. In evaluating these self-assessments, a reader becomes aware that unconscious assumptions about our relationship to the universe are inextricably involved, as well as unconscious assumptions about what constitutes "manhood."

Chapter 10 considers whether Crane's novel is "prowar" or "antiwar." Answering this question directs us once again into a study of underlying yet unconscious assumptions—or perhaps "myths"—about the effect of combat upon men. This chapter explains why Crane repeatedly entices readers into imposing their own assumptions, about the probable course of an individual's experience, about the human predicament in the universe, and about the effects of combat, upon the experiences of Fleming and his fellow infantrymen.

"Literature as mousetrap" is this book's awkward definition, advanced in Chapter 11, for this unusual strategy of enticement. By enticing his readers into imposing their own unconscious assumptions—or myths—upon the chaos of existence, Crane shows exactly how powerful is the human tendency to use such myths to impose some sense of order, no matter how dire, upon chaos. Despite repeated disappointments and despite steadily accumulating evidence, Crane's readers typically persist in imposing their presuppositions—about the nature of reality, about the nature of "manhood," about the effect of combat on young men—upon the narrative. Readers themselves thus exemplify this peculiarly human tendency, which is one of the profound subjects of Crane's novel. Chapter 11 locates similarly devised fictional narratives from elsewhere in American literature, in particular from Flannery O'Connor and from Herman Melville, in order to render Crane's employment of this (very unusual) strategy more clearly defined.

The Conclusion isolates the particular brilliance of Crane's novel by comparing it to a book with which it has many clear affinities, Leo Tolstoy's *Sebastopol Sketches*. Despite obvious similarities in the way the two works apprehend war, Crane's narrative strategy achieves a vividly different and distinct impact. In Crane's book not only are truths about mid-nineteenth-century warfare powerfully rendered, but profound truths about human nature are effectively brought into the imaginative lives of its readers. Crane's novel has that effect, though, only if a reader is capable of seeing it as in itself it really is. Such capability depends, in turn, upon an awareness of the historical realities upon which Crane, with researched accuracy, established his book.

Chapter 1

Crane's Fiction and Crane's Research

In the autumn of 1862, Henry Fleming had withdrawn from school and, defying his widowed mother's arguments, left their New York dairy farm to enlist in the company forming in a nearby town. On the morning of May 2, 1863, he finds himself in a line of battle advancing through the part of northern Virginia known as the Wilderness of Spotsylvania. Alongside him on this May morning are two other fictional enlisted men from that company, John Wilson and Jim Conklin, with whom he has shared a hut during the army's winter encampment. The terrain through which they are now advancing is dense in underbrush, saplings, and second-growth pine, matted unevenly with marshy "runs," traversed by few roads, and giving few vistas.

Fleming, Wilson, and Conklin are private soldiers in a center company of their regiment. Their company's second in command is the fictional Lieutenant Hasbrouck. The name of the captain commanding the company is not given. He will be dead in a matter of hours.

The company is one of ten comprising the fictional 304th New York Volunteer Infantry Regiment, under the command of fictional Colonel MacChesnay. The 304th is one of the regiments in the fictional "Grandpa" Henderson's brigade. It is raw and untested, but at least two of Henderson's other regiments are veterans (*RBC* 205).

The number of the division to which Henderson's brigade belongs is not given, nor is the name of the general commanding it, although these private soldiers know him on sight: he is General William French, a historical figure who in fact commanded a Federal division on operations in the Wilderness of Spotsylvania on the morning of May 2, 1863. The corps to which this division belongs is likewise not named in *The Red Badge of Courage*, but it is clearly the historical Second Corps, commanded by the historical General Darius Couch.

This corps was one of the seven that, along with cavalry and supporting formations, constituted the Army of the Potomac, under the command of Major General Joseph Hooker. Fleming and his fellows will soon be engaged in combat with Confederate soldiers from Major General Lafayette MacLaws's division of the Army of Northern Virginia, commanded by General R. E. Lee.[1]

Two of Lee's divisions, under the command of Lieutenant General James Longstreet, had been absent on operations in southeastern Virginia since mid-February. This reduction of the strength of the Army of Northern Virginia determined Hooker to undertake an offensive. His plan of campaign was brilliant, his logistical arrangements innovative and effective, and except for the blundering of his cavalry, his army's deployment had been flawless. Lee was outnumbered, as usual, but he had also been outmaneuvered. A substantial portion of Hooker's army had appeared to his rear, and in overwhelming strength. Lee had to divide his depleted army even further and had spent much of the previous day, May 1, rushing troops toward the Wilderness to face this altogether unexpected threat.

Hooker had placed his forces precisely where and when he intended, but his nerve was starting to crack. Given his huge superiority in men and artillery, the tangled Wilderness was no place for him to fight a battle. He should have cleared it as soon as possible and reached the open landscape beyond, where he could bring his superior numbers into play. The previous afternoon his two leading corps had pushed well out of the Wilderness onto separate, built-up roads, before encountering significant rebel formations. The commanders of these corps had asked for reinforcements so they could continue their thus far

---

1. The overview that follows is based upon Vincent J. Esposito et al., *The West Point Atlas of American Wars*, vol. 1, maps 84–91, and Jay Luvaas and Harold W. Nelson, *The U.S. Army War College Guide to the Battles of Chancellorsville and Fredericksburg*, in which passages from the *Official Records* and other historical sources constitute most of the narrative and are keyed to the maps. The literature about the Chancellorsville campaign is vast. Among the best narrative histories are Edward J. Stackpole, *Chancellorsville: Lee's Greatest Battle, Second Edition*; Bruce Catton, *Glory Road: The Bloody Route from Fredericksburg to Gettysburg*; Stephen W. Sears, *Chancellorsville*; Richard Wheeler, *Lee's Terrible Swift Sword: From Antietam to Chancellorsville, an Eyewitness History*; Ernest B. Furgurson, *Chancellorsville, 1863: The Souls of the Brave*; Edward G. Longacre, *The Commanders of Chancellorsville: The Gentleman versus the Rogue*. The relevant portions of *Battles and Leaders* and the *Official Records* have not only formed part of the subject of this book but have informed my understanding of the campaign.

entirely successful advances, but Hooker instead had ordered them to retire, so as to concentrate his forces in an enclave arrayed on the defensive. This concentration brought them back into that daunting terrain.

General Hooker's decision dismayed his senior commanders who found it inexplicable, though the rank and file, not recognizing what was happening to their campaign, still admired him. By the second morning, though, most of them who are still alive will agree with Private Henry Fleming's assessment: "Now, I'd like to know what the eternal thunders we was marched into these woods for anyhow, unless it was to give the rebs a regular pot shot at us. We came in here and got our legs all tangled up in these cussed briers, and then we begin to fight and the rebs had an easy time of it" (*RBC* 160–61). But this will be Fleming's opinion tomorrow morning. At this moment nearing the noon hour on May 2, he has quite other things on his mind.

If Hooker's boldness had deserted him, this was not at all the case with R. E. Lee. Although his 55,000 remaining rebels faced over 130,000 Federal soldiers, at dawn that morning he had yet again divided his army and had sent General Thomas J. Jackson with 30,000 of them on a twelve-mile march that would circle Hooker's army and fall altogether unexpectedly, at about 6 o'clock that evening, upon its exposed right flank. The result was Lee's most brilliant and most costly victory, which would come to be known as the battle of Chancellorsville.[2]

Crane's Research

From mid-autumn of 1892 to the early summer of 1893, unable to find a regular position as a journalist and living a hand-to-mouth existence as a freelance writer, Stephen Crane shared a rooming house with medical students on Avenue A near Fifty-seventh Street in Manhattan. In the early spring of 1893, he spent hours lounging in the studio of his friend Corwin Knapp Linson, reading through old copies of the *Century Magazine* from a famous series entitled "Battles and Leaders of the Civil War," which had run in the magazine from 1884 to 1887. This much is established fact. Crane's important but unreliable biographer, Thomas Beer, wrote that Crane then borrowed a set of "books" also entitled "the *Century's* 'Battles and Leaders,'" sending them back on April 2 with a note thanking the lender for the loan of "the books," which, however, "won't tell me

---

2. Harold R. Hungerford, "'That Was at Chancellorsville': The Factual Framework of *The Red Badge of Courage*." Although the battle of Chancellorsville was always widely assumed to be the basis for Crane's novel, Hungerford's essay was of seminal importance in confirming the fact. I will diverge considerably from significant portions of Hungerford's argument, so an interested reader should consult his article, which is often (and deservedly) reprinted.

what I want to know so I must do it all over again I guess." This book-borrowing incident does not, alas, pass muster with the meticulous authors of *The Crane Log*, but it is worth defining what "books" were putatively involved. In November 1887, the *Century Magazine* pulled together the illustrations and articles from the "Battles and Leaders" series, added an equal number of new articles, and amplified the whole with maps, orders of battle, footnotes, and the like, to issue all of this together as a four-volume set of books entitled *Battles and Leaders of the Civil War*.[3]

To return to what is certain: in the early summer of 1893 while he was living a Bohemian life among cheap Manhattan tenements and studios, Crane began composing the book that would eventually be entitled *The Red Badge of Courage*. He was engaged upon this throughout the summer, his city-pent labors occasionally refreshed by extended visits to his brother's home in Lake View, New Jersey. In the early autumn, Crane moved into the Art Students' League Building on East Twenty-third Street, and there he finally completed the rough draft of the novel. One of his three roommates, R. G. Vosburgh, gives an eyewitness account of Crane amid his sources:

> For seven or eight months, from one autumn until the following summer, the four men lived together. It was during that time that *The Red Badge of Courage* was written. At the time he came to live in the studio, Crane was reading over the descriptive articles on the Civil War published in the *Century*. War and fighting were always deeply interesting to him. . . . . The articles in the *Century*, then, were full of interest and fascination for Crane, and when he moved to the studio on Twenty-third street he borrowed the magazines and took them with him to read and study. All of his knowledge of the war and of the country depicted in *The Red Badge of Courage* was gathered from those articles and from the study of maps of that region. . . . . Crane spent his afternoons and evenings studying the war and discussing his stories.[4]

3. Wertheim and Sorrentino, *Crane Log*, 69, 89; Robert U. Johnson and Clarence C. Buel, eds., *Battles and Leaders of the Civil War: Being for the Most Part Contributions by Union and Confederate Officers*, 1:ix; Thomas Beer, *Stephen Crane: A Study in American Letters*, 97–98; Wertheim and Sorrentino, *Crane Log*, xviii–xix. In Robert W. Stallman's monumental *Stephen Crane: A Biography*, the account of Crane's research is infected by Stallman's reliance upon the now discredited Beer. I do not believe scholars adequately understand the considerable difference between the material on the battle of Chancellorsville that appears in the *Century Magazine* series "Battles and Leaders" and the far more extensive material that appears in the four-volume book edition *Battles and Leaders*. See, for example, J. C. Levenson, "*The Red Badge of Courage* and *McTeague*," 175n11; James B. Colvert, *Stephen Crane*, 53; Joseph Katz, "Introduction," viii.

4. Wertheim and Sorrentino, *Crane Log*, 69, 92, 94.

But one of the novel's preeminent scholars states, "What Crane read is harder to establish than what he was writing."[5] I believe that Crane must have carried his research much further. The *Century* addressed the battle of Chancellorsville in its September 1886 issue, which consists of just five essays and a single map. The pieces themselves are variously and narrowly focused and quite partisan (understandably). There is the losing general's account of things in "Chancellorsville Revisited by General Hooker," and an essay upon "Jackson's Attack Upon the Eleventh Corps" by General O. O. Howard, whose division was virtually destroyed by that event. (Howard's profound concern with abolition, freedmen's issues, and African American soldiers in the U.S. Army would be memorialized in the name of the nation's preeminent black college.) There is a speculative essay upon "Lee's Knowledge of Hooker's Movements" and an account of "Sedgwick's Assault at Fredericksburg," which took place at some remove from the battlefield Private Fleming is just now tentatively entering. Finally, and accompanied by the *Century*'s only map of the campaign, there is an essay, "The Successes and Failures of Chancellorsville," by the ineffable General Alfred Pleasanton, a figure who was remarkably ludicrous in his own day for the unreliability of his reports and the constant drumbeat therein of his self-promotion.[6]

The steel engravings accompanying these pieces are dramatic and imaginatively stimulating, and there is a great deal of equally stimulating general worth in other issues of the magazine. But nothing in this material has anything to do with the sector of the battle in which Private Fleming will be engaged. Vosburgh says Crane studied "maps of that region," but there is only one in the *Century*'s Chancellorsville issue. What other maps was he studying? And what else could he have spent his "afternoons and evenings" studying for those "seven or eight months"?

The account of the battle of Chancellorsville in the four-volume edition of *Battles and Leaders* is much longer. It includes a study of "The Chancellorsville Campaign" by Major General Darius Couch (see below). There are footnoted rejoinders to Pleasonton, and four accounts of the experience of the Eighth Pennsylvania Cavalry (see Chapter 6). An Ohio gunner gives a brief account of "The Artillery at Hazel Grove," which Private Fleming is destined to see. There is an account of "Stonewall Jackson's Last Battle" by a rebel chaplain, and an account of "Hooker's Appointment and Removal" by a staff officer who "occupied

---

5. J. C. Levenson, "Introduction," xxxviii.
6. Stephen W. Sears, *Chancellorsville*, 502–3.

responsible and confidential positions at the headquarters of the Army of the Potomac and in the War Department." Footnotes fill up most of the pages. There is an order of battle, listing in detail and giving casualty returns for "The Opposing Forces in the Chancellorsville Campaign." There are three more maps of the campaign, of which two are of remarkably particular focus and will be immediately relevant to Fleming's upcoming experience this evening. One of these shows the "Position of the 11th Corps at 6 p.m., May 2, 1863"; the other shows how the Federal forces will be defensively arrayed during that night and into the morning of May 3. All of this material would have been of incalculable value to the "studying" Crane did in his preparation for, or in tandem with, his composition of this novel based upon the battle of Chancellorsville.[7]

Where then might Crane have gained access to this set of expensive books? New York City was served during these months by two libraries, the Astor and the Lenox. The Astor was on Lafayette Street, between East Fourth and Astor Place; the Lenox was on East Seventieth, between Madison and Fifth. Although books from the first did not circulate and access to the second was limited, both libraries were famous sources for research and intellectual stimulation. By May 1895, they would be combined into a single institution, the New York Public Library.[8] It seems probable to me that Crane used one or both of these libraries to continue his research. And, if he found his way to the folio-sized four volumes of *Battles and Leaders*, in one of these libraries, why would he not have sought further along its shelves?

Even with the far greater amount of information available in the four-volume edition of *Battles and Leaders*, its coverage of the battle of Chancellorsville is still not particularly informative about the quadrant of the battle in which Private Fleming will soon receive his baptism of fire. In General Darius Couch's article surveying "The Chancellorsville Campaign," there are only two sentences that bear upon the action on the afternoon of May 2 in the Second Corps's sector. General Couch offers nothing further, nor is there a single sentence to be found anywhere else in *Battles and Leaders* about the action on this specific front.

An intelligent argument holds that the experiences of Private Fleming and the 304th are closely based upon the experience of the 124th New York Infantry and thus can be located with some precision on the Third Corps's portion of the front, that is, facing to the south rather than to the east of positions held by

7. Johnson and Buel, *Battles and Leaders*, 3:239. All subsequent references will be given parenthetically in the text as *BL*.

8. History of the New York Public Library, http://www.nypl.org/pr/history.

the portion of the Army of the Potomac that was operating in the Wilderness this May morning. But Couch's account of that part of the battle does not accord at all with what Fleming and his regiment will experience: "Sickles [this is General Daniel Sickles, the sometimes disastrously flamboyant commander of the Third Corps] received orders at 1 p.m. to take two divisions, move to his front and attack, which he did, capturing some hundreds of prisoners" (*BL* 3:163). The experience of Crane's fictional regiment will be quite different.

In the libraries, just a shelf or two past *Battles and Leaders*, however, Crane could have found the 128 volumes of the U.S. War Department's *War of the Rebellion: Official Records of the Union and Confederate Armies*. The compilation of these records was established by act of Congress in 1874, and sets of them were distributed throughout the nation by an act of Congress in 1882: "Eight thousand three hundred copies shall be sent by the Secretary of War to such libraries, organizations, and individuals as may be designated by the Senators, Representatives, and Delegates of the Forty-seventh Congress." The volume containing the after-action reports of the Chancellorsville campaign, volume 25, was published in 1889 (*OR* iii).

—⁂—

"Research" of any sort at all is hardly a self-evident fact about *The Red Badge of Courage*. At first encounter, the novel's impressionistic style instantly befogs the reader's understanding, and the landscape through which its hero journeys and the scenes of battle he witnesses seem random and chaotic. The novel seems a purely imaginative projection. But Stephen Crane was not a veteran of combat, and yet thousands of Civil War veterans were still alive while he was composing his "Episode" of that war. Consider the challenges thus facing him.

He would desire to keep his principal characters and the officers and units named in the book free from possible association with any "real" soldiers, officers, and units. Suppose there really had been a Federal junior officer named Hasbrouck at the battle of Chancellorsville, or a colonel or brigadier general named Saunders who really had commanded a brigade or a regiment? To avoid such unintended associations, Crane would be compelled to seek the most detailed and most reliable indexes, rosters, and orders of battle currently accessible. There are no such things offered in the *Century* magazines. They are indeed available in *Battles and Leaders*, but in minute print. The only index is in the fourth volume and is limited to names and formations listed in the edition's quite varied selection of essays and articles. On the other hand, tables of battle occupy page after page of the *Official Records*, and they are authoritatively detailed.

And each *OR* volume offers two massive indexes, one for all the men named in the volume and the other for all organizations mentioned. In such extraordinary reference material, the name of an individual or of a unit (a name such as Saunders, for instance) could be sought with both alphabetical ease and entire confidence.

Crane would also have desired to be as accurate as possible in portraying his hero's experience. He would have wanted to avoid any obvious blunders, such as depicting soldiers marching farther than physically possible, enduring combat for an implausible amount of time, being fed or sheltered on a campaign in inaccurate ways. The best way to avoid such errors, to assure that the basic historical details of his fiction were accurate and persuasive, would have been to select an actual battle, with the actual Federal formations that participated in it, and to place his fictional soldiers and units into these, thus building his fictional narrative within a framework of historical fact.

The problem of actually specifying historical moments and historical figures and units would still remain, of course. To do so would risk causing offense or, worse, deflecting a reader's attention from the fiction to the historical fact ("General French? Didn't he go on to ruin the Third Corps?" and so on). How detailed could the historical framework be, then, without the need to identify "real" historical facts in his fiction?

Private soldiers engaged in a battle would be altogether ignorant of the name by which it eventually would be known. And it was not at all necessary for Crane to show his private soldiers thinking or talking about the corps or the division to which they belonged. It would not be at all discordant or a violation of the probable and ordinary for such never to arise in their thinking or in their conversation. For the Civil War soldier, the regiment was the formation that engaged his identity and esteem. In some rare and special cases, his self-identification may have extended to the brigade, such as in the Stonewall Brigade or the Iron Brigade, but the "division" as a particular locus of a soldier's pride and identification was a development of the great world wars of the twentieth century.[9] So, in Crane's novel, his soldiers think often of their regiment—and once, wistfully, of their slain brigadier, "Grandpa" Henderson. But beyond these fictional and explicitly named formations (single entities amid the welter of many hundreds of regiments and many scores of brigades in the main Union field army in the

---

9. R. Ernest Dupuy, *A Compact History of the United States Army,* 224; Philip R. N. Katcher, *The Army of the Potomac,* 7; Michael P. Musick, "The Little Regiment: Civil War Units and Commands."

eastern theater of operations), the framing historical facts of battle, army, corps, and division are not explicitly designated in the novel itself.

Thus, by focusing upon only the experience of ordinary soldiers and their company officers, Crane felt himself free to select, from the historical record, the specific battle and the major formations in it that would best serve his fiction. Here, too, the *Official Records* volumes constitute the perfect source. The records of the Union armies' campaigns are arranged by corps and descend down the chain of command. In other words, Crane would have found himself presented first with a given corps commander's official report of a campaign, then with the report of the commander of the first division of that corps, then with the official report of the officer commanding the first brigade of that division, and then with the reports of each separate regimental commander in that brigade. His eye would then carry him back up to the official report of the commander of the second brigade of that same division of that same corps, and so on. It is a mass of rich, if unevenly detailed, material reporting the experiences of scores of brigades and hundreds of individual regiments—the reports out of which he could begin fashioning his story of a private soldier in the (fictional) Henderson's brigade and the (fictional) 304th New York Volunteers, all framed rigidly within the larger patterns of the formations (corps, division, brigade) above them.

On this matter, one crucial final note: although I claim that Crane may have carried his research much further than is normally noted, this does not mean I believe Crane expended treasures of time and energy on the task. He need hardly have surveyed a very great deal of the massive OR volume 25, part 1, *Reports: Operations in Northern Virginia, West Virginia, Maryland, and Pennsylvania, Jan. 26–June 3, 1863; Chancellorsville.* In fact, its very size would have simplified his research. Crane was surely interested in the experience of the 124th New York Infantry Regiment, and in five minutes he could have found his way to the two-page report of its colonel, A. Van Horne Ellis (OR 163). Colonel Ellis's report is embedded in five pages of reports concerning the brigade under which the 124th served, which themselves constitute a third of the fifteen pages of reports from the formations in the Third Division of the Third Corps. Crane could have read all this material in half an hour, and then, having chosen the historical corps (the Second) and division (French's Third) into which to insert his fictional formations (the 304th New York Infantry Regiment, of Henderson's brigade), he could also have easily found his way to the clutch of reports most immediately relevant to his project.

Nor would he have needed to digest a great deal of factual material from that particular clutch. Crane was not a historian, nor was he embarked upon a historical project. He was already steeped in the reminiscences of veterans, in popular writings about the Civil War, and in his own imaginative lucubrations.[10] In conducting focused research into more recondite sources and perhaps even into these *Official Records*, he was under no compulsion to secure therefrom any historical precision. He was looking only for details. Germane to this is the nature of Crane's own relatively indifferent career as a journalist. To this point in mid-1893, he had only written "sketches," for the *New York Herald Tribune*. His relish for the telling visual detail is apparent in his sketch of the "average summer guest" at Asbury Park, "a rather portly man, with a good watch-chain and a business suit of clothes, and about three children," and in another, of the parade of the Junior Order of United American Mechanics: "The procession was composed of men, bronzed, slope-shouldered, uncouth." These pieces show no interest at all in the facts, the backgrounds, the aspirations, or the economic realities undergirding such people's lives. In researching his novel, he would have been looking not to accumulate or validate facts but to seize upon catalyzing details.[11]

To compare much lesser things to great: my own effort to give fictional embodiment to the Fort Pillow episode in the Civil War received considerable praise for its (seeming) historical accuracy and for the (putative) depth of the research that produced it. This praise remains gratifying to my vanity, but it is not entirely deserved. I spent perhaps four or five hours securing, reading, and taking brief notes from the apposite volume of the *Official Records*. Given Crane's much greater imaginative resources, he would surely have needed even less time with the volume relevant to his selected battle. A few mornings in a library reading room would quite probably have sufficed.

Company, Regiment, Brigade

Of all the formations to which he belonged, it was the regiment, identified by number and state (Tenth Alabama, for instance, or Fourth Ohio), that gave the Civil War infantryman or cavalryman his essential identity. When Henderson's

10. Charles J. LaRocca, "Stephen Crane's Inspiration"; Lyndon U. Pratt, "A Possible Source of *The Red Badge of Courage*"; H. T. Webster, "Wilbur F. Hinman's *Corporal Si Klegg* and *The Red Badge of Courage*." See also Patrick K. Dooley, "*The Red Badge of Courage*," in *Stephen Crane: An Annotated Bibliography of Secondary Scholarship*, for a list of secondary sources of particular importance on the much visited subject of influence and inspiration, and for annotated assessments of specific arguments.

11. Wertheim and Sorrentino, *Crane Log*, 69; Levenson, "Introduction," xiv.

brigade is "halted in the fringe of a grove" awaiting action, rumors pass up and down the ranks of the 304th New York Infantry Regiment. To identify the man who passed along one rumor, the soldier identifies him by regiment: "I met one of th' 148th Maine boys an' he ses his brigade fit th' hull rebel army fer four hours over on th' turnpike road an' killed about five thousand of 'em. He ses one more sech fight as that an' th' war'll be over" (RBC 48). The vast majority of Civil War soldiery were infantrymen. Compared to the infantry regiments that were assembled in their hundreds, cavalry regiments were very few. Unless specifically or contextually identified as "cavalry" (Fourth Ohio Cavalry, for example), a formation identified only by number and state would inevitably be an infantry regiment. So the informant's regiment—the 148th Maine Infantry Regiment—is given, not his brigade, division, or corps, and that should suffice.[12]

The 304th New York and the 148th Maine are the only regiments fully identified in the novel by both number and state. To preclude any possible confusion between these fictional regiments and "real" historical regiments, Crane has given them impossibly high numbers. Regiments in both the Union and the Confederate armed forces were numbered sequentially as they were mustered into service, and no state provided anything close to three hundred regiments for the Union army. The highest-numbered New York regiment in the Army of the Potomac during the Chancellorsville campaign was the 157th. In the index to *Battles and Leaders*, the highest-numbered New York regiment is the 179th; the highest-numbered Federal regiment is the 211th Pennsylvania. The small state of Maine produced fewer regiments: the Twentieth Maine is the highest-numbered regiment listed in the Federal order of battle for the Chancellorsville campaign, and the Twenty-eighth Maine is the highest to be found in the *Battles and Leaders* index.

In this national service of regiments identified by number and state, however, there were a few exceptions. In the order of battle for the Federal cavalry and infantry in the Chancellorsville campaign, there were two regiments identified as "U.S. Sharpshooters" in the *Official Records*, and there were four cavalry and about a dozen infantry regiments identified as "United States," such as the Eighth U.S. Infantry. These were regiments from the "regular" (professional or permanent) U.S. Army. But less than one regiment in forty was "regular." The vast majority were regiments raised solely for service in this great national crisis. They were raised by individual states and furthermore raised by voluntary enlistment, and they were proud of both facts. In their reports, they typically identified

12. Musick, "Little Regiment."

themselves as "Volunteers": for example, Major Samuel K. Wilson of the "Twenty-Eighth New Jersey Infantry" signed his report as "Major, Commanding Twenty-Eighth New Jersey Volunteers" (OR 97). This would soon change, however. In early 1863 the Congress of the United States passed an act calling for nation-wide conscription, and soon the term "Volunteers" would no longer be auto-matically applicable to infantry regiments in the Federal service.

The 304th New York Infantry is a new regiment. One mark of its newness this particular May morning is its uniformity of dress: "Also, there was too great a similarity in the hats. The hats of a regiment should properly represent the his-tory of headgear for a period of years" (RBC 34). During its previous day's march toward the front, the 304th has purged itself of a good deal of equip-ment: "few" of them are now carrying "anything but their necessary clothing, blankets, haversacks, canteens, and arms and ammunition" (33). This appears merely practical, but it constitutes an unwarranted departure from one of Hooker's best innovations.

Trying to maneuver large armies across the sparsely settled American land-scape made Civil War logistics a nightmare. Hooker's staff had studied the problem exhaustively and had found a plausible new model in the "flying columns" of the French army on campaign in North Africa. Under that model, the infantryman's individual burden weighed forty-five carefully calculated pounds. This was certainly heavy, but it was also quite manageable. As a result of this brilliant logistical innovation, Hooker's Army of the Potomac had not had to assemble massive animal-drawn convoys at the very outset of this cam-paign, and its marching columns had not had to stick to built-up highways upon which those convoys could also march. But having so cavalierly disburdened themselves of their personal supplies, the soldiers in the 304th New York had better hope that the weather will not turn chill (it is May 2, and still mid-spring in northern Virginia), and that the campaign will not continue much longer at such a distance from the army's railheads.[13]

From these details in the novel, we can envision Private Henry Fleming and his fellows with some confidence. They are obviously wearing regulation head-gear, "forage caps" of the sort familiar from photographs and statues, which were caps of dark blue wool whose flat crowns stiffened with cardboard flop for-ward over leather visors. During the Civil War period, the insignia of the in-fantry was a circular brass hunting horn: Fleming and his fellows might have once worn this insignia on the crown of their caps, with their company initial above

13. Edward Hagerman, The American Civil War and the Origins of Modern Warfare: Ideas, Organ-ization, and Field Command, 72–73.

or within it, but few photographs from this midyear of the war show men retaining these insignia, so they should probably not be added to our envisioning.

They would be wearing fatigue "blouses," dark blue flannel jackets extending about midway down the thigh, with falling collars and four brass buttons stamped with an eagle-and-shield device. Corporal Simpson (*RBC* 131) would be wearing two sky blue inverted chevrons, about six inches wide, on his sleeve between shoulder and elbow. The men have "shed their knapsacks" (33), backpacks that carried personal supplies and upon which their blankets could be strapped. Shedding these not only frees them from weight but relieves them of constricting chest straps. They are now carrying their blankets in rolls slung over their left shoulders and tied under their right arms: the blankets are dark gray, and some of them are wrapped in dark rubber groundsheets (137). Their "necessary clothing" is most likely wrapped inside their blanket rolls.

Over the left shoulder, the men are wearing black leather shoulder belts, about three inches wide, bearing in the center of the chest a circular brass plate stamped with an eagle surrounded by wreaths and constellations. These belts support black cartridge boxes on the right hip, big waterproof double-flapped boxes divided inside by tin compartments, and bearing on the outside flap a brass oval, marked "US," that is heavy enough to weigh down the flap when unfastened for battle. The soldiers also wear wide, dark brown leather waist belts, which buckle under oval "US" plates similar to those on the cartridge boxes. On its right front, the waist belt carries a small leather waterproof box for copper percussion caps. On the left hip, the waist belt supports the soldier's bayonet, an eighteen-inch blade in a leather scabbard. The cartridges and caps and the bayonet are for the infantryman's weapon, the .58 caliber U.S. Rifle Musket, Model 1861, known as the Springfield (see Chapter 3 for a detailed description of this firearm).

Over the right shoulder, the men sling their canteens and their haversacks. The tin canteens, slung on white cotton straps, are made of two dish-shaped halves soldered together and covered in wool, and they carry a quart of water. Haversacks, slung on leather straps, are foot-square waterproof leather sacks with a canvas food bag inside that contains the soldiers' rations—tough cracker-like hardtack, pork (*RBC* 42), and coffee (132).

Their trousers are sky blue; those of the noncommissioned officers, the corporals and sergeants, are marked by inch-wide dark blue stripes down the seams. Sometimes the trouser cuffs are stuffed into the tops of thick gray socks, but this is evidently not the practice in the 304th New York (*RBC* 134).

The officers are dressed differently. Lieutenant Hasbrouck wears either a forage cap like those of the enlisted men or a black slouch hat. He wears a dark blue single-breasted frock coat, probably with a standing collar, whose skirts reach three-quarters of the way down his thigh, and his light blue trousers have a half-inch dark blue stripe down the seam. "Shoulder-bars" indicate his rank. These are rectangular badges of infantry-blue cloth framed in gold thread that are sewn front-to-back over the top edge of each shoulder. Were he a second lieutenant, there would be no badge of rank within these bars, but since he will assume command of the company upon his captain's death, he is surely a first lieutenant and is wearing one gold bar at either end of each shoulder bar. Entitled to wear a crimson sash beneath the sword belt around his waist, he probably has elected not to do so. Officers' uniforms are distinctive enough already, and while this serves order and morale, the officers in Henderson's brigade are very shortly to pay the price for their distinctive dress. He wears a holstered pistol on his right hip, and a sword in a scabbard on his left.

A modest fraction, perhaps one in thirty, of the volunteer regiments in the Union army styled themselves Zouaves. These wore, with varying degrees of authenticity and color, uniforms reflecting the French colonial soldiery upon which they based themselves: short blue jackets with red cuffs and decorative facings, red baggy trousers and white gaiters, and sometimes white turbans and red fezzes. Soldiers so uniformed did fight in the Chancellorsville campaign (OR 100; see the uniformed mannequin sometimes on display at the National Park Service museum at the battlefield). These Zouave regiments were not distinguished as such in the battle order, but the 304th New York is obviously not one of them. There is not a single reference in *The Red Badge of Courage* to suggest that Private Fleming, Lieutenant Hasbrouck, or any one of their fellows is outfitted with such uniforms.[14]

U.S. Army regulations specified that each volunteer infantry regiment should consist of ten companies. Each company consisted of eighty-two private soldiers, two musicians or drummer boys, eight corporals, four sergeants, and a first or "orderly" sergeant. There are three commissioned officers—a captain, a first lieutenant, and a second lieutenant.[15]

Private Fleming's company has only one lieutenant, Hasbrouck (*RBC* 40); its

14. Katcher, *Potomac*, 5–20, plates and notes; Philip Haythornthwaite, *Uniforms of the Civil War, 1861–1865*; James I. Robertson Jr. et al., *Tenting Tonight: The Soldier's Life*, 72–78. Most important, Bell Irvin Wiley, *The Common Soldier in the Civil War*, an edition containing both *The Life of Johnny Reb* and *The Life of Billy Yank*, serves as the reliable old warhorse on the subject of soldiers' lives during the Civil War. The volumes by Katcher, Haythornthwaite, and Robertson are less detailed but give vivid, immediate pictorial witness and are entirely reliable.

15. Katcher, *Potomac*, 5–6; Brent Nosworthy, *The Bloody Crucible of Courage: Fighting Methods and Combat Experience of the Civil War*, 137; Jack Coggins, *Arms and Equipment of the Civil War*, 21–22.

other lieutenant must have fallen prey to illness during the army's long winter encampment. A new regiment at full strength should number above a thousand, but the 304th New York Infantry will shortly enter its first battle at a strength of seven hundred (53). Most of the missing men are victims of disease: measles, dysentery, malaria, typhus (known as camp fever), or perhaps "hospital gangrene," a disease that defies modern diagnosis because it became extinct once the war was over. The most widely accepted general estimate is that, for every one Union soldier killed in battle or subsequently dying of battle wounds (over 110,000 men), another two die of disease (225,000). Another estimate puts this number much higher, at one to six. Medical practices in the Civil War were uninformed by any knowledge at all of bacterial infection, or the causes of sepsis, or the reasons for the transmission of diseases, and one shudders to read of the surgical practices of the period. There is no mystery about why the 304th New York has lost about a third of its number before it even enters combat.[16]

Companies within a regiment were identified by letters "A" through "K," there being no Company J. When a regiment was new, the senior companies were companies A and B, the first being that of the captain whose date of commissioning identified him as the senior captain, the second that of the next-most-senior captain. In line of battle, Company A was posted on its regiment's right flank, the position of honor dating from spear-and-shield times when warriors on a host's right flank were in the greatest danger because their unshielded right side was exposed to the enemy. Company B was posted on its regiment's left flank. So flank companies were commanded by the regiment's most senior and presumably most experienced captains. They were of particular importance because they had to maintain contact with neighboring regiments in the heat of battle or the confusion of maneuver.[17]

---

16. It is stunning to survey the progress achieved in medicine during the fifty years between the Civil War and World War I. In sharp (and quite relieving) contrast, the treatment of Frederic Henry's wounds in Ernest Hemingway's *A Farewell to Arms* includes X-rays, sun lamps, and mechanized rehabilitation; Frederic Henry himself is a lieutenant in the Italian army's motor ambulance service. On the Austro-Hungarian side in that war, Sigmund Freud was called as an expert witness in a case involving psychological trauma. World War I was the first in human history where combat casualties exceeded those caused by disease. See Robertson, *Tenting Tonight*, 97, 78, 91; William H. McNeill, *The Pursuit of Power: Technology, Armed Force, and Society since a.d. 1000*, 336; K. R. Eissler, *Freud as an Expert Witness: The Discussion of War Neuroses between Freud and Wagner-Jauregg*. See as well John Keegan's hugely (and appropriately) influential *The Face of Battle*, which remarks particularly upon the advances in the treatment of casualties between the Battle of Waterloo and the Battle of the Somme.

17. Nosworthy, *Crucible*, 138; Paddy Griffith, *Battle in the Civil War: Generalship and Tactics in America, 1861–1865*, 13.

Private Fleming's company is not identified by letter, but we know it is not either of these flank companies. A regiment of seven hundred arrayed in its customary two-deep formation would be about 250 yards long, so the men in the flank companies would be a football field's length away from the colors, which were carried in the center of the regimental line. Fleming, when in his proper position in the battle line, is quite close to the battle flag, close enough this afternoon to observe details about the "color sergeant" carrying it (*RBC* 51).

Union regiments typically carried two flags, each six feet tall and six-and-a-half feet wide: a blue infantry flag with the regimental name on a scroll beneath a heraldic American eagle, and a national color with the regiment's name and number in gold letters on the center (red) stripe. The 304th New York is evidently carrying only the national banner (an unusual but hardly unprecedented situation), but then, in the battle that will shortly follow, Fleming's eyes never seem to pick out any blue regimental flags. Flags were carried into battle by selected noncommissioned officers, for such service was one of great danger and great honor. Flags were crucial rallying points and position markers amid the smoke of the battlefield (the British tradition of "trooping the colours" commemorates the ancient practice of annually parading a regiment's colors before its soldiers in order to make the colors familiar to the men). This means that colors inevitably drew enemy fire. It was not uncommon for a regiment to lose a half-dozen men from the color guard during an engagement. Captured enemy colors were much prized: soldiers in the Union army who captured rebel flags were routinely awarded the Medal of Honor. In the Confederate Army of Northern Virginia, either the loss of a regiment's own colors or the capture of a stand of Federal colors required a separate addendum to a regiment's official report of its conduct during a campaign.[18]

At the beginning of the war, regiments traveled with bands of a score or more musicians, but this practice had largely been discarded by the third year. The 304th New York probably has a small drum-and-bugle corps, a half-dozen or so, who supplement the twenty company drummers. As with the regimental flags, these drummers and buglers are not merely ornamental. Instruments in military bands are traditionally percussion and brass, because their sounds can penetrate the blare of combat. Bugle calls and drum calls were used to convey orders, both in camp and in battle. In battle, the regimental bandsmen served also as

---

18. Coggins, *Arms and Equipment*, 25. For the awarding of the congressional Medal of Honor, see the text citations for those awarded during the Civil War in the "Medal of Honor" chapter at www.army.mil/cmh.

medical personnel, the only soldiers automatically excused from the line of battle to help wounded soldiers to the rear. Otherwise there would have been a steady depletion of soldiers from the firing line, as men excused themselves from that deadly realm under the pretense of helping their wounded comrades. But the useful practice of having distinctive uniforms for musicians had by now been dropped, because it made them too conspicuous.

A regiment at full strength was commanded by a colonel. The 304th New York is commanded by Colonel MacChesnay (*RBC* 202), a name that appears neither in the order for battle for the Chancellorsville campaign as given in the index to the *Official Records* Chancellorsville volume nor in the index to *Battles and Leaders* (Crane surely availed himself of at least one of these sources; the one in the *Official Records* would have been the more detailed and authoritative). This pattern is true throughout the novel: all the proper names are fictional and cannot be confused with those of any "historical" people.

Remember that a regiment at full strength would number above a thousand men. But after some months in camp, even a rookie Union regiment would have considerably fewer (seven hundred, in the case of the 304th New York), and by the spring of 1863, a typical veteran Union regiment would rarely still enroll as many as five hundred. This is because there was no systematic reinforcement of veteran regiments. New volunteers (and, when the Federal government would begin drafting men in the summer of 1863, new draftees) would not be sent to the line as replacements for casualties in veteran regiments. They were instead formed up into new regiments. This practice makes little military or psychological sense, but the reasons for it were several. New regiments meant that there were new colonelcies to be awarded by state governors to friends, political supporters, and the like, and new commissions to extend to soldiers desirous of promotion into or up the ladder of the commissioned ranks. But on a less cynical note, these state regiments were not permanent institutions of a regular standing army (as is, say, the 101st Airborne Division or the Seventh Cavalry of the current U.S. Army, or the Coldstream Guards or the Black Watch of the British). They were raised specifically for the national crisis caused by the rebellion in the Southern states. Commissioned and noncommissioned officers in these regiments were occupied serving in the field, or on home leave, or in hospital. Hence they were unavailable to serve as cadres back home for recruiting new soldiers to their specific regiments. Too, administrative work necessary to reinforce veteran regiments would be far more complex than that required to establish brand-new ones. Thus, for instance, there would not be recruiting booths for the Fourth Ohio Volunteer Infantry Regiment, raised in east-central Ohio in April 1861, on the public squares of Newark or Marion or Mount Vernon. A man recruited from the Mount Vernon area in 1862 would likely find himself in the newly raised Fifty-fourth Ohio Infantry.[19]

The result is stark: "veteran regiments in the army were likely to be very small aggregations of men" (*RBC* 33). Indeed they might be so greatly reduced that they would be broken up and the men distributed into other formations. In contrast to such veteran regiments is the still unblooded 304th New York: "Once, when the command had first come to the field, some perambulating veterans, noting the length of their column, had accosted them thus: 'Hey, fellers, what brigade is that?' And when the men had replied that they formed a regiment and not a brigade, the older soldiers had laughed, and said, 'O Gawd!'" (33–34). Regiments were brigaded together for field service. Crane's depiction of the 304th as typically fighting as a part of its brigade (50), but on occasion detached for a specific service (157), is quite consistent with battlefield practice.

Brigades were supposed to be commanded by officers of brigadier-general rank, but brigade commanders direct their part of the battle personally and closely and often became casualties. Brigadier General Henderson himself will be killed this day (*RBC* 205), so privates Wilson and Fleming, searching for water tomorrow morning, will recognize their division commander but not the new officer commanding their own brigade (174 ff). Their brigade's new commander is surely the senior, by date of his appointment to the rank of colonel, of the brigade's regimental commanders. Colonels very often commanded brigades.

There is no indication as to how many regiments comprise Henderson's brigade, though two are called by their numbers alone, the Twelfth and the Seventy-sixth (*RBC* 175). Tomorrow morning our two privates will overhear the new brigade commander intimate that he has inherited a brigade consisting of more than just three regiments. Brigades of only three regiments were rare during the Chancellorsville campaign. The *OR* order of battle gives only five: in Hooker's army, eighteen brigades had four regiments, twenty-two had five, eleven had six, and one brigade had seven. Brigades of veteran (and thus depleted) regiments were reinforced by adding entirely fresh regiments, and the 304th New York itself has clearly been assigned to Henderson's brigade in order to bring it back up to nominal brigade strength.

Three brigades in the novel are identified by the names of their commanding officers: Saunders's (*RBC* 50), Taylor's (73), and Henderson's (205). These names

---

19. Nosworthy, *Crucible*, 204.

are so common in the general population that it is noteworthy that there were no officers so named who commanded brigades during the Chancellorsville campaign. This I consider further proof of Crane's research into the *Official Records*, each volume of which presents a reader with two massive indexes, one of men named in the volume and the other of organizations mentioned. There are no similar sources, and it is hard to believe mere luck would account for this phenomenon. The novel names two other officers commanding formations probably of at least brigade size: Perry (47) and Whiterside (174). Again, the order of battle in OR shows no Federal commanders so named. One of Crane's artillery batteries is identified by the (ungrammatically rendered) name of its commander "Hannises' batt'ry" (47). Batteries were almost always commanded by captains, and the Federal order of battle for the campaign shows, again, no battery commanded by anyone named Hannis (or, for that matter, Hannises).

The 304th New York Volunteer Infantry and Henderson's brigade are both fictitious. So it might seem fruitless to search for any historical formations into which Crane may have slotted them. But beneath the superficial welter of confusion and discordance achieved by his impressionistic style, Crane's novel is quite accurate in its details concerning the historical campaign at hand.

A rumor retailed by Private Jim Conklin opens the dialogue in the novel: "We're goin' t' move t'morrah—sure. We're goin' 'way up the river, cut across, an' come around in behint 'em" (*RBC* 2). Once challenged, Conklin says, "Didn't the cavalry all start this morning? The cavalry started this morning. They say there ain't hardly any cavalry left in camp. They're going to Richmond, or some place, while we fight all the Johnnies" (15). This is an accurate account of the plan of campaign as of that moment in mid-April. There will be "much scoffing" at Jim Conklin the "next morning" when these infantrymen do not break camp. The "mistake" (18), however, is not Conklin's but, rather, that of the Federal cavalry general George Stoneman.

In the spring of 1863, Lee's army was entrenched on the western bank of the Rappahannock at Fredericksburg, Virginia. The Union Army of the Potomac was facing it on the eastern bank, at the hamlet of Falmouth. A direct frontal assault against the rebel entrenchments the previous December had resulted in a devastating repulse. Major General Ambrose Burnside had been dismissed as its commander and replaced by Hooker.

In mid-April, Hooker's plan was to force the Confederates to retreat from Fredericksburg by a huge turning maneuver around their left flank. He massed his cavalry under General Stoneman, who was to lead off the campaign by encircling the rebel army from the north-east to the south. This massive raid was to sever their communications with their capital at Richmond and hold them in place, so that Hooker could then crush them with his infantry. Thus, "the cavalry started this morning." But the Union army had not yet developed the logistical or command skills necessary to handle large cavalry formations effectively: Stoneman was slow in getting underway, he then could not get the majority of his cavalryman across the Rappahannock before the river's spring rise submerged his bridges, and thus he was delayed even more. Since the campaign schedule for the entire Army of the Potomac was keyed to the cavalry's advance, Hooker, infuriated, had no choice but to delay his offensive.

Hooker then decided to shelve his reliance upon his cavalry, sending the majority of them off on a distant and less consequential raid, and to depend, instead, upon his infantry to turn Lee's army out of its Fredericksburg defenses. He improved his strategy and, two weeks later, did exactly what Private Conklin foretold. He left about forty thousand of his command facing the Confederates at Fredericksburg, and in a move of strategic and logistical brilliance, directed the rest of his army, some ninety thousand men, on a well-coordinated sequence of westward marches "way up the river" where, at several points, they "cut across" the Rappahannock and then, marching south and east, came "around in behint" the Confederates.

So from the outset, Crane established the "real" battle of Chancellorsville as the underlying skeleton of his novel, and he selected a specific "real" corps, the Second, in which to place Henderson's brigade and the 304th New York Infantry Regiment. Hooker intended to conduct almost all of his westward deployment in secrecy. The Fifth, Eleventh, and Twelfth corps, marching for Kelly's Ford on the Rappahannock over twenty miles west of Fredericksburg, were not allowed evening campfires. On the other hand, the divisions of the Second Corps were set on the march toward United States Ford (sometimes called the United States Mine Ford), only eight miles west of Fredericksburg and defended by rebel entrenchments. Hooker thus intended to distract Lee from that critical flanking maneuver much farther upriver. These Second Corps divisions were under constant rebel observation, so they bivouacked at night around campfires, according to usual campaigning practice. "At nightfall the column," in which the 304th New York was on campaign, "broke into regimental pieces, and the fragments went into the fields to camp. Tents sprang up like strange plants. Camp fires, like red, peculiar blossoms, dotted the night" (*RBC* 26).

The Fifth, Eleventh, and Twelfth corps crossed the Rappahannock at Kelly's Ford on a single pontoon bridge and then crossed the tributary Rapidan at Ely's Ford. They had hardly been challenged. Hooker's campaign was off to a brilliant start, with forty thousand Federal soldiers now established on the south bank of the Rappahannock, and in the rear of Lee's entrenchments at Fredericksburg. These three corps then advanced eastward, compelling the rebels to abandon their fortifications at United States Ford—the military term is "uncovering" them.

In contrast, the divisions of the Second Corps had only the Rappahannock to cross, and by the time they descended to it, army engineers were able to put down two pontoon bridges at United States Ford. These two divisions began crossing in the afternoon, but formations were still crossing in the evening. "When another night came" (the second night of the campaign, for the 304th New York Infantry Regiment), "the columns, changed to purple streaks, filed across two pontoon bridges" (*RBC* 32).

The Second Corps was the first of three that crossed the Rappahannock at United States Ford; Major General Daniel E. Sickles's Third Corps crossed these pontoon bridges at United States Ford in their wake. But in order to mask the scale of his great turning maneuver, Hooker had ordered these Third Corps formations to mask their own westward deployment, and at places on the river roads where their route could be observed from the rebel-controlled south bank, they had to leave the roads and force their way through ravines and fields. This exhausting march took them all the day and well into the evening of April 30. While the 304th New York Infantry Regiment is being "routed out" from its sleep "with early energy" (*RBC* 32) on the morning of May 1, the Third Corps is just beginning its daylight crossing of the Rappahannock.

The First Corps was ordered into action in front of Fredericksburg, to further fix Lee's attention there, until Hooker would order it westward early on May 2. The First Corps will spend all of that day marching to United States Ford and will not arrive at the Chancellorsville battlefield until the night during which Private Fleming is being led, dazed from a head wound, back to the ranks of the 304th.

This shows that, as a soldier in the Second Corps, Private Fleming has enjoyed the shortest, easiest, and most comfortable approach to the test of battle that Crane could find in his research. For the soldiers of the three corps (the Fifth, Eleventh, and Twelfth) who were sent on Hooker's ambitious westward sweep and who forded the Rapidan as well as the Rappahannock, the march itself was vivid and memorable. Soldiers in the other two corps who crossed at United States Ford had either had a day of hacking their way across country or had a day of combat followed by a day of forced marching before arriving at the Wilderness battlefield. But by locating Henderson's brigade and the 304th New York Volunteer Infantry Regiment in the Second Corps, Crane allowed his fictional characters an easy march and an unremarkable river crossing. Crane's research takes Fleming from a comfortably familiar routine and plunges him into the bewilderments of combat more suddenly than any other historically valid possibility. Crane sets Fleming's quite extraordinary perceptions ("Camp fires, like red, peculiar blossoms, dotted the night") amid the least strenuous, most routine approach of any of the Federal formations to the battlefield of Chancellorsville.

Crane may have initially been attracted to the idea of placing his fictional regiment in the Third Corps, rather than the Second. The regiment raised in his hometown of Port Jervis, in Orange County, was the 124th New York. It served in the Third Corps during the Chancellorsville campaign. He evidently read the Third Corps reports in the *Official Records,* for he included details of the campaign that I have not been able to find elsewhere. The report of Lieutenant Colonel George H. Woods, "Chief Commissary of Subsistence" of the Third Army Corps, is remarkably detailed (and remarkably aggrieved) about discarded supplies: "following the march of the troops, in very many places I found where knapsacks had been emptied of their contents, and in many places the knapsacks themselves were slung into the bushes" (OR 109). This might be a source for Crane's description of the men of the 304th discarding their knapsacks on this campaign, although the novel implies that such disburdening was the ubiquitous "practice" in the Union army (*RBC* 33).

Not so common is the next incident he probably derived from Third Corps's official reports. As the 304th is retreating from battle on the afternoon of May 3, a soldier describes Private Bill Smithers's experiences in the Union army hospital the previous night: "he ses he'd rather been in ten hundred battles than been in that heluva hospital. He ses they got shootin' in th' nighttime, an' shells dropped plum among 'em in th' hospital. He ses sech hollerin' he never see" (*RBC* 231). Compare official report no. 110, "Report of Surg. Thomas Sim, U.S. Army, Medical Director," from the "Headquarters Third Army Corps," about events on the night of May 2, the night of the rebel breakthrough "on the Plank Road" that drove "the Eleventh Corps in ignominious retreat":

> The fleeing Dutchmen [that is, the soldiers of German ethnicity in the Eleventh Corps] actually ran over our hospital. This and the rapid approach of the rebels made the position untenable, so the surgeons pro-

ceeded to evacuate, but they succeeded in conveying their wounded (except those killed by the shells) to the white house . . . as the principal depot. In the meantime a few others [wounded] of our corps and several of other corps had been brought in by our stretcher-bearers, and were properly attended to by the surgeons; but soon the enemy appeared to have got the range of this hospital, for the shells came thick and fast, and I thought it best to order the wounded removed to the woods on the opposite side of the road leading to the ford, the medical officers, of course, to accompany them. (OR 110)

This report gives Crane historical warrant ("several of other corps") to have a private of the Second Corps, William Smithers, find himself in a Third Corps hospital.

Why not, then, place the 304th in the Third Corps? That Crane in fact did so is the thesis of Charles LaRocca's eloquent and influential argument. It seems to me that the evidence indicates otherwise, however. The march of the Third Corps on April 30—where they were hustled along on an eighteen-mile march, portions of it through ravines choked with spring vines and under-brush—would have been unusual enough to have made its own forcible impact upon the soldiers' impressions (OR 108). But on his advance to battle, Private Fleming was unencumbered by anything so strenuous and was free to brood.[20]

The Third Corps was handled quite differently in the battle itself. Sickles, not a professional soldier, was energetic to the point of recklessness, and his corps was blessed with those two regiments of "U.S. Sharpshooters," hand-picked marksmen in green uniforms and armed with breech-loading rifles, which gave him a cadre of men who were unusually effective in the sort of wilderness fighting at hand. Those brigades of the Third Corps that went into combat during the morning and afternoon of May 2 were constantly on the offensive, and they enjoyed considerable success, carrying off hundreds of rebel prisoners. They were preying, in fact, upon Stonewall Jackson's supply columns, as Jackson's command marched across the southern face of the Federal army's semicircular position, and both the offensive character of their operations and the success they enjoyed do not correspond with the experiences of Henderson's brigade and the 304th New York during those hours, a fact that is readily apparent

20. LaRocca, "Inspiration"; Wertheim and Sorrentino, *Crane Log*, 150–52; Sears, *Chancellorsville*, 509–11. The Third Corps crossed the river on pontoon bridges during the morning hours (OR 108, 162), whereas the Third Division of the Second Corps (and the 304th New York Infantry Regiment) crossed the pontoon bridges during the night (OR 101, 102; *RBC* 32).

in LaRocca's own gracefully developed, "Historically Annotated Edition" of *The Red Badge of Courage.*[21]

The Third Corps was next in line to and just to the southeast of the Eleventh Corps on the army's exposed western flank. A soldier fleeing from a regiment in the Third Corps would not have had much space to roam in thereafter, nor would he have had to make his way very far through the woods in order to see what happened when Jackson's twilight assault struck the Eleventh. When the Eleventh Corps collapsed under that assault, all the formations of the Third Corps, both those previously in action and those in reserve, were hastily redeployed to face Jackson's victorious onslaught. It would have made far less sense for a soldier returning that night to a Third Corps regiment to explain his absence by saying he had been "Way over on th' right. Ter'ble fightin' over there" (*RBC* 130). The Third Corps units would have been reformed toward the right, and indeed, many of them would have been involved in that fighting.

The sequence of events leading to Private Fleming's "red badge of courage" is crucial to the novel's major themes and conceptions. Had Fleming been in the Third Corps, there would have been little warrant in the historical record for his regiment's defensive posture, and even less to suggest that his personal failure was in some way typical. There would have been little time and less space for his subsequent wanderings. To be true to his historical sources (and that he aimed for such truth is a central thesis of this study), Crane would have to show Fleming defecting from a regiment in an active and victorious brigade, and thereafter Crane would not have enough room in which to let him roam.

Only the First and Third divisions of the Second Corps's three divisions crossed the Rappahannock into the Wilderness. Brigadier General John Gibbon's Second Division remained behind near Falmouth, compelling the rebels to con-

---

21. Charles J. LaRocca, *Stephen Crane's Novel of the Civil War: The Red Badge of Courage, an Historically Annotated Edition.* LaRocca imaginatively and intelligently annotates the novel by interleaving pictures, explanations, definitions, and historical documents into the text of *The Red Badge of Courage.* This illuminates the book superbly; it also enables a reader to see readily enough the difference between the deployment of the 124th New York and Franklin's brigade during the battle of Chancellorsville and the deployment of the 304th New York and Henderson's brigade in Crane's novel. The reader is particularly invited to consider the contrast between the historical records and the fictional narrative as they each depict combat during the day of May 2, 1863. (LaRocca, *Annotated Edition,* 48–62). The 124th New York and Franklin's brigade were everywhere on the offensive, moving forward against or actually assaulting rebel units. The 304th New York, in contrast, is arrayed defensively, in a reserve line. The contrast between historical and fictional narratives is not as stark in the pages concerning the experience of the 124th New York and that of the 304th during the combat on the morning of May 3, but it is clear that the 124th enjoyed far greater success than the 304th New York during those hours.

tinue guarding Banks Ford. Then the Second Division supported Sedgwick's assault on the rebel lines at Fredericksburg on May 3. The division was lightly engaged in the campaign, suffering only 8 men killed, and 150 casualties altogether. (To put this in perspective, the Fourth Georgia Regiment and the 124th New York Regiment each took over 150 casualties during the battle.)

Major General Winfield Hancock's First Division of the Second Corps was one of the army's best and was deployed forward immediately upon its arrival in the Chancellorsville area, in support of Sykes's division (Fifth Corps) in the spearhead of the army's advance along the Orange Turnpike toward Fredericksburg. On the afternoon of May 1, the first day after it crossed the Rappahannock, the First Division in its entirety was in combat.

The 304th New York Volunteer Infantry Regiment, on the other hand, will have at least an entire day's grace between its river crossing and its battlefield initiation (*RBC* 32–34). This initiation unquestionably falls on May 2, which slots the experience of the regiment precisely into the calendar of Major General William H. French's Third Division of the Second Corps: having crossed the Rappahannock on the night of April 30, French's Third Division of the Second Corps saw no action on May 1 but, confused by congested roads and countermanded orders, spent the day in sporadic maneuver, "hustled along" various "narrow" roads "that led deep into the forest" (32). In the "real," historical record, its formations did not go into action until the afternoon of May 2. So, down to and including their first engagement with the enemy on the midafternoon of May 2, the experience of Henderson's brigade and the 304th New York Volunteer Infantry Regiment corresponds exactly to what a brigade and a regiment in the Third Division of the Second Corps would have experienced during the Chancellorsville campaign. Their experience does not correspond to that of any other regiment or brigade in any other division of any other corps in the Army of the Potomac during that campaign.

Thus the historical record of the first days of the campaign locates Crane's fictional brigade and fictional regiment in French's Third Division of Couch's Second Corps. What then befalls them during the two days of the battle will correspond exactly (with one signal exception) to what two of French's three brigades experienced. In particular, Private Fleming's fictional experiences can be plotted with precision upon the historical record, by keying his perceptions to the landscapes dictated by the deployment of French's brigades. Such precise correspondences cannot be established between Crane's fiction and any other of the Federal units that fought in the Chancellorsville campaign. The "one signal exception" does not work against the thesis that Crane located his characters in

the Third Division of the Second Corps. In fact, it may be the single most compelling piece of evidence that Crane had indeed studied the crucial historical
documents pertaining to French's Third Division of the Second Corps while
formulating his story—although the argument to this effect, I confess, is a paradoxical one.

For the moment, the reader may add one last detail to Fleming's uniform.
When Hooker assumed command of the Army of the Potomac and began to re-
organize it and to rebuild its morale, he ordered each of his corps to adopt a distinctive cap badge. These badges were made of red cloth for the first division of
each corps, white cloth for the second, and blue cloth for the third. So, to the
crown of Fleming's forage cap, visible from the front because of its slouch, we
can now add a trefoil badge (like the clubs design on playing cards) made of
light blue flannel and about two inches in width. During the afternoon of May
2, Private Fleming will lose his cap (*RBC* 69), and as a result, an Ohio soldier
giving him assistance later that evening will have to ask him which corps his regiment belongs to (126).[22]

In the four-volume *Battles and Leaders*, the principal account of the battle of
Chancellorsville was written by General Couch, who had commanded the
Union army's Second Corps during this campaign. About the battle on the
Second Corps's front on May 2, Couch wrote: "At half-past two that afternoon
the Second Corps' lines were assaulted by artillery and infantry. Just previous to
Jackson's attack on the right a desperate effort was made by Lee's people to carry
the left at Mott's Run, but the men who held it were there to stay" (*BL* 3:163).
This describes a rebel "assault" of some weight ("a desperate effort") on the
"left" of the Union position. Mott's Run is one of the mazy watercourses on the
eastern face of the Union army's deployment. This passage specifies that rebel
attacks in the area were underway by midafternoon ("Half-past two") on May 2,
that these attacks were "previous to Jackson's" more massive, violent, and successful assault, and that the Union formations involved "held" fast against
them.

To examine the Third Division's specific experience this afternoon, I believe
Crane turned to General French's after-action report in the *Official Records*.
French also wrote about the battle that morning and afternoon (note the erroneous "3d" where he obviously means May 2, as the passage itself and the preceding and following paragraphs both make absolutely clear):

22. Katcher, *Potomac*, 28–31; LaRocca, *Annotated Edition*, xxvii–xxviii; Coggins, *Arms and Equipment*, endpapers.

On the morning of the 3d [sic], my First Brigade was placed . . . to form the line of defense, connecting with the First Division, Second Corps, on the right, and Sykes' Division, Fifth Corps, on the left, making rifle-pits and strengthening the front by felling trees. The enemy, who had been feeling our lines during the morning, made his principal attack on the right of our position, and, driving back the troops which held it, uncovered the masses in the rear and center, of which my division formed a part.

This seems to fit in with Couch's account in *Battles and Leaders*. After a "morning" during which the rebels "had been feeling" the Second Corps's defensive "lines," they finally delivered a "principal attack" there. The passage adds further significant details: this "attack" was powerful enough to "drive back" Union "troops" who were "on the right of" the Third Division's "position."

French's formations themselves were evidently in a second or reserve line, for the collapse of those soldiers on their right "uncovered" their own "part" of the Federal line. French then goes on to describe the steps he took to repair the situation in, so it seems, the sector held by his division:

Taking a portion of my staff, I made a rapid reconnaissance of the roads leading through the woods to the Plank road, preparatory to making an attack upon the enemy's flank in his pursuit. On my return to the division, I found that my Second Brigade (Hays') had been taken off by a staff officer from corps headquarters. I followed it to Chancellorsville, and afterward saw it taking up a position to support the division of Major-General Berry. The general commanding the Second Corps sending me word that the Second Brigade was not [sic] [now?] under his orders, I confined my attention to the First and Third. (*OR* 93)

So French's immediate professional instinct was to put in a counterattack, "to make an attack" upon the momentarily victorious (the "pursuing") rebels. This crisis obviously caused some moments of frenzied enterprise in the Second Corps's command structure, as one of French's brigades was taken away from his division and redeployed by "corps headquarters." But in the event, as Couch above and the record everywhere else indicate, French and his fellows in this sector were successful. Whatever success Jackson's attack achieved on Hooker's "right" or western flank, the Union lines east of Chancellorsville were never breached.

It is worthy of note, then, how precisely these two documents define the experiences of the 304th New York and of Henderson's brigade in their first experience of battle. They spend the morning being maneuvered into various defensive alignments, entrenching themselves each time with "barricades" and "protective piles of earth and stone" (*RBC* 41, 43). "In the afternoon," then, "the skirmish fire increased," artillery near them goes into action (43, 44), and a major rebel attack develops on their front. It falls, specifically, upon "A brigade ahead of them and on the right" (45). That brigade is "Saunders's" and is driven off in a rout (50), which exposes "the reserves" (52) in the second line of defense and, among those "reserves," the 304th New York Infantry Regiment and the "veteran regiments" aligned on their "right and left" (50).

After some "moments of waiting" (*RBC* 53), the rebel assault descends upon them in their reserve position. The one Federal "division" commander (72) that we see in this area is understandably "much harassed," and his orders are confused as he "irritably" deploys a "brigade" to meet this threat (73). The reserve line holds through two or more rebel attacks, and as the novel's attention shifts rearward and away from this part of the battlefield, we see the Federal "general of division" sending in a counterattack: "Yes, by heavens, they've held 'im! They've held 'im!" (74), this "general of division" exclaims, watching the final rebel assaults fail. As Couch himself said in his summary of the action at that very time (the afternoon of May 2, 1863) and place (the sector of the Union defensive position held by the Second Corps, on the left of Hooker's position): "the men who held" the left, including the fictional Henderson's brigade and the fictional 304th New York Volunteer Infantry Regiment, "were there to stay."

It seems to me, then, that Crane studied these two passages—Couch's article from *Battles and Leaders* and French's *Official Report*—and drew from them the historical basis for his fictional account of the 304th in this battle. The reiteration and detail of this exposition has not, I hope, suggested there is anything very complex about these two "military" circumstances: the historical one that emerges or seems to emerge from the two historical documents, and the fictional one that lies just beneath the welter of Private Fleming's perceptions. Both historical and fictional accounts outline relatively simple military narratives, and (albeit in quite different styles) both narratives present the same single and quite recognizable moment in the battle of Chancellorsville.

The obvious sharing of this moment is not the only or even the most compelling reason I believe Crane had exactly these two documents, Couch's and French's, before him when he created Private Fleming's first experience of combat. I am led to this belief because Crane could not have found historical evidence (such circumstances as these, so portrayed) anywhere else in any of his sources about the battle of Chancellorsville. The basic historical facts are (1) that General Couch's article is inaccurate and (2) that Crane, through no fault of his own, was confused by General French's official report.

In Crane's portrayal of the campaign down to the afternoon of May 2, 1863, his narrative has unquestionably and quite accurately fitted Henderson's brigade into French's Third Division of Couch's Second Corps. But Crane's portrayal of its experience of battle on the midafternoon of May 2 does not coincide with the experience of the actual historical division. Indeed, it does not coincide with the experience of any of the historical Third Division's formations that rendered official reports.

It is inconceivable to me that Crane would have ceased to use the historical record as the armature for his narrative at the very moment that the battle began for Private Fleming and his fellows. Not a veteran himself, Crane would have been especially eager to find a historical structure for the first engagement for Henderson's brigade and the 304th New York. So far, he has painstakingly developed their story according to historical details of the Chancellorsville campaign. This moment would have been the last—not the first—at which he would have liberated them completely from historical sources. Couch and French, taken together, have misled him.

First, let us consider French's report: it is not only careless (saying, for instance, May "3d" where it can only have been May 2) and eye-glazingly dull, but the paragraph given above is actively misleading for anyone trying to understand the experience of French's division on the afternoon of May 2. Throughout the paragraph, he seems to be concerned only with the experience of his particular division. He would thus seem to mean that the "principal attack on the right of our position," which occasioned the stampede of some unspecified Union formation, happened in front of his Third Division. His repetition of the possessive "our" twice in this crucial sentence would seem to make this fact crystal clear: surely "our lines" and "our position" refer to the same part of the battlefield. But this is not his point at all. Believe it or not, he is testifying not to drama on his division's front during the midafternoon but to its virtual inactivity.

It is only after some study of this passage in the context of other reports from the Third Division that a reader comes to understand what French means. Not a single report from anyone else in French's Third Division (OR 94–107) mentions any significant action during the midafternoon. At some time after "5 p.m.," Hays's brigade of the Third Division was "ordered to move in support of Major General Berry, Third Army Corps, to the right of Chancellorsville" (OR 101). Hays's brigade was one of the Federal formations hastily redeployed to the army's right flank, to face Jackson's attack as it bore down upon them from the "right," or west. So French's "the right of our position" means the right flank of the entire Federal army. This is French's befuddling way of reporting Jackson's devastating twilight attack upon Howard's Eleventh Corps, not an afternoon attack delivered upon his Third Division of the Second Corps. Far from depicting a moment of crisis in front of the lines of the Third Division, his report is actually explaining that the Confederates limited themselves to "feeling" the lines of the Third Division and delivered their "principal attack" quite elsewhere.

Most of the Third Division of the Second Corps in fact spent the whole day in reserve, engaged in digging field fortifications. Some units may have come under rebel artillery fire, and some may have exchanged rifle fire with the rebels on the skirmish lines, though I find no accounts confirming this. In the *Official Records,* there is no report of action of the sort witnessed by Fleming and his fellows, viz. rebel attacks on their immediate front of sufficient weight and violence to rout a full Federal brigade, to penetrate to their reserve lines, and to compel the Union commanders in their sector to mount a full-bore counterattack.

In fact, the rebels in that sector had very compelling reasons not to initiate any vigorous action at all. Lee had to retain ten thousand men in defensive positions in his rear at Fredericksburg, facing Sedgwick's force of forty thousand, which Hooker left deployed at Falmouth. The departure of Jackson's thirty thousand men, on the circuitous march that would take them across the southern face of Hooker's army while heading for its right flank, left Lee with seventeen thousand soldiers facing a Union array of over seventy-three thousand on his immediate front. Lee's own position was a precarious one until the hour Jackson struck. Any energetic Federal move against his position would be ruinous to the Army of Northern Virginia. If Lee's slender forces were not overwhelmed by such a move, they would at least be compelled to withdraw from the battlefield. Either outcome would abandon Jackson's command to its own fate. So Lee had to keep the enemy on his front occupied, to suggest offensive intent of his own, so as to keep them behind their field fortifications—but without precipitating a major engagement until Jackson could come into action.

On the morning and afternoon of May 2, these two divisions of Couch's Second Corps were facing only three rebel brigades, from Major General McLaws's division. General McLaws's orders for May 2 "were to hold my position; not to engage seriously, but to press strongly so soon as it was discovered that General Jackson had attacked" (OR 315). This was the attack signaled by the "crimson roar" (RBC 82) Private Fleming will hear some hours and some miles away from the time and place of the 304th New York Regiment's afternoon engagement.

There was energetic Confederate skirmishing all day against Hancock's First

Division of Couch's corps, pursuant to Lee's intention to keep the Union army occupied and on the defensive. Couch's first report in the *Official Records*, written on May 9, 1863, states, "*May 2d.*—The corps in line between Meade and Slocum. A strong picket, on the road leading to Fredericksburg, held its position under Colonel Miles, Hancock's division, after repeated assaults. The enemy felt our lines. Toward evening Hays' brigade, French's division, ordered to support Berry. My whole line entrenched" (OR 63). Eleven days later he wrote:

> By the morning of the 2d, Hancock got into a new position, his right connecting with Slocum's left at Chancellorsville. Colonel Miles, of the Sixtyfirst New York, with a strong body of skirmishers, held some rifle pits in the forest to the front, and was attacked by the enemy, but unsuccessfully. I succeeded that day in intrenching my entire line. Major-General French connected with Hancock's left, and at sunset sent Brigadier-General Hays, with his brigade, to support Major-General Berry. (OR 63)

These initial reports are quite consistent, both with each other and with the tactical situation on that part of the field: Confederate forces skirmishing, sometimes intensely, and the First Division of the Second Corps resisting with its own skirmish (or "picket") lines, while entrenching its main positions. General Hancock, closer to the action, necessarily saw things more intensely:

> On May 2, the enemy frequently opened with artillery from the heights toward Fredericksburg and from those on my right, and with infantry assaulted my advanced line of rifle pits, but was always handsomely repulsed by the troops on duty there [three regiments, plus some detachments from others, in other words, a heavy skirmish line]. During the sharp contest of the day, the enemy was never able to reach my principal line of battle, so stoutly and successfully did Colonel Miles contest the ground. (OR 65)

However intense the skirmishing may have become, then, the "principal" battle line of the First Division of the Second Corps was never engaged.

Brigadier John C. Caldwell, commanding the first brigade of Hancock's First Division, reported that Colonel Miles's command "skirmished all day long with the enemy, and at 3 p.m. repulsed, with signal loss, a determined attack of the enemy, made in two columns on each side of the road." He added that Miles "with a single line of skirmishers, deployed at 3 paces," had "repelled a determined attack of the enemy made in column, a feat rarely paralleled" (OR 68).

As one might expect, Colonel Miles's account is the most vivid of all:

At about 3 p.m. the enemy commenced massing his troops in two columns, one on each side of the road, flanked by a line of battle about 800
yards in front, in the woods. Their orders could be distinctly heard. They
soon advanced with a tremendous yell, and were met with a sure and
deadly fire of one simple line. A very sharp engagement continued about
an hour, when the enemy fell back in disorder. Their charge was impetuous
and determined, advancing to within 20 yards of my abatis, but were hurled
back with fearful loss, and made no further demonstrations. (OR 69)

To question the accuracy of Miles's account is not to accuse him of deliberate
falsehood. One of the most persuasive qualities of *The Red Badge of Courage* is its
emphasis on how men engaged in battle rapidly lose perspective on distance,
time, and numbers. Further, the wooded terrain in the Wilderness on Hancock's front was such that panoramic vistas were rare, and vision was often limited to twenty or thirty yards. But in light of the rebel intention to convince the
Union forces they were indeed under attack, and in light of the unexpected success a skirmish line seemed to enjoy in repulsing a supposedly "determined"
and "heavy" rebel assault, and in light of Miles's own reiterated reference to the
sound rather than the actual size of the forces facing him, what actually happened seems clear. This was an affair of skirmish lines on both sides—utterly serious to men whose lives were at stake but nothing approaching the significance
it was given in some reports. To put it more succinctly, the rebel bluff worked especially well in the cases of Colonel Nelson A. Miles, Brigadier General John
Caldwell, and Major General Winfield S. Hancock.

Consider the rest of the evidence from the *Official Records*. Some of the reports
from Caldwell's brigade and other formations of the First Division do note a
strong rebel effort against Miles's "pickets" (OR 70, 75, 78, 81), but they unanimously specify that this effort reached no further than those pickets. Other
First Division reports (OR 76, 79, 80) remark only artillery fire and general skirmishing, for example: "The left of my line of skirmishers had passed over the
ground where there had been a skirmish; several of the dead lay in the woods,
and the ground was strewn with the knapsacks of friends and foes" (OR 79).
Most striking, a lieutenant of Miles's own regiment who was actually on the
picket line on "the afternoon of the 2d instant" did not experience anything significant enough to be worth mentioning in his report (OR 71). One reporting
participant uses exactly the metaphor chosen by both Couch and French: "The
enemy was engaged in feeling our lines all day, but could make no impression"
(OR 77). Keep in mind that these are all reports from Hancock's First Division.

What of French's Third Division? Not a single report mentions any infantry combat at all on May 2, until the evening after Jackson's attack (OR 93–107).

From the Confederate side, reports from McLaws's division confirm that no forces larger than skirmish lines were advanced during the afternoon. Only "thirteen companies" (forming a body barely larger than a single regiment) advanced from Kershaw's brigade into "the dense wood in my front" (OR 316). Only five companies were advanced as skirmishers in front of Semmes's Georgia brigade (OR 318). In obedience to McLaws's specific orders, they undertook "desultory skirmishing, sometimes growing quite sharp, which continued throughout the day" (OR 317).

What, then, of General Couch's claim in *Battles and Leaders*, that, at "halfpast two that afternoon the Second Corps' lines were assaulted" and that "just previous to Jackson's attack" there was a "desperate effort . . . by Lee's people to carry the left"? The simplest explanation is that his name should be added to the list of those Union officers who were effectively misled by McLaws's rebel skirmishers. To the names of Miles, Caldwell, and Hancock, add the name Darius Couch.

This list of names progresses right up the chain of command, and Couch would have had no reason to question claims advanced with such unanimity, especially given the admiration Hancock and his division enjoyed throughout the Army of the Potomac. If Couch accepted the accuracy of these reports at the time, nothing in the months or years after the battle of Chancellorsville would have caused him to question them thereafter. Hancock continued to grow in esteem, succeeding Couch as commander of the Second Corps, in which post he would be severely wounded at Gettysburg. He returned from his wounds to serve throughout the campaigns of 1864 and, after the war, became the 1880 Democratic candidate for the presidency of the United States. Caldwell had a less spectacular but nonetheless very solid career. And then there is the obscure Colonel Nelson Miles, his name becoming prominent for the first time in these official reports about the action on the Second Corps front on the afternoon of May 2, 1863. Twenty-four at the time of this battle, by the age of twenty-six he would be the commanding officer of the Second Corps himself, by twenty-seven, a major general. In the years after the war, Miles would achieve national fame, leading campaigns against the First Nations. In 1892 he would be awarded the Medal of Honor for his conduct at Chancellorsville. And from 1895 until 1900, he would be the commander in chief of the U.S. Army. It is not clear when Couch wrote his Chancellorsville article for *Battles and Leaders*, but, during the years between the end of the war and Couch's death in 1897, two of the men in his corps who wrote those reports about the battle on May 2 were as famous, accomplished, and distinguished as anyone among the living veterans of the Army of the Potomac. As Couch recalled his experience of the battle itself, his wartime association with these now-so-prominent men must have been a source of the greatest satisfaction.

Furthermore, Couch was so disgusted with Hooker's blundering during the Chancellorsville campaign that, after its conclusion, he asked to be relieved as commander of the Second Corps. Although he became a division commander in the West in 1864, he never again held such high command: as the senior corps commander at Chancellorsville, he had been second in command of the Army of the Potomac itself. Revealingly, his account of the steadfastness of his "Second Corps' lines" is not placed in the article in chronological order, but after he has given his version of the collapse of the Eleventh Corps under Jackson's attack, and his explanation for it—that the numbskull "conjecture of Hooker" that Lee was in retreat had put "the superior officers of the right corps . . . off their guard" (BL 3:163). In sweet contrast to which he presents two sentences (actually irrelevant to this part of his article, which is dealing with Jackson's 6 p.m. attack) about the steadfastness of his own corps: "At half-past two that afternoon the Second Corps' lines were assaulted by artillery and infantry. Just previous to Jackson's attack on the right a desperate effort was made by Lee's people to carry the left at Mott's Run, but the men who held it were there to stay" (BL 3:163).

So what was in fact a successful rebel bluff and a combat limited to skirmish lines was perceived at the time as something remarkable. In the postwar years, the small affair swelled even more significantly in the retired general's mind, not so much through active embroidery as through satisfied recollection: "the men who held it were there to stay." His pride is palpable in his understated style.

Crane evidently did note a discrepancy between the general situation on the Second Corps's front that afternoon, as established in most of the Federal and rebel reports, and the implications in Couch's and French's accounts. Those two latter accounts, especially when taken together, do suggest that something significant—an action of sufficient intensity to make a "brigade-size" catastrophe plausible—had happened there; but such a situation is not confirmed elsewhere in the *Official Reports*. Crane's fiction implicitly acknowledges this discrepancy (see Chapter 3). His portrayal of the rout of "Saunders's" brigade will at least intimate that the reason lay not in the strength of the rebel attack so much as in the brigade's own faulty deployment. Thereafter, he will undercut the 304th New York Regiment's rookie impression about the magnitude of the rebel attack ("the hull damn' rebel army" [*RBC* 66]) that they faced. But later that afternoon, Private Fleming himself will conclude that this "affair" had actually been "meek and immaterial" (*RBC* 83–84). So, to the list of those Federal soldiers taken in that afternoon by the bluff of McLaws and his rebels could also be added the fictional names of Colonel MacChesnay, and (for a time) Private Henry Fleming and his fellows.

But, faced with this discrepancy, why did Crane settle for such subtle (even supersubtle) compromises, instead of doing further, more meticulous reading in order to achieve the greatest possible certainty about what actually happened in front of French's division during the midafternoon of May 2, 1863? Such further labor might not have appealed to him, given the creative and original impulses his research was intended to buttress. The *Official Reports* of the operations of brigades and regiments consist almost entirely of dry factual recitals—movements, deployments, orders, statistics, exact locations in reference to other units at each stage of the battle—and inert, cliche-ridden depictions of action, such as, "The men of the Sixty-fourth worked coolly and steadily, taking good aim, and but few shots were thrown away" (*OR* 79). This is hard going; it is impossible not to skim. This is the very writing that Crane was impatient to turn inside out, so to speak. He was eager to enliven the arid facts and bloodless narratives, even to the extent of deleting most "facts" altogether, in order to present instead what those narratives deliberately eschew: the sensations of battle. It is hardly surprising that he turned from research to writing, once a (seeming) sufficiency of fact established itself in his imagination.

Further, he took pains to avoid identifying any of his brigades or regiments with historical ones. To have descended further than (what would have seemed to him) necessary into the records of specific historical brigades and regiments at Chancellorsville might well have struck him as not merely supererogatory but even a little risky to the fictional purity of his invented formations. And even if he did read those records more deeply or more thoroughly, it is not at all certain he would have seen the errors in French's and Couch's accounts. The general commanding the Third Division (seemingly) testified to the breakdown of Federal formations on his own right front.

Human nature being what it is, few if any of the *Official Records*, written in each case by the commanding officer of the given formation, admit to humiliating failure. Nor is sheer mendacity involved. Crane, a master in the study of human self-delusion, would have known better, and he would have been signally unsurprised to find precious few brigade or regimental commanders reporting the abject defeat of their units. Brigadier General Charles Graham, commanding a brigade in the Third Army Corps, forwarded the report of one of his colonels (Collis, commanding the 114th Pennsylvania) with the following "indorsement": "it is incumbent upon me to say that it is a complete romance from beginning to end" (*OR* 119). Since these were Third Corps formations, Crane probably did read this "exchange"; if so, surely with mordant pleasure. So he certainly would not have anticipated finding any frank confirmation of failure by those who had failed. After all, he would not have believed he needed them. Did he not have the clear, direct testimony of the commander of the division, about what happened to his front on the afternoon of May 2?

It must have seemed to Crane that testimony had given him exactly what his plot needed. Soldiers in General Henderson's brigade in the "reserves" (*RBC* 52) will find battle descending upon them with the collapse of a brigade to their right front. This gives Crane a warrant to portray soldiers failing the test of courage that Private Fleming has been dreading, even before Fleming himself is confronted by it. The rout of "Saunders's brigade" ratchets up a reader's concern about Fleming's response, by making a soldier's failure of courage more than merely plausible—by showing it happening to an entire formation. So if Fleming does not fail, the ironic sequence (his fear of failure, the failure of many others, and then his actual success) will add hugely to a reader's satisfaction and relief—and, of course, to Fleming's own satisfaction and relief. On the other hand, if Henry Fleming does fail when his own moment arrives, his cowardice will not seem a bizarre and rare phenomena but, instead, something common enough on the field of battle—a fact of considerable importance in a reader's moral judgment of him and, needless to say, in Fleming's own judgment of himself.

With the narratives of Couch and French thus providing his armature, Crane must have been eager to shape this part of his novel upon it, perhaps too eager to return to the dense print and mind-numbing dullness of other accounts in the *Official Records*. The substance of my argument, however, is not that Crane did too little research but that he did considerably more than is usually recognized. And however he may have been misled in this one detail, it is clear that in preparing his novel he did read the most significant sources accessible to him (or to a student of the Civil War, even a century after him) with imagination and attentiveness.

—⁓—

A reader may be understandably inclined to doubt whether this long-after-the-fact evaluation is plausible, privileging as it does the after-action report of rebel officers over those of Federal officers, one of whose accounts (Couch's) was found of sufficient stature to merit publication in volume 3 of *Battles and Leaders*. A reader knowledgeable about American military history might well be inclined to doubt this argument altogether, given the reputation for brilliance that Hancock enjoyed at the time, and the glittering subsequent record both he and Miles would accomplish. Such doubts are probably reinforced by the word "rebel" itself, used consistently by Unionists from Abraham Lincoln down to a raw private soldier in the 304th New York Infantry (*RBC* 66). "Rebels" does connote a less-than-professional armed force, a rabble in arms, banditti, an assembly of guerrillas. It is in this fashion that Private Fleming has imagined them: "gray, bewhiskered hordes who were advancing with relentless curses and chewing tobacco with unspeakable valor," or "fierce soldiery who were sweeping along like the Huns," or "tattered and eternally hungry men who fired despondent powders" (12). This impression is compounded by the homespun, raffish, sometimes barefoot appearance of the Southern soldier himself (and by the more recent adoption of that soldier's principal symbol, his battle flag, by the most deliberately illiberal and defiantly uncultured elements in our nation).

The Army of Northern Virginia has justifiably gone down as one of history's great armies. At the time of the battle of Chancellorsville, it was at the top of its game. Whatever problems this Confederate army had with logistics and supply, at every level it enjoyed combat leadership that was thoroughly professional—more so, in most every case, than that to be found in the Army of the Potomac. This superior professionalism and, conjoined with that, a greater relish for combat are reflected in the *Official Records*. Reports from rebel officers are almost always more lucid and engaging than those of their Federal counterparts. The best proof, however, is the historical record itself. For over a year, this army had consistently defeated Federal armies that were far larger in numbers and that enjoyed incomparably better equipment and supply.

The "rebel" army was the product of cultures that particularly celebrated the warrior, whether of the cavalier or the border-captain tradition. During the previous century, forebears of these "rebels," themselves wearing homespun motley, had repeatedly defeated the best professional soldiers in the world, the British army under Ferguson, Tarleton, Cornwallis, and the duke of Wellington's own brother-in-law. And this Southern army was also, less happily, the product of that garrison-state mentality necessitated by the institution of racial slavery. For example, John Brown's effort to spark a slave rebellion drew down upon the raiders in the isolated village of Harpers Ferry over five thousand armed men (both formed militia and eager "civilian" allies), in a matter of hours.

Knowledge of weaponry, a readiness to join in concerted military action, a willingness to accept leadership, and an upper class trained both formally and informally to provide such leadership, these aspects were endemic in the culture from which the rebel armies were raised, and they produced a superb soldiery. The evidence ranges from the fictional record of *Adventures of Huckleberry Finn* to the *Official Records of the War of Rebellion*.[23] So, in leadership, skill, discipline, inclination, and esprit, these "rebels" were quite capable of deceiving Federal commanders as talented as Hancock and Miles.

—⁓—

It is interesting that Crane is not alone in being misled about the events of May 2 on the Second Corps's front. Edward J. Stackpole's 1958 study of Chancellorsville is the work of a professional soldier and is considered "the book of record for its time and its subject." In light of Miles's subsequent career, the praise given him in the various official reports inevitably seized Stackpole's attention. But Stackpole also recognized the midafternoon action on the Second Corps's front for what it was: "The skirmishing along the lines was especially severe on the front occupied by Hancock's division of Couch's Second Corps. . . . . At no time, however, did it assume the aspect of a decisive attack and consequently, after a number of local exchanges, the Federal troops appraised the Confederate exercises for what they were, mere distractions." Confronted by this contradiction, Stackpole resolved it by shifting his depiction of Miles's action to a later hour of the battle, and by identifying a "vicious" rebel attack on the "center" of the Union position, immediately following upon Jackson's twilight assault upon the Union army's right:

> His ear acutely cocked to sounds from the west, Lee acted promptly to order into action the divisions of Anderson and McLaws as soon as the noise of the conflict on the Turnpike [that is, Jackson's assault] reached him. The two Confederate generals threw their divisions . . . into a vicious attack on Hooker's center at Chancellorsville. . . . . Hancock's division of the Second Corps was posted at the center across the Turnpike and thus received the heaviest weight of the collateral Confederate blow, delivered with artillery and infantry by Lee's two divisions. The strongly fortified front line on Hancock's sector was under the command of an unusually keen young officer named Nelson A. Miles, whose skillful and determined

23. David Hackett Fischer, *Albion's Seed: Four British Folkways in America*, 212–25, 642–50, 859–62.

handling of the battle at that point, in refreshing contrast to much that happened elsewhere that afternoon of May 2, would win for him a retroactive Congressional Medal of Honor. Repeatedly and violently the Confederates concentrated their attack on Miles' regiment, but each time were vigorously repulsed.

This time scheme is flatly contradicted by all the Union accounts of Miles's action, however. All of them specify that it took place hours before Jackson's attack.[24]

For that matter, no Union or Confederate narrative in the *Official Records* reports that Lee pressed any such attack upon the Second Corps at all. Not a single report from anyone in either the First Division (OR 65–82) or the Third Division (OR 93–107) mentions any such major assault. For example, the report of the colonel commanding the Fourth Brigade of the First Division states that after "[Jackson's] attack commenced on the right (the Eleventh Corps) . . . our front was comparatively relieved from any vigorous assault by the enemy" (OR 77). R. E. Lee himself reports:

> As soon as the sound of cannon gave notice of Jackson's attack on the enemy's right, our troops in front of Chancellorsville were ordered to press him strongly on the left, to prevent re-enforcements being sent to the point assailed. They were directed not to attack in force unless a favorable opportunity should present itself, and, while continuing to cover the roads leading from their respective positions toward Chancellorsville, to incline to the left so as to connect with Jackson's right as he closed in upon the center. (OR 309)

Obviously Lee did not want to commit McLaws's and Anderson's thin divisions against Federal formations that still heavily outnumbered them, until he could make contact with Jackson's assault driving in from his left and thus reunify his army. Until that reunification, the divided state of the Army of Northern Virginia remained precarious. General McLaws confirms this particularly in his report: "It was not until late in the evening that it was known General Jackson had commenced his assault, when I ordered an advance along the whole line to engage with the skirmishers, which were largely reinforced, and to threaten, but not attack seriously; in doing which General Wofford became so seriously engaged that I directed him to withdraw" (OR 315). In sum, Stackpole's response

---

24. Stackpole, *Chancellorsville*, William C. Davis, "Foreword," 227, 247–48.

to the reports about Miles's "skillful and determined handling of the battle at that point" was to invent an entirely fictional rebel attack on the Union army's Second Corps, in which to place it, just as Crane unwittingly created an entirely fictional crisis in the Union army's Second Corps upon which to base his novel.

I recognize the paradoxical nature of this argument—that the fact Crane's portrayal of the 304th New York Volunteer Infantry Regiment's baptism of fire is historically inaccurate is proof not that he did little research, but of the contrary: that he researched the battle of Chancellorsville thoughtfully and in the depth commensurate with his literary ambition. It seems to me that he turned to exactly the sources one would anticipate, to the account of the battle according to the commander of the corps he had selected, and to the official record of the battle as presented by the commander of the division he had selected out of that corps. They both misled him: one through pure rhetorical sloppiness; the other for a complex of reasons, beginning with the effectiveness of rebel tactics on the afternoon of May 2, and then because of understandable psychological responses. Crane might have heard of the nightmare shelling of the Federal field hospitals from veterans reminiscing about the Chancellorsville campaign beneath the monument to the 124th New York in the Port Jervis town park. But from nowhere else except these two documents (Couch's and French's) could he have derived the misconception that rebel attacks managed to rout an entire brigade in the sector of the Second Corps at midafternoon on May 2.

The fact remains, however, that all this is indeed paradoxical. Let me anticipate two criticisms. Both have the undeniable virtue of simplicity, and the second has ramifications that are significant enough to warrant the full attention of the final portion of this chapter.

The first objection is finally irrefutable. All I can do is offer the choice between it and my own contention. Crane may well have just created a fictional division in which to locate Henderson's brigade—let us call it the Fourth Division of the Second Corps. This would be consistent with the rest of the novel, in which no formation or character actually depicted is "historical." As with "Grandpa Henderson" and with the new officer (riding like a cowboy) who replaces him in command of the brigade, so perhaps with the general commanding the division: these could all be fictional. If this is the case, Crane seems to have slotted this Fourth Division more or less in between Geary's Second Division of the Twelfth Corps on its right and Hancock's First Division of the Second Corps on its left. If you prefer to believe that Private Fleming is in a fictional Fourth Division, then please substitute in your mind's eye an orange or green badge on his cap, in place of the light blue one you were invited to imagine above.

The second objection is indeed the simplest rejoinder imaginable, namely, that all this speculation is pure nonsense, given what is perhaps the major theme of the novel. Is not *The Red Badge of Courage* a study, and a brilliant one, of the meaninglessness, the chaos, the utter pointless randomness of war? Is it not Crane's point that war is by its very nature without reference, clarity, or comprehension? Is it not Crane's point that Fleming and his fellows are lost in its fog? To try to discern any "real" historical pattern, then, is not only a pointless exercise but one that, carried to its own misleading end (after all, ambitious imaginations can always discern patterns in instances of sheer chaos), would do an active disservice to students of the novel.

This would certainly be a plausible objection concerning any of several great fictions coming from the Great War of 1914–1918. Authors often found the perfect outward and visible image of the (supposed) meaninglessness of that war in the horrific confusion of those Western Front battlefields. A confusion, a profound dislocation, a strange isolation is implicit even in the titles of several of the best: *All Quiet on the Western Front, The Enormous Room, The Middle Parts of Fortune, Company K, Through the Wheat.* To try to track down the German formations to which Paul Bauer is supposed to belong in *All Quiet on the Western Front* would indeed be a misleading and misled undertaking.[25]

But great literature based upon the face of battle will develop its themes out of the particular details of the particular "face" produced by any given historical moment. The (supposed) end of meaning in the Great War is often imaged in its literature—in portraying, for example, the very real erasure of the landscape itself under the impact of the massive heavy artillery used for the first time in human history in that war. On the other hand, though, it is in Pierre's journey from the false and Europeanized St. Petersburg to the truly Russian world of wintertime Moscow, a journey parallel to and occasioned by Napoleon's 1812 invasion, that the hero of *War and Peace* finds meaning sufficient to redeem his life. We should not read *The Red Badge of Courage* with a predisposition dominated by fictions set during a war that happened fifty years later, involving weapons of destruction (among them poison gas, armored vehicles, aircraft, and battlefield artillery big enough to obliterate the landscape) that were unknown to the soldiers of the 304th New York Volunteer Infantry Regiment.

25. But see Michael Reynolds's *Hemingway's First War: The Making of "A Farewell to Arms,"* which traces Frederic Henry's military career on the Isonzo front with extraordinary, informative, detailed precision.

Crane's characters are not universally lost in a "fog of war." Lieutenant Hasbrouck is obviously as innocent of combat experience as the rest of his fellows, but even in his first battle, he sees things clearly and performs his duty capably. Although he is "shot in the hand" (*RBC* 49), with the enormous burden of company command descending upon him with the death of his captain in the first exchange of fire (60), the lieutenant nonetheless challenges deserters and, despite his own wound, somehow helps a panicked soldier reload his rifle (59, 69). Battle excites him into language that borders on the delirious (169), but his perceptions are acute, and he leads and directs his company with clarity and effectiveness (186, 194–95), motivating his men with praise as well as censure (168, 40), perceptive about their individual performances in even in the most disorienting moments of battle, and quick to report on their conduct to his commanding officer (206–7).

It could be objected that officers are exceptional in their appetite or capacity for combat, that they are selected as officers because they are exceptions to the rule, and that Private Fleming is representative of the typical, ordinary mass of men for whom battle must be "appalling," and that the real truth about war can be seen in Fleming's "blind" panic-stricken confusion (*RBC* 69). But such an objection must be based upon two claims about Fleming himself: that he is typical, and that his blind confusion results from the horrors of combat. Neither of these claims will stand examination. We shall consider his personality and his actions more closely later, but for the time being, please note: Private Henry Fleming's vision is "befogged" this afternoon, but not by the realities of the infantry combat he experiences, and his vision will not seem "befogged" at all on the second day, when he will stand "erect and tranquil" (209) and watch the battle of May 3 with a vision as arrogant as it is wide-ranging. But it is time to examine the historical realities of the battle that Private Fleming is about to encounter. We will consider the military and technological developments that led to a war in which two combatant armies, both molded out of the military heritage of the Western world, could be entirely armed with muzzle-loading rifles, and the particular kind of infantry combat dictated by that gruesome fact.

Chapter 2

The Rifled Musket

Infantry Combat in the Civil War

The American Civil War was the first major war in which the rifle was the standard infantry weapon on both sides of the battle line. A novel set in the Revolutionary War or the Napoleonic wars that used the term "rifle" as ubiquitously as Crane employs it would be altogether inaccurate. On the walls of the hut shared by privates Wilson, Conklin, and Fleming "three rifles were paralleled on pegs" (*RBC* 4). Had these three soldiers been at Valley Forge under Washington rather than at Falmouth under Hooker, they almost surely would have had three "muskets" paralleled on pegs. One of Private Fleming's first glimpses of rebel infantry will be of them coming toward him and "swinging their rifles at all angles" (*RBC* 54). Were Private Henry Fleming facing Napoleon's attack at Waterloo rather than Lee's at Chancellorsville, he certainly would have seen the French bearing down upon him "swinging their muskets at all angles." And when, for instance, Barbara Tuchman repeatedly uses the term "riflemen" in *The First Salute* to refer to rank-and-file American infantry during the Revolutionary War, or the term "rifle fire" to refer to infantry fire, she is committing a (very common) error.[1]

In writing that dates from the time of the Civil War itself, the problem is

---

1. Barbara Tuchman, *The First Salute: A View of the American Revolution*, 284.

reversed. In the 1860s, the use of the word "musket" as the defining term for the infantryman's long firearm was so traditional that the weapon which nowadays would be called a rifle was then officially designated a rifled musket. During the Civil War, the general term for infantry fire was "musketry": "at 11 p.m. [there was] a heavy musketry firing on our left" (OR 96). This usage was perhaps dated even then and can certainly prove misleading today. By the outbreak of the Civil War, advances in technology (particularly in milling machines) made it possible to equip entire armies with reliable "rifled muskets." By the time of the Chancellorsville campaign, over 70 percent of the Federal regiments were armed with Springfield or Enfield rifles. The result upon battlefields was dramatic: the advantage passed (and hugely) from the offense to the defense.[2]

The Red Badge of Courage constantly elicits a reader's judgment upon the conduct of Private Fleming and upon the 304th New York Volunteer Infantry Regiment. After Private Fleming's first experience of combat, for example, he will judge his conduct as having been "magnificent" (RBC 64), and tomorrow morning, the 304th will indulge in some "grim rejoicing" about their performance in an early morning engagement: "By thunder, I bet this army'll never see another new reg'ment like us!" (RBC 169). Such self-evaluations abound throughout the novel, and they invite a thoughtful reader to consider whether they are accurate. Knowing something about battle tactics in the Civil War, and the weapons that led to the development of those tactics (knowledge in which Crane himself was obviously steeped, and which he assumes in his readership) will help a modern reader make more accurate judgments. That reader should always keep in mind the crucial fact (just stated above): with the universal employment of rifles, battlefield advantage passed—and radically so—from the attacking side to the defending side.[3]

To the untutored eye, rifles of the Civil War period look exactly like muskets of the Revolutionary or Napoleonic wars: three metal bands secure a metal barrel to a wooden stock, with a trigger and guard underneath and an external hammer on the right side. There are two significant differences, however. The earlier weapon was a flintlock and a smoothbore; the later weapon was a percussion

---

2. Griffith, Battle in the Civil War, 27; Nosworthy, Crucible, 183–84.

3. Battle tactics in the Civil War have become a subject of great scholarly interest. Of particular interest are McWhiney and Jamieson's Attack and Die (although the Celtic cultural dimension of the book's concluding portion seems questionable), Griffith's Battle Tactics, and Nosworthy's Crucible. The last two works challenge the generally accepted notion that the long range of the rifle explains entirely how the defensive came to be superior on the battlefield, negating the effect of the bayonet. A reader not wishing to become immersed in the subject might seek out Coggins's Arms and Equipment and Griffith's Battle in the Civil War, works that are simply drafted, profusely illustrated, and absolutely reliable on factual matters.

weapon and a rifle. A flintlock's firing was initiated by a shower of sparks produced by the striking of a flint upon metal, which ignited a small charge of powder in a pan below, which then, through a small touch-hole, ignited the powder in the barrel. And the term "smoothbore" means that the barrel was a simple smooth tube (modern shotguns are smoothbores). The smoothbore musket, constructed by supervised artisans, had been the standard infantry weapon for well over a century: the Brown Bess version served the British army, essentially unchanged, from the early eighteenth century to the mid-nineteenth, from the time of Marlborough to the time of Wellington. The standard ammunition for the smoothbore musket was a round ball loaded from the muzzle and molded to be considerably smaller in caliber than the muzzle itself, to enable quick reloading. Thus the "windage," the difference between the width of the ball and the width of the barrel, was relatively great. The musket was accurate only up to fifty yards; at a hundred yards it could not be relied upon to hit a man-sized target, and beyond that it was almost completely inaccurate.

The loading of the smoothbore musket was almost identical to the loading of the rifle. Most well-trained professional soldiers could probably fire three times a minute. With the fouling of the barrel during combat because of accumulating detritus from the residues of powder, the rate would fall off. Since a running man can cross fifty yards in ten seconds, and even a line of soldiers advancing elbow-to-elbow at the "common pace" could cross fifty yards in thirty seconds, defensive tactics were based on the sheer weight of gunfire, rather than accuracy. And until the advent of smokeless gunpowder late in the nineteenth century, accuracy would be inhibited in any case by clouds of powder smoke. Musket-armed soldiers awaiting attack at Blenheim, Bunker Hill, or Borodino would form in lines two or three deep. Their officers would give the order to fire only when the enemy came within certain range and would then try to sustain a heavy fire by having each rank give its volley in sequence, so the first rank was reloading while the rear rank fired, and the first rank could deliver its second volley as the rear rank was reloading in its turn. The weapons were so inaccurate and so cumbersome that Frederick the Great trained his Prussians to point their musket barrels at the ground twenty feet away, to compensate for the kick of the weapon and the tendency of the soldier to fire into the air. Pumping out an overpowering weight of fire—achieved by the disciplined speed of reloading and firing—was inevitably paramount. Seeking to take accurate aim was both futile and time-consuming.[4]

4. Brent Nosworthy, *The Anatomy of Victory: Battle Tactics, 1689–1763*, 189–92; Christopher Duffy, *The Military Experience in the Age of Reason*, 110–15, 204–14. Duffy's volumes about eighteenth-

This explains much about the curious stateliness of the drill and maneuvering of the period. Strict alignment in attack and defense were crucial, so the officers could bring their firepower to bear in unison, at precisely the time and place where it would be most effective. The regiment or battalion was essentially the weapon, not the musket itself, and it was aimed by the officer commanding it.[5] Commanders of the day aspired to have their own men formed into lines two or three men deep at the critical moment, so that all their muskets could be brought into play—and preferably upon an enemy formation still in column, where only the score of soldiers of the enemy's first rank could fire. Since musketry distances were short ("Don't fire until you see the whites of their eyes"), there was much reliance upon the bayonet. These were fitted to the musket barrel before a formation went into battle and either carried into the enemy's line in a final last surge or used in self-defense as the lines closed.[6]

The inaccuracy of the musket at any distance also explains why European states in the eighteenth century almost exclusively employed professional standing armies rather than citizen-soldiers assembled for limited periods of active service. Frederick the Great thought it took two full years to develop a reliable infantryman. To load the musket was a complex task and rendered more so by the need to load it in sequence with fellow soldiers. Fighting in tight-packed formations required endless drill, so the soldiers could be deployed effectively while maintaining alignment. Consider the difficulties inherent in keeping a line—one mile long and three men deep—in alignment as it advances a mile or more across woodland, field, and hill, crossing stone walls and streams. The consequent slow development of a battle demanded unflinching courage in the men, which was probably best secured through severe discipline to produce ubiquitous, immediate, and unquestioning obedience. Only professional soldiers could be expected to stand such drilling and disciplining, men for whom the military calling was a genuine one, or men in straits so desperate that the military was a last resort. The European states' decision in this matter was vindicated on almost every battlefield of the Revolutionary War where regular forces were pitted against untrained American militia.

---

century warfare are among the best on the subject in English. Nosworthy's is also excellent, though mired perhaps in drill specifics. My argument here is indebted to both. A reader seeking a brief introduction would be well served by Donald E. Graves's *Red Coats and Grey Jackets: The Battle of Chippawa, 5 July 1814*, 46–54, about the War of 1812.

5. There is surely a harmonic convergence of sorts, however subtle, in the similarity between eighteenth-century infantry drill and the predominance of the couplet in eighteenth-century poetry.

6. Graves, *Red Coats and Grey Jackets*, 46–54.

In all this, the advantage lay generally in attack. The aggressors' momentum and freedom of movement allowed the infantry to concentrate and strike the weakest part of the enemy's line, which had to await the impact in rigid formations or risk losing the effectiveness of its studied volley fire. Morale was generally higher among attackers; their advance would leave their own casualties behind whereas the dead and wounded would pile up amid a defending formation.

This was the general tactical situation in the eighteenth century for the infantry, the combat arm trained to fight on foot. The horse-mounted arm is the cavalry, and charging cavalry could cross a fifty-yard distance far more rapidly than infantry. It was difficult for cavalrymen to force a way through unbroken ranks, because their horses instinctively shied away from crashing into people and inevitably balked at hedges formed by long steel bayonets. But the cavalry's mobility allowed it to exploit any gaps in enemy lines and to constitute a standing menace against its flanks. In the charge, the horse-and-rider combination produced an impetus where the total was far more than the sum of its parts; it could be decisive against infantry whose battle lines had become ragged from the firefight, and catastrophic against infantry whose formations were broken. A good percentage of European cavalry was intended for battlefield use and was termed "heavy," that is, dragoons, who were essentially mounted infantrymen, and cuirassiers, big men wearing body armor and mounted on big horses. The cavalry's other major military functions, such as reconnaissance and raiding, were performed by horsemen much more lightly armed and mounted: hussars, lancers, and *chasseurs*.[7]

The third combat arm is the artillery, consisting of crew-served weapons that can engage enemy forces at considerable distance. The smoothbore artillery of the eighteenth century was accurate at five hundred yards or more, and a six-pound cannonball could cut through nineteen men or seven feet of earth at six hundred yards, so it greatly outranged the smoothbore muskets. Cannon could be massed together in front of enemy lines to subject them to steady bombardment while remaining immune to their musketry. If the defenders lacked sufficient artillery for "counter-battery" fire or had no way of sheltering themselves, their formations could be broken or forced to retire before the opposing infantry or cavalry were even committed to the battle. Thus the advantage in battle based upon the smoothbore musket lay generally with the side that could seize the offensive and commit its army to the attack.[8]

7. Keegan, *Face of Battle*, 153–59; Ernest Hemingway, "Introduction," *Men at War*, 11.
8. Graves, *Red Coats and Grey Jackets*, 51.

During much of the eighteenth century, soldiers from the German states were generally considered superior. Their perfection in drill, maneuver, and alignment was legendary, the result of their ability to endure and profit from strict discipline, itself the result of their pride in such ability and their belief that it constituted a particular quality of their Germanic temper. German officers were admired for their attention to alignment and formation. The most admired soldiers were the Prussians, and the most admired soldier of the eighteenth century was Frederick the Great. So thorough was the Prussian command of maneuver, so schooled their soldiers in instant obedience, that their commanders could place Prussian battle lines at the precise time and place for their fire to be the most devastating, and this no matter the terrain, weather, or enemy response. In this way they could take better advantage of the smoothbore musket (or, more properly, better reduce its inherent shortcomings) than any army of their age. Witnesses said admiringly that the Prussians moved "like clockwork," which was the appropriate and inevitable term of praise in the Age of Reason and of Deism, when forward thinkers conceived of God Himself as the great "watchmaker." (Frederick the Great and Voltaire were close friends.)[9]

The French Revolution and the fall of the ancien régime brought about sweeping changes in the military world, changes presaging the great wars of the twentieth century, but these changes did not include the technology that armed the common soldier. The smoothbore musket remained the standard weapon for the infantryman throughout Europe, so the basic realities of the battlefield remained unchanged. Yet changes in other aspects of warfare further enhanced the power of the offensive. Within twenty-five years of his death, the "clockwork" drill of Frederick's Prussian army had become a term of contempt rather than admiration. This was because the offense, as practiced by the most famous soldier of the new nineteenth century, was indeed so dominant.

The French royal army had been officered almost exclusively by the nobility of France, so with the Revolution, the old French professional army was wrecked. Impelled both by revolutionary zealotry and by the bankruptcy it had imposed upon France, the French nonetheless went to war with most of Europe. Desperately engaged on many fronts, they found their solution in the *levée en masse*, the "nation in arms." Where revolutionary fervor waned, conscription began, and the French fielded armies of barely trained new soldiers against the professional armies (traditionally small in size, because so expensive to maintain) of their foes.[10]

9. Duffy, *Military Experience*, 21–25; Christopher Duffy, *Frederick the Great: A Military Life*, 18–19 et seq.

10. John R. Elting, *Swords around a Throne: Napoleon's Grande Armee*, 5–25.

The French lacked both the time and the officers to inculcate the intricacies of drill into these new armies. Instead, they developed a new style of infantry combat, still based upon the smoothbore musket but drawing upon those qualities that the French assumed to be innately theirs: *élan*, spontaneity, audacity, individuality. French tactics emphasized the attack. They made a cult of the bayonet: using it required that you hurl yourself at your opponent, so it was the preeminent offensive weapon. Their raw soldiers were arrayed for the assault in the simplest of military formations: columnar blocks of men clustered beneath their revolutionary banners. Well-disciplined lines of professional soldiery could ordinarily shatter such columns through the massive weight of their musketry, which could, in a two-deep formation, put a musket at every eleven inches of its front, while in a column anyone not among the score or so in the forward rank would be helpless to return fire.

The French, however, also advanced large, loose arrays of skirmishers well in advance of their columns—arrays huge in comparison to anything known before, and loose enough to release that enterprise and individual dash the French assumed innately theirs. "Swarms," their opponents called these formations, or "clouds." Unopposed by similarly large skirmish lines, the French would work their way by short spontaneous rushes into musketry range of the enemy's battle lines and submit them to a stinging fire.[11] To try to chase away these swarms of skirmishers with massed countercharges would inevitably disorder your own defensive posture, and the French columns would roll through the gaps. To return volley fire would blind your own officers with its smoke, foul your weapons, and reduce the rate of your fire when the time came to oppose the assault columns. And it would waste your ammunition, since the French skirmishers were scattered across the landscape rather than concentrated in packed formations. This was the new military doctrine that the greatest captain of the age, Napoleon Bonaparte, inherited.[12]

11. Here is another possible harmonic convergence. At the same time, in the poetry of the early nineteenth century, the couplet fell entirely out of favor, to be replaced by blank-verse columns, and by the blocks of the ballad form and the ode.

12. Gunther Rothenberg, *The Art of Warfare in the Age of Napoleon*, 95–124. The literature upon Napoleon's military career, even in English, is vast. David Chandler's *The Campaigns of Napoleon: The Mind and Method of History's Greatest Soldier* is the acknowledged standard study. Among the most accessible works in English are Corelli Barnett's *Bonaparte*, Michael Glover's *The Napoleonic Wars: An Illustrated History, 1792–1815*, and Elting's *Swords around a Throne*. The general influence of these works upon what follows should be assumed. For anyone not interested in becoming submerged in the subject, see Vincent J. Esposito and John R. Elting, *A Military History and Atlas of the Napoleonic Wars*, "Introduction" (see especially the "Summary"), for an excellent brief description.

Napoleon had also inherited from the revolutionary regimes the belief that war should pay for war, and his logistics were based essentially upon confiscation from the local population. The French revolutionary and then imperial armies fed off the lands through which they campaigned, which generated continent-wide enmity that would last at least a half-century and which also doomed their armies when they invaded the least arable areas of Europe such as Russia and the Iberian Peninsula. In contrast, the Habsburg armies—for raisons d'état having to do with the very survival of their monarchy—were far more professional in their respect for the realms through which they campaigned. In the short run, this logistical equation meant that Napoleon's armies were unencumbered by the massive supply columns that slowed the operations of his major foes.

As Napoleon's star ascended, he surrounded himself with an increasingly professional army, officered by men who achieved their rank entirely through merit as displayed at musket-range on the battlefield (natural selection with a vengeance). His armies at their apogee were tactically sophisticated; the French imperial infantry formations could be deployed, arrayed, then maneuvered across the battlefield with great flexibility. Pinned in place by an assault of swarming skirmishers and clawed by their fire, enemy lines were primed for assault by the French infantry, whose formations were being adjusted to the particularities of topography and psychology even as the enemy was beginning to waver.

Bonaparte took steps to enhance the offensive power of the other two arms, the cavalry and the artillery. In order to emphasize the cavalry's ability to destroy enemy formations through frontal assault on the battlefield, Napoleon decreed a massive increase in the percentage of heavy cavalry in the French army and provided heavier helmets and breastplates for his cuirassiers. Napoleon's own military training had been in the artillery arm, and he took a particular interest in developing its offensive power. Artillery had traditionally been parceled out to give direct support to the infantry's battle lines. Napoleon both increased the number of cannon in his armies and taught his subordinates to mass them together in order to batter gaps in enemy positions. In the French republican and imperial armies, such massed artillery was typically thrust forward, ahead of the infantry's advance, to take full advantage of the fact that smoothbore artillery so greatly outranged smoothbore muskets.[13]

13. The study of Napoleon's battlefield tactics has also been burgeoning. Probably the most cited work in English is Rothenberg's *Art of Warfare*, which seems more a textbook than a narrative. Keegan's study of Waterloo in *The Face of Battle* is probably the most widely read. Books by Sir Arthur Bryant (especially *The Great Duke; or, The Invincible General*), Michael Glover (for exam-

Napoleon's tactics were based essentially upon the combining of these three combatant arms—the infantry (numerically dwarfing the other two), the cavalry, and the artillery. His armies prospered in the fertile lands of western Europe but lost a great deal of effectiveness in those parts of the continent where the native agriculture was thin. When the two arms dependent upon horses—the cavalry and the artillery—began to lose their effectiveness as the number of their animals dwindled, the efficiency of his forces decayed apace.[14]

Napoleon Bonaparte's ascension to world-girdling status was based upon these fundamentally simple tactics, developing as they did the offensive capacity of the large French armies he had inherited from the revolutionary years. Even a quick survey of the Napoleonic Wars suggests that from first to last, from the Italian campaigns of 1796 to Waterloo twenty years later, the French always seized the tactical offensive—this, no matter the strategic situation, relative strength of armies, or anything else. And while Napoleon's own overweening strategic ambitions led to the attrition of his forces in Spain and to his defeat in Russia and thus a year later in Germany, it is impossible to find a battle right down to Waterloo that he lost because his men were outfought. Their tactics, based upon seizing and sustaining the offensive, repeatedly both proved successful and generated a great moral advantage, an esprit, an instinct for seizing the offensive.

Their enemies were rarely able to devise answering tactics. Continental professional armies were initially overwhelmed by the French numbers as well as by their tactics. Continental rulers had no choice but to answer the French conscription with conscription of their own, at the cost of professional standards of

---

ple, *The Peninsular War, 1807–1814: A Concise Military History*), and Jac Weller (for example, *Wellington at Waterloo*) are informative and compelling, but these are based upon the general Anglophone understanding, developed by Sir Charles Oman in the nineteenth century, that the firepower of the English line repeatedly proved successful against the clumsy columnar tactics of the French. Recent studies challenge this orthodoxy and demonstrate that French battlefield tactics were far more flexible and imaginative: Brent Nosworthy's *With Musket, Cannon, and Sword: Battle Tactics of Napoleon and His Enemies* goes into more detail as it is based upon memoirs. George Nafziger's *Imperial Bayonets: Tactics of the Napoleonic Battery, Battalion and Brigade as Found in Contemporary Regulations* is rich with diagrammatic and tabular information. Rory Muir's *Tactics and Experience of Battle in the Age of Napoleon* stresses the "experience." I am indebted to all these works in what follows.

14. To leapfrog into future considerations, by way of defining what we, and Private Henry Fleming, encounter in the Civil War: only with the return of the combined-arms tactics of World War II armies (with the role of the cavalry necessarily taken over by mechanized armor and with the role of the artillery hugely increased by tactical airpower) would the offensive once again come to predominate in Western warfare. See, for example, Russell A. Hart, *Clash of Arms: How the Allies Won in Normandy*, 409–19.

drill and discipline. One has the impression that, while Napoleon's opponents opposed him with ever-increasing grimness and with ever-larger armies, their soldiery became less rather than more effective during those decades of battle. Austrian professionals stood up well enough against him in the early campaigns in Italy, but the Russian, Swedish, Prussian, German, and Austrian formations during the titanic campaigns of 1813 and 1814, even though frequently enjoying numerical and strategic superiority, more often than not were overmastered at the knife-edge of battle itself. They found themselves unable to carry their own assaults through to success or to maintain their own defensive positions against French assaults.[15] It is significant that the one European power that sustained a purely professional army throughout the Napoleonic Wars was the one that dealt most effectively with the French offensive tactics, whether employed by Napoleon's chosen marshals or (as at Waterloo) by the emperor himself. Let me confess immediately that this will be a particularly Anglophilic argument. A century ago, quite different claims about which powers were ultimately successful against Napoleon would have been rendered by military historians in Berlin or Vienna; even today, quite different claims are advanced by military historians in Moscow. There is no question that the continental powers, most inveterately the Austrian, did the heavy lifting. But the British battlefield accomplishment was significant, and it is a matter of historical record; the British battlefield accomplishment was based in part upon the rifle, which would become the battlefield weapon of significance from the mid-nineteenth century on.

The entirely professional and brutally disciplined British soldiers remained unshaken by the French skirmishers. When French columns were sent against them, their disciplined volleys shattered those columns on battlefield after battlefield. So repetitive is this pattern that the one battle (Salamanca) in which the British seized the tactical offensive is even now to be studied with some surprise, though a modern student's surprise is nothing compared to the surprise with which the British thrust fell upon the French army of Auguste-Frederic-Louis Viesse Marmont. For the rest, the same pattern reappears repeatedly: at the climax of the battle, the British lines, assisted by the most stable of their allies (the Portuguese, or the Hanoverian) shatter the French assault columns.[16]

The Prussians had been the preeminent soldiers of the Age of Reason, and

15. See, for example, Esposito and Elting, *History and Atlas*, maps 127–54.
16. Rory Muir, *Salamanca 1812*, 69–83. This fascinating study illustrates, among much else, that achieving entire and ironclad certainty about military operations is a chimera.

trapped in their "clockwork" drill they had been mauled by Napoleon. Why did the British succeed? The major reason is that their major European land campaigns were commanded by Lord Wellington, one of the great commanders of history. He was a great battle captain with a brilliant eye for terrain, who took pains to shelter his men on the battlefield and to feed them on their way to and from it. Wellington, schooled in India, was a master of maintaining his armies through sophisticated logistical structures that originated with the flour and gunpowder mills in England.[17]

Other contributing reasons lie in specific institutions peculiar to the British army of the period. In the first place, the British had long institutionalized "light infantry." Regiments in the British service were formed into battalions of ten companies each. The tallest and most prepossessing soldiers were formed into each regiment's grenadier company, which was expected to set the standard for courage. The quickest, most independent, and resourceful were formed into each regiment's light company, which served the battalion as its scouts and skirmishers. During the American Revolution, these light companies achieved a high degree of effectiveness. On the eve of Britain's entrance into the Napoleonic Wars, army reform not only stressed the role of the light infantry in particular but further institutionalized the concept by converting a number of regiments, such as the Forty-third and the Fifty-second, into "light infantry," soldiers extensively trained to fight in "open order" as skirmishers. There is every evidence that the professional competence of these companies and regiments more than compensated for the "dash" of the French skirmishers.

A second reason is that no army of this period made as great and effective use of riflemen as the British. During the Napoleonic Wars, several battalions of line regiments were equipped with rifles, and a new regiment of three battalions, the Ninety-fifth, was raised for service explicitly and entirely as riflemen. However minuscule this force, it combined professional discipline and long-range firepower to a degree unmatched by any other European power of the time. Clothed in green uniforms, wearing equipment of blackened leather, and armed with the short Baker rifle, these soldiers were the most lethally effective skirmishers in the world, capable of hitting targets at ranges far beyond those reached by the French skirmishers' smoothbore muskets.[18]

---

17. Esposito and Elting, *History and Atlas*, "Biographical Sketches"; Elting, *Swords around a Throne*, 507.

18. Elting, *Swords around a Throne*, 723.

This brings us to the peculiarities and capacities of the weapon known as the rifle. In the process called rifling, which gives the weapon its name, spiral grooves are cut into the interior of the weapon's barrel. If these grooves engage the projectile, they impart a spiral to its flight, which increases its accuracy tremendously. It is the difference between throwing a football (the rifle bullet) and throwing a soccer ball (the smoothbore musket ball). Rifles were used in combat for most of the century preceding the Napoleonic period. It was Natty Bumppo's accuracy with his frontier "long rifle" that gave him his fame and a couple of his nicknames. During the Revolutionary War, the rifle shot that killed General Simon Fraser was critical in the Saratoga campaign, and the battle of King's Mountain was decided entirely by the superiority of the rifle over the musket. The British experience with the accuracy of the American rifleman during the French and Indian wars was one of the reasons that during the Revolutionary War they sought German rather than Russian mercenary allies. Companies of Jaegers from the smaller German principalities, soldiers armed with short European hunting rifles, matched up well against the Patriot riflemen.

In wars in the eighteenth century, however, if rifle-equipped soldiers appeared at all, they were always in small, specialized contingents that supplemented the big musket-equipped battalions. The hand-production of rifles was expensive and time-consuming. Hundreds of hours could go into the production of one Kentucky or Pennsylvania long rifle. By the Napoleonic era, advances in technology had enabled the mass production of rifles, but the British were still hesitant about equipping entire brigades with rifles, because riflemen's rate of fire remained much lower than that of musket-armed men. In a rifle, in order to be gripped properly by the rifling inside the bore, the projectile had to fit tightly. The "windage" was nonexistent. If a rifle could be breech-loaded (that is, loaded by opening the rear of the barrel and inserting the projectile and the powder there), this would be no problem, and the projectile could be of exactly the same caliber as the barrel itself. But metal-working and metallurgy technologies had not yet reached the point where long infantry weapons could be reliably breech-loaded. Metal tolerances remained too imprecise, and the gases generated by the discharge inevitably escaped from the breech area, to the detriment of the weapon's effectiveness and the discomfiture of its user. The world's armies, including their riflemen, remained inevitably wedded to long guns whose barrels were breechless closed tubes that had to be loaded from the muzzle. Riflemen had to force tightly fitting or tightly wrapped projectiles all the way down the barrels of their weapons. In consequence, European military rifles had short barrels, and German and British riflemen were issued mallets to hammer the loads all the way home, a detail suggesting the effort and the time it took to load these rifled weapons—three times as long as it took to load smoothbore muskets. This explains why riflemen remained specialists, and why the brunt of the Napoleonic battles fell on infantry armed with muskets.[19]

The problem could be solved by some kind of muzzle-loaded projectile that would expand inside the barrel when the rifle was fired. In 1843, French army captain Claude Etienne Minié perfected the most famous and widely adopted solution: a cylindroconoidal projectile (that is, it was shaped like a bullet rather than a ball) with a plug at its base that caused it to splay outward at the base upon discharge, thus sealing tightly into the rifling. This was adopted by the U.S. Army in 1852 and, simplified by the removal of the plug and counting upon the hollow-shaped base of the bullet to accomplish the same end, became the famous (and variously spelled) minié ball of the Civil War.[20]

So, while the Springfield rifle in the hands of the statue of the Union infantryman on his pillar in the town square of Mount Vernon, Ohio, may look just like the flintlock musket in the grasp of the Minuteman on his plinth at the Rude Bridge, the real thing was a far different weapon—one that would utterly alter the infantryman's battle. In the first place, the firing of the Springfield rifle was initiated by a copper percussion cap, containing one half grain of fulminate, upon which the hammer fell. The older flintlock system was more complex mechanically and became useless in wet weather when the powder in the pan absorbed moisture. The sealed percussion-cap system was simpler, more instantaneous in its discharge, and effective in all weather.[21]

Far more important, the Springfield rifle could be fired as rapidly as that flintlock musket, but it was accurate at over five times the range (at three hundred rather than at fifty yards) and in the hands of brilliant marksmen could strike targets at five hundred yards and beyond. The long-range accuracy of the rifle made it the supremely "democratic" firearm. The efficiency of the smoothbore musket depended upon its use in mass, which in turn required an officer caste capable of maneuvering masses of enlisted men. Just as Achilles led his Myrmidons and the Black Prince led his knights, so it was still necessary to have aris-

---

19. This point is often made. See, for example, F. Myatt, *The Illustrated Encyclopedia of Nineteenth-century Firearms: An Illustrated History of the Development of the World's Military Firearms during the Nineteenth Century*, 24–25.

20. Nosworthy, *Crucible*, 23–35.

21. Myatt, *Firearms*, 19–23.

tocratic officers—Wolfe at Quebec, Washington at Chadds Ford—to provide physical leadership to lines of musket-armed solders. Aristocratic and feudal traditions that sustained the ideals of privilege and noblesse oblige, the codes of personal honor and chivalry, the systems of hierarchy, and an elite freed from commercial engagement were hardly atavistic, given the realities that still obtained in smoothbore-armed infantry combat. These were, in fact, of incalculable worth to any national or imperial state. But by May 1863, given the range of every private soldier's rifle, such leadership not only was no longer necessary but was downright suicidal. The Federal major general John Sedgwick, commanding that portion of Hooker's army at Falmouth this May morning, had a year and a month left to live. His last words were spoken less than a mile from this place: "They could not hit an elephant at that distance."[22]

Yet the fact that the common infantryman was now fitted out with a weapon of such phenomenally enhanced and lethal long range did not transform the nineteenth-century battlefield as one might at first have thought, even if one were, say, Captain Pierre Gillium of the Belgian artillery, who predicted in 1856 that the rifle's greater range would "take from" the individual infantryman "all thought of danger," would allow him to conduct himself on the battle line with complete "coolness and sangfroid," and would have the immediate tactical effect of replacing "close-order formations" with infantrymen deployed as skirmishers.[23] In the first place, the rifled musket had an extraordinarily low muzzle velocity, which meant that, while its projectile could indeed hit a target at five hundred yards, it did so only by carving a very high parabola in its flight. A minié ball aimed at an advancing enemy soldier 300 yards away would be seven feet above the ground at 150 yards. Riflemen had to be scientists in estimating ranges correctly; and the more experienced (or the more cynical) military theorists doubted whether an ordinary infantryman experiencing the psychological stresses of combat would be much better off with such a weapon after all. With a smoothbore, he and his officers at least had a fair idea of the effective range of their weapons. With these new rifles, you could fire entirely over (or entirely short of) an enemy soldier even though the bead on your barrel was squarely upon him.[24]

America's leading soldiers were not ignorant men, and they were fully aware

22. Noah Trudeau, *Bloody Roads South: The Wilderness to Cold Harbor, May–June 1864*, 145.
23. Nosworthy, *Crucible*, 45.
24. Ibid., 53.

of the far greater range and accuracy of the rifle. But in addition to these yet un-proved theoretical issues concerning the effectiveness of the rifled musket in combat, there was the weight of experience. The offense had proved superior to the defense in battles throughout the course of the eighteenth century. It had proved of even greater ascendancy during the wars of the nineteenth century's greatest soldier, Napoleon I, and had reconfirmed its superiority during the Mexican War, where maintaining the offensive throughout had brought Amer-ican arms remarkable military success.

Certain ineluctable realities about the armaments themselves, especially as they would be used in the landscape of mid-nineteenth-century America, would count heavily against the effectiveness of the rifle's long range. The dense smoke from the weapons' discharge would obscure vision. The wooded character of most potential battlefield sites would mean that enemy soldiers could rarely be seen—much less, fired at—at ranges beyond three hundred yards. Even with a high-powered modern rifle, few people today can hit a man-sized target at much beyond three hundred yards.[25]

Throughout its history, American military theory had been profoundly molded by French theory and practice, and (incredible as it may seem today) in the years before the Civil War Napoleon III was esteemed the leading statesman and the greatest soldier of his day. (Had Napoleon III had the good fortune to die in 1869, he might yet enjoy such esteem.)[26] During their long campaigns in North Africa, French imperial soldiers had become increasingly disenchanted with long-range fire, because estimating range was "too slow and too difficult." The French army had taken the decision to remove the back-sights (necessary to elevate the muzzle effectively for long-range fire) from their rifles. When they then handsomely defeated the rifle-armed Austrians at Magento and Solferino, the lesson seemed clear: the tactical offensive and the spirit of the bayonet still ruled the battlefield. Americans were so impressed that militia units began adopting Zouave dress, honoring the dash and fire of the North African shock troops of Napoleon's armies. To say that American military men on the eve of the Civil War were obsessed with "Napoleonic" tactics is but to say that they had closely studied the most recent examples of toe-to-toe battle in the Euro-pean tradition.[27]

25. Coggins, *Arms and Equipment*, 38–39.
26. Griffith, *Battle Tactics*, 22; John Milner, *Art, War, and Revolution in France 1870–1871: Myth, Reportage and Reality*, 4–5.
27. Nosworthy, *Crucible*, 58–60 (59).

The latest American infantry manuals not only were directly influenced by but sometimes were even literal translations of the latest French manuals. The most significant and influential American military theorist in the years before the Civil War was Dennis Hart Mahan, professor at West Point. His was the standard American work on infantry tactics, incorporated into army regulations. It insisted upon taking the offensive, upon seizing the initiative or wresting it away from the enemy with the countercharge and the bayonet. Confronting the vastly increased range of infantry firepower, theorists so schooled envisioned an increased use of skirmish lines and an increased speed for infantry deployment, always to the end of successful offensive attack.[28]

There is a complicating fact. West Point was administered by the Corps of Engineers because it was expected to produce not only army officers but men capable of building up the infrastructure of the new nation. The Corps of Engineers was the elite of the U.S. Army and it culled the very cream of the academy graduates, those top-ranking cadets who could choose their branch. They in turn became the most influential and significant officers in the service, and true to their training and their elected field, they stressed the construction of field fortifications in combat. They argued that such fortifications—trench systems, firing pits, bunkers—were particularly suitable to war conducted by the American Republic because they could shield unprofessional citizen soldiers and the small, irreplaceable professional officer corps that would direct them. Mahan himself was an engineer and published both that book about infantry tactics stressing the offensive and also *A Complete Treatise on Field Fortification*. Such professional and intellectual schizophrenia at the highest levels of the army's doctrinal and educational institutions evidences a troubling fact: as April 12, 1861, approached, there were profound issues about the conduct of war that had yet to be resolved.[29]

Concerning the defense, on the other hand, although the long range of the unprecedentedly accurate rifled muskets might not live up to promises, these rifles were also over five times more accurate than the musket at shorter distances, an accuracy enhanced by the scouring effect of the minié ball, which reduced the fouling of the barrel during action. Even if advancing enemy infantry could but rarely be engaged at five times the range obtaining on Napoleonic battlefields, as the range closed to seventy-five or fifty yards, soldiers could put rifle

28. Ibid., 78–84; McWhiney and Jamieson, *Attack and Die*, 59–68.
29. Griffith, *Battle Tactics*, 123–27.

fire into the enemy's ranks that was five times more accurate. Clearly there could be individual soldiers capable of utilizing the range and accuracy of these new weapons with murderous effect. Under the exigencies of real combat, most soldiers were probably incapable of the cool thinking necessary to achieve effective long-range fire. But even if 95 percent of the 304th soldiers would be unable to do anything other than fire "without apparent aim into the smoke" (*RBC* 59), this would still leave over thirty capable of utilizing their Model 1861 .58 caliber U.S. Rifle Musket to its full advantage. If each of them achieved a 50 percent hit rate with the eight shots he could take during a four-minute engagement, almost a hundred and twenty minié balls would have struck an enemy force. To a rebel regiment of five hundred, such a casualty rate would be shattering.[30]

Napoleon's successes were achieved by combining the individual efficiencies of the three combat arms. In the days of the First Empire, cavalry was always a threat on the battlefield: its impetus in the charge could break wavering infantry; its mobility always threatened to find a formation's exposed flanks; it could slaughter and terrorize broken formations, turning a retreat into a rout. The consequence was that infantry formations had to keep their ranks tightly formed and their regiments and brigades closely aligned. The enhanced accuracy and range of the infantry rifle effectively banished true cavalry, the men trained to fight from horseback using weapons (sword, pistol) wielded by one hand while the other handled the reins. The horse presents a large target; a dismounted cavalryman, hobbled by his boots and spurs and lacking a personal weapon with the range of the enemy rifles, is out of action.[31] Cavalry remained critically important in scouting, foraging, and raiding, but there was no heavy cavalry in the Civil War. and very few cavalry charges on major battlefields (Private Fleming will be privileged to see the outset of one of them); no cavalry charge on any major field achieved anything other than the slaughter of men and animals.[32]

The most brilliant cavalryman of the war was Nathan Bedford Forrest, who led not cavalry as classically understood but mounted infantry, soldiers armed

---

30. Nosworthy, *Crucible*, 590–91.

31. Automatic weapons will complete this banishment, as World War I will reveal. Consider the moment in the film "The Untouchables" when mounted government agents charge into submachine gun fire. Not a horse is hit; the logic of this invites consideration.

32. H. Hattaway and A. Jones, *How the North Won: A Military History of the Civil War*, 45–46; Nosworthy, *Crucible*, 42.

with rifles who used their horses for mobility and did most of their fighting on foot. Forrest assumed the tradition of Tennessee and the Southern frontier. Andrew Jackson's campaigns fifty years earlier depended upon the Tennessee mounted riflemen, known as the "dirty shirts." (Could something about the terrain or the agriculture of middle Tennessee and adjacent Southern regions have produced men especially capable of this kind of warfare?) Forrest prefigures the Boer commandos of thirty years later, even Erwin Rommel's Afrika Korps of the next century. But the fact is that the traditional cavalry arm—the most purely offensive of three major military arms in spirit, capacity, and effect—no longer belonged on the battlefield.

The artillery, on the other hand, could still lend weight to an offense, but this was the sum of its offensive capacities. Fifty years earlier, Bonaparte had said, "It is with artillery that one makes war." Fifty years later, artillery would dominate World War I, scarring both the landscape and the psyche of Europe. But during the American Civil War, artillery was effective principally as a defensive weapon.

The technology of the era had produced rifled artillery firing bullet-shaped projectiles that could be accurate at distances of more than a mile and a half. But the wooded terrain characteristic of most Civil War battlefields tended to negate this enhanced accuracy, and Civil War cannoneers also lacked any way of gauging the effectiveness and correcting the range of long-distance fire. Entrenched enemy soldiers would be sheltered from solid shot by banks of earth and logs, so the only kind of artillery fire that could substantially help infantry in the attack would be fire that could explode powder-filled shells above an entrenched enemy, causing casualties through the bursts and the downward spray of skewering projectiles. But the technology of the age had not yet produced effective fuses to detonate such projectiles. The fuse remained the same crude device it had been a century earlier, a powder-impregnated cord cut off at what the gunner estimated to be an appropriate length and set alight by the cannon's discharge. Even when fuses became more reliable (which would be soon, under the hothouse technological development that warfare always achieves), the bullet-shaped shells fired by rifled artillery tended to bury themselves harmlessly in the earth. So long-range shellfire from rifle artillery was unreliable and relatively ineffective.

Smoothbore cannon, especially the twelve-pounder "Napoleons" (developed by Napoleon III himself and firing projectiles of twelve pounds), were greatly preferrable to rifled artillery pieces. They had larger bores, inflicted more widespread damage at close range, and could be loaded more rapidly. The Napoleon had a maximum range of about two thousand yards, but its real damage was done at closer distances, and with solid shot and grape and canister. Solid shot were round twelve-pound cannonballs, effective to 650 yards, aimed so as to bounce and ricochet through successive lines of infantry. Grape shot and canister consisted of bags or cans filled with iron balls of an inch and a half in diameter, or sometimes canvas bags of scrap metal. This converted smoothbore cannon into giant shotguns and was murderous at close range but ineffective beyond about 350 yards. Neither solid shot nor grape and canister was effective against entrenched infantry in defensive array, because banked-up earth absorbs or deflects the projectiles. Smoothbore artillery could also employ shell, but the problems with fuses remained. In any case the Napoleon, far and away the best of the smoothbores, lacked the long-range accuracy of the rifled cannon; solid shot was effective to about 650 yards, canister only to 350. In warfare of the Napoleonic era, smoothbore artillery outranged smoothbore musketry by hundreds of yards and was often pushed forward on the battlefield to blast the way for attacking infantry. In the Civil War, on the other hand, artillery was genuinely effective against enemy infantry only at ranges that brought gun crews and their horse teams well within reach of enemy marksmen. Artillery unsupported by infantry was always at risk, even in defensive deployment, and to press artillery pieces forward in the Napoleonic tradition was to invite the slaughter of teams and crews.[33]

Thus Civil War artillery alone could not dislodge entrenched infantry in defensive array, or even contribute much to its own infantry when committed to assaulting such arrays. The most significant effort in the war to use artillery alone to pave the way for an infantry offensive would happen on the third day at Gettysburg, when Lee asked his batteries to prepare for "Pickett's charge," and the bombardment proved a signal failure. The rebel artillery officer who commanded it would (loyally) claim that the fault lay not in the theory but in the practice. The fact remains that the enemy lines were entirely unshaken by a barrage that could be heard as far away as Philadelphia, and the subsequent infantry attack ended in complete, bloody, famous failure. Civil War artillery came into its brutal own, however, against attacking or counterattacking infantry formations caught in the open. In dramatic contrast to Lee's massed guns at Gettysburg was

---

33. Coggins, *Arms and Equipment*, 63ff; Griffith, *Battle in the Civil War*, 26–27; Nosworthy, *Crucible*, 438ff.

McClellan's massed artillery in defense of his positions at Malvern Hill the previous July, which crushed repeated rebel assaults.[34]

Field artillery was rarely, if ever, massed at all in the Civil War, in fact. Instead, batteries were doled out in support of infantry brigades and divisions, to contribute to their defensive strength. This undercut the prestige of the artillery service considerably, since infantry officers now commanded the work of the artillery officers (a dramatic reversal since the great Bonaparte, who was an artilleryman by trade). Looking around on the afternoon of May 2, Private Fleming will be able to see exactly this: "From a position in the rear of the grove" where the 304th New York had just held its line, "a battery was throwing shells over it" in support (*RBC* 61). On the morning of May 3, the 304th New York will experience the effect of artillery when they attempt a counterattack: for the first stages of their charge they will be brought under shellfire (181); when they close they will endure canister (183). The artilleryman's typical combat experience during the war was to be thus employed, or sometimes to be engaged in counterbattery fire: "The refined joy of planting shells in the midst of the other battery's formation" (71).

Despite the relative inefficiency of shellfire as opposed to solid shot or canister, it is notable that Private Fleming is far more conscious of the former. As they witness Saunders's disaster, "A shell screaming like a storm banshee went over the huddled heads of the reserves. It landed in the grove, and exploding redly flung the brown earth" (*RBC* 49). Fleming will be especially aware of shells throughout these two days (65, 70, 162, 173). He will even see one rebel shell that performs exactly as intended. As the 304th launches a counterattack, the shell tumbles "directly into the middle of a hurrying group" to explode there "in crimson fury. There was an instant's spectacle of a man, almost over it, throwing up his hands to shield his eyes" (180–81). But by midmorning on the second day, Fleming will have developed a veteran's contempt for long-range shellfire (209).

On the other hand, solid shot and canister—infantry-killers both, and the kind of artillery an infantryman should be particularly aware of—hardly seems to figure in his consciousness. Neither term is ever used in the novel. This is not an oversight on Crane's part, but an indicator of Private Fleming's particular mentality. Fleming clearly will encounter canister fire on the second day. As the

34. Edward Porter Alexander, *Fighting for the Confederacy: The Personal Recollections of General Edward Porter Alexander*, 251–52.

men of the 304th press a counterattack, they are brought under it: "from the top of a small hill came level belchings of yellow flame that caused an inhuman whistling in the air" (*RBC* 183). These rebel guns are no longer elevated for distance but are "level," as they fire at the Union troops who have closed into canister range; the "whistling" of the canister is distinctly different to his ear from the "screaming" (49, 70) of the shells from rifled artillery or the "swirling" (65) and "flip-flapping and hooting" (173) of the less-accurate smoothbore shells.

So Civil War artillery enormously augmented the defensive firepower of the infantry, but it was of little value to an army committed to the assault. At this moment in military history, the weight and effect of the artillery arm contributed little to soldiers exposed while undertaking offensive operations. In contrast artillery contributed decisively—murderously—to the strength of formations entrenched in defensive positions.

With neither the cavalry nor the artillery capable of supporting infantry in the offensive, and facing the powerfully enhanced lethal ability of the weapon arming the individual infantrymen, direct assaults against entrenched infantry rifle fire proved ruinously expensive. Two early bloodbaths of 1862, Shiloh in Tennessee and Antietam in Maryland, produced casualty lists so large as to numb the nations whose men collided there. Field fortifications were not used in either battle. Grant, before the battle of Shiloh, was specifically ordered to see to them but did not. His army was surprised by the Confederates under Albert Sidney Johnston and was nearly destroyed. Johnston had absorbed the belief that the smaller side must compensate by seizing the offensive (a truth repeatedly proved by Frederick and Napoleon) and committed his army to headlong assault. R. E. Lee's failure to build field fortifications outside of Sharpsburg in Maryland is amazing. Despite the day's grace permitted by McClellan's cumbersome advance and despite Lee's observation of the massive size of the army McClellan was concentrating upon him, Lee's army dug no trenches and erected no barricades. McClellan himself, given a miraculous chance to destroy Lee's army, uncharacteristically (and in the event ineptly) committed the Army of the Potomac to an entirely offensive battle. In both these 1862 battles, attack and counterattack was the order of the day. Men were slain in windrows; formations vanished in the teeth of rifle fire at ranges dwindling from two hundred yards to ten paces. Both battles saw fire intensity and displays of raw courage that veterans remembered as unequaled in the rest of the war. Both battles, revealingly, were shaped by features of terrain—a declivity of the ground and a thicket at Shiloh, a sunken farm lane at Antietam—that became de facto field fortifications. The rebel inability to seize or bypass the "Hornet's Nest" until far too late doomed their assault at Shiloh, as did the Union army's inability at Antietam to carry, until too late, the "Bloody Lane."[35]

No subsequent major battle conferred immortality upon this kind of topographical feature, because the soldiers learned their lesson. Thereafter they dig "at the ground like terriers" (*RBC* 41) at every opportunity. Note that on this May morning two years into the war, even the raw soldiers of the 304th New York Volunteer Infantry Regiment will be constructing field fortifications at every opportunity, guided by the frenzied labors of the veterans in the regiments around them.

Napoleon had always sought to seize the initiative on the battlefield, to put his army on the offensive. The generals who were the most Napoleonic in character in the Civil War were probably two Confederates, T. J. Jackson and John Bell Hood. Jackson's vigorous offensive spirit succeeded brilliantly in his early campaign in the Shenandoah, conducted against raw, indifferently commanded Federal forces. Thereafter, under Lee's command, Jackson's enthusiasm for offensive action was constrained by Lee's relatively more cautious nature (though Lee himself was inclined to strike rather than await a blow). John Bell Hood, taking command of the Army of Tennessee in 1864, was under no such constraint, and he hurled his army into sequential head-on assaults against Sherman at Atlanta, losing men ruinously and finally abandoning Georgia. Undaunted, he launched an offensive campaign into Tennessee. Frustrated by failures of command, on November 30, 1864, and without artillery preparation, he threw his army of twenty-seven thousand men against twenty-eight thousand Federal soldiers under General John Schofield, in an assault that had to cross two miles of open ground against a well-entrenched enemy. In five hours, a quarter of the Army of Tennessee were killed, wounded, or missing; five Confederate generals were killed, thirty-five battle flags lost. After five months of enjoying such thoroughly Napoleonic leadership, the Army of Tennessee could only await, like a stunned animal, the killing blow, which General G. H. Thomas administered to it on the hills outside of Nashville.

So completely did the defense now dominate the field of battle that only by "turning" maneuvers (that is, by turning a foe's flank to achieve enfilade fire and to menace his rear) could a single formation or an entire army compel an enemy

---

35. Bruce Catton, *Mr. Lincoln's Army,* 258; Shelby Foote, *The Civil War, a Narrative: Fort Sumter to Perryville,* 1:340–51, 685–700; William A. Frassanito, *Antietam: The Photographic Legacy of America's Bloodiest Day,* 103. The narrative histories of Catton and Foote are deservedly famous. Frassanito's book is to me the single most fascinating and compelling book about the war.

to abandon a position. On the afternoon of May 2, 1863, and in his first experience of combat, Private Fleming will witness a good example of a turning maneuver at the tactical level—at the level of warfare in which combatant forces are locked in immediate battle with one another (see Chapter 3). At twilight on this same afternoon, Private Fleming will witness the consequences of a successful turning maneuver at the strategic level—at the level of warfare in which forces are maneuvered against each other at some distance, seeking to achieve tactical advantages that are widespread enough to determine the outcome of an entire campaign (see Chapter 6).

Chapter 3

Private Fleming's Regiment
Enters Combat

During General Joseph Hooker's wintertime preparation of his army, as his soldiers were "drilled and drilled and reviewed, and drilled and drilled and reviewed," Private Henry Fleming had "grown to regard himself merely as part of a vast blue demonstration" (*RBC* 11). He had returned to the precocious cynicism that characterized his initial response to the "war in his own country" (5). "Greeklike struggles would be no more. Men were better, or more timid. Secular and religious education had effaced the throat-grappling instinct, or else firm finance held in check the passions" (11). But with the first rumors of a coming campaign, "some new thoughts . . . had lately come to him" (4), and "[h]e tried to mathematically prove to himself that he would not run from a battle" (13). The novel's point of view was initially sweeping: "the retiring fogs revealed an army stretched out on the hills, resting" (1). Then it narrows down to Private Fleming's perception of the world, carrying with it the reader's interest. Fleming's concern "that perhaps in a battle he might run" (13) is so plausible that it is possible to overlook something very unusual about this private soldier's fears.

Private Fleming is only a few months away from being a schoolboy, and from this very first instance he continues to think of his problem in terms and images drawn from the classroom. "He was forced to admit that as far as war was concerned he knew nothing of himself" (*RBC* 13); "He recalled his visions of broken-bladed glory, but in the shadow of the impending tumult he suspected them to be impossible pictures"; "Whatever he had learned of himself was here of no avail. He was an unknown quantity. He saw that he would again be obliged to experiment as he had in early youth. He must accumulate information of himself" (14).

> For days he made ceaseless calculations, but they were all wondrously unsatisfactory. He found that he could establish nothing. He finally concluded that the only way to prove himself was to go into the blaze, and then figuratively to watch his legs to discover their merits and faults. He reluctantly admitted that he could not sit still and with a mental slate and pencil derive an answer. To gain it, he must have blaze, blood, and danger, even as a chemist requires this, that, and the other. (18–19)

The dominant image is that of a test in school, albeit with one great difference. Instead of proving his competence in a subject, this test will "prove himself."

As he conceives his situation, the potential penalty for failure and the potential reward for success are those of a school examination. If he is even suspected of lacking confidence in himself, he may find himself "derided" (*RBC* 20). But if he succeeds, he may secure "glory." Just as important, there will be the relief of having "passed" the test, of having it over with. Everything will be "settled forthwith," the "load" will be lifted. Thus during the two weeks' delay necessitated by Stoneman's mismanagement of the cavalry, it is the delay itself that is most onerous. "In his great anxiety his heart was continually clamoring at what he considered the intolerable slowness of the generals. They seemed content to perch tranquilly on the river bank, and leave him bowed down by the weight of a great problem. He wanted it settled forthwith. He could not long bear such a load, he said. Sometimes his anger at the commanders reached an acute stage, and he grumbled about the camp like a veteran" (21). Crane's reader cannot help but comprehend Private Fleming's emotional condition, all the more so because, nowadays, the reader is probably in an academic setting, and very probably not in any life-endangering circumstance.

Private Fleming's indifference concerning the cause to which the Union army is committed—that of the preservation of the American republic—is immediately obvious in even a cursory reading of *The Red Badge of Courage* and is certainly of considerable significance in any assessment of his character and of the novel itself. But Crane's success in involving his reader with Fleming's self-absorbed "problem" may obscure something even more surprising about this young man.

To put it simply, he has no idea what he is facing. This is because he has no idea what he is; he has no perspective at all upon his situation or his circumstance. None of these "new thoughts" with which he is wrestling has anything to do with the very real possibility that, in the course of taking this particular test, he may be shot dead, or maimed for life. Once brought out into the open, all this suddenly seems too obvious to need stating: that he is not facing a classroom examination but a battle in which he may very well lose his life. This is not at all obvious to Private Fleming. He is not even conscious of the fact.

This may be a good thing. This curious blindness may produce in him an ability to behave with great courage. On the other hand, it may cost him his life: "What like a bullet," Melville writes, "can undeceive!"[1] But whatever the outcome, this state of oblivion is surely atypical. The novel convinces us that a youth could indeed be as blind to his own mortal condition as Henry Fleming is. But upon sober reflection, it seems hardly possible that the generality of soldiers facing combat would be so ignorant—not stoic, but ignorant—about the possibility that the coming campaign may well bring an end to their earthly existence. Private John Wilson of the 304th, for example, is so secretly consumed with this possibility that it has become for him not a probability but a certitude. He seems altogether more typical. When a brigade "ahead of them and on the right" goes into action and combat approaches their ranks, he will tell Fleming that "I'm a gone coon this first and—and I w-want you to take these here things—to—my—folks" (RBC 45–46). Nor will one day's experience of battle "cure" Wilson of this foreboding awareness of the possibility of his own death. In the midst of battle the next morning he will say to Fleming, "Well, Henry, I guess this is good-by—John" (194). For nothing can cure us of the awareness of our own mortality.[2]

This awareness Private Fleming does not have, but it is part of Crane's strategy in the novel to obscure the fact. His principal techniques are the sudden narrowing of vision, which successfully traps us in Fleming's perceptions; the easily understood paradigm of the academic test; and a reader's ready appreciation of the fear of failure, which must face anyone contemplating a first experience of combat. But it is hard to imagine fear of failure alone would be the only

---

1. Herman Melville, "Shiloh. A Requiem," line 16.
2. Alfred Habegger, in his excellent "Fighting Words: The Talk of Men at War in *The Red Badge*," finds instead that this is Wilson's "slightly humorous invocation of the colloquial phrase, 'good-bye-John'" (237). But in the Appleton edition, the punctuation is as given here, and "by[e]" is separated from "John" with a dash rather than a hyphen. And although the colloquialism "a Dear John (letter)" is of course familiar, "good-bye-John" is not, to me.

fear generated in most of these "fresh fish" (*RBC* 17) of the 304th New York Volunteer Infantry Regiment.

In trying to deal with his newfound "little panic-fear" at the prospect of his possible cowardice (*RBC* 13), Private Fleming to this point has been particularly ill-served by the Union army's practice of forming its new recruits into completely new regiments. He has been "afraid to make an open declaration of his concern, because he dreaded to place some unscrupulous confidant upon the high plane of the unconfessed from which elevation he could be derided" (20). The absence of veteran soldiers in the ranks of the 304th means he has had no one to turn to with admiration for their proven steadfastness or with curiosity about their reactions to their first taste of battle.

All the men in the 304th are in the same situation, and no one else has confessed to such a fear of fear. Even if every other soldier feels the same way, a confession would reveal the presence of such fear. And this, in and of itself (regardless, so Private Fleming's mind works, of how one actually comes to behave), would give others an opportunity for public derision, which would be a devastating weapon in the competition in which one's own esteem can be enhanced at the expense of others. Even worse, the absence of veterans in the regiment leaves him with no examples of "proved men" (*RBC* 163) against whose familiar personalities, psychologies, and histories he could measure his own:

> In regard to his companions his mind wavered between two opinions, according to his mood. Sometimes he inclined to believing them all heroes. In fact, he usually admitted in secret the superior development of the higher qualities in others. He could conceive of men going very insignificantly about the world bearing a load of courage unseen, and although he had known many of his comrades through boyhood, he began to fear that his judgment of them had been blind. Then, in other moments, he flouted these theories, and assured himself that his fellows were all privately wondering and quaking. (20)

His efforts to tease out the truth about their expectations from the phlegmatic but violence-prone Jim Conklin and the loud, pompously modest John Wilson produce much hot temper and little satisfaction.

So his government's practice in the raising of its new regiments brings him to this May morning with his "problem" still unsettled and still unsettling. His nervous energy distorts his own conception of himself: "it occurred to him that he had never wished to come to the war. He had not enlisted of his own free will. He had been dragged by the merciless government" (*RBC* 36). It also distorts his perception of the world around him: "The regiment slid down a bank and wallowed across a little stream. The mournful current moved slowly on, and from the water, shaded black, some white bubble eyes looked at the men" (36). The nerve-wracked moment at hand conspires with the busily curious cast of mind that had brought him into the Federal service to begin with (6). Private Fleming "tried to observe everything" (37), and what he noticed in particular are the skirmishers ahead of him. "The brigade was formed in line of battle, and after a pause started slowly through the woods in the rear of the receding skirmishers, who were continually melting into the scene to appear again farther on" (36–37).

In the Civil War, soldiers were sent out in loose skirmish lines as much as five hundred yards in advance of the main battle line. A regiment might be detached from an advancing brigade or division to perform this task, or perhaps just one or two companies from a regiment. Their responsibility was to shield the main battle line from surprise; to fire upon the enemy's main line if they could, seeking to kill its officers and rattle its courage before the main lines engaged; and to suppress enemy skirmish fire upon their own battle line. The employment of skirmishers, a major element in Napoleonic warfare, was ubiquitous in the Civil War, and as is the case on the front of the 304th New York, they typically became engaged in dueling. "They were always busy as bees, deeply absorbed in their little combats" (RBC 37).[3]

The advancing line of battle comes upon the body of a rebel skirmisher, killed in one such "little combat." "He lay upon his back staring at the sky. He was dressed in an awkward suit of yellowish brown" (RBC 37). The corpse is wearing homespun clothing that had been home-dyed with "butternut," a dye produced out of various concoctions such as nutshells and rust. The color was ubiquitous throughout the Southern ranks, so much so that "Butternut" became one of the nicknames given them by Union soldiers. Beginning with a much smaller industrial base than the North and hampered throughout the war by a ramshackle logistical system, the Confederate government was rarely able to supply its soldiers efficiently. The rebels were not only often clad in homespun uniforms, they were also very poorly shod, and so with this casualty: "the soles of his shoes had been worn to the thinness of writing paper, and from a great rent in one the dead foot projected piteously." The way Private Fleming's mind works upon this is characteristic and revealing: "it was as if fate had betrayed the soldier. In death it exposed to his enemies that poverty which in life he had per-

---

3. Griffith, *Battle in the Civil War*, 32–33.

haps concealed from his friends" (37). In Fleming's mind, death has no meaning; it is the loss of prestige that is all important, even to a corpse.[4]

After a measured advance, during which Private Fleming is chastised by Lieutenant Hasbrouck for skulking (*RBC* 40), the brigade is halted in a forest. Without orders from their own officers but in emulation of veteran regiments "on the flanks who were digging at the ground like terriers," the soldiers of the 304th dig and build field "intrenchments" (41). The staggering casualty lists from the first and second years of the war (the battle of Antietam on September 17 of the previous year was the bloodiest day in the history of the American people, producing over twenty-five thousand casualties) brought home to the common soldier the truth about the murderous efficiency of Civil War weaponry. Formations inevitably entrenched themselves at every opportunity, until the battlefields of 1864 and 1865 would foreshadow those of the 1914–1918 Western Front. Henderson's brigade is moved twice more through the noon hour, the men entrenching or barricading their front each time.[5]

After lunch they are moved yet again, across the "same ground" (*RBC* 43) they crossed in the morning, and then on into territory that is new to them. Private Fleming's "problem" grows with renewed strength, such that "Once he thought he had concluded that it would be better to get killed directly and end his troubles." Death before shame, then—but Crane makes it clear Fleming is only "regarding death thus out of the corner of his eye." He conceives of it as a journey to "some place where he would be understood." He is looking "to the grave for comprehension" (44).

The test is nearly upon him. The firing of the skirmish lines grows in intensity, they can hear the high-pitched rebel yell, artillery opens fire, and the Union skirmish lines come running back, withdrawing before a rebel assault. Saunders's brigade "ahead of them and on the right went into action with a rending roar" (45). Private Fleming's curiosity, his "busy" mind (6, 45), engages itself in the moment.

"The brigade was halted in the fringe of a grove" (*RBC* 47). On the afternoon of May 2, the Army of the Potomac lay in a great saucepan-shaped deployment running some five miles from the Fifth Corps's positions on its left or eastern flank to the Eleventh Corps's position—the handle of the saucepan—on its right, or western flank. Its three center corps, the Second, Twelfth, and Third, were arrayed in that order in a southern arc from east to west that

4. Haythornthwaite, *Uniforms*, 179–80.
5. Paddy Griffith, *Battle Tactics of the Civil War*, 117–18; Nosworthy, *Crucible*, 533ff.

enclosed the map-reference point known as Chancellorsville Crossroads. The Second Corps was deployed facing east. It was formed to the east of a road into which funneled roads from the various river fords to the north. Just south and just to the rear of the Second Corps's position, this north–south road entered Chancellorsville Crossroads. The name Chancellorsville derived from the Chancellor House, a large plantation manor at the crossroads, where General Hooker established his headquarters. The conjoined Old Orange Turnpike and Orange Plank Road came in from the west, and at the crossroads these bifurcated again and led off on their separate ways east toward Fredericksburg.

The Third Division of the Second Corps formed a second line behind the First Division and constituted its "reserves" (RBC 49). It was "occupying the edge of the woods on the left [that is, just to the east] of the road" from the fords (see OR 94, 95, 96). During the day, the Third Division was assembled in this position in a way that would have indeed seemed "apparently aimless" (RBC 41) to common soldiers in the ranks. There had been much redeployment of individual regiments and brigades to maintain their alignment with the Fifth Corps to their north and the Twelfth to their south. The First Division to their front was posted more thickly in the woods of the Wilderness and had been engaged all morning in skirmishing with the rebels. Some brigades and regiments of the Third Division had also dispatched skirmishers during all of this jockeying and maneuvering (OR 97).

So at this afternoon hour, "Grandpa" Henderson's brigade stands "halted in the fringe" of the woods of the Wilderness. The novel makes no mention of field entrenchments during this deployment, but since it has been their practice to build them at every opportunity and since they manifestly have time and there is timber and earth at hand, there is no reason to think they are not doing so now, with action so imminent. They will be erecting barricades of branches between the second-growth pine and oak around them, piling up stones, and digging at the earth with their bayonets and mess plates.

This is also a time for the new men of the 304th to exchange confidences (RBC 45) and nervous gossip. "I met one of th' 148th Maine boys an' he ses his brigade fit th' hull rebel army fer four hours over on th' turnpike road an' killed about five thousand of 'em" (48). The reference is to fighting the previous day, when Hancock's division of the Second Corps supported Sykes's division of the Fifth Corps in a fairly stiff engagement with rebel soldiers of Anderson's and McLaws's divisions on the Old Orange Turnpike east toward Fredericksburg.

Then "bullets began to whistle among the branches and nip at the trees. Twigs and leaves came sailing down" (RBC 49). A distinctive feature of the Civil War battlefield was the whistle of the minié balls. Rifled muskets, because of their low muzzle velocity, when aimed at distant targets threw bullets in very high trajectories. The bullets passing over the ranks of the 304th are probably aimed at Saunders's brigade ahead of them on their right and, missing Saunders, pass through the trees overhead. It might also be that the 304th is in the zone beaten accidently by the fire of rebels who are miscalculating distances and overshooting Saunders's lines. Or perhaps some of the rebel soldiers (skirmishers, possibly, now that the Union skirmish lines directly before the 304th have withdrawn) are indeed aiming at Private Fleming's battle line. Lieutenant Hasbrouck, his officer's frock coat an obvious target, is "shot in the hand." The wound is bleeding, and his captain binds it with a handkerchief (49).[6]

Lieutenant Hasbrouck's response to this wound is stoic. It must be painful, but he will carry on without reference to it, and once the battle reaches their position and he is thrust almost instantly into command of the company, he will manage to ignore it so completely that no one else in Private Fleming's purview (essentially the reader's range of vision for the length of the novel) mentions it during the course of the next twenty-four hours. Fleming himself forgets about it, so most readers probably do as well. The company enters battle without its second lieutenant, and Hasbrouck's remarkable endurance may be because there is no other commissioned officer who can replace him. As extraordinary as his endurance is at this moment, he will surpass it on the next day. He will be shot in the arm, such that he cannot bend it or swing it without "multiplied pain" (RBC 191). But even this will not incapacitate him. He will return to the company after finding a "bandage" for it (213), rather than securing more rigorous medical attention for himself, which, for all his doughty heroism, he should. The cause of blood poisoning was unknown, so even the most trivial of wounds could prove deadly. Hasbrouck will suffer two wounds to the same limb—otherwise he would not be able to hold a weapon or continue commanding the company. If dirt or flecks of his uniform find their way into these wounds, his arm may soon become gangrenous, and the only cure will be amputation. During the night of May 2, Confederate General T. J. Jackson was wounded in the hand and arm by North Carolina pickets of his own command, when, scouting ahead of his lines, he was mistaken for the enemy. His arm was broken, so his wounds were more immediately incapacitating than Hasbrouck's, but they were of the same order of magnitude. In ten days, Jackson was dead.

Given Private Fleming's insignificance and his current "trance of observation"

---

6. Coggins, Arms and Equipment, 26–27, 38–39; Nosworthy, Crucible, 33ff, 580–81.

(*RBC* 45), and given that his perception and the novel's point of view are virtually identical, the 304th's tactical situation at this moment is not immediately clear. Henderson's brigade is explicitly in a "reserve" (49, 52) position. This would normally mean they are about two hundred and fifty yards directly behind a front line, and so relatively immune to rifle fire aimed at that front line.[7] But Henderson's brigade actually seems to be arrayed in a sort of checkerboard or echelon pattern, to the left and rear of Saunders's brigade. "The din in front" (49) of them does not seem to involve any other formation than Saunders's brigade ahead of them to their right (45), for the men in this reserve line point "their restless guns out at the fields" (47) on their own immediate front, and they obviously would not do this if fellow Union soldiers were arrayed there.

If this is indeed the case (that Saunders's brigade is in advance, to their right, and there is no Federal formation directly ahead of them), it is a foolish and dangerous deployment for a force in a defensive posture. Yet, since their own skirmishers have just been driven back upon their main lines (*RBC* 44), the reserve is halted (47), and the general officer commanding this part of the front intends to hold the enemy's attack (74), this is pretty clearly their situation. There is no Federal force on Saunders's left flank: in military terms, that flank is "in the air."

The *Official Records* are full of accounts of the care with which Union formations of every size, from corps down to individual regiments, maintained contact with friendly forces on both flanks. This is one aspect of the official reports that makes them so hard to read. See, for example, this report from the officer commanding the Fourth Ohio Infantry in the First Brigade of French's division: "we again changed our position, in line of battle facing the wood in the direction of the Plank Road, with the Fourteenth Indiana on our right and the Seventh Virginia (Union) on our left" (*OR* 98). They took such care with good cause, for a defensive formation finding its flank exposed could not hope to keep its position before an energetic, pressing enemy. Soldiers arrayed in the normal two-deep battle formation presented, to an enemy coming at them from their front, a row of potential targets that was everywhere only two men deep. When an enemy force could flank or enfilade those soldiers, it meant the enemy could fire at them down the length of their battle formation. Soldiers in a regiment of six hundred would then present two thick targets—the front rank and the rear rank, each of some three hundred men. In the sights of the enemy riflemen, these targets would then consist of crowded, overlapping human flesh

7. Coggins, *Arms and Equipment*, 24.

about two hundred yards deep. Then it would not be necessary to gauge distances with precision, and it would be unusual for a minié ball not to find some lodgment somewhere in that mass. There was also always the catastrophic possibility that, once an enemy formation achieved a position on your flank, elements might then work around to your rear.

There is no suggestion that the denseness of the Wilderness at this point in the Federal line explains its curious deployment. Private Fleming can see what is happening to Saunders's brigade at some "distance" (*RBC* 45, 50), and there are open "fields" (47, 54) on his own front. The 304th is posted in one of the relatively open areas of the battlefield. There is no feature of the natural terrain, such as an impassable copse or a deep stream bank, that could anchor the left of Saunders's brigade and thus protect its left flank.

Out of the "haze" of Saunders's engagement emerge "running men. Some shouted information and gestured as they hurried" (*RBC* 47). Since the skirmishers from Henderson's brigade have already returned (44), these running men are almost certainly soldiers from Saunders's brigade: either messengers sent back to seek support for their flank, or men panic-stricken because of the manifest danger of their situation. Whatever "information" they shout, the rumors produced along the 304th's line of battle portend disaster. The general commanding the division to which Saunders's brigade belongs may have responded by sending a battery "at a frantic gallop" (49) to Saunders's support, but more likely this is a battery withdrawing from Saunders's impossible position. The most logical move would be to order Henderson's brigade forward to secure Saunders's flank, but no such orders come.

The flag upon which Private Fleming fastens his vision is obviously the flag closest to him, that of Saunders's leftmost regiment. "It seemed to be struggling to free itself from an agony," then "horizontal flashes" appear in the smoke surrounding the position (as the rebels close upon it, the muzzle-flashes of their rifle fire can be seen), the flag falls, and "the whole command was fleeing." Fleming can hear the "wild yells" of the rebels' celebration "from behind the walls of smoke" (*RBC* 50).

The veteran regiments in Henderson's brigade "jeer" at this "moblike body" (*RBC* 50) of routed men. Officers of Saunders's brigade—including Saunders himself—rage, bawl, and strike at them with their swords (51). But it is hardly the enlisted men's fault: Crane has depicted in brief but sufficient detail a disastrous deployment, and what inevitably befalls it. Given the relative quiet of this part of the Union army's line (83), it is the critical weakness of Saunders's disposition that draws the rebel attack upon it (the Army of Northern Virginia had officers at every level alert to such possibilities, and steeped in the tradition of seizing them) and then guarantees its success.

It is the fault of the commanding officer of the division to which Saunders's brigade belongs. It would be tempting to think it is the fault of General French himself. The sloppiness of his official report reveals careless habits of thought and a lack of attention to detail. A West Point graduate, forty-eight at the time of this battle, French would be promoted to command of the Third Corps in July 1863, when his administrative incompetence would be cruelly exposed. His inability to move his corps efficiently wrecked the Mine Run campaign of October 1863 and ended the Union army's efforts on the Virginia Front for the year. French himself was held directly responsible and removed from further field command. The Third Corps, destroyed as an effective formation under his misdirection, was disbanded.[8]

In the long run, however, it seems this disaster cannot be attributed to General French. The historical record shows that French's Third Division was deployed entirely in the reserve line, so no brigade under French's command would have been positioned ahead of the other brigades and in such immediate contact with rebel infantry. Private Fleming will soon have occasion to pass near the "general of division" (RBC 72) who is in command of the battle along this part of the battlefront, and he does not identify him as the general commanding his division, whom Fleming does indeed know by sight (174). This unfamiliar officer is a "quiet man" who looks "mouse-colored" (72) on his horse, whereas French was tall, bulky, and red-faced. That Saunders's and Henderson's brigades belong to different divisions might help to explain why Henderson's brigade was not advanced to protect Saunders's left flank. This nameless division commander seems quite as capable of mishandling a combat situation as French himself: he will instruct an aide to "go over an' see Taylor, an' tell him not t' be in such an all-fired hurry; tell him t' halt his brigade in th' edge of th' woods; tell him t' detach a reg'ment—say I think th' center 'll break if we don't help it out some; tell him t' hurry up" (73). These vague, impatient, contradictory orders suggest the kind of leadership that, earlier, could have directed Saunders's brigade to a hopeless deployment.

General Henderson has sensibly placed the 304th New York in between two veteran regiments of his brigade (RBC 50), which should stiffen them. When Saunders's brigade is routed and comes streaming past, the veteran regiments

8. Catton, Glory Road, 353; Mark M. Boatner III, "French, William Henry," in The Civil War Dictionary.

jeer and joke, whereas the "fresh fish" are stunned and appalled (51). As the battle-front approaches, their nervous responses are discordant and confused (52).

At this moment they are formed in two lines, with their commissioned and noncommissioned officers to the rear as "file closers," responsible for keeping men in their positions through encouragement or discipline, and for directing their fire. Hasbrouck will prove capable at both. The soldiers are arrayed behind whatever entrenchments or barricades they have been able to construct. The major problem they face is that their Springfield Model 1861 rifles must be loaded from the muzzle, which means that each cartridge's load of powder and bullet will have to be rammed home with a ramrod. The total length of the rifle barrel and the ramrod when the latter is fully extended above it for the thrust is about eight feet, and the rifle's butt must be grounded for that thrust home. The rifle is most conveniently and quickly loaded by a standing man—but to stand up deprives the soldier of most of his cover. It is possible to load the rifle while kneeling, but this is also more awkward and the rate of fire declines. To lie prone would offer the soldier the most protection, but the rifle would be very difficult indeed to load in that position. Breech-loading rifles can be loaded by a prone man, and the technology of the time can produce breech-loaders and even repeating rifles. But breech-loaders are about three times as expensive and repeaters are up to six times as expensive as Springfields. There are 130,000 men in the Army of the Potomac alone. By the end of the war, the Federal government had purchased over three million muzzle-loading weapons. It provided the men in its thousands of regiments with the best weapons it could afford.[9] In any case, the rebel soldiers who appear before them as "a brown swarm of running men who were giving shrill yells" (54) are similarly armed. Since they are on the offensive, they lack the protection of any field fortifications at all.

At this moment a "hatless general pulled his dripping horse to a stand near the colonel of the 304th" and yells repeatedly, "'You've got to hold 'em back!'" (RBC 54). Who is this general? Only MacChesnay's own brigadier should give orders to regimental commanders in this brigade, and this man is obviously not Henderson, whom the private soldiers know and like (205). Has Henderson already been killed? Is this his replacement? It does not seem likely. They have hardly been in action. If Henderson had been shot down in these first moments, army headquarters would not have replaced him with another general. The most senior of his colonels would have taken command on the spot, as Hasbrouck soon

9. Griffith, *Battle in the Civil War*, 32; Coggins, *Arms and Equipment*, 21–22; Nosworthy, *Crucible*, 610–11; Griffith, *Battle Tactics*, 80–81.

will do with Fleming's company. It is more probable that this is Saunders himself; or a general officer from the division to which Saunders's brigade belongs, unnerved at the spectacle of the brigade's collapse. His falling so unexpectedly upon MacChesnay has precisely the wrong effect: the colonel is so startled he can only "stammer" in reply and wonder about the quality of his regiment (54).

The captain of Private Fleming's company orders his men in "endless repetition" to "'Reserve your fire, boys—don't shoot till I tell you—save your fire—wait till they get close up—don't be damned fools'" (*RBC* 55). This is a traditional order, dating from the time of unrifled muskets and immortalized in Putnam's famous order to his own inexperienced soldiers at Bunker Hill not to fire until they see "the whites of the eyes" of the British soldiers advancing upon them. The Springfield rifles with which the 304th is equipped far outrange the smoothbore muskets with which Putnam's men were armed, but this is an entirely appropriate order. It takes skill to estimate ranges in order to bring enemy soldiers under effective fire at any significant distance; it takes about thirty seconds to reload; above all, these are untried and inexperienced soldiers. The captain's effort to impose a tight fire control is surely appropriate.[10]

Private Fleming ignores the order completely, however, and in undisciplined haste, throws "the obedient, well-balanced rifle into position and [fires] a first wild shot" at his very first glimpse of the enemy (*RBC* 55–56). Whether other men of the 304th are better disciplined is uncertain. The impression is that, perhaps triggered by Fleming's unsoldierly first wild shot, they also panic and fire. "The regiment was like a firework that, once ignited, proceeds superior to circumstances until its blazing vitality fades." The "noise" of their fire "gave [Fleming] assurance" (56), and he is surely not alone: in the Civil War raw troops were notoriously eager to take comfort in the all-absorbing noise of their own fire, which is exactly why company commanders sought to control them lest they waste their ammunition in blind panic.[11]

Private Fleming's experience of his first battle can be fairly well summarized: under the rush of nervous energy and the sensations of the firing line in action, his consciousness splinters. He perceives the world in disconnected, frenzied fashion. Given the novel's point of view, this befalls the reader as well. In light of some understanding of infantry tactics in the Civil War, what can we observe concerning the behavior of the 304th New York Infantry during its first action that Fleming himself is not capable of noting?

10. Griffith, *Battle Tactics*, 81–86.
11. Ibid., 83.

Regiments going into action, in either assault or defensive formations, were arrayed two-deep. Given two feet for each soldier, this means the 304th battle-front is around seven hundred feet long, that is, over two hundred yards. The smaller veteran regiments on each side will occupy shorter fronts. The 304th have not been told to fix bayonets. The regiments in Henderson's brigade are on the defensive. Were they on the attack, the bristling appearance of the bayonets would probably give them impetus and effect. And although the bayonet still has considerable psychological power, the infantry fight in the Civil War is generally decided by firepower, not steel. The socket where the bayonet is fitted on the muzzle obscures the front bead sight (though the 304th do not seem committed to accurate marksmanship in their first battle). When it is fixed, the eighteen-inch blade makes loading even more difficult.[12]

The two-rank formation dissolves as the regiment starts firing at the oncoming rebel assault. Smoke from the black powder obscures their front after the first discharge. Some men bolt; the officers drive them back (*RBC* 59). Most of them crowd forward, loading and firing as quickly as they can. Despite their improvised field fortifications and entrenchments, they take casualties from the outset. The captain of Private Fleming's company is one of the first (59–60). This means the rebels' forward surge slows at the first volley from the Union line, as the rebels pause to return fire. The rebel infantrymen may continue to work closer, but the action is turning into a firefight, an exchange of gunfire at close range. The men in the 304th load in furious haste, jerk their rifles to their shoulders, and fire, often "without apparent aim into the smoke or at one of the blurred and shifting forms which upon the field before the regiment had been growing larger and larger" (59).

Loading these Springfields is a cumbersome process (*RBC* 57). Each gun weighs nine pounds and measures four-and-a-half feet in length. After each shot, the soldier grounds his rifle, takes a cartridge from beneath the unfastened flap of his cartridge box (58), brings it to his mouth. The cartridge consists of a charge of powder below a conical bullet, contained in a paper wrapping. The cartridge is about two inches long and weighs a solid ounce or more. The soldier tears open the powder-filled end of the cartridge with his teeth, empties the powder down the barrel, pushes the bullet into the muzzle of the barrel with his thumb. He takes out the steel ramrod by sliding it from the bands holding it under the

---

12. Griffith, *Battle in the Civil War*, 40–41; Griffith, *Battle Tactics*, 140–42; Grady McWhiney and Perry D. Jamieson, *Attack and Die: Civil War Military Tactics and the Southern Heritage*, 76–80; Nosworthy, *Crucible*, 594–608.

rifle barrel, presses the cup-shaped end down upon the bullet, rams the charge down to the end of the barrel (58). The ramrod is then returned to its slot under the bands, or a soldier will tilt it against anything handy so as to get at it more quickly. The hammer on the right side of the barrel is pulled back to half-cock, which exposes a small nipple. The soldier takes a small copper percussion cap from his cap box (on the right front of his belt), fits it thereupon, pulls the hammer back to full cock, raises his rifle to his shoulder, takes aim (or, in the case of many of the 304th, does not), pulls the trigger, and fires the weapon.[13]

The best, most experienced soldiers could get off three shots a minute. For all their furious haste, it is hard to imagine that the soldiers of the 304th New York are averaging less than thirty seconds each, to reload and fire. Private Fleming has no conception of time, so the reader does not either. The 304th are firing long enough for their rifle barrels to get hot (RBC 58), which perhaps means about ten shots by each soldier, or an engagement that lasts about five minutes. This may not sound long, but it would give the regiment enough time to fire off over six thousand bullets at the rebel attack.

The attack is repulsed. "The enemy were scattered into reluctant groups. He saw a man climb to the top of a fence, straddle the rail, and fire a parting shot." This is an incident worth remarking because it shows there are marksmen in the enemy ranks who know how to aim at targets on the battlefield despite the smoke. "The waves had receded, leaving bits of dark debris upon the ground" (RBC 60). The word "bits" hardly constitutes a testimonial to the effectiveness of the fire of the 304th New York Infantry. They are "fresh fish" after all; perhaps they will develop as soldiers.

Such thoughts are far from Private Fleming's mind at this moment. He is refreshed by a drink of water, interested in details of the battle (a battery in action and the like) that he has not noticed, thrilled by the sight of the national flags in the woods around, and astonished at the undisturbed beauty of the May afternoon. He is in "an ecstasy of self-satisfaction." He thinks, "So it was all over at last! The supreme trial had been passed." He credits himself as being "a fine fellow," and "even with those ideals which he had considered as far beyond him" (RBC 64). He smiles "in deep gratification," feels "tenderness and good will" toward his fellow soldiers, and even more, "the bonds of tied hearts." And his fellow soldiers share his mood; they grin "sociably," sprawl out "luxuriously," share "handshakings and deep speeches" (65).

"He helped a cursing comrade to bind up a wound of the shin" (RBC 65)—a

13. Coggins, Arms and Equipment, 26–33; Griffith, Battle Tactics, 86–90.

scratch or scrape, obviously, since anything worse, anything displaying the appalling effect of the soft-lead minié balls upon a shinbone, could not have been so readily treated. In his euphoria at having passed the test, he gives no further attention to the casualties. Despite their field fortifications, however, his company seems to have been hit not only early but often.

During the fight Private Fleming was dimly aware of men falling around him, even of the death of his company commander, but his mind records them merely as "bundles" (*RBC* 59). Indeed to an innocent, distracted eye, the dead could register as mere bundles of dirty clothing. Even now, after the fighting, Fleming shows more interest in the appearance of these "few ghastly forms" than comprehension of their condition: "Arms were bent and heads were turned in incredible ways. It seemed that the dead men must have fallen from some great height to get into such positions. They looked to be dumped out upon the ground from the sky" (61). His attention roams from his dead comrades to marvel at the working of nearby artillerymen, then it falls for another second upon his wounded regimental comrades, "going drearily toward the rear" (62). They seem to him "a flow of blood from the torn body of the brigade," a metaphor accurate enough, but lacking awareness of how acute the suffering of individuals in that "small procession" must be (62). His own mood is anything but dreary, so he turns his attention upon other details of the battle.

Fleming's jubilant mood is understandable enough, given his earlier nervous tension. But is his judgment of himself correct? "Standing as if apart from himself, he viewed that last scene. He perceived that the man who had fought thus was magnificent" (*RBC* 64). Consider what he and his fellows have managed to accomplish, keeping in mind the basic facts of the Civil War battlefield. To reiterate: with the universal employment of rifles, the advantage has passed from the offensive side to the defensive. Unlike Saunders's unfortunate brigade, Henderson's brigade was not turned but received a rebel assault from directly in front. The 304th New York probably had the advantage of field fortifications. They certainly had the advantage of being completely on the defensive. That they "helt 'em back" (61) comes as no surprise: it is the outcome dictated by the very nature of infantry combat in the Civil War.

What is surprising is that they seem to have taken so many casualties while doing this. The captain of the company has been killed, the lieutenant wounded. An enlisted man had "grunted suddenly as if he had been struck by a club in the stomach" and then "sat down and gazed ruefully"—as well he might for, because of blood poisoning, stomach wounds were almost inevitably fatal. Another enlisted man "farther up the line" from Fleming "had had his knee joint splintered by a ball" (*RBC* 60); if he survives this first fight, he can count on having the leg amputated above the knee, the alternative being death from gangrene. Within Private Fleming's own narrow range of vision during the battle, he has witnessed one death, one mortal wounding, one very serious wounding, and lesser wounds to his lieutenant and to a panicked soldier. What would constitute a "few" dead forms "under foot" (61)? Five or six, perhaps? So within Fleming's own range of vision, there have been about ten casualties. Even if his company suffered no more casualties than these he has remarked (a highly improbable circumstance, given the characteristic self-absorption of this particular soldier and the fact that during the battle the company would have occupied some sixty square yards), it has nonetheless lost, in this one ten-minute engagement, over 10 percent of its strength.

Immediately after this first day's battle, the company will "'count'" itself short by "'forty-two men'" (*RBC* 131), an appalling figure. Many, separated in one way or another, will return during the night—indeed so many that later in the evening the corporal will add hopefully, "if they keep on a-comin' this way, we'll git th' comp'ny all back by mornin' yit" (131). The captain will never return, however, nor the man shot in the stomach, nor the one with the shattered kneecap, nor any of the motionless "ghastly forms" at Private Fleming's feet at this afternoon moment. The company, with more action awaiting, has already been hit hard.

What of the 304th generally? Tomorrow morning Private Wilson will say, "Th' reg'ment lost over half th' men yestirday. I thought a course they was all dead, but, laws, they kep' a-comin' back last night until it seems, after all, we didn't lose but a few. They'd been scattered all over, wanderin' around in th' woods, fightin' with other reg'ments, an' everything" (*RBC* 146–47). There is no way of knowing what constitutes a "few" casualties in Wilson's thinking at this moment. Keep in mind the inexperience of these private soldiers, the casualties their company suffered (Private J. Conklin, at least, will be added to the casualty list in the morning's roll call), the death the first day of the brigade commander himself, and above all, Wilson's initial impression that the 304th New York "lost over half th' men." A loss of 10 percent would indeed seem few if you believed for a time that half your regiment had been killed or wounded; but a loss of 10 percent is still a stunning figure, especially given the tactical advantages it had enjoyed.

Both the casualties they took and the collapse of the 304th's cohesion as a formation ("They'd been scattered all over") illustrate their raw inexperience and lack of discipline. Private Fleming himself ignored his company commander's explicit, oft-repeated order and fired the instant he got his first "glance" at the rebel advance, "Before he was ready to begin" (*RBC* 55). His comrades instantly joined him, so his frenzy was clearly typical. Both he and they probably ignored the protection of their entrenchments just as they ignored their captain's single order: taking false comfort instead in the noise of their weapons, buried in a "battle sleep" (58).

It is not at all clear that the attack they repulsed was particularly serious. The historical facts confirm no major, intentional, or sustained rebel assault on their part of the Federal line at that time. Crane's narrative implies that the rebels spotted the glaring fault in Saunders's deployment and took savage advantage. Henderson's line, on the other hand, was at least partially fortified, and its flanks were secure: the battlefield skill displayed by the rebels in their success against Saunders's brigade suggests they would not have gone on to hurl full-scale, headlong assaults against such a strong Federal position. Instead, as the historical record shows them doing throughout the afternoon on this part of the Union front, they probably advanced skirmish lines of company strength, which these raw troops would believe to be major attacks. The "field" seemed "foe-swarming" (*RBC* 55) at Fleming's first glance. But his frenzied mental condition does not suggest he was an accurate observer at that moment.

As he now looks across the field, after the rebel "waves had receded" and they had been "scattered into reluctant groups" (*RBC* 60), he sees to "the right and to the left" the "dark lines of other" Federal "troops" (62), which reiterates the continuity of their defensive position. "Far in front he thought he could see lighter masses protruding in points from the forest." These are obviously rebel formations uniformed in regulation gray, which appears "lighter" in contrast both to the "dark" blue uniforms of the Federals and to the butternut and brown rebel uniforms he had seen before. "They were suggestive of unnumbered thousands" (62). This is precisely the "suggestive" effect Lee and McLaws and the other rebel commanders on this part of the front wish to achieve at this hour.

What then of the number of casualties suffered by the 304th? Do they not suggest an attack of some weight? They surely could have been inflicted by a few companies of cool, experienced soldiers upon a raw, frenzied, undisciplined regiment. That both of the company's officers were hit suggests keen rebel marksmanship. Also, the sheer weight of fire put down by the 304th New York—over six thousand minié balls—seems to have done little execution. "Bits of dark *debris*" (60) is an imprecise description of rebel casualties, but those casualties would surely have been heavier, if they had been from real "waves" of rebel infantry, surging toward the 230 yards of the 304th's regimental front.

The main reason to think the 304th New York did not participate in repulsing a full enemy assault is to be found in an observation Private Fleming himself
will make when he has had the opportunity to observe more of the battle.
When toward "twilight" this afternoon he will hear the "tremendous" (*RBC* 82)
sound of Jackson's surprising and massive assault on the Federal right, it will
suddenly occur to him "that the fight in which he had been was, after all, but
perfunctory popping. In the hearing of this present din he was doubtful if he
had seen real battle scenes." He will see "a sort of a humor in the point of view
of himself and his fellows during the late encounter. They had taken themselves
and the enemy very seriously and had imagined that they were deciding the
war" (83). To be sure, Fleming will have reasons of his own at that twilight hour
for looking with contempt upon his regiment's earlier conduct, but these perceptions are quite in keeping with the historical record. "Perfunctory popping"
echoes the report of General P. J. Semmes concerning McLaws's division of the
Army of Northern Virginia, whose brigade was engaged with the Union lines
where Crane locates the 304th that afternoon: "Saturday morning came, and
with it desultory skirmishing, sometimes growing quite sharp, which continued
throughout the day, from which the brigade suffered some slight loss" (*OR* 317).

Jackson's assault, on the other hand, was delivered by thirty thousand men,
two-thirds of the army Lee had assembled for battle that day. It was anything but
perfunctory or desultory. That twilight attack was the defining feature of the
battle of Chancellorsville. Soldiers of the Eleventh Corps—upon which it fell—
reported its "suddenness and great fury" (*OR* 246), its "heavy force" so strong
"as to completely envelop us" (*OR* 244), and the "tremendous fire of musketry
and grape and canister from artillery" (*OR* 244) with which it developed.

So how well did Private Fleming and his fellows conduct themselves in their
first engagement with the enemy? Were they "magnificent" (*RBC* 64), as they
thought? Fighting in a war where the advantage lay entirely with the defense,
they succeeded in holding their position. It seems from the evidence that the attack was a light one, perhaps a probing of the Union position in the wake of the
rebels' stunning tactical success against Saunders—but probably a feint, purposefully and skillfully designed to be "suggestive" of the presence of "unnumbered thousands" on this front, while thirty of those thousands were at that
moment marching away toward the opposite end of the Union position. In repulsing this attack, the 304th's blind indiscipline caused them to take casualties
out of all proportion to the situation they were in. They will soon have another
chance to earn "handshakings and deep speeches" (*RBC* 65), thanks to General
R. E. Lee and the Army of Northern Virginia, for it was still only midafternoon.

Chapter 4

Private Fleming's "Well-Meaning Cow"

The Implications of Crane's Literary Style

Until this midafternoon moment of Private Henry Fleming's "ecstasy of self-satisfaction" (*RBC* 64), Crane's novel, with one signal exception, is remarkably faithful, in both general and specific detail, to the historical facts of the battle of Chancellorsville as they can best be understood. He shows men fighting as the weaponry of the Civil War dictated they must. He shows both the terrain in the Wilderness of Spotsylvania in northern Virginia, and the battle in which the Third Division of the Second Corps of the Army of the Potomac was immersed on the afternoon of May 2, 1863.

Even the one signal exception—the rout of a full federal brigade on an afternoon of "desultory" or "perfunctory" combat—shows not so much Crane's indifference to the historical record but, rather, his reliance upon the most significant documents available to him, the relevant reports in the *Official Records of the War of Rebellion*. A close look at the novel reveals how Crane works to reconcile what he recognized was a problematic inconsistency. Concerning those officers whose commands he had selected as the "home" of and the models for both his fictional Henderson's brigade and his fictional 304th New York Volunteer Infantry Regiment, it turns out there was a discrepancy between the official report of Major General French, on the one hand, and the official reports of his immediate superiors, subordinates, and antagonists on the other.

This close assessment of the historical accuracy of Crane's novel is based, however, upon an overview that is completely absent from both the structure and the stylistic texture of the novel itself. The point of view in the novel is almost always identical to Private Fleming's own, and this is extraordinarily reinforced by the fact of Crane's impressionistic style, as we will soon see. We are entirely immersed in the world of his physical and tactile perceptions, his emotional responses, and his mental evaluations. There are no authorial intrusions to challenge the flow of Fleming's perceptions and responses, or the accuracy of his evaluations of himself. Such intrusions would elevate our perceptions above his and would interrupt our personal and immediate experiencing of his states of mind and his ways of understanding his world.

In the absence of such intrusions, Crane employs a variety of generally subtle and ironic ways of suggesting that Private Fleming may not be seeing things accurately and may not be assessing himself accurately. We saw a dramatic example in Fleming's radical revision of his personal history as he is driven toward his initiation in combat: "he had never wished to come to the war. He had not enlisted of his free will. He had been dragged by the merciless government" (*RBC* 36). We saw a subtler example in the unconscious tentativeness of Fleming's perceptions about the size of the rebel forces facing the part of the Union left-center flank held by Henderson's brigade: "he thought he could see lighter masses"; "They were suggestive of unnumbered thousands" (62). And Crane most particularly has been assuming that a reader's own knowledge of Civil War realities will be steadily fretting at the edges of the persuasiveness of Private Fleming's conceptions and evaluations. Knowledge of the actualities of Civil War battle would not deny the soldiers of the 304th their raw courage, and it would not discount what a "ghastly" and frightening thing Civil War combat was. But it surely would challenge Fleming's belief that he and his fellows are "magnificent" (64) in their first battle.

In addition to the subtle ironies in its narrative and to the closely researched accuracy of its depiction of battle, a third aspect of Crane's novel invites and directs a reader's judgment. This is his extraordinary style. Crane's portrayal of Fleming's first experience of battle is an immense literary accomplishment. Indeed perhaps it is too immense. Even sophisticated readers remember his firing-line experience this first day, May 2, 1863, whereas they forget how he experiences combat on the morning and the afternoon of May 3. This portrayal of Fleming's first experience of battle is vividly engaging and immensely persuasive, and the more so because Crane's historical sources could hardly have helped him here. You look in vain in *Battles and Leaders of the Civil War* or the *Official Records* for any verbal depiction of the actualities of Civil War combat that might have informed his presentation. Instead, the historical sources gave him a framework of verifiable details. They thus liberated his imagination to find an answerable style in which to evoke Private Fleming's experience in the imagination of a reader.

To consider exactly how that style works and, further, the kinds of judgment deeply embedded within it, we shall examine the twenty-one paragraphs in which Crane presents Private Fleming's baptism of fire. This examination will remove us once again from our close consideration of Fleming's experience on the afternoon of May 2, 1863, but the close assessment in this case will be literary rather than historical; and to achieve an understanding of the breakthrough Crane achieved in the style of his novel, and to understand how that style is in itself an implicit instrument for evaluating character, we will use literary rather than historical documents. The first is a paragraph from James Fenimore Cooper's *The Spy: A Tale of the Neutral Ground.* This romance was published in 1821, early in the period in American literature that can usefully if loosely be called "the Romantic Period" or the "American Renaissance," a period that would reach its fruition in the literature of Ralph Waldo Emerson, Nathaniel Hawthorne, Henry Thoreau, Herman Melville, and Walt Whitman, and which ended with the outbreak of the Civil War. The second two-paragraph passage is from John William DeForest's *Miss Ravenal's Conversion from Secession to Loyalty,* which was published in 1867, early in the period of American realism, a literary movement that was a response to the Civil War and an implicit rejection of the idealism that had led to it. DeForest's great contemporary realists were William Dean Howells, Mark Twain, Henry James, and Edith Wharton.

These two passages are quite different, but taken together they will reveal that if Crane could find no useful models in contemporary historical texts for his evocation of battle, the literature of his nation would not serve him much better. Approaching Crane through these passages will reveal the extraordinary nature of his stylistic achievement. Comparing the three styles will define the point of this chapter, which is that Crane's style is not only famously evocative, it also profoundly and subtly directs a reader's judgment.

The passage from Cooper is one of the very few passages in which an author of canonical stature in the American Romantic period endeavored to portray field combat between formed bodies of soldiers. In Cooper's Leatherstocking romances, guerrilla warfare is the norm, that is, combat between informal bands of men in forested terrain. Guerilla warfare stresses the sudden ambush, the sharp exchange, the duel between personalities, and it constitutes altogether the perfect setting for Natty Bumppo's superhuman qualities of marksmanship, woodcraft, and rhetoric. (In these matters, these Leatherstocking romances exactly prefigure Ernest Hemingway's own fictions about war a century later.) In contrast, this particular passage from *The Spy* depicts the climactic moment in formally conducted battle between American dragoons and British infantry:

In the meanwhile, great numbers of the English, taking advantage of the smoke and confusion in the field, were enabled to get in the rear of the body of their countrymen, which still preserved its order in a line parallel to the wood, but which had been obliged to hold its fire, from the fear of injuring friends as well as foes. The fugitives were directed to form a second line within the wood itself, and under cover of the trees. This arrangement was not yet completed, when Captain Lawton called to a youth, who commanded the other troop left with that part of the force which remained on the ground, and proposed charging the unbroken line of the British. The proposal was as promptly accepted as it had been made, and the troops were arrayed for the purpose. The eagerness of their leader prevented the preparations necessary to ensure success, and the horse, receiving a destructive fire as they advanced, were thrown into additional confusion. Both Lawton and his more juvenile comrade fell at this discharge. Fortunately for the credit of the Virginians, Major Dunwoodie re-entered the field at this critical instant; he saw his troops in disorder; at his feet lay weltering in blood George Singleton, a youth endeared to him by numberless virtues, and Lawton was unhorsed and stretched on the plain. The eye of the youthful warrior flashed fire. Riding between this squadron and the enemy, in a voice that reached the hearts of his dragoons, he recalled them to their duty. His presence and word acted like magic. The clamor of voices ceased; the line was formed promptly and with exactitude; the charge sounded; and, led on by their commander, the Virginians swept across the plain with an impetuosity that nothing could withstand, and the field was instantly cleared of the enemy; those who were not destroyed sought a shelter in the woods. Dunwoodie slowly withdrew from the fire of the English who were covered by the trees, and commenced the painful duty of collecting his dead and wounded.[1]

---

1. James Fenimore Cooper, *The Spy: A Tale of the Neutral Ground*, 85–86.

DeForest was a veteran of the Civil War. His realistic portrayal of combat is the most striking quality of his novel, and Crane had probably read it. Here the hero, Colburne, is directing his company's advance, as skirmishers, upon rebel fortifications at Port Hudson.

"Get down!" reiterated Colburne; but the man had waited too long already. Throwing up both hands he fell backward with an incoherent gurgle, pierced through the lungs by a rifle-ball. Then a little Irish soldier burst out swearing, and hastily pulled his trousers to glare at a bullet-hole through the calf of his leg, with a comical expression of mingled surprise, alarm and wrath. And so it went on: every few minutes there was an oath of rage or a shriek of pain; and each outcry marked the loss of a man. But all the while the line of skirmishers advanced.

The sickishness which troubled Colburne in the cannon-smitten forest had gone, and was succeeded by the fierce excitement of close battle, where the combatants grow angry and savage at sight of each other's faces. He was throbbing with elation and confidence, for he had cleaned off the gunners from the two pieces in his front. He felt as if he could take Port Hudson with his detachment alone. The contest was raging in a clamorous rattle of musketry on the right, where Paine's brigade, and four regiments of the Reserve Brigade, all broken into detachments by gullies, hillocks, thickets and fallen trees, were struggling to turn and force the fortifications. On his left other companies of the Tenth were slowly moving forward, deployed and firing as skirmishers. In his front the Rebel musketry gradually slackened and only now and then could he see a broad-brimmed hat show above the earthworks and hear the hoarse whistle of a Minie-ball as it passed him. The garrison on this side was clearly both few in number and disheartened. It seemed to him likely, yes even certain, that Port Hudson would be carried by storm that morning. At the same time, half mad as he was with the glorious intoxication of successful battle, he knew that it would be utter folly to push his unsupported detachment into the works, and that such a movement would probably end in slaughter or capture. Fifteen or twenty, he did not know precisely how many, of his soldiers had been hit, and the survivors were getting short of cartridges.[2]

Now let us look at those twenty-one paragraphs from Crane's novel, *The Red Badge of Courage*, in which he depicts Fleming's first direct experience of infantry combat. The passage begins with the first glimpse of the oncoming rebels and

2. John William DeForest, *Miss Ravenal's Conversion From Secession to Loyalty*, 286–87.

concludes with the depiction of the casualties taken by Fleming's company during the fight.

(1) Across the smoke-infested fields came a brown swarm of running men who were giving shrill yells. They came on, stooping and swinging their rifles at all angles. A flag, tilted forward, sped near the front.

(2) As he caught sight of them the youth was momentarily startled by a thought that perhaps his gun was not loaded. He stood trying to rally his faltering intellect so that he might recollect the moment when he had loaded, but he could not.

(3) A hatless general pulled his dripping horse to a stand near the colonel of the 304th. He shook his fist in the other's face. "You've got to hold 'em back!" he shouted, savagely; "you've got to hold 'em back!"

(4) In his agitation the colonel began to stammer. "A-all r-right, General, all right, by Gawd! We-we'll do our—we-we'll d-d-do—do our best, General." The general made a passionate gesture and galloped away. The colonel, perchance to relieve his feelings, began to scold like a wet parrot. The youth, turning swiftly to make sure that the rear was unmolested, saw the commander regarding his men in a highly resentful manner, as if he regretted above everything his association with them.

(5) The man at the youth's elbow was mumbling, as if to himself: "Oh, we're in for it now! oh, we're in for it now!"

(6) The captain of the company had been pacing excitedly to and fro in the rear. He coaxed in schoolmistress fashion, as to a congregation of boys with primers. His talk was an endless repetition. "Reserve your fire, boys—don't shoot till I tell you—save your fire—wait till they get close up—don't be damned fools—"

(7) Perspiration streamed down the youth's face, which was soiled like that of a weeping urchin. He frequently, with a nervous movement, wiped his eyes with his coat sleeve. His mouth was still a little ways open.

(8) He got the one glance at the foe-swarming field in front of him, and instantly ceased to debate the question of his piece being loaded. Before he was ready to begin—before he had announced to himself that he was about to fight—he threw the obedient, well-balanced rifle into position and fired a first wild shot. Directly he was working at his weapon like an automatic affair.

(9) He suddenly lost concern for himself, and forgot to look at a menacing fate. He became not a man but a member. He felt that something of which he was a part—a regiment, an army, a cause, or a country—was in a crisis. He was welded into a common personality which was dominated by

a single desire. For some moments he could not flee no more than a little finger can commit a revolution from a hand.

(10) If he had thought the regiment was about to be annihilated perhaps he could have amputated himself from it. But its noise gave him assurance. The regiment was like a firework that, once ignited, proceeds superior to circumstances until its blazing vitality fades. It wheezed and banged with a mighty power. He pictured the ground before it as strewn with the discomfited.

(11) There was a consciousness always of the presence of his comrades about him. He felt the subtle battle brotherhood more potent even than the cause for which they were fighting. It was a mysterious fraternity born of the smoke and danger of death.

(12) He was at a task. He was like a carpenter who has made many boxes, making still another box, only there was furious haste in his movements. He, in his thought, was careering off in other places, even as the carpenter who as he works whistles and thinks of his friend or his enemy, his home or a saloon. And these jolted dreams were never perfect to him afterward, but remained a mass of blurred shapes.

(13) Presently he began to feel the effects of the war atmosphere—a blistering sweat, a sensation that his eyeballs were about to crack like hot stones. A burning roar filled his ears.

(14) Following this came a red rage. He developed the acute exasperation of a pestered animal, a well-meaning cow worried by dogs. He had a mad feeling against his rifle, which could only be used against one life at a time. He wished to rush forward and strangle with his fingers. He craved a power that would enable him to make a world-sweeping gesture and brush all back. His impotency appeared to him, and made his rage into that of a driven beast.

(15) Buried in the smoke of many rifles his anger was directed not so much against the men whom he knew were rushing toward him as against the swirling battle phantoms which were choking him, stuffing their smoke robes down his parched throat. He fought frantically for respite for his senses, for air, as a babe being smothered attacks the deadly blankets.

(16) There was a blare of heated rage mingled with a certain expression of intentness on all faces. Many of the men were making low-toned noises with their mouths, and these subdued cheers, snarls, imprecations, prayers, made a wild, barbaric song that went as an undercurrent of sound, strange and chantlike with the resounding chords of the war march. The man at the youth's elbow was babbling. In it there was something soft and tender like the monologue of a babe. The tall soldier was swearing in a loud voice.

From his lips came a black procession of curious oaths. Of a sudden another broke out in a querulous way like a man who has mislaid his hat. "Well, why don't they support us? Why don't they send supports? Do they think—"

(17) The youth in his battle sleep heard this as one who dozes hears.

(18) There was a singular absence of heroic poses. The men bending and surging in their haste and rage were in every impossible attitude. The steel ramrods clanked and clanged with incessant din as the men pounded them furiously into the hot rifle barrels. The flaps of the cartridge boxes were all unfastened, and bobbed idiotically with each movement. The rifles, once loaded, were jerked to the shoulder and fired without apparent aim into the smoke or at one of the blurred and shifting forms which upon the field before the regiment had been growing larger and larger like puppets under a magician's hand.

(19) The officers, at their intervals, rearward, neglected to stand in picturesque attitudes. They were bobbing to and fro roaring directions and encouragements. The dimensions of their howls were extraordinary. They expended their lungs with prodigal wills. And often they nearly stood upon their heads in their anxiety to observe the enemy on the other side of the tumbling smoke.

(20) The lieutenant of the youth's company had encountered a soldier who had fled screaming at the first volley of his comrades. Behind the lines these two were acting a little isolated scene. The man was blubbering and staring with sheeplike eyes at the lieutenant, who had seized him by the collar and was pommeling him. He drove him back into the ranks with many blows. The soldier went mechanically, dully, with his animal-like eyes upon the officer. Perhaps there was to him a divinity expressed in the voice of the other—stern, hard, with no reflection of fear in it. He tried to reload his gun, but his shaking hands prevented. The lieutenant was obliged to assist him.

(21) The men dropped here and there like bundles. The captain of the youth's company had been killed in an early part of the action. His body lay stretched out in the position of a tired man resting, but upon his face there was an astonished and sorrowful look, as if he thought some friend had done him an ill turn. The babbling man was grazed by a shot that made the blood stream widely down his face. He clapped both hands to his head. "Oh!" he said, and ran. Another grunted suddenly as if he had been struck by a club in the stomach. He sat down and gazed ruefully. In his eyes there was mute, indefinite reproach. Farther up the line a man, standing behind a tree, had had his knee joint splintered by a ball. Immediately he had dropped his rifle and gripped the tree with both arms. And there he

remained, clinging desperately and crying for assistance that he might withdraw his hold upon the tree. (*RBC* 54–60)

A reader might well bring an initial assumption to these three fictions that, as they become more "modern" and less "romantic" (Cooper is writing in the tradition of the historical romance), a greater human compassion and a greater concentration upon the human cost of combat would appear. And to some extent such a change obtains, in the contrast between Cooper and DeForest. George Singleton and Lawton have been personalized for us, but their stylized portraits as casualties does not get much purchase in our minds. The nameless soldiers hit beside Colburne hardly have individualized personalities, but the specific details provided about their wounds (the "incoherent gurgle" of the man shot "through the lungs," for example) make the pain and death of a battle line much more forcibly apparent.

So perhaps it is surprising that in Crane's, the most "modern" of the three, there is far less concern for casualties than in either of the other two. The casualties are not named. They are described in reductive figurative language or in narrative patterns that make them more ridiculous than pitiable: "The men dropped here and there like bundles"; the dead captain looks like a "tired man resting," albeit looking "astonished and sorrowful" as though "some friend had done him an ill turn." A man struck in the body "grunted suddenly as if he had been struck by a club" and gazes "ruefully"; a man with a "splintered" knee clings ludicrously to a tree. They are rendered solely in terms of visual impressions; the humanity implicit in the Irish soldier's "comical" mixture of emotions in DeForest's account is denied them.

Each passage uses the third-person point of view. But in each succeeding example, this point of view comes steadily closer to the individual. In Cooper's passage, we are not hampered by the smoke that masks the British retreat, or by the anger Dunwoodie feels but manages to channel into effective action. Such emotions obviously are present in Captain Colburne, which DeForest's account specifically witnesses: fear ("sickishness") earlier, and now "He was throbbing with elation and confidence" and "felt as if he could take Port Hudson with his detachment alone." He is, however, only "half mad" and still quite capable of exercising judicious restraint.

In Crane's narrative, on the other hand, we are blinded by the smoke, alongside Private Fleming. All Crane gives us are the emotions, in the bewildering sequence as they surge over Fleming. Colburne and Dunwoodie are experienced officers, granted, whereas Fleming is an inexperienced private soldier. But when juxtaposed to DeForest's sober and realistic account, Crane's passage appears other than "realistic," even at first glance. Compare "He developed the acute exasperation of a pestered animal, a well-meaning cow worried by dogs" (no. 14), with "He was throbbing with elation and confidence, for he had cleaned off the gunners from the two pieces in his front." Which thought pattern seems more "realistic," in the sense of being more probably true of a man in armed combat? How many infantrymen are likely to think of themselves as a "well-meaning cow"?

The focus in Crane is upon the sensory impressions of battle, which is not the case in the other two. But consider the implications of what is revealed about Private Fleming's mental condition. In *The Spy*, there is smoke and confusion and fear; indeed, the dragoons are thrown into confused disorder. Cooper's focus is not on these, however, but on the commanders' leadership; their encouragement, direction, and deployment of their men in response to clearly perceived situations. In the passage from DeForest's *Miss Ravenal's Conversion*, there is more stress on the sights, sounds, and emotions of battle, and considerable attention paid to the emotions sweeping through the hero. But again, these do not explicitly interfere either with Colburne's intelligent command of his men or with his understanding of the nature of the action in which they are engaged.

In Crane's novel, Private Fleming's emotions and sensory perceptions are stressed to the exclusion of everything else. The central paragraphs in this portion can each be catalogued according to a single sensory impression or a single emotion: in no. 7 it is perspiration, in no. 8 panicked firing, no. 9 loyalty, no. 10 the racket of their gunfire, no. 11 brotherhood, no. 12 work, no. 13 the tactile world of fleshly sensations, no. 14 rage, no. 15 smell, no. 16 voices, no. 17 numbness, no. 18 the sight of their firing line. Further, these paragraphs are arrayed without order, in deliberate incoherence: clearly no. 8 should follow no. 1 directly, but a sweep of disordered impressions intervenes, confirming that Fleming immediately loses all sense of time.

One of the first (famous) consequences in Crane's depiction is a specific repudiation of conventional glamor: here there is no eye that flashes fire. "There was a singular absence of heroic poses" (no. 18) among the men, while the officers "neglected to stand in picturesque attitudes" (no. 19). There are no heroic poses in DeForest's account, either, where solid paragraphs reflect Colburne's mind, in which "the glorious intoxication of successful battle" is controlled by wisdom and discipline, just as reference to those emotions is buried in a paragraph of sober narrative. What Colburne sees (the increasing scarcity of "broadbrimmed" hats above the rebel parapets) provides him with information from which to make decisions. Crane's style conveys just the opposite: as the narrative disintegrates into unconnected fragments and random emotions, perceptions, and impressions, so too (it is implied) does Private Fleming's mind.

This is not the case of everyone on the firing line. Lieutenant Hasbrouck, as inexperienced as Private Fleming, behaves with extraordinary intelligence. He blocks the flight of a fear-struck private, drives him back into the ranks, and despite his own wounded hand somehow manages to help him reload his gun. The point of view is so close to Fleming that a reader instinctively attributes to Fleming himself the admiring assessment of Hasbrouck's soldierly conduct: "Perhaps there was . . . a divinity expressed in" Lieutenant Hasbrouck's "voice . . .— stern, hard, with no reflection of fear in it" (no. 20). Compare the concept of "divinity" with Colburne's businesslike mein: "Fifteen or twenty, he did not know precisely how many, of his soldiers had been hit, and the survivors were getting short of cartridges."

These three passages have quite different rhetorical styles. Cooper's metaphorical range is slight and utterly conventional: "the horse" is a standard eighteenth- and nineteenth-century synecdoche for cavalry. "The eye of the youthful warrior flashed fire" is so conventional as to find no purchase in the reader's mind. So is the claim that his voice "reached the hearts of his dragoons," or that "His presence and word acted like magic."

DeForest is writing about the most cataclysmic and significant war in American history, a war he had witnessed as a serving officer, yet his style is as minimalist as any current novelist writing about bored, affluent collegians. His skirmish fire has literally, not metaphorically, "cleaned off" the rebel gunners from their artillery pieces. There is not a single example of figurative language in these two paragraphs. This is not always the case with DeForest, but generally he is determined to show things with the clarity of flat depiction, to show things as they are.

With Crane, it could almost be said he chooses figurative language in such a way as to show how things were not. The range of his figurative language and style is startling. There are unexpected, often ironic or paradoxical similes. Colonel MacChesnay begins "to scold like a wet parrot" (no. 4); the captain speaks to his company "as to a congregation of boys with primers" (no. 6); Private Fleming's face is "soiled like that of a weeping urchin" (no. 7); the regiment in action is "like a firework that, once ignited, proceeds superior to circumstances until its blazing vitality fades" (no. 10); in action on the firing line, trying to kill rebel soldiers, he is "like a carpenter who has made many boxes, making still another box" (no. 12); his eyeballs are "like hot stones" (no. 13); the babbling of one soldier in battle is "like the monologue of a babe," while a complaining soldier speaks "like a man who has mislaid his hat" (no. 16); Fleming, engaged in combat, "heard this as one who dozes hears" (no. 17); approaching rebel infantry, glimpsed through the smoke, seem to have been "growing larger and larger like puppets under a magician's hand" (no. 18).

There are likewise unexpected and often paradoxical metaphors. To his own fragmented perception, Private Fleming's "sweat" is "blistering" rather than cooling (no. 13). The appropriate "red rage" of the battle experience devolves into the bizarre metaphor of "the acute exasperation of a pestered animal, a well-meaning cow worried by dogs" (no. 14). This metaphor refers to a soldier in an army that has invaded an enemy's land, who has had a winter of training, who is armed with the most murderous weaponry his government can afford to put in his hands. His enemies seem to him to be "swirling battle phantoms," which is appropriate enough to the difficulty of seeing through the smoke; but these "phantoms" are "choking him, stuffing their smoke robes down his parched throat," and he fights against them "as a babe being smothered attacks the deadly blankets" (no. 15). It is a rifle and not a soldier that is "obedient" (no. 8); flaps of the leather cartridge boxes bob "idiotically" (no. 18). There are bizarre dual sensory appeals: "jolted dreams" (no. 12), "blistering sweat," a "burning roar" (no. 17).

Crane's style is by far the most vivid of the three. Cooper's style is so conventional we must stimulate our own imagination (which proves hard indeed) in order to envision his portrait of combat. The flatness of DeForest's style, his reliance upon narrative alone to carry us, is what we are schooled to expect by much of the literature of our day. What we are perhaps not prepared for is the hero's (and DeForest's own) unalloyed commitment to the Union cause: his flat style remains, surprisingly to our anticipation, uninflected by irony.

In contrast, Crane's style is inflated, at times overly so (he sometimes becomes his own best, or worst, parodist). It is violently stimulating to the imagination. The paradoxical imagery of "blistering sweat" and the dual sensory appeal of "burning roar" demand a vicarious response. The same is true of the extraordinary, ironic, "inappropriate," or paradoxical range of figurative language. Yoking a private soldier in the Army of the Potomac, who is firing his rifle furiously in combat, to a "well-meaning cow" presents such an anomaly it snags our attention, and the image registers in a way utterly beyond anything achieved by Cooper when his hero's eyes flash fire.

Crane's style dovetails precisely with the achievement of the structure of this passage; the style also insists upon the bizarre and utter chaos of Private Fleming's experiencing of this moment. The steady, almost leechlike attachment of the novel's point of view to Fleming's own individual perception means that we implicitly credit him with these reactions, just as we tend to credit him with seeing something akin to divinity in Hasbrouck's competent performance of his job. "He developed the acute exasperation of a pestered animal, a well-meaning cow worried by dogs" (no. 14). We assume not only that Fleming feels this "exasperation" but also that the image of the cow is his own. Instinctively we assume that this very image flashed into his own, individual, consciousness. And our assumption about this specific impression (that it is Fleming's own) is reinforced by other memories of the cows of his mother's farm, which came to him earlier (*RBC* 7, 27) at particularly significant or vivid moments.

That these figures—of a carpenter making boxes, a babe fighting against blankets, or that cow—are to be attributed to Private Fleming himself is a hard thing to "prove," but it seems to me that this is the way Crane's style works upon us. We know that Fleming does, himself, feel the "blistering sweat" (no. 13) as such, and that he does himself hear the man at his elbow babbling "like the monologue of a babe" (nos. 16 and 17), and that this is how he imagines the noise to himself. It seems consistent then that these other images cross his attention, as part of those "jolted dreams" that "were never perfect to him afterward, but remained a mass of blurred shapes" (no. 12).

This "fact" about the style—that this figurative language "belongs" uniquely to Private Fleming—is made more certain by the fact that, upon reflection, we know we are "seeing" what Fleming saw. We understand that this is distinct from what Lieutenant Hasbrouck was seeing, or the way he was seeing it. Otherwise, Hasbrouck could not have performed as he did. Likewise with Fleming's fellow enlisted men: the salient difference between Fleming and Private Jim Conklin is the former's "busy mind" (*RBC* 6); Conklin, in stark contrast, is prone to violence but phlegmatic and unimaginative (16–17), given to measuring sandwiches and to the "blissful contemplation of the food he had swallowed" (43). So Conklin's reactions to his first battle were appropriately different: he "was swearing in a loud voice. From his lips came a black procession of curious oaths" (no. 16). We are surely not to believe that the extraordinary range of impressions in the passage above is at all akin to what was crossing Conklin's mind at this moment. We will have reason, also, before this night is over to believe that Fleming's experience of this afternoon's battle was vastly different from Private Wilson's experience of it.

Metaphors and similes are ways of ordering perception, of orienting ourselves in the world, of demonstrating an intellectual and human control over experience. When they are thus wildly inappropriate, we have the sense that the mind to which they are "credited" cannot orient itself. This dovetails with the discon-nected, disordered narrative, centered upon that stream of conflicting emo-tions. Our strongest sense is that Private Fleming in this action was incapable of making sense of his experience.

The reasons? His perception was obviously distorted by an inevitable surge of adrenalin and nervous energy. But it also seems he was paying the price for his stored-up nervousness: hence his panicked surrender of self-discipline to the raw sensory details of battle, especially in the "assurance" he took from the all-enveloping "noise" of its rifle fire (no. 10). His characteristic self-absorption was ratcheted up into monstrous blindness to what was really going on around him. Thus Private Fleming's consciousness is dominated by his physical senses and his crazily excited imagination; his mind cannot pull the details of his world into significant patterns; he cannot (unlike Colburne) discipline his emotions; he cannot (unlike Hasbrouck) discipline his mind; he cannot discipline himself. Some such lack of discipline surely affected to a greater or lesser degree his fel-low soldiers, which in its turn explains why they took such egregious losses in this first exchange.

If the range of figurative language credited to Fleming's imagination is star-tling, it is not without a pattern, one that we have seen consistently and that is peculiar to this soldier. Crane consistently calls Private Fleming "the youth." The reader tends to accept this as an alternative identification for him, and the term thus loses its meaning, but it is in fact a telling identification.

Recall that as he wrestled with his fear of failing the test of combat, Fleming conceived of it in schoolroom terms, in childish terms, without revealing any full or mature awareness of what was in store for him. The potential rewards he also conceived of in exactly such terms. If successful, he would pass a test he would not have to retake. The potential penalties for failure were public scorn and humiliation. Of the real possibility of death, wounds, and the like, he had no conception. Indeed, in his furtive glance at it, death was preferable to the agony of suspense he was undergoing: it was only "some place where he would be understood" (*RBC* 44).

As the 304th New York Volunteer Infantry Regiment was enduring the last moments before the rebel assault reached their position, "the youth thought of the village street at home before the arrival of the circus parade on a day in the spring. He remembered how he had stood, a small, thrillful boy, prepared to fol-low the dingy lady upon the white horse, or the band in its faded chariot" (*RBC* 53). Three more sentences follow, all dedicated to his memory of awaiting the circus parade; this paragraph offers more details about a moment from Fleming's childhood than any other single paragraph in the novel. Fleming was then in an agony of nervousness, commingled with his characteristic curiosity (52), but the moment was quiet on the battle line, and the paragraph makes clear how Fleming's mind works even without the numbing stimulus of combat. A thing he awaits in anguished nervousness is reduced to a thing (the circus parade from his childhood) that produced a nervous excitement of its own; but one that was benign, happy, unthreatening, utterly different. Such a mental reaction is his unconscious way of preparing himself for the oncoming "supreme trial," by thus masking its true nature behind this sustained moment of childhood memory. This is a plausible human reaction, though the extraordinary detail of his memory is peculiar and reinforces our awareness of the childishness of his nature. Whether this mental trick was "useful" to him or not, he was clearly not facing the reality of his present circumstance while he was buried in this detailed recollection.

Notice that throughout his first experience of battle, without exception his mind characterizes things in ways that render them more benign than they are, and in ways that almost always partake of his childhood world: "a congregation of boys with primers," "a weeping urchin," "a firework," "brotherhood" and "a mysterious fraternity," "a carpenter making boxes," "a well-meaning cow," "a babe" entangled in its blankets, "the monologue of a babe," "puppets under a magician's hand," officers nearly standing "upon their heads." This is not to say that Fleming's mind is untouched by other, more appropriate consciousness, including "red rage," a wish "to rush forward and strangle" the enemy. He even experiences one moment of selfless loyalty—though he mentally shuffles through an uncertain list of what the object of that loyalty might be ("a regiment, an army, a cause, or a country"), and this particular emotion is placed so as to suggest it is occasioned by the comforting roar of the regiment's own gunfire that is submerging him.

Looked at all together, this recurrence to things of peacetime and childhood looms inordinately large and confirms a characteristic peculiar to "the youth": he is not only young, he is still a child, and this is what marks him out. He conceives his world in childish terms: battles in terms of tests to be won. The rewards he seeks and the penalties he fears are childish: public adulation, or public scorn. It is instructive to look at his parting from his fellow schoolmates, and particularly the schoolgirls (*RBC* 10). His sexuality is of the most immature kind, and this is not because more mature sexual expression was unknown in the 1860s or not deemed suitable for expression in print (as *Miss Ravenal's Conversion* readily demonstrates). He has a child's vivid visual curiosity and eagerness to "see it all" (6), "to get a view of it" (52) at whatever cost to the sensibilities of others or the possible price to himself. He has a child's unawareness of his own mortality, and he has no awareness of the reality of death. In the aftermath of the battle, in his "ecstasy of self-satisfaction" (64) and with dead fellow soldiers at his feet, he remains untouched by its reality, unaware of the possibility that he too could be one of those "ghastly forms"; his "busy mind" is engaged solely with the curious appearances of the corpses (61). He is equally untouched by the agony of his wounded comrades. He has a child's general indifference toward the suffering of others, whether a hut-mate (104), a chance comrade (105), or his own mother (9–10). He distinctly does not have an adult's imaginative consideration of others; he has no awareness that other people actually exist, save as they play into his own desiring. Above all else, he has that monstrous self-absorption that we identify with childhood, a self-absorption that is utterly solipsistic.

Is it unfair to characterize Private Fleming in this stark way, on the basis only of his behavior and his mentality during his first experience of combat? His personality during battle is quite consistent with the personality that has preceded it in the novel down to this afternoon of May 2 and his "ecstasy of self-satisfaction" (*RBC* 64). Look at an even earlier moment, when battle was only a distant prospect. Recall that Crane has chosen for the 304th New York the simplest, easiest approach to the Chancellorsville battlefield of any presented in the historical record, one of the reasons he chose to place Henderson's brigade in the Second Corps. Fleming's first night in the field on this campaign generates the following perception:

> At nightfall the column broke into regimental pieces, and the fragments went into the fields to camp. Tents sprang up like strange plants. Camp fires, like red, peculiar blossoms, dotted the night.
>
> The youth kept from intercourse with his companions as much as circumstances would allow him. In the evening he wandered a few paces into the gloom. From this little distance the many fires, with the black forms of men passing to and fro before the crimson rays, made weird and satanic effects.
>
> He lay down in the grass. The blades pressed tenderly against his cheek. The moon had been lighted and was hung in a treetop. The liquid stillness of the night enveloping him made him feel vast pity for himself. There was a caress in the soft winds; and the whole mood of the darkness, he thought, was one of sympathy for himself in his distress. (*RBC* 26–27)

In his self-absorption and self-pity, Private Fleming's childish mentality registers the mundane experiences of this evening's bivouac as "strange plants," "red, peculiar blossoms," and "weird and satanic." For it is in that human world that he knows he will be tested, and in his anxiety he registers the human world as alien. His mentality now finds human comfort in the natural world: grass "blades" press "tenderly against his cheek," the winds "caress" him, "the whole mood of the darkness . . . was one of sympathy for himself in his distress." Most startling of all, "the moon had been lighted and was hung in a treetop." Obviously he does not literally believe this, but it does occur to his mind at some level of his consciousness, which demonstrates the extraordinary reach of his self-pity and his self-centeredness. Anyone who has ever been punished as a child will recognize this tendency to find the human world alien and the natural world comfortingly human. This is, though, a tendency of childhood; and Private Fleming of the 304th New York Volunteer Infantry Regiment seems not only still immured in a childhood world, but immured to a depth beyond that reached by most children.

Private Fleming's equally untried fellow soldiers evidently shared to some degree his panicked, undisciplined response to combat: the narrative shows as much, and it is confirmed by the disproportionate losses they suffer. But this particularly childish cast of mind seems peculiar to Fleming. It characterizes neither Lieutenant Hasbrouck nor Private Conklin, and a reader will soon learn it is not true of Private Wilson either. It is this particular soldier's peculiar mentality that lies at the heart of Crane's novel: it is a study of solipsism of an extraordinary degree. When the regiment subsequently offers him a welcome haven that evening, replete with sympathy, care, and blankets after he has taken a blow to the head, he will think of the wilderness space it occupies as a "low-arched hall," with the stars visible "through a window in the forest" (*RBC* 135).

It is the fog of Private Fleming's peculiar mentality that is under study in this novel, rather than the "fog of battle." Yet it is probably the case that many readers regard Fleming's experience on this May afternoon as typical, and that he stands as a sort of "Everysoldier," the typical infantryman for this or any other war. This is true even of readers of considerable sophistication (see Chapter 5). How could Crane's portrayal of such an extraordinary mentality produce this?

In the first place, what is extraordinary about Private Fleming is the degree of his solipsism. Self-absorption is a human tendency we all share, and it is probably only when Fleming's condition is teased out of the narrative for display that its monstrous degree becomes apparent. All of us have feared failure of some sort and have brooded in self-absorption over it. So Fleming at first glance strikes us as "one of us." In his humdrum anonymity the word "typical" seems appropriate. But I doubt that very many of his readers past the earliest ages of childhood have ever, at any level of consciousness and however fleetingly, thought that "the moon had been lighted and was hung in a treetop."

Other things conspire to make us assess Private Fleming as "one of us," and hence, "typical." His fears are familiar, as is his fear of being ridiculed for expressing those fears. He fears combat, which is legitimate for any sane mentality. What is often overlooked is the peculiar nature of his fear—at no moment does he worry about dying, or being maimed or severely wounded. He does not approach battle confident of his own abilities, and we suspect that we would not, ourselves. It is instructive to note that Colburne's very success in *Miss Ravenal's Conversion* has a quality that separates him from us. We are not at all sure we could do as well as he does in battle, and the reverse is true for Fleming. We do not contrast ourselves to him in our imagination, for we can readily conceive of being just as uncertain, and we readily enter his mentality. After all, we have all been children. The quality of his curiosity we have all shared. It is something we all remember as being indeed entrancing. But presumably most of us have developed more mature kinds of imagination, through which we develop qualities of sympathy and compassion.

The qualities of style herein—themselves generated by his extraordinary mental condition—tend to render familiar that which in our own imaginations we dread: battle. The power of Crane's vivid style makes the battle quite "envisionable" to us, so we can experience it with vicarious excitement. Anything rendered so accessible to our imagination loses its strangeness and can be seen as part of our world, which in imagination it has indeed become. As Fleming's childish mind reduces the details of combat to things we are familiar with from our own childhood and our own mundane experiences (for instance, the way our minds do "career off in other places" while we are absorbed in some repetitive routine), battle becomes not so weirdly different from ordinary life. It becomes plausible, perceptible, "typical." Since Fleming in his solipsism is indifferent to the dead of his own company and to the suffering of the wounded, what marks combat as an extraordinary kind of human activity, utterly different from anything else, is forgotten: it seems "typical." But, in fact, Private Fleming is "typical" only in the sense that Milton's Satan, possessing sins all too familiarly ours, can be seen as "typical."

What happens next to Private Fleming confirms that it is upon his monstrous self-centeredness that Crane's novel is particularly focused. We left our close consideration of him while he was enjoying an "ecstasy of self-satisfaction" because "The supreme trial had been passed." These ecstatic "moments" will not last very long, however, and a "sudden" few moments later he will be fleeing "like a proverbial chicken" (*RBC* 64–65, 68–69). Henry Fleming's panic-stricken failure is surely the most renowned fact about this novel, familiar to people who know it only through its film versions, or by reputation.

Pausing at this cliff-edge moment allows us to recognize two crucial facts about the catastrophe that is just about to befall Private Fleming. In the first place, he did "pass" his first "trial." The unaccustomed blare, smoke, haze, confusion, and proximity to death did not panic him into flight, at first, nor did some raw instinct for survival impel him to flee the first time this survival was threatened (it seems he did not even know it was threatened). To establish this helps to isolate the specific reason he ran. Elements common to most instances of military panic are surely present: a belief that the line is not being supported against superior enemy forces (*RBC* 66, 67); "nervous weakness," "exhaustion"; a fearful exaggeration of "the endurance, the skill, and the valor" of the enemy (67). A "few" of his fellows panic because of a mixture of these things, and when Fleming sees them, a blind herd instinct consumes him with the thought that "the regiment was leaving him behind" (68).

What is so striking in Fleming's case is that these debilitating thoughts are generated in him by his self-centered blindness. He is dwelling in a fictional drama of his own devising: that, as in the academic world, there will be one "supreme trial"; that, having passed this, "The red, formidable difficulties of war" will have "been vanquished"; that by passing this one trial, he will achieve some permanent personal condition, immune to future failure. So, having passed the trial, "He felt that he was a fine fellow. He saw himself even with those ideals which he had considered as far beyond him" (*RBC* 64). It never occurs to him, in his childlike self-absorption, that circumambient reality—composed of other human beings, their own plans, intentions, and agendas—might not conform to this private drama he knows will shape his own life. Nor does it occur to him that his own psychology might not work as he is confident it will.

Circumambient reality first appears in the form of Major General Lafayette McLaws and about six thousand soldiers of the Army of Northern Virginia. In his moment of "self-satisfaction," Private Fleming's solipsism has erased them from existence. So when they attack again, Fleming's initial response is revealing, hilarious, and characteristic: "Surely, he thought, this impossible thing was not about to happen. He waited as if he expected the enemy to suddenly stop, apologize, and retire bowing" (*RBC* 66).

The refusal of the world to conform to the fiction his self-absorption has produced about himself is effective cause of Private Fleming's collapse. This refusal leads to the psychological reactions that follow in most animals when their conditioned expectations are violated: "Into the youth's eyes there came a look that one can see in the orbs of a jaded horse. His neck was quivering with nervous weakness and the muscles of his arms felt numb and bloodless. His hands, too, seemed large and awkward as if he was wearing invisible mittens. And there was a great uncertainty about his knee joints" (*RBC* 67). All this is perfectly appropriate to the moment, because Fleming, in his solipsism, has been privately conditioning himself to believe in a reality that does not exist.

Nor does his own psychology work as he has conditioned himself to believe it will. Before the battle he was "resolved to remain close upon his guard lest those qualities of which he knew nothing should everlastingly disgrace him" (*RBC* 14). But his private view of the world—which, given his solipsism, is the only reality of which he is aware—has evidently been convincing him that if he passes the trial, he will enter into some new and permanent condition "even with those ideals which he had" before "considered as far beyond him" (64), so he will no longer need to be on such guard. But he has not entered into any such condition, and those "qualities" of "nervous weakness," "exhaustion," and the like—generated in his case by his failure to be even vaguely aware of elemental realities about the world around him, that is, the continuing active presence of rebel soldiers—are loosened, unmonitored, and panic him into "blind" flight (69).

Earlier, on the line of battle, his mind had churned up relatively comforting images from the world of his childhood. Now, as his self-centered reality has been shattered, his mind produces horrifying images, most of them still from the world of childhood but this time from nightmare. "To the youth" the rebel probe "was an onslaught of redoubtable dragons. He became like the man who lost his legs at the approach of the red and green monster. He waited in a sort of a horrified, listening attitude" (*RBC* 68). "On his face was all the horror of those things which he imagined"; his lieutenant was a "peculiar creature"; "noises of battle were like stones; he believed himself liable to be crushed" (69). He is being followed by "dragons" determined on eating the fleeing soldiers; "he imagined [rebel shells] to have rows of cruel teeth that grinned at him" (70).

Fleming's failure, needless to say, does nothing to make him seem any less "typical" in most readers' responses. Uncertain whether we ourselves could "pass" the "trial," we have sympathized with his fear of failure from the outset, and we sympathize with him now. Crane's brilliance in selecting and depicting the patterns of Fleming's thought while he runs draws us quite vicariously into them. Yes, "Death about to thrust" us "between the shoulder blades" would seem far more dreadful than "death about to smite" us "between the eyes" (*RBC* 69). Yes, we too would take "one meager relief" in knowing that "the initial morsels for the dragons" pursuing us would be those men fleeing behind us (70). Yes, given the experience we have shared so vividly with Fleming, artillerymen standing to their pieces would seem to be "Methodical idiots! Machine-like fools!" and the "youthful" mounted officer trying to control his horse in their midst would probably strike us too as "a man who would presently be dead" (71). So again, our ready willingness to assess ourselves in "ordinary" and unheroic ways in responding imaginatively to portraits of battle, and to sympathize with Fleming's example, makes him still seem "typical" at this juncture.

It is not "typical" at all for soldiers to desert in battle, however. This is not to say that panic is unknown on the battlefield. It has upon occasion seized entire formations and entire armies, as well as individuals, and it did so during the Civil War. Nor is it to claim that unflinching heroism is the norm. The Civil War shows many examples of even brave, "proven" soldiers giving way to raw panic. Such panic befell many of the most veteran regiments and brigades of the rebel Army of Tennessee at Chattanooga in 1863 and Nashville in 1864. But it is the entire purpose of military discipline and training to ensure that panic remains atypical. This is surely the case even with these "fresh fish" of the 304th New York Volunteer Infantry Regiment. Whatever Fleming thinks in his blind panic, only a "few fleeting forms" (*RBC* 68) deserted when he did.

Chapter 5

Private Fleming and
Stereotypes of Modern War

Private Henry Fleming is a very unusual soldier, both in the extent to which childish solipsism grips him and in the way his military career unfolds. Yet my impression is that nowadays he appears to be a very typical soldier to most first-time readers. I am sure that Fleming is often taken to be typical, even arche-typal, by many extraordinarily sophisticated readers whose assessments appear in their scholarship and criticism. An example appears in Y. N. Harari's 2005 study of "Martial Illusions: War and Disillusionment in Twentieth-Century and Renaissance Military Memoirs," where he wrote, "On the literary front, Stendahl's *Charterhouse of Parma*, Tolstoy's *Sebastopol in August, 1855* and *War and Peace*, Stephen Crane's *Red Badge of Courage*, and several short stories by Ambrose Bierce, all narrate the familiar story of how a young man full of romantic martial dreams is disillusioned by the cruel realities of war."[1] This is a succinct example of a phenomenon that is widespread in the contemporary critical estimation of Crane's novel. To understand and appreciate the significant aspects of *The Red Badge of Courage* that vanish when this template is placed upon it, we will examine four instances in detail.

---

1. Yuval Noah Harari, "Martial Illusions: War and Disillusionment in Twentieth-century and Renaissance Military Memoirs."

—⁓—

In his revisionist study of World War I, *The Smoke and the Fire*, John Terraine says this about Private Fleming: "The ordinary soldier's experience of battle seems to me to be a constant. I know no better description (out of hundreds) of that private world of mysterious movement, incomprehensible behaviour, abrupt outrage and devouring fear than Stephen Crane's *The Red Badge of Courage*, a story of the American Civil War which first appeared in 1895." High praise, and from one of the best of a superior class of current British military historians, one whose work is knowledgeable, original, and tough-minded.[2]

This claim is perhaps true enough down to the moment at hand, when "devouring fear" sends Fleming running "like a blind man" (*RBC* 69). It would not seem "ordinary" for soldiers to desert in combat, however, and certain images that have occurred to Private Fleming seem extraordinary indeed. Unmistakably, what follows this moment is anything but "ordinary."

Having deserted the 304th New York Volunteer Infantry Regiment, Private Fleming will be free to see a great deal of the battle of Chancellorsville, including a division commander in operation amid his headquarters staff, the spectacular rout of General O. O. Howard's Eleventh Corps, artillery massing, an elite brigade moving up to establish a new defensive line, and one of the rare appearances of mounted cavalry in action on a major Civil War battlefield. Through a fortuitous and quite extraordinary sequence of events, Fleming is then returned to the 304th New York so outfitted as to escape any discovery of his desertion. He is welcomed with admiration and kindness. The ordinary fate of battlefield deserters was quite different. Exactly one year after the events recounted in this book, when these same two armies again engaged in battle in this same landscape, a Union soldier who deserted from the line was summarily executed by firing squad.[3]

The next day, May 3, Private Fleming will fight with such blind ferocity as to win the praise of Lieutenant Hasbrouck, undoubtedly "th' best off'cer in this here reg'ment" (*RBC* 231). Thereafter, privates Fleming and Wilson will have the extraordinary opportunity to overhear a discussion between Major General French and the new brigadier who replaces Henderson, which enables the two privates to prophesy to their fellow soldiers exactly what the next movement of the 304th New York will be. During this action, Fleming will seize the flag of

2. John Terraine, *The Smoke and the Fire: Myths and Anti-myths of War, 1861–1945*, 218.
3. Noah Trudeau, *Bloody Roads South: The Wilderness to Cold Harbor, May–June 1864*, 80, 210.

the regiment from the dying "color sergeant" (187) and will keep it to the front of the 304th with such efficiency that—despite the failure of the regiment's effort—he earns extraordinary praise from Colonel MacChesnay himself: "He kep' th' flag 'way t' th' front. I saw 'im. He's a good 'un"; privates Fleming and Wilson "deserve t' be major generals" (207).

Carrying the regiment's colors thereafter releases Private Fleming from the frenzy of action on the firing line. The battlefield, for him, ceases to be that "private world of mysterious movement and incomprehensible behaviour."[4] His survey is extraordinarily wide for a private soldier. It embraces the withdrawal of distant infantry, rearguard combat involving both infantry and artillery, and events at the Chancellor House just moments before Hooker's headquarters abandons it in decisive defeat.

In the 304th New York's last action, Private Fleming leads a countercharge wherein Private Wilson captures a rebel flag. For this, Wilson will surely be awarded a congressional Medal of Honor, a customary practice in the Federal service in the Civil War, and Fleming's conduct before and during that countercharge could earn him a Medal of Honor as well. One particular, very extraordinary reward will certainly come to Fleming alone, and in the very near future. In Union regiments, flags were carried by picked noncommissioned officers. Colonel MacChesnay has already praised him in public for keeping the flag properly to the front, and MacChesnay now has a rebel trophy to assuage his embarrassment over the general failure of his regiment. Henry Fleming's days as a private are numbered. He will most surely be promoted to color sergeant of the 304th New York Volunteer Infantry Regiment.[5] In sum, after Fleming's initial experience of panic, his battlefield experience is absolutely extraordinary (in some ways, nearly miraculous); his military conduct is not only extraordinary but exemplary, both above and beyond the call of duty.

—⁊⁊⁊—

James Reston Jr. in his effort to find a "metaphorical" link between *Sherman's March and Vietnam* wonders: "Was the experience of the Civil War soldier really so different from the Vietnam soldier? Did a profound belief in the cause really keep" the Civil War soldier rather than the Vietnam soldier "in the ranks"? Reston's book depends upon detecting similarities between American soldiers in these two different wars, so his answer must be "no."

4. Terraine, *The Smoke and the Fire*, 218.
5. Trudeau, *Bloody Roads South*, 289.

It is said that over 60 percent of the American soldiers who fought in Vietnam either opposed the war or did not understand why it was being fought. To be sure, the reasons for the American Civil War were more easily comprehensible to the common foot soldier. But if the pollsters had been busy then, would they have found the understanding and the support so much greater? To understand is not necessarily to support, but [for a soldier] not to understand and to leave the exercise of "duty" on the level of blind obedience to the state is that much more tragic. For me, Stephen Crane's youth remains a point of reference.

"As the common Civil War foot soldier," Reston claims, "the youth of Stephen Crane [Private Fleming] or the youth of the Vietnam era was always given relief for treason or desertion . . . and the relief was given instantly after the divisive conflict was over."[6]

In fact, Crane's Private Fleming was decidedly not "given relief for desertion," because he did not need it: no one ever found out he deserted. Consider Reston's more significant claim that, for him, Fleming serves as a "point of reference." Reston is disinclined to believe that "the common Civil War soldier" was possessed of a "profound belief in the cause," or even a basic "understanding" of it. Fleming did not understand the reasons for the war, so therefore most "common foot soldiers" probably did not either. Fleming deserted because he did not have this "understanding." Thereafter, however, he returned to do his "duty," because of a "tragic" and "blind obedience to the state." This not only implies that Fleming's act of desertion occurred because he had no "profound belief" to sustain him in the ranks, it also suggests that his desertion was all but a purposeful act of conscience—he could not support a war the causes of which he could not "understand." Thus it is "tragic" that he subsequently surrendered his private conscience out of "blind obedience to the state."

Let us turn from Reston's work to the novel itself. To begin with, it is not clear that Private Fleming does not understand the reasons for the war. He just is not concerned with them. His motivation for enlisting came from a child's "prolonged ecstacy of excitement" (*RBC* 7) at the prospect of witnessing and participating in "great movements" involving "much glory." His mother "had affected to look with some contempt upon the quality of his war ardor and patriotism" (6), evidently recognizing the immaturity therein. Nonetheless, at the time of his entering the service, he was a volunteer, not a bewildered or dubious draftee.

6. James Reston, *Sherman's March and Vietnam*, 98–99, 100, 102, 219–20.

Further, his reasons (so to speak) for desertion had absolutely nothing to do with a failure to "understand" or an unwillingness to accept the Union cause: it is ludicrous to suggest that some disaffection with the Union cause was in any way involved (see Chapter 4). Nor does his return to the 304th involve some sort of relinquishment of his private conscience because of "blind obedience to the state." Dazed by a blow to the head (*RBC* 125), he is led back to the 304th by a stranger (128) and settles in gratefully to the warmth, care, and sustenance provided by his hut-mate John Wilson (132–37). For all we know, Private Fleming may both completely understand and completely accept the reasons for the Union war effort; or he may be childishly indifferent to them altogether. What Crane reiterates is that Fleming's main motivations involve quite other things.

To return to Reston's claim that Private Fleming is a "common foot soldier": according to Crane's novel, Fleming's career in combat during the battle of Chancellorsville reveals he is about as "common" an American "foot soldier" as Alvin York or Audie Murphy. In action on the second day, "When the enemy seemed falling back before him and his fellows, he went instantly forward," and "when he was compelled to retire again, he did it slowly, sullenly, taking steps of wrathful despair." So intense is his "hate," so "engrossed" is he in the combat, that he continues firing, unaware that a "lull" has fallen over his portion of the field. His fellow soldiers are all "staring with astonishment at him." Lieutenant Hasbrouck says, "By heavens, if I had ten thousand wild cats like you I could tear th' stomach outa this war in less'n a week!" (*RBC* 167–68).

As the 304th New York Infantry Regiment falters in a charge, Private Fleming joins Lieutenant Hasbrouck: "They galloped together down the regimental front. [Private Wilson] scrambled after them. In front of the colors the three men began to bawl: 'Come on! Come on!'" (*RBC* 186). As the charge falters yet again, Fleming, now the color-bearer, joins Lieutenant Hasbrouck in haranguing "his fellows, pushing against their chests with his free hand" (192). In this failed charge, Fleming is decidedly uncommon. Crane portrays him repeatedly as set apart from his fellows by superior courage and ferocity.

—⁂—

Daniel Aaron in his excellent *The Unwritten War* surveys the American literary response to the war and posits that *The Red Badge of Courage* is "an antiwar tour de force in which deluded people misread the laws of the universe and were overwhelmed." He considers Crane's work "a profane parable against war and its glorifiers and apologists." In support of this reading, Aaron produces a dense volley of images from it, some of them of diabolism and insanity, or parodies of traditional religious imagery and usage. He concludes that Crane's war is "cruel and purposeless, especially for the foot soldiers. It turns men into animals or machines and blurs the distinction between fools and heroes."[7]

Much in Aaron's short account of the novel is persuasive and to the point. But is *The Red Badge of Courage* really "an antiwar tour de force"? This does not seem right. The reason lies in the unpersuasiveness of the rest of the statement. Although Crane's hero may have indeed "misread the laws of the universe," in the end he was manifestly not "overwhelmed." Throughout his panic-stricken flight, perhaps, but following his return to the ranks of the 304th New York, he succeeded splendidly and achieved unblurred "distinction" as one of the regiment's few genuine "heroes."

Nor, in the aftermath of these two days of battle, does the "War" seem "cruel and purposeless" for Private (soon to be Color Sergeant) Henry Fleming. Four paragraphs from the end of the novel, the "purposes" the war has served in his particular case seem to him very clear indeed. The war has transformed him utterly, and for the better: "He felt a quiet manhood, nonassertive but of sturdy and strong blood. He knew that he would no more quail before his guides wherever they should point. He had been to touch the great death, and found that, after all, it was but the great death. He was a man" (*RBC* 232). Aaron notes that Fleming is "reading his own seraphic contentment into the universe" here, and there is warrant to understand that this moment is indeed imbued with Crane's characteristic irony.[8]

It is nonetheless this particular private soldier about whom Crane has constructed his novel: a private soldier whose conduct has been atypical throughout, especially in the heroic record he achieves on the second day, a record that is indeed publicly significant and replete with martial virtues, a record that is the opposite of what Aaron's general statements about the novel seem to imply about its plot. Private Fleming may be wrong about himself, but he is not "overwhelmed," and the war has not thus far proved "cruel and purposeless" to him. The typical foot soldier may have found the battle experience overwhelming, and the war "cruel and purposeless," but Crane has chosen to present the narrative of a very atypical private, especially in his actions on the second day at the battle of Chancellorsville. *The Red Badge of Courage* may indeed be "an antiwar" novel in some ways, but not in the ways Aaron claims.

—⁓—

7. Daniel Aaron, *The Unwritten War: American Writers and the Civil War*, 215, 218, 217.
8. Aaron, *Unwritten War*, 217.

John Fraser, in his seminal study *Violence in the Arts*, says that *The Red Badge of Courage* is "the most brilliant account of modern battle I know . . . and it is brilliant precisely because the breakdown of stereotypes is one of its central preoccupations and because the details of battle that don't accord with its youthful hero's preconceptions have" an unprecedented "vividness."[9] In *The Red Badge of Courage* almost exactly the opposite obtains, however. To begin with the last part of Fraser's statement, Private Fleming had a number of "preconceptions" about battle, and some of them do seem to have been stereotypical: "In visions he had seen himself in many struggles. He had imagined people secure in the shadow of his eagle-eyed prowess" (*RBC* 5). But before his enlistment, his general attitude toward the war was quite cynical: "But awake he had regarded battles as crimson blotches on the pages of the past. . . . . There was a portion of the world's history which he regarded as the time of wars, but it, he thought, had been long gone over the horizon and had disappeared forever." The "war in his own country" seemed "some sort of a play affair. He had long despaired of witnessing a Greeklike struggle. Such would be no more, he had said. Men were better, or more timid. Secular and religious education had effaced the throat-grappling instinct, or else firm finance held in check the passions" (ibid.).

It is true that immediately after his enlistment, while the 304th New York Infantry was being feted on their way to the front, "the youth had believed that he must be a hero" (*RBC* 10). And "he had had the belief that real war was a series of death struggles with small time in between for sleep and meals," which seems a plausibly stereotypical preconception. But "months of monotonous life in a camp" had disabused him of both these beliefs. "He was brought then gradually back to his old ideas," which Crane repeats, almost word for word: "Greeklike struggles would be no more. Men were better, or more timid. Secular and religious education had effaced the throat-grappling instinct, or else firm finance held in check the passions" (11).

Once Private Fleming found himself on campaign, his sudden new concern about his own possible failure of courage absorbed him completely. It generated within him a new preconception that was virtually the reverse of his earlier, stereotypical "belief that real war was a series of death struggles." Now in his childish self-absorption, he assumed this battle was arranged solely as a "supreme trial" for him, and that, if he passed it, all would be over. This "preconception" is perhaps understandable but it is hardly "stereotypical": "bizarre" would seem closer to the mark (*RBC* 64).

9. John Fraser, *Violence in the Arts*, 74–75.

Fraser quotes a passage from Private Fleming's first experience of combat, which does indeed specifically refute stereotypes: "Another [man] grunted suddenly as if he had been struck by a club in the stomach. He sat down and gazed ruefully. In his eyes there was mute, indefinite reproach. Farther up the line a man, standing behind a tree, had had his knee joint splintered by a ball. Immediately he had dropped his rifle and gripped the tree with both arms. And there he remained, clinging desperately and crying for assistance." It is also true that the portrayal of Fleming's first experience of combat is extraordinary for its vividness, and that portrayal does reflect various "breakdowns" in Fleming's mental condition. These "breakdowns" are not, however, of stereotypical preconceptions. They are breakdowns of self-control and discipline, and of coherent thought and perception. These "breakdowns" unleash Private Fleming's vivid imagination, and it is his own peculiar imagination that produces this array of unquestionably vivid and unstereotypical images: of a worker making boxes, of a well-meaning cow, of the monologue of a babe, and all the rest.

In the wake of Private Fleming's first cataclysmic experience on the afternoon of May 2, and as he becomes increasingly acclimated to "modern battle" during the morning of May 3, the imagery crossing his consciousness adjusts itself. It becomes more, not less, "stereotypical." This is apparent in the animal imagery his mind applies to himself and his predicament as the novel develops. To begin with, after he was swept by successive spasms of bewilderment, fear, and excitement on the regiment's foray into battle: "The swift thought came to [Fleming] that the generals did not know what they were about. It was all a trap" (*RBC* 38). "He thought that he must break from the ranks and harangue his comrades. They must not all be killed like pigs; and he was sure it would come to pass unless they were informed of these dangers. The generals were idiots to send them marching into a regular pen" (39). Seeing helpless people as pigs on the way to the slaughter pen may be stereotypical, but here the image is inappropriate. These men were not helpless. They were armed with modern, quite lethal Springfield rifles and were engaged in offensive operations against their enemy.

The pivotal, absolutely unstereotypical image amid Private Fleming's first taste of battle is that of the cow. "He developed the acute exasperation of a pestered animal, a well-meaning cow worried by dogs." This is extraordinarily vivid, and radically discordant with his actual condition as a fully armed soldier. "He had a mad feeling against his rifle, which could only be used against one life at a time" (*RBC* 57).

As he panicked during the subsequent rebel probe, into his "eyes there came a look that one can see in the orbs of a jaded horse" (*RBC* 67). This image is

vivid, but not clearly ascribable to Private Fleming's own consciousness. A fleeing soldier beside him "ran like a rabbit" (68). Then Fleming himself in his
panic "was like a proverbial chicken" (68–69). These are both stereotypical images of human terror but, given that the hero of the novel was himself panicking, quite untypical in their application.

Then consider images that occur as Private Fleming, with one day's experience of battle (and flight) behind him, awaits action on the second day, May 3,
1863. General French is redeploying formations of his division toward the west,
to face the continuing rebel offensive from that direction. Fleming is frustrated
and angered: "Good Gawd," he says, "we're always being chased around like
rats! It makes me sick. Nobody seems to know where we go or why we go. We
just get fired around from pillar to post and get licked here and get licked there,
and nobody knows what it's done for. It makes a man feel like a damn' kitten in
a bag" (RBC 160). His anxiety of the previous day has been replaced by a focused
anger. This morning the imagery (cornered rat, kitten in a bag) has become
more appropriate to his situation and more, not less, stereotypical than the imagery (those pigs, that well-meaning cow) that preceded them.

The process continues, as his mind develops images about himself that come
gradually closer to the reality of the given moment. "Yesterday, when he had
imagined the universe to be against him, he had hated it, little gods and big
gods." Now, as the rebel battle line approaches, "he hated the army of the foe
with the same great hatred. He was not going to be badgered of his life, like a
kitten chased by boys, he said. It was not well to drive men into final corners; at
those moments they could all develop teeth and claws" (RBC 164). The basis of
the image "badgered" is metaphorical: the badger's stout resistance requires a
particular pertinacity in overpowering it, which led to the cruel sport of "badger-
baiting" and hence created the verb "to badger" (the Oxford English Dictionary
gives the earliest printed example from 1792). This image has become a stereotype lacking in evocative power for most readers. Private Fleming's mind, influenced at some level by his earlier use of the image of the kitten, then equips that
animal with entirely stereotypical accessories, "teeth and claws."

Then the regiment becomes fully engaged: "To the youth, the fighters resem-
bled animals tossed for a death struggle into a dark pit" (RBC 165). "When the
enemy seemed falling back before him and his fellows, he went instantly forward, like a dog who, seeing his foes lagging, turns and insists upon being pursued" (167). The image of the dog has been applied to the common soldier in
literature from Shakespeare to Robert Stone.

That these images progressively become more appropriate to his situation as an armed soldier in combat is a part of Crane's portrayal of Private Fleming's growing familiarity with battle and growing confidence as a combat infantryman. This is also a device that commits Crane to a steadily greater use of traditional (that is to say, stereotypical) images. In the regiment's final action on the second day, Fleming as flag bearer leads a counterattack: "He plunged like a mad horse" (unarmed himself, his imagination replaces the ferocity of the dog with the wild speed of the horse) at a rebel regimental flag and the small color-party defending it. "His own emblem, quivering and aflare, was winging toward the other. It seemed there would shortly be an encounter of strange beaks and claws, as of eagles." This last image is vivid because it is unusually developed, but the basic image itself is utter stereotype. The flag winging above the battle line is a conventional image that often takes physical shape in the metallic American eagle atop the pole. This conventional physical object in its turn seems to have triggered Fleming's impression that the flags themselves will clash with "beaks and claws" (*RBC* 221).

It is interesting to trace another progression of images, those that Private Fleming associates with enemy shellfire during these two days of battle. One screamed "like a storm banshee" over the head of the regiment while it was in reserve (*RBC* 49). Enemy shells preceding the second rebel probe on the afternoon of May 2 "looked to be strange war flowers bursting into fierce bloom" (65). As his panic peaked, so too did the imagery applied to enemy shells: "They hurtled over his head with long wild screams. As he listened he imagined them to have rows of cruel teeth that grinned at him" (70). But on the second day, "The [Union] guns in the rear, aroused and enraged by the shells that had been thrown burlike at them, suddenly involved themselves in a hideous altercation with another band of guns" (162).

Depicting artillery as "throwing" shells is not necessarily an image at all but an appropriate application of one clear meaning of the verb "to throw." The *OED* gives the first example of such usage as 1726. Crane himself will soon use it again. The usage abounds in Civil War accounts, for example, "the batteries in our rear were throwing shells which exploded directly over my line" (*OR* 107). What is original here is the modifying adverb "burlike." Observed from a distance, the whitish smoke and the metal fragments generated by a shell burst could well suggest a bur: the image is tamer and more appropriate than seeing them as "strange war flowers."

Later, "Near where they stood shells were flip-flapping and hooting" (*RBC* 173), an image bizarre enough to call attention to itself. This image seems to return to the undisciplined imagination that produced those "strange war flowers" on the first day. The underlying thought is appropriate, however, of the harm-less overhead passage of a flight of birds. Not only is it thus a fairly tame envi-sioning, devoid of the menace of "strange flowers bursting into fierce bloom," and also one based upon the actual sound of spherical case shot tumbling in flight overhead. Certainly the description of canister as "an inhuman whistling in the air" (183) is not so much an image as an accurate depiction of its sound. Finally, "When the woods again began to pour forth the dark-hued masses of the enemy the youth felt serene self-confidence. He smiled briefly when he saw men dodge and duck at the long screechings of shells that were thrown in giant handfuls over them" (209). Crane returns to the stereotypical usage of artillery "throwing" shells. But in this instance he develops the stereotype so as to en-hance its potential as an image rather than as a simple verb. The barrage falls in "giant handfuls," which depicts the shells as balls or objects thrown in some kind of game. This is quite consistent with other images in the two following paragraphs, which compare infantry combat to a boxing match, and then to a childhood prank (209–10).

So my point is that, rather than a "breakdown of stereotypes," as Fraser would have it, they actually tend to accrue. As Private Fleming becomes more fa-miliar with battle and more self-confident, the imagery investing his compre-hension of the world becomes more comfortably traditional. As he becomes the typical soldier-hero, the imagery becomes more stereotypical. One reason that relatively few readers pay much attention to the second day of battle in *The Red Badge of Courage* is almost surely because its portrayal is precisely so stereotypical, so tame, in contrast to the more vivid portrayal of the first day.

This is not to say that this range of imagery is more accurate, however. The wild range of imagery generated by his experience of battle on the first day was childish in nature, first reducing the facts of the battlefield to those of a child's world; then, when overtaken by panic, overinflating them with the monsters and dragons of a child's nightmare. Now publicly praised by both the lieutenant commanding his company and the colonel commanding his regiment, his heroic status confirmed by serving as the flag-bearer of the 304th New York Volunteer Infantry Regiment, Private Fleming adopts the laconic ease of a veteran, under-stating the real nature of combat as proof of his "serene self-confidence," and that he is indeed a "good 'un" (*RBC* 207). The tone of these last paragraphs is not unlike General Couch's tone in his proud note about the conduct of his own corps during the battle: "a desperate effort was made by Lee's people to carry the left at Mott's Run, but the men who held it were there to stay" (*BL* 3:163).

In among this developing panorama of images, Crane every now and then plants a single descriptive sentence that reminds us of the murderous, exhausting reality of battle. Shells may not have teeth but neither are they as benign as balls thrown in a game. "One tumbled directly into the middle of a hurrying group and exploded in crimson fury. There was an instant's spectacle of a man, almost over it, throwing up his hands to shield his eyes" (*RBC* 180–81). Charging infantrymen are not puppets, dogs, or mad horses. The counterattack by the 304th New York "was a blind and despairing rush by the collection of men in dusty and tattered blue, over a green sward and under a sapphire sky, toward a fence, dimly outlined in smoke, from behind which spluttered the fierce rifles of enemies" (218). These sentences devoid of imagery offer occasional, but rare, instances of counterpoint to Private Fleming's metaphor-laced perceptions.

Finally, in light of Fraser's claim that *The Red Badge of Courage* is "the most brilliant account of modern battle" that he knows, "precisely because the breakdown of stereotypes is one of its central preoccupations," consider two of the novel's most critical moments.[10] First, in the wake of his "fine, wild" performance on the battlefield on the morning of May 3, which earned him the praise of Lieutenant Hasbrouck, Private Fleming ponders his conduct. "He had been a tremendous figure, no doubt. By this struggle he had overcome obstacles which he had admitted to be mountains. They had fallen like paper peaks, and he was now what he called a hero. And he had not been aware of the process. He had slept and, awakening, found himself a knight" (*RBC* 168–69). The moment is pivotal, as he himself recognizes, in his military career. Accordingly he applies, quite consciously, the most stereotypical of all martial terms—"hero" and "knight"— to his conduct.

While ironies may abound in the context of the moment, and perhaps even in some of the more abstruse connotations of these two terms, there is no discrepancy between the conventional meaning of the two stereotypical terms and the quality and kind of conduct Private Henry Fleming of the 304th New York Volunteers had just exhibited for all the world (or at least, for his company and his company commander) to see. Then the penultimate paragraph in the novel surveys things later that same morning:

It rained. The procession of weary soldiers became a bedraggled train, despondent and muttering, marching with churning effort in a trough of liquid brown mud under a low, wretched sky. Yet the youth smiled, for he saw

10. Ibid., 74.

> that the world was a world for him, though many discovered it to be made of oaths and walking sticks. He had rid himself of the red sickness of battle. The sultry nightmare was in the past. He had been an animal blistered and sweating in the heat and pain of war. He turned now with a lover's thirst to images of tranquil skies, fresh meadows, cool brooks—an existence of soft and eternal peace. (*RBC* 232–33)

Far from Fraser's "breakdown of stereotypes," it is to an entirely new edifice of stereotypes that the youth's experience has emboldened him to turn. Somehow the "red sickness of battle" has reaffirmed in him the common belief that "the world was a world for him." The last "images" before him are entirely banal—"tranquil skies" and all the rest—leading to the triumphant last stereotypical belief that "an existence of soft and eternal peace" extends before Private Fleming.

What is extraordinary about this last moment is that these conventional images and beliefs (unlike those of that morning, concerning his "knighthood") are contradicted by the actual evidence accumulated during the last two days, especially by the massive evidence immediately before him this morning: his army, defeated and retreating down muddy roads. His images here, then, are the worst of all stereotypes because they are completely false—but they are the stereotypes that his experience with violence has generated in his mind. It could be argued that "modern battle" should have "broken them down" in Fleming's mind. But Crane's conclusion makes it clear: Fleming's stereotypes have actually been reinforced. The other, more "typical" soldiers are "bedraggled and despondent"; Private Fleming is anything but.

—⁂—

All of these confident and sophisticated assertions about Private Fleming's typicality prove, then, to be not only unsupported but contradicted by what the text itself clearly displays about him. Why do astute and knowledgeable readers assume Fleming is "typical"? Why do they virtually reverse the actual pattern of his combat record during these two days of battle? Why do they misrepresent Fleming's own perception of that record?

The explanation lies in the impact upon both literature and popular fiction of a cataclysm that would have been unimaginable to Stephen Crane as he lay dying in 1900, that is, World War I, "the Great War," the war that transformed central and fundamental understandings about the ways in which literature is significant, the ways in which it signifies, and the ways in which it is to be professionally studied. That transformation devalued in the critical mind two of the most significant qualities of *The Red Badge of Courage*: Crane's brilliant and subtle development of the plot, and his meticulous attention to the realities of his hero's world.

World War I also generated a staggering number of imaginative responses in fiction, verse, film, and drama. These responses vary enormously in quality, detail, and influence, but a huge majority of them are based, surprisingly, upon a single paradigm. Over the last seventy-five years, this paradigm has become virtually omnipresent in narrative forms of art dealing with warfare. Thus even very sophisticated readers will often bring, all but unwittingly, that paradigm to bear upon Crane's novel.

—⚭—

Over the last forty years, the direly contrapuntal relationship between World War I and Western literature has generated a vast corpus of critical and theoretical appraisal. Paul Fussell's 1975 *The Great War and Modern Memory* is the best known, but it did not initiate the subject. In his 1967 *World War I and the American Novel*, Stanley Cooperman noted that "Major American works of the twenties and thirties tended toward the obliteration—through formal structure no less than philosophical emphasis—of any rhetorical statement whatsoever." Recall that, in previous notes, I tentatively suggested that there was a convergence between the heroic couplet in the eighteenth century and the infantry tactics dominant in the Age of Reason, and a similar convergence between the forms of verse in the first decades of the nineteenth century and the infantry tactics employed by the armies of the Napoleonic period. Cooperman argued that such a convergence between the novel and the unprecedentedly devastating nature of warfare in World War I was exactly the reason for that obliteration of meaning in fiction. "No longer one subordinate element among many contributing to a total aesthetic structure, environment—the war itself—became a chief protagonist; when this happened readers were left foundering in a situation where the traditional critical instruments simply could not be applied."[11]

In a variety of amplified forms and through a multiplicity of reiterations, in studies of the relationship between World War I and literary modernity this thesis has become "orthodoxy," and "sacrosanct."[12] The thesis involves far more than

11. Stanley Cooperman, *World War I and the American Novel*, 35, 194.

12. Martin Stephen, *The Price of Pity: Poetry, History, and Myth in the Great War*, xiii; Jay Winter, *Sites of Memory, Sites of Mourning: The Great War in European Cultural History*, 3. In addition to the works cited in this chapter, two studies are of particular worth because they add breadth and depth to one's knowledge of this field of study. In his refreshing work cited above, Stephen challenges the "orthodoxy" described here. Hugh Cecil, in his excellent *Flower of Battle: How Britain Wrote the Great War*, carries the "orthodox" Great War thesis into heretofore untilled fields with grace and significance. Neither author has reason to mention Crane.

just an argument that World War I produced absurdity, disillusionment, and horrific surrealism in literature about war. Ambrose Bierce, lieutenant of infantry (Ninth Indiana) and staff officer (provost marshal, topographical engineer) in the American Civil War, proved capable of finding his way to such things without having to contend with poison gas or the obliterating effect of high explosive.[13] Paul Fussell articulates the far more sweeping claims of the orthodox thesis:

> The Great War was perhaps the last to be conceived . . . within a seamless, purposeful "history" involving a coherent stream of time running from past through present to future. . . . . The Great War took place in what was, compared with ours, a static world, where the values appeared stable and where meanings of abstractions seemed permanent and reliable. Everyone knew what Glory was, and what Honor meant. It was not until eleven years after the war that Hemingway could declare in *A Farewell to Arms* that "abstract words such as glory, honor, courage, or hallow were obscene beside the concrete names of villages, the numbers of roads, the names of rivers, the numbers of regiments and the dates."

This breakdown, according to Fussell's critically important amplification of the thesis, collapsed the human capacity to categorize things intelligently: "The drift of modern history domesticates the fantastic and normalizes the unspeakable. And the catastrophe that begins it is the Great War."[14]

In *A War Imagined*, Samuel Hynes develops this argument further and more explicitly. World War I engendered a "sense of a gap in history," which "entered post-war consciousness as a truth about the modern world." So "time" in literature "must be disordered," and "a style [must be] created that denies its own past, and in which the act of denial is often a part of the work's statement." Jay Winter in *Sites of Memory, Sites of Mourning* says that "Gone is the comfort of conventional art and literature, for example, the safe, sentimental narrative of Dickens' prose." Critical imaginations schooled in these understandings could hardly be expected to attend closely to Crane's meticulous attention to the temporal schedule in which the battle of Chancellorsville developed, or to his evocative use of perhaps the most "conventional" of all narratives (see Chapter 6).[15]

13. Ambrose Bierce, *Phantoms of a Blood-stained Period: The Complete Civil War Writings of Ambrose Bierce*, 7–12.

14. Paul Fussell, *The Great War and Modern Memory*, 21, 74.

15. Samuel Hynes, *A War Imagined: The First World War and English Culture*, xiii, 191; Winter, *Sites of Memory*, 4.

In *Postcards from the Trenches*, Allyson Booth again posits the case for a convergence between the particular nature of World War I and the particular nature of modernist literature. "Readers impatient with modernist novels complain that nothing happens, but nothing happening is precisely what war devolved into when attrition became its organizing policy and staying alive its motivating goal." She identifies a "Modernist impatience with a linear time that moves straight forward from lunch to dinner and with ladder-like narrative structures." This impatience, she says, "signals an abrupt shift in ideas about what the novel was and issues to which it should attend." Such a shift leaves Crane, with his extraordinary command of "narrative structures," hopelessly dated. She defines, furthermore, an aspect of the modernist critical mentality that derides Crane's determination to base his novel in historical fact: "the guidelines implicit in a category like factuality are overwhelmed." In *The Great War and the Language of Modernism*, Vincent Sherry says that the war rendered ludicrous "the propositional logic of the narrative plot" in fiction, or "the additive meaning of its serialized incidents." But the brilliant evocative power of *The Red Badge of Courage* lies exactly in the way in which it entices its readers to respond to the "additive meaning of its serialized incidents."[16]

The subject of the fictional responses to World War I is tangential at best to this study of Crane's novel, but I cannot forebear offering a modest rejoinder to these articulations of the orthodox thesis about the consequences of that war upon literature. If I were to compose a list of the most evocative, famous, and influential novels dealing with World War I (to prepare, say, a syllabus for an undergraduate course in "Great War novels"), to me the most inevitable choices would almost without exception be conventionally plotted novels, in which linear time moves in a very straightforward—sometimes a brutally straightforward—way, and which derive a very great deal of their power from the palpable "factuality" of the specific time and specific place in which each is set. My list would include *A Farewell to Arms*, *All Quiet on the Western Front*, *Education before Verdun*, *Paths of Glory*, *The Enormous Room*, *Winged Victory*, *The Case of Sergeant Grischa*, and *The Forty Days of Musa Dagh*. These novels do share one quite powerful post–World War I paradigm, but they are all based upon conventionally fashioned, ladderlike narrative structures in which a very great deal happens. This is the case with *The Good Soldier Schweik* despite its titular antihero. *Parade's End* is discomfiting because of Ford's narrative tic wherein each volume begins with a

16. Allyson Booth, *Postcards from the Trenches: Negotiating the Space between Modernism and the First World War*, 109, 111, 87; Vincent Sherry, *The Great War and the Language of Modernism*, 226.

scene that the ensuing pages then labor to explain, but it is quite conventionally coherent in that we follow a crucial passage in the history of a central figure from beginning to end. *Company K* is the only World War I novel that I can imagine adding to the list that is nonconventional in its narrative shape. And would it not seem an entirely willful, theory-dictated act to supplant two or three of these with, say, *To the Lighthouse, Ulysses,* and *The Sound and the Fury?*[17]

In this chapter, though, we are seeking to understand why so many readers, including so many very sophisticated students of literature, find Private Fleming to be typical and even archetypal, despite what is so clearly displayed by the novel's plot and so clearly reiterated by the historical reality of its setting. A substantial part of the answer lies, as we have seen, in the way in which the dominant critical and theoretical response to the literature of World War I undermined confidence or even interest in conventional narrative and undermined belief in the significance or even the possibility of historical accuracy. Recent trends in critical and theoretical inquiry into the relationship between war and literature go even further. For scholars who have continued in the field so powerfully limned by Fussell, World War I and the wars following it have evidently erased the necessity for factual precision, or for normally understood categorization.

Back in 1967, Cooperman argued that "Fleming becomes a man through confrontation, fear, cowardice, resignation, and courage," and that "War, for all Crane's irony, is still the magnificent proving ground." I will consider this and similar claims narrowly (see Chapters 6 and 7) and will argue that this kind of response to the novel falls into a literary mousetrap—a mousetrap that Crane has deliberately placed and carefully baited (see Chapters 10 and 11). So while Cooperman's response is questionable, it is understandable. It is a response that is invited by aspects of the book that are there to be seen.[18]

Compare Margot Norris's assertion in *Writing War in the Twentieth Century* that *The Iliad* is a "martial spur" for the soldiers in *The Red Badge of Courage*, who "mentally carry Homer's *Iliad* into the Civil War with them."[19] Did not Private Fleming explicitly assure himself, twice, that "Greeklike struggles would be no more" (*RBC* 5, 11)? It is surely hard to imagine that Jim Conklin's mental baggage includes the tragic stories of Achilles, Hector, Priam, and Andromache.

17. Hemingway, *A Farewell to Arms*; Erich Maria Remarque, *All Quiet on the Western Front*; Arnold Zweig, *Education before Verdun*; E. E. Cummings, *The Enormous Room*; V. M. Yeates, *Winged Victory*; Arnold Zweig, *The Case of Sergeant Grischa*; Franz Werfel, *The Forty Days of Musa Dagh*; Jaroslav Hasek, *The Good Soldier Schweik*; Ford Madox Ford, *Parade's End*; William March, *Company K*; Virginia Woolf, *To the Lighthouse*; James Joyce, *Ulysses*; and William Faulkner, *The Sound and the Fury.*

18. Cooperman, *World War I*, 47.

19. Norris, *Writing War*, 37, 24.

"But gradually, as he chewed, his face became again quiet and contented. He could not rage in fierce argument in the presence of such sandwiches" (*RBC* 43). Does Private Wilson remind a reader of Patroclus? "I'm a gone coon this first time and—and I w-want you to take these here things—to—my—folks" (*RBC* 45–46). I find no evidence that any of Crane's figures, even including Lieutenant Hasbrouck, find *The Iliad* to be "a martial spur." Norris sees "Crane's naturalism" as "playing its minutiae of fear, pain, and bafflement off the clarity of the epic's graphic violence," but even this allusion to *The Iliad* does not seem to me an accurate representation of the epic. The "clarity" of its "violence"? After thirty readings, I still find it difficult to figure out whether warriors are being slaughtered by Trojan or Achaean bronze.[20]

Compare, too, John Limon's postmodern attention to the novel in *Writing after War: American War Fiction from Realism to Postmodernism*: "For Stephen Crane, heir of the realists but not a war-evader, modernism consisted in the discovery that the best literary substitute for the Civil War was the Civil War." This critical appraisal is bewildering to me, in its rejection of ordinarily understood categorizations. Does the following statement about *The Red Badge of Courage* assist a reader in seeing the novel as in itself it really is? "When an imaginary Chancellorsville *becomes* Chancellorsville, realism loses its rationale."[21]

But then the "real," historical battle of Chancellorsville itself is presented in *Writing after War* in a bizarrely weighted fashion: "its distinguishing feature seems to have been the breakdown of the Northern telegraphic communication" and the failure of "semaphore signaling and, due to heavy winds, balloon and telescopic observation. It was fought to a large extent blindly; for this reason, among others, an atavistic frontal assault resulted in a very costly Southern victory."[22] What can one make of this? Had the (nonexistent) Confederate States balloon service not been grounded by the weather, T. J. Jackson might not have been killed? This claim entirely ignores the narrative that most widely (indeed, almost universally) obtains concerning the battle of Chancellorsville; the narrative established at the time by participants; the narrative developed, adumbrated, and repeated by historians having paid meticulous attention to documentary, statistical, and topographical evidence for over a hundred and fifty years; the narrative reiterated with varying emphasis and focus by the dozen volumes listed in this study and at least fifty more beyond these. Limon's claim focuses entirely upon one or two isolated "facts," to which he has been directed by the literary theory driving his argument. Thus his claim can stand as an excellent

---

20. Ibid., 24.
21. John Limon, *Writing after War: American War Fiction from Realism to Postmodernism*, 36, 56.
22. Ibid., 55.

example, from the realm of history, of those approaches to fictional narratives that particularly obtain in the field of postmodern, post–World War I literary study.

The postmodern theoretical bases under which Limon studies *The Red Badge of Courage* thus liberate him not only from ordinarily understood categorizations but also from any responsibility toward the historical record. Similarly those theoretical bases liberate him from any responsibility toward the plot of the novel. As with the historical record, so with Crane's text: Limon is free to pick and choose among Crane's striking and sometimes not altogether fortunate images, as here in an exposition upon the "badge of courage" Private Fleming receives from the rifle butt of a fellow Union soldier:

> That wounds are both inside and outside is a physical fact that turns epistemological when Henry finally receives his badge. "He saw the flaming wings of lightning flash before his vision" (RB, 60). [Limon is using the Binder edition.] This *is* a vision, or almost—the flaming wings of lightning suggest an inchoate mythologizing of the battlefield, a partial descent of the beautifying goddess, who is later incarnate as the American flag: "It was a goddess, radiant, that bended its form with an imperious gesture to him" (RB, 90). That is not to say that Henry did not literally see his vision. The wound is a hybrid of visionary and visible fact—superfluously visible and visionary, since of all the visions that flash before eyes, the most redundantly appropriate one is a flash.[23]

This critical appraisal seems to me to be bewildering in itself, and strikingly indifferent to the basic facts of Private Fleming's wounding. As we shall see in Chapter 6, if this "epistemological" wound teaches him anything about supernatural presences, it is surely not that he was "beautified" (could Limon mean "beatified"?) by a descending "goddess" but, rather, that "retribution was a laggard and blind" and that "the dragons" of the battlefield were "inaccurate" in supervising human conduct (*RBC* 150–51). "That is not to say that Henry did not literally see his vision"? That is also "not to say" or even to intimate that, according to Crane's plot, Henry Fleming's wound is above all things *ironic*.

—〰—

In the Western world, the response in fiction to modern war—from World War I to the present—is one of remarkable sameness (the starting point alike for Harari and Fussell), which fact is all the more striking if the category is appro-

23. Ibid., 57.

priately understood to include film.[24] Modern war is universally portrayed as hideously murderous and meaningless, mutilating to both the flesh and spirit, obscene and random in its destructiveness, indeed obscene exactly because it is so random in its destructiveness. This last aspect is manifest in the irony of the title of Erich Maria Remarque's *All Quiet on the Western Front* (the official summary from the battlefront on the day the novel's hero is killed), and it is given succinct expression in *A Farewell to Arms*: "The killing came suddenly and unreasonably."[25] The "unreasonable" randomness of death in modern war is the central point in fictions set in the air, at sea, and on land.[26] In the lurid glare of modern firepower, from the artillery of World War I to the air strikes of Vietnam, traditional soldierly virtues of courage and skill count for very little. Other virtues, those of comradeship and love, become by contrast all the more important, but important for the solace they can bring to the maimed soul—manifestly these humane virtues are no more efficacious, no more capable of affecting events or preserving the lives of those who possess them, than are those traditionally martial ones.[27]

There are scattered exceptions to this general rule, but the only significantly different "schools" in novels and films about modern war are those that produced essentially patriotic (and limited) works during World War II, and those that nowadays produce essentially escapist (and ludicrous) "entertainments" of the Rambo variety.[28] Otherwise, these statements are true for virtually the entirety of the body of literature from Hemingway's *A Farewell to Arms* to Paul Watkins's *Night over Day over Night*; for virtually the entirety of drama from "Journey's End" to "Streamers"; for virtually the entirety of film from "All Quiet on the Western Front" to "Full Metal Jacket."[29]

The most famous, significant, and celebrated fictional responses to modern war share one single, rudimentary plot device by which this shared general vision of the destructive randomness of war is driven home. This device is that the

24. In the lists of works that follow, the titles of novels will be rendered in italics; the titles of films and plays will be given in quotation marks. Playwrights' names will be given but not directors' names.

25. Hemingway, *Farewell to Arms*, 218. Further references to this work will be given parenthetically in the text as *FTA*.

26. Remarque, *All Quiet on the Western Front*; Hemingway, *A Farewell to Arms*. For fictions set in the air, see Jim Shepard, *Paper Doll*; Derek Robinson, *Piece of Cake*. For fictions set at sea, see "Mister Roberts" (1955); "The Boat" (1981). For fictions set on land, see Thomas Boyd, *Through the Wheat*; James Jones, *The Thin Red Line*; "Hamburger Hill" (1981).

27. For example, *All Quiet on the Western Front*, *A Farewell to Arms*, or "Mister Roberts."

28. For a few exceptions to the general rule, see Ernest K. Gann, *The Company of Eagles*; M. Fagyas, *The Devil's Lieutenant*; "Patton" (1970); "Pork Chop Hill" (1959).

29. R. C. Sherriff, "Journey's End"; David Rabe, "Streamers"; "All Quiet on the Western Front" (1930); "Full Metal Jacket" (1987).

most devastating wounds, whether psychic or physical, are inflicted by one's own side. Sometimes these are profound psychic wounds occasioned by the impact upon the hero of brutality toward helpless civilians: sometimes through actual military necessity, or because of an inhuman power-crazed logic that passes as such. These also happen because of racism, panic, or mindless technology; because of sadistic officers or vicious enlisted men. Sometimes these psychic wounds are occasioned by brutality toward a captured or helpless enemy, because of seeming military necessity, brutal indifference for life, or sheer blood lust. More often, however, these wounds (whether psychic or physical) are incurred by soldiers themselves. Sometimes such wounds are incurred early, when idealisms or romanticisms imposed upon youths by their mentors or societies prove empty or murderously misleading in combat itself.[30]

This device is always central to the fiction when combat itself is not centrally involved. The "evil" attributed to the enemy is sometimes personified instead in brutal instructors in training camps. In a number of instances these wounds are caused by the callousness of military law, or the brutality of military police and the punishment camps they maintain.[31]

In combat, soldiers are sacrificed by their commanders, because of military necessity, or because of their officers' cowardice or their ready willingness to sacrifice nominal "allies." Soldiers are sacrificed because of their commanders' stupid adherence to dated values, attitudes, and practices, or their dumb theories; because of inhuman regulations, or manifestly erroneous information. Soldiers are needlessly sacrificed because of their commanders' blind fanaticism, mad ambition, personal animus, or desire to cover up their own crimes or errors.[32]

---

30. For military necessity, see Nicholas Monserrrat, *The Cruel Sea.* For power-crazed logic, see Kurt Vonnegut, *Slaughterhouse-five or the Children's Crusade: A Duty-dance with Death.* For racism, see John Hooker, *The Bush Soldiers;* "Casualties of War" (1989). For panic, see "Apocalypse Now" (1979). For technology, see Thomas Pynchon, *Gravity's Rainbow;* Len Deighton, *Bomber.* For sadistic officers, see Joseph Heller, *Catch-22.* For vicious enlisted men, see "Platoon" (1986); Nelson DeMille, *Word of Honor.* For brutality toward prisoners, see *Company K;* Paul Watkins, *Night over Day over Night.* For blood lust, see Frederick E. Smith, *A Killing for the Hawks.* For idealism proving empty, see Joseph Roth, *The Radetzky March.* For idealism or romanticism proving murderously misleading, see Remarque, *All Quiet on the Western Front;* John Masters, *Now, God Be Thanked;* "Born on the Fourth of July" (1989).

31. For brutal instructors in training camps, see Irwin Shaw, *The Young Lions;* "Full Metal Jacket." For the callousness of military law, see Zweig, *The Case of Sergeant Grischa;* Humphrey Cobb, *Paths of Glory;* "King and Country" (1964); Geoffrey Wagner, *The Killing Time.* For military police, see Hemingway, *A Farewell to Arms;* James Jones, *From Here to Eternity;* "The Jewel in the Crown" (1984). For the punishment camps, see Cummings, *The Enormous Room;* "The Hill" (1965); Kenneth Brown, "The Brig."

32. For military necessity, see Sherriff, "Journey's End"; Frederic Manning, *The Middle Parts of Fortune;* "Dawn Patrol" (1938); Len Deighton, *Goodbye, Mickey Mouse;* Derek Robinson, *The Hornet's*

Accidental deaths at the hands of one's own side figure frequently. Such occur, for instance, because of the worn barrels of one's own artillery, the panic of one's own rearguard, the automaton functioning of one's own radar, or the inexperience of one's own fellow soldiers. Sometimes enlisted men just kill each other (or try to), for the slenderest of motives, or for no clearly perceptible motive at all.[33]

Conflict between central characters is central to fiction, of course, and our culture's earliest fictions are shaped by plots wherein characters who are bound by ties of loyalty or family cause terrible wounds to one another. *The Iliad* is our seminal text about warfare, and it begins when the Achaean field marshal Agamemnon arrogantly brutalizes his best combat leader. What I wish to identify, here, is the omnipresence and centrality of this plot device in fictions since the 1914–1918 war. This device is not found in *The Spy*, and (while pale versions of it could possibly be identified in the hero's confession that Union campaigns were mismanaged, or in the indifference accorded him upon his return), it is not at all central to *Miss Ravenal's Conversion*. Nor is such a device central to the portrayal of war in Tolstoy's *War and Peace* or even in Zola's *The Debacle*.

On the other hand, so central and stereotypical nowadays is this device, wherein the worst wounds are caused by one's own side, that it occurs in contemporary historical fiction concerning past wars in which the actual face of combat was quite different from that obtaining since 1914. The device is central to recent novels and films about the Revolutionary War, the Crimean War, the Civil War, and the Zulu War, and it is typically the central device in recent fictions about wars with the First Nations. It is the central device in the most famous film about warfare in feudal Japan, and it appears in a variety of ways in a seminal film about the Boer War.[34] This device is so stereotypical that, just as

---

Sting. For cowardice, see Herman Wouk, *The Caine Mutiny, a Novel of World War II*; Walter Baxter, *Look Down in Mercy*. For sacrificing "allies," see "Gallipoli" (1981); Evelyn Waugh, *Sword of Honour*. For stupid adherence to dated practices, see "Oh! What a Lovely War!" (1969); Geoffrey Wagner, *Sands of Valor*; "King of Hearts"; "How I Won the War" (1967); Timothy Findley, *The Wars*; Robinson, *Piece of Cake*. For dumb theories, see John Harris, *Covenant with Death*; Shepard, *Paper Doll*. For inhuman regulations, see Heller, *Catch-22*. For erroneous information, see Cobb, *Paths of Glory*; Jones, *Thin Red Line*; "Gallipoli"; William Boyd, *An Ice-cream War*. For commanders' blind fanaticism, see Norman Mailer, *The Naked and the Dead*; "The Bridge on the River Kwai" (1957); "The Battle of the Bulge" (1965); "Apocalypse Now"; Watkins, *Night over Day over Night*. For mad ambition, see Jack D. Hunter, *The Blue Max*. For personal animus, see Ford, *Parade's End*. For commanders' crimes or errors, see Zweig, *Education before Verdun*; Jack D. Hunter, *The Flying Cross*.

33. For artillery, see Remarque, *All Quiet on the Western Front*; for rearguard, see Hemingway, *A Farewell to Arms*; for radar, see Deighton, *Bomber*. For fellow soldiers, see Derek Robinson, *Goshawk Squadron*, and Robinson, *Piece of Cake*. For the slenderest of motives, see Watkins, *Night over Day over Night*; for no motive at all, see Roger McDonald, *1915*.

34. For the Revolutionary War, see Howard Fast, *The Hessian*; Bernard Cornwell, *Redcoat*. For the Crimean War, see "The Charge of the Light Brigade" (1968); Tim Jeal, *Until the Colors Fade*.

modern British theater largely seeks to achieve purchase upon audiences steeped in Shakespeare or country-house mysteries ("The Mousetrap") by confounding their expectations ("The Real Inspector Hound"), so at least one recent television miniseries ("Anzacs"), one recent film ("Lighthorsemen"), and one recent novel about World War I (*A Soldier of the Great War*) array moments charged with this stereotype in order to refute them.[35]

The nature and employment of this device explains a good deal about the difference in stature and power of the two most ambitious contemporary series of historical novels based upon the Napoleonic wars. This device is omnipresent in Bernard Cornwell's series on the English infantryman Richard Sharpe, appearing in every single volume.[36] Those figures from whom Sharpe receives his most crippling wounds are always Englishmen or their allies: among others, Sergeant Hakeswill, whose viciousness finally results in the murder of Sharpe's Spanish lover; the half-Danish captain of foot guards, who is a traitor; the cavalry officer who seduces Sharpe's English bride; the incompetent Netherlandish princeling who gets Sharpe's men needlessly killed at Waterloo. With the exception of the French agent Ducos, the French themselves are, in comparison, almost benign. The series is based upon painstaking research and presents the face of infantry combat informatively and persuasively, but the ubiquity of this plot device finally becomes not only tiresome but claustrophobic.

Consider in contrast Patrick O'Brian's Jack Aubrey–Stephen Maturin series. From the first volume in the series, where the Royal Marine on sentry outside Captain Aubrey's cabin nods his happy approval as Aubrey explains to an appalled Maturin the Royal Navy's patently unfair but superbly efficient prize system, to one of the last volumes, where Aubrey embarrasses himself (and misses a shot at a pheasant) because he has let slip a mild criticism of the navy, these heroes are thoroughly at home in their service.[37] Their effectiveness is directed against foreign enemies—Bonaparte, the Dutch and American navies, pirates, slavers, and a host of others—and although English miscreants and traitors are to be found, these heroes' actions are undistracted by constant over-the-shoulder glances. Maturin's director in the English secret service is a rotund man who cares deeply about Maturin and who loves collecting beetles (the equivalent for-

---

For the Civil War, see Stephen Becker, *When the War Is Over*; for the Zulu War, see "Zulu Dawn" (1979). For the First Nation Wars, see Thomas Berger, *Little Big Man*; "Dances with Wolves" (1990). For the wars of feudal Japan, see "The Seven Samurai"; for the Boer War, "Breaker Morant."

35. Agatha Christie, "The Mousetrap"; Tom Stoppard, "The Real Inspector Hound"; "Anzacs" (1985); "Lighthorsemen" (1987); Mark Helprin, *A Soldier of the Great War*.

36. Bernard Cornwell, *Sharpe's Enemy*; Bernard Cornwell, *Sharpe's Prey*.

37. Patrick O'Brian, *Master and Commander* and *The Yellow Admiral*.

eign office official in the Sharpe series is an unscrupulous aristocratic fop who has the throat of one of Sharpe's lovers, the beautiful Astrid Skovgaard, slit). The O'Brian series registers far differently in consequence: each volume opens out into new worlds and new experiences, both literally and figuratively. It is an ebullient, powerful, and compelling achievement, liberated because O'Brian eschews this by now tediously familiar device. Indeed this device has recently achieved an apotheosis of sorts in Tom Connery's three (initially very promising) novels about a Royal Marine officer named Markham whose career and series come to abruptly simultaneous ends when he is betrayed by a typically craven and typically villainous and thus inevitably aristocratic "milord." The sequence of titles says it all: *A Shred of Honour, Honour Redeemed, Honour Be Damned.*

To return to fiction dealing with modern wars: the hero's progress almost always falls into a stereotypical pattern as well. In some few of the works set in World War I, heroes at the outset begin with stereotypical ideals and preconceptions. Inevitably these ideals are shredded, and then replaced—by calloused cynicism at best, but more frequently by despair, paralysis either mental or physical, or death itself. Innocence once lost to a culture or a hemisphere cannot be regained. So these fictions more often deal with heroes who are alienated to some degree at the outset, and who are then carried into further dimensions thereof: into self-serving cynicism, rebellion against the brutality or tyranny of one's own military compatriots, or into protest against war itself. Frequently central characters desert their service; so frequently, in fact, that this too has become a stereotype of a plot device, to be found at the center of an array of works.[38]

⁓⁓⁓

Into this ubiquitous paradigm, remark how precisely, even how wearisomely, *The Red Badge of Courage* can seem to fit. Death comes to Private Fleming's company of the 304th New York with a randomness familiar from all these later fic-

---

38. For stereotypical ideals and preconceptions, see Remarque, *All Quiet on the Western Front*; Henry Williamson, *Patriot's Progress: Being the Vicissitudes of Pte. John Bullock*; Dalton Trumbo, *Johnny Got His Gun*; Masters, *Now, God Be Thanked*; Derek Robinson, *War Story*; Sherriff, "Journey's End"; "Dawn Patrol." For self-serving cynicism, see Hasek, *Soldier Schweik*.

For rebellion against the brutality or tyranny of one's own military compatriots, see Zweig, *Education before Verdun*; "Mister Roberts"; Becker, *When the War Is Over*; "The Hill"; "Casualties of War." For protest against war itself, see Siegfried Sassoon, *Memoirs of an Infantry Officer*; "Born on the Fourth of July." For central characters who desert their service, as a stereotypical plot device, see Hemingway, *A Farewell to Arms*; John Dos Passos, *Three Soldiers*; "King of Hearts"; Findley, *The Wars*; Heller, *Catch-22*; Watkins, *Night over Day over Night*; "Apocalypse Now"; Tim O'Brien, *Going after Cacciato*.

tions: "Men dropped here and there like bundles" (*RBC* 59). Fleming, in his
extraordinary childish solipsism, is untouched by the reality of death, and un-
moved by compassion for his fallen comrades. His mind records them in ways
ignorant of the horror in their condition: "The captain of the youth's company
had been killed. . . . . His body lay stretched out in the position of a tired man
resting, but upon his face there was an astonished and sorrowful look, as if he
thought some friend had done him an ill turn" (60). Fleming's response, then,
approaches the laconic style with which benumbed heroes in many of the later
fictions record battle deaths: "Aymo lay in the mud within the angle of the em-
bankment. He was quite small and his arms were by his side, his puttee-wrapped
legs and muddy boots together, his cap over his face. He looked very dead" (*FTA*
214). This stylistic similarity is produced by radically opposed mentalities:
Fleming's childish ignorance "produces" a style matching that of Lieutenant (in
Italian, *Tenente*) Frederic Henry, but the latter results from a consciousness so
overfreighted with the experience of meaningless death that it is disciplined to
concentrate only upon superficial detail. The characters' opposite mentalities
have produced identical styles. The similarity between them cannot be ignored
and must suggest, to someone familiar with the post–World War I tradition,
that these works are themselves radically similar.

Completely in keeping with this all but ubiquitous central stereotype in modern fiction about war, Private Henry Fleming is wounded by a soldier of his own
side. "'Well, then!' bawled the man in a lurid rage. He adroitly and fiercely swung
his rifle. It crushed upon the youth's head. The man ran on" (*RBC* 120). This
wound drives Fleming to the ground (121) and leaves him physically staggered
(122), terrified (123–24), and at one moment almost delirious (124–25). Save
for the miraculous intervention of a passing stranger, Fleming might have collapsed (125), been captured by advancing rebels, or exposed, helpless, to rifle
and artillery fire in the intense confused action that continued on this front
throughout the night of May 2–3. This is the only wound Private Fleming receives during the battle of Chancellorsville.

Further, in seeming conformity to this paradigm, Crane's hero deserts from
the army. His thinking during his hours of delinquency is not very profound,
but during that time his thoughts touch many of the bases visited by other deserting heroes in their own various fictions. Tenente Frederic Henry deserts
from the Italian army when "mindless" young *carabinieri* (battle police) are about
to execute him as a "German agitator" (*FTA* 224). After his desertion, Tenente
Henry finds himself with a new perspective upon the war; he is "seeing now very
clearly and coldly"; "Anger was washed away in the river along with any obliga-

tion. Although that ceased when the carabiniere put his hands on my collar"; "I was not against them. I was through. I wished them all the luck. There were the good ones, and the brave ones, and the calm ones and the sensible ones, and they deserved it. But it was not my show any more and I wished this bloody train would get to Mestre and I would eat and stop thinking" (FTA 232).

With this, compare Private Fleming, who also believes he has been "betrayed" by "the blind ignorance and stupidity" of soldiers of his own side (RBC 76). He also now finds himself in "rebellion against his fellows" and "war in the abstract" (77), choosing instead "life" and "the religion of peace" (78). He, too, has come to a "new point of view" concerning "himself and his fellows" after his desertion (83). In fact, Fleming goes further in his repudiation of the "show" he himself has just left and enthusiastically contemplates "a defeat for the army" (112, 114, 115) from which he has just deserted.

If The Red Badge of Courage is engaged by an imagination steeped in this post–World War I tradition, these similar aspects of Crane's book stand out. Then those aspects of the novel that are radically different from the tradition— especially Private Fleming's courageous conduct on the second day, the (justly merited) praise it is accorded, and his own pride and contentment thereafter with his newfound prominence in the 304th New York—can slide off, unnoticed, into the shadows. Recall, for instance, Reston's implication that Fleming deserted because of his inability to "understand" the reasons for the Civil War, and the claim that, as a "common foot soldier, the youth of Stephen Crane was given relief . . . for desertion."[39] The issue of Fleming's "understanding" of the war never arises in the novel, however, and obviously has nothing whatever to do with his desertion. Nor is he "given relief for desertion," because no one ever knows he did desert. The only possible explanation for these startling errors is that Reston is "seeing" Fleming against such characters as Tenente Henry, Captain Yossarian in Catch-22, and Private Cacciato in Going after Cacciato, soldiers who did indeed desert for conscious reasons having to do with a repudiation of the war they found themselves in.

It is quite probable that Terraine's claim that Private Fleming's experience of battle is "ordinary" is based upon Terraine's own familiarity with a great deal of post–World War I work, both historical and literary, which leads him to assume that the "mysterious movement, incomprehensible behavior, abrupt outrage and devouring fear" that indeed surround Tenente Henry (for instance) embrace Fleming as well. It also seems certain that Aaron assumes a "deluded"

39. Reston, Sherman's March, 102, 219–20.

Fleming is "overwhelmed" by war because this unquestionably happens to Remarque's romantic German schoolboys in *All Quiet on the Western Front*, Sherriff's idealistic English public school youths in "Journey's End," and Cobb's
atomized French peasant soldiers in *Paths of Glory*, who were indeed overwhelmed, all of them, and beyond a doubt. It seems plausible that Fraser believes that "the breakdown of stereotypes is one of the central preoccupations"
in Crane's novel and that "the details of battle . . . don't accord with its youthful hero's preconceptions," because such things are unquestionably at the very
heart of most of the post–World War I works alluded to here. So too with
Norris's catalog of "the minutiae of fear, pain, and bafflement," which are indeed visited upon most of the heroes in the works surveyed above.

To make such assumptions about *The Red Badge of Courage*, however, is to misread the novel Crane actually presents. Just as a seeming similarity of style in the
portrayal of casualties actually involves, paradoxically, a polar difference in the
mentalities of Crane's Private Fleming and Hemingway's Tenente Henry, so
the other raw similarities that Crane's novel seems to share with the post–World
War I fictional tradition are actually mirror-image reversals. Fleming is indeed
wounded by a soldier of his own side; but far from driving home to him the
meaninglessness of war, this wound fortuitously enables him to return to the
304th New York by completely masking the fact of his desertion. His desertion
not only has nothing to do with any conscious repudiation of his army, his
country's cause, or war itself; it also occurs before, not after, he receives his
wound. Above all, Fleming is not only not alienated because of his experience
of combat, at the end of the novel he is surely the least alienated of any hero in
significant American fiction.

For all the enormous, wary sophistication of Limon's postmodern response
to the book, his imagination is still immured in the same post–World War I
misperception of the novel we have been tracing. Exercising the justification
given him by postmodernist theories to ignore how Crane has consciously
shaped his material, Limon concludes his study of *The Red Badge of Courage* as
follows: "To imagine war, imagine war imagining you. If war is the subject, we
are its objects. Who is writing? Hell is writing."[40] Well, in fact, this is not correct: Stephen Crane is—or was—writing.

Consider the concept of "Hell." Whose? Not Private (soon to be Color Sergeant) Fleming's. He is feeling "gleeful" and "assured," he is "smiling" because
"the world was a world for him." Private Wilson is quietly exultant in his pos-

40. Limon, *Writing after War*, 58.

session of the rebel battle flag; Lieutenant Hasbrouck ("th' best off'cer in this here reg'ment" [*RBC* 231]) is basking in the praise of his soldiers. Limon's "Hell" manifestly does not belong to the characters in Crane's novel but, rather, to Philippe Paris in *Paths of Glory*, or Paul Baumer in *All Quiet on the Western Front*, or Joseph Yossarian in *Catch-22*.

Ironies abound here. Sherry summarizes perfectly the essential "initiative" of critics such as Norris and Limon who belong to the "imaginative program" of postmodern theoretical criticism: "insurgent, counterprivilege, underclass."[41] Their theories, however, deliver them into affirming the authority of the single most traditional, privilege-implying, aristocratically based paradigm of them all—the paradigm seen as the special province of the educated male youth of the Eurocentric world; of Paul Baumer, George Sherston in *Memoirs of George Sherston*, Frederic Henry and Catherine Barkley's fiancé in *A Farewell to Arms*, the young Aussie mates in "Gallipoli," and all those doomed public schoolboys in all those spiffing squadrons in the Royal Flying Corps in *Winged Victory*, "Dawn Patrol," and *War Story*.[42] In the process, these critics miss exactly how "insurgent," how mordantly and rewardingly subversive is Crane's deliberate, efficient, and effective control of this material in *The Red Badge of Courage*.

Just as Crane could not have envisioned the changes in war witnessed in World War I, so he could hardly have envisioned the tradition this war would establish in the fictional portrayal of war, nor how this tradition would so thoroughly dominate the field down to the present day. He could hardly have anticipated how aspects that seemed so singular to him as he conceived his novel—a hero whose portrayal is so radically isolated from the social or political world of his time that the entire novel consists only of a portion of his military experience, a hero who is a private soldier and never rises into the company of the great people or the critical crises of his day, a hero who flees, a hero who is wounded by a soldier of his own side—would in less than three decades become, in scores of portraits of alienated, isolated, cog-like, disillusioned, and betrayed central characters, absolutely stereotypical in the portrayal of modern war. What Crane portrayed was the extraordinary experience of Private Henry Fleming, whose extraordinarily "youthful" mind not only was never awakened into "manhood" by combat (the supposed great rite of passage) but carried the youth at first into the depths of failure and possible disgrace and thereafter, unchanged altogether, carried him subsequently to the heights of success and public fame. What many of his readers and some of

41. Sherry, *Language of Modernism*, 19.
42. V. M. Yeates, *Winged Victory*; "The Dawn Patrol" (1938); Robinson, *War Story*.

his most informed critics have come to find, instead, is an altogether "typical" episode of youthful idealism collapsing, through the meaningless horrors and betrayals of battle into hellish disillusionment and alienation.

In the course of achieving this transformation of Crane's fiction, such modern readers have necessarily forgotten, ignored, or undervalued Private Fleming's conduct on May 3, 1863. They may have overlooked the "historical" specificity of the novel's subtitle as well, which defines the particular war from which this episode arises. It is the American Civil War—not World War I, World War II, the Vietnam War, or any other war in history—that is the central thesis of this study.

They have surely mistaken the central point of Crane's novel. The stereotypical plot of the modern-war fiction, so often and so erroneously applied to *The Red Badge of Courage*, is so omnipresent it has achieved a tyranny over the literary and cultural imagination. Yet the "message" or "lesson" this stereotypical plot so insistently brings to us is fully as romantic, fully as subjective an assertion imposed upon objective reality, as any of the romantic notions of warfare that this plot purports to refute. To claim that any young soldier outfitted with idealistic commitments will inevitably become disillusioned, to insist that his own "side" must inevitably give him his most brutal injury, to reiterate that any such tale must finally end in death or alienation—all this is to insist there is a shape or structure or pattern to reality. Just because this pattern may be ironic, malign, or disillusioning does not make its imposition any less gratuitous. To insist that some cosmic force will inevitably strip the heroic illusions from any young warrior is no different, except in the specific spiritual assumptions underlying it, than to insist that God will always strip Satan of his illusions of independence. Crane's novel in contrast—and especially as it continues to develop this "Episode" after Private Fleming speeds "toward the rear in great leaps" (*RBC* 69)—insists that reality is utterly random, utterly chaotic, utterly devoid of any pattern. Crane's world is not dominated by Hemingway's antagonistic "Them," but by the white, faceless "Weaver God" of Melville's *Moby-Dick*.[43] To lose *The Red Badge of Courage* amid this plethora of fictions about modern war (which Crane could never have anticipated) is to lose this critical understanding.

What Crane could have foreseen, on the other hand, and what he would have relished is the central fact at work in this kind of misreading. It is wonder-

---

43. Herman Melville, *Moby-Dick, or, The Whale*, 401.

fully ironic that this novel, which so steadily shows how solipsism can shape experience despite reality, has itself been "reshaped" in the reading by the preconceptions brought to it by even the best historical and cultural imaginations. What is absolutely true about Private Fleming himself—that his personal mentality everywhere dominates his perception, preventing (or saving) him from ever seeing the thing itself as in itself it really is—has evidently become true for a number of his readers.

The dislocations and the categorical confusions that Crane employed so effectively to evoke the activity of Private Fleming's mind during his first experience of combat should not be confused with the monstrously overinflated versions to be encountered (and justified, and celebrated) in post–World War I fictions and the criticism attendant thereto. In Crane's novel, these were techniques consciously and brilliantly employed to work upon a reader's own mind. And so they do still, after the passage of a century. Far from witnessing the helplessness, isolation, and ineffectuality of human intelligence, far from giving paradoxical witness to the limitations of linguistic intercourse, that passage of twenty-one paragraphs from chapter 5 in particular and Crane's novel in general illustrate exactly the opposite. To a reader sufficiently disciplined (or perhaps just sufficiently willing) to surrender to Crane's astonishing control of his medium, the novel can be a rewarding celebration of the imaginative powers of a human agent (Stephen Crane) and can demonstrate how much community yet exists between human beings; how marvelously capacious, alert, insightful, even good-humored the individual human mind can be; and how purposeful, informative, definitive, and transforming linguistic structures can still become.

Chapter 6

Private Fleming's Evening Hegira

"He Must Be a Hero"

The following is from the first chapter of *The Red Badge of Courage*. Consider how it probably registers in a reader's mind—and why. "On the way to Washington his spirit had soared. The regiment was fed and caressed at station after station until the youth had believed that he must be a hero. There was a lavish expenditure of bread and cold meats, coffee, and pickles and cheese. As he basked in the smiles of the girls and was patted and complimented by the old men, he had felt growing within him the strength to do mighty deeds of arms" (*RBC* 10–11). A reader is completely certain that Private Fleming at this moment is in the grip of an illusion. Were he to march from Washington directly to the field of battle and there immediately prove that his belief about his heroism is correct, a reader would be flabbergasted.

Not only do readers know exactly what to anticipate from this paragraph, they already (and far in advance) have anticipated encountering it and already (likewise far in advance) have anticipated that it will be significant enough to remark, register, or (if they are students in a course of literature) underline it. These anticipations are so confident, in fact, they quite likely cause the typical first-time reader to highlight this passage in such a way as to overvalue it, and then to ignore the three subsequent paragraphs, which show that Private Fleming's assumption of his own "heroism" here is only momentary. It is soon submerged in the dreary wintertime routines of the Army of the Potomac.

Why do readers bring such confident anticipations to the text? Reflection suggests that these anticipations do not arise from some "statistical" or "historical" investigation of human behavior. It is just as likely that a soldier believing such things about himself will go on to prove them true as that he will find them only illusory. Autobiographies repeatedly demonstrate such: soldiers whose training prepared them perfectly well for combat. Were Lieutenant Hasbrouck—"I was willin' t' bet they'd attack as soon as th' sun got fairly up" (*RBC* 160)—to write an autobiography, it would present exactly such a story. Nor is it necessarily the case that an inexperienced soldier must have any illusions at all about his own heroic potential. Autobiographies rarely show raw recruits who are possessed by such monumentally phrased, elevated concepts of themselves. The phlegmatic Private Jim Conklin manifestly does not think of himself in this fashion—"But if everybody was a-standing and a-fighting, why, I'd stand and fight" (17).

Most readers, I believe, do nonetheless have such confident anticipations and are so possessed by them that, when Private Fleming does prove (in his own eyes) "magnificent" (*RBC* 64) in his very first test, they instinctively "know" his assumption about himself cannot be true here. They are absolutely confident that some situational irony is about to unfold that will prove this assumption illusory as well. They push ahead confidently to find it. Again, why such confidence? It is not inevitable that Fleming will shortly fail—or even that he must soon be "tested" once again. Suppose that McLaws's rebels fell back completely after their initial probe? If Fleming had a full evening in which to rest and bask in his own self-esteem, what kind of soldier would he prove to be in battle on May 3? The reason for this confidence is that any reader brings anticipations to any work of fiction, anticipations generated by that reader's experience with literature and with all other forms of narrative art. The more that this experience reinforces any given anticipation, through steady repetition, the more a reader may come to assume that this anticipation reflects "life" itself, or that it constitutes some truth about human nature. In fact, however, the reader's perception of "life" has come to imitate art.

I think no pattern in literary tradition is quite as pervasive as the one influencing a reader here. Just as readers instinctively "know" that King Lear will not "unburden'd crawl toward death" (*King Lear* 1.1), precisely because at the opening of the play that bears his name he says he will, so a reader "knows" that Private Henry Fleming will not immediately prove a "hero," precisely because, at the beginning of the novel in which he is the central character, he believes (however fleetingly) he is a "hero." A reader looks for such initial, inevitably illusory declarations. They signal what is going to happen, and where a reader can most immediately discern the significance in it.

In the last chapter I sought to account for a peculiar pattern of misreadings of *The Red Badge of Courage* by pointing to a trap the post–World War I tradition in fiction poses for imaginations steeped in that tradition. Crane could not have anticipated this tradition, nor the way in which it would affect readings of his Civil War novel. On the other hand, for the imagination trained in the canon of Western literature, *The Red Badge of Courage* poses a potential trap of a different sort; and one that Crane deliberately fashioned as a crucial part of his strategy for affecting his readers' response.

—⁂—

At first glance, *The Red Badge of Courage* would seem to fit precisely into what is the most pervasive pattern in the narrative literature of the Western world; a pattern manifest in *The Iliad*, validated or at least recommended by Aristotle, and embracing subsequent works as diverse as Sophocles' *Oedipus the King*, Shakespeare's *King Lear*, Dickens's *Great Expectations*, Melville's *Moby-Dick*, George Eliot's *Middlemarch*, Henry James's *The Ambassadors*, Hemingway's *A Farewell to Arms*, and John Fowles's *The French Lieutenant's Woman*. This pattern presents a central figure who experiences failure and its consequences and then achieves a moment of redemption (in tragedies, the moment of such redemption may be brief indeed). This itself is overlaid upon a basic "psychological" pattern, from which the significance of the story depends. At the outset of the narrative, the hero is possessed by some sort of illusion; failure leads to a shattering moment of recognition; the hero, after suffering or sacrifice, will at last achieve "success"; but this "success" will be established on the basis of a new, more profound comprehension of reality. The mark of the hero's new wisdom is that this ultimate success will be altogether different from the success that he (more rarely, she) first sought to achieve.

The Iliad is the earliest of these works. This is not to say (of course not, since we are dealing with Homer) that this pattern is simple therein. Consider the epic in a general overview. Achilles' choice of a short but glorious life rather than a long quiet one is made while he is under at least two illusions. The first is that the rewards to be found in such a short life can be the same as those that "ordinary" warriors, under no such literal deadline, aspire to earn (women prisoners, contemporary fame, wealth, and so on). The second is that, for his own close entourage, his death will subsume all death—that his dear friend Patroclus will inevitably survive, and in his survival, Achilles himself will live on, vicariously. The epic strips him brutally of both these illusions: the first at the outset, when Agamemnon proves how nugatory normal pleasures are; and the second quite late, when Patroclus is killed in (with perfect ironic appropriateness) Achilles' literal stead. Thereafter follows Achilles' tremendous, lonely anguish, when he gives expression to the awful truths he now understands: that the price of his immortal glory will be the sacrifice of those satisfactions taken in "normal" pleasures (he neither bathes nor feeds himself in his grief) and utter loneliness (for friendship is also one of the pleasures of the world of normal life). Then when he finds himself in absolute power over Priam, the father of the man who killed his great friend, he also finds his way to a "satisfaction" or "success" of a sort that would be unrecognizable to any one of his fellow Achaean officers, and which is hard even today to articulate clearly as a success. He is compassionate with the old man, rather than holding him for some vast ransom, and he returns his son's body to him. Had the later Achilles not found satisfaction in these gestures, he would not have made them, but it is obviously satisfaction of a sort unimaginable to the earlier Achilles, at the outset of the epic, who flew into a rage when a concubine was taken from him.

This pattern, in which a hero undergoes failure and disillusionment and thereafter journeys through suffering and isolation into some new awareness, is so thoroughly ingrained in Western literary tradition that authors can build works that deliberately take advantage of readers' anticipations. Shakespeare's *Tempest* works on the basis that readers will "grant" the first stages of it (a hero's failure based upon illusion, and a subsequent new undeluded understanding of reality, which comes to the hero now isolated in the natural world) as Prospero explains his history to Miranda. The history all makes sense, instantly, and enables Shakespeare to dramatize only the last stages of the pattern. Counting upon the prevalence of similar anticipations, Joseph Conrad in *Heart of Darkness* and F. Scott Fitzgerald in *The Great Gatsby* focus attention not upon the central figures in the pattern, Kurtz and Gatsby (given what they know their readers will immediately comprehend, there is no need to) but upon those figures' principal biographers, Marlowe and Nick Carraway, and the effect of these instances of the pattern upon them. Flannery O'Connor knows a reader will anticipate finding a hero's newly heightened perceptions, summarizing the "truth" of things, toward the conclusion of a narrative fiction. So at these places in her stories (as in "A Good Man Is Hard to Find," "Good Country People," or "The Artificial Nigger"), she offers instead the most crack-brained idiocies, in order to test a reader's intelligence of soul (or lack thereof), which will be measured in the reader's ability to overcome the force of the tradition or pattern, in order to reach spiritual truth.

So, this omnipresent pattern teaches a reader to anticipate that the hero, at the outset of a fictional narrative, will be in the grip of an illusion—just exactly as the yet untested Private Fleming, stuffed with pickles and undeserved praise, believes "that he must be a hero." This omnipresent pattern also teaches a reader to anticipate that, after the inevitable failure generated by this illusion, the hero will then achieve some moment of disillusioned or undeluded recognition, and that this moment will fall at some place in the fiction between the halfway point and the very end. Thus in *King Lear* "I am a man / More sinn'd against than sinning" (*Lear* 3.4) initiates several newly insightful comments upon the human condition. Other moments from this play may fulfill this expectation more satisfactorily for other readers: for instance, the later moment where Lear is reconciled to Cordelia with the admission that he is "a very foolish fond old man" (4.7). I do not advance a study of *King Lear* here, but rather call attention to the singular fact that a reader will bring to the play an expectation that such a moment of accurate recognition will inevitably be there to be found. Yet again, this expectation is not based upon any "real" or statistical evidence about "actual" human nature, human history, or human psychology. Surely many more people have been swept straight to destruction still in the grip of their illusions, and especially upon battlefields, than have been brought first to see any kind of light. Rather, this expectation is something that the dominant literary tradition of our world instills in us.

Then consider how this tradition invites us to respond to the following moment of recognition midway through *The Red Badge of Courage*: "A moral vindication was regarded by the youth as a very important thing. Without salve, he could not, he thought, wear the sore badge of his dishonor through life" (*RBC* 114). The singular significance of this moment in meeting a reader's anticipations seems unmistakable. It appears at exactly the right place, viz. roughly halfway through the novel; its language is inflated with terms of ultimate human significance ("moral vindication," "dishonor"); it has obvious reference to the "badge" in the title of the novel. Moreover, at this particular moment, the hero is alone, so the recognition clearly comes from within his own experience and from his private reaction to it; he is in a wild natural landscape, the most customary and appropriate landscape for such a discovery; he has suffered extended anguish because of his own culpable behavior; and he has witnessed the death of a friend.

So after this moment, thanks to the omnipresent literary pattern, a reader confidently anticipates that, through suffering or sacrifice, the hero Private Fleming will achieve a final triumph, of some entirely unanticipated kind. In *King Lear*, this "triumph" surely comes when Lear, who at last sees what it is he truly "needs" (2.4), finds himself at last in possession of it: not "an hundred knights" nor "The name, and all the additions to a king" (1.1), but the generous and spontaneous love of his daughter with whom he is now reunited, "We two alone," in happy, defiant indifference to the sordid world of "court news," power, and prestige (5.3). This happy moment in *King Lear* proves brief. But the narrative involving Private Fleming's "Episode" ends quite otherwise than tragically, with the hero instead in firm possession of his newfound success. Earlier, we marked his justifiable pride and satisfaction with his own performance, and his delight in the well-merited public praise it garnered: "He saw that he was good. He recalled with a thrill of joy the respectful comments of his fellows" (*RBC* 229).

Now comes the conclusion we have anticipated all along. Mark how perfectly it, too, seems to fulfill our expectations. First, Private Fleming himself believes he has now happily progressed far beyond his earlier illusions. "He found that he could look back upon the brass and bombast of his earlier gospels and see them truly. He was gleeful when he discovered that he now despised them" (*RBC* 232). Second, very serious aspects of the human condition—maturity, courage, mortality—are invoked in the kind of "big speech" that, even if we do not exactly understand it, reeks of ultimate truth and significance: "He felt a quiet manhood, nonassertive but of sturdy and strong blood. He knew that he would no more quail before his guides wherever they should point. He had been to touch the great death, and found that, after all, it was but the great death. He was a man" (232). Third, this is succeeded by a sequence of images of the most positive and affirmative sort: "Scars faded as flowers," "the youth smiled, for he saw that the world was a world for him." "He turned now with a lover's thirst to images of tranquil skies, fresh meadows, cool brooks—an existence of soft and eternal peace." The entire conclusion itself ends with "a golden ray of sun" appearing through "hosts of leaden rain clouds" (*RBC* 232-33).

Just as Crane planted those earlier moments at exactly the strategic places we would anticipate finding them, all his tactics are designed at this moment to fulfill our trained anticipations. It is not surprising that the published record of literary intelligence concerning *The Red Badge of Courage* is, in large part, a history of efforts to reconcile Private Fleming's "Episode" with this literary tradition. But this is exactly where a modern student of the novel encounters a problem—or perhaps even *the* problem. I will now endeavor to sort out major trends and controversies in this record of scholarship in order to illustrate exactly how captivating is the narrative pattern that Crane so deliberately evokes, though I will not attempt a complete survey of all the scholarly criticism attending to the career of Private Fleming, and I know I will probably do some disservice (however unwitting) to some of the works upon which this will touch.

—⚂—

In his magisterial bibliography on Crane scholarship, Patrick Dooley notes that *The Red Badge of Courage* "has inspired a minor industry of critical response." No division of that industry is quite as large as the one that addresses the question of Private Fleming's transformation from one of the seven hundred "fresh fish" of the 304th New York to the regiment's most celebrated private soldier, who will very soon become its color sergeant. At least fifty of the "Articles, Book Chapters, and Study-Guide Pamphlets" in Dooley's survey trench upon that crucial issue, and it inevitably looms large in the books devoted to Crane.[1]

The issue arises, as Stanley Wertheim puts it in his equally magisterial *Stephen Crane Encyclopedia*, because the novel confronts a reader with "two oppositional voices," one voice "expressing Henry Fleming's affirmations of growth," and a second voice that is "detached, ironic," and "undercutting." Exactly so—and the first of these two "voices" is, as we have been measuring, powerfully amplified by the novel's seeming to fall so clearly into this great paradigm, so manifestly dominant in the Western canon, so explicitly evidenced in *King Lear*, and so obviously the template for works from *The Iliad* through, say, "The Godfather." Thus, as Wertheim succinctly puts it, a very great proportion of the criticism of the novel has inevitably engaged the question of whether Private Fleming's "transmutation indicates true growth toward maturity or remains self-deception."[2]

The critical works addressing this issue sort themselves into three categories. The first category consists of the critical works based upon the "undercutting voice" and the argument that Private Fleming's positive assessments of himself reflect the egocentricity and self-deception that have characterized him throughout. The second category consists of works based upon the "affirming voice," and the argument that Fleming has indeed grown in a positive way during the course of the novel. The third category, slender in numbers, consists of works that do not support either of these "voices" but seek to account for the fact that both voices are undeniably present. In establishing these categories, three points about the criticism addressing the issue of Fleming's development be-

1. Dooley, *Annotated Bibliography*, 72–109 (69).
2. Stanley Wertheim, *A Stephen Crane Encyclopedia*, 108.

come immediately clear. In the first place, the less narrowly a critic is focusing upon *The Red Badge of Courage* itself and the more he or she is concerned with other matters, the more readily he or she reads the book as a relatively uncomplicated example of this great tradition. In the second place, among those critics who deal closely and centrally with the novel, those who deny that Private Fleming has "grown toward maturity" have the incomparably easier task. In the third place, the "undercutting" arguments vary in force and focus but they all are quite similar in the evidence and the explanation they advance to support their conclusion, while the "affirming" arguments scatter themselves widely as they seek to account for the moment or the occasion or the nature of Private Fleming's "growth."

—⁂—

The "undercutting" or negative voice is found in three book-length studies of Crane's career when they consider the hero of Crane's most famous work. For Richard Halliburton, "although the later Fleming has acquired experience, he is as much as ever the creature of his imagination." According to George Monteiro, "he has emerged from the valley of death and is safe again—for the moment, anyway." For Linda Davis, "an ironic last line" shows that Fleming remains in the grip of "the same old delusions."[3]

Of the novel's most significant students, a significant percentage are ranged in this "negative" category. This is essentially the argument of John Berryman (albeit after some wavering), Jean Cazemajou, James Cox, William Dillingham, Alfred Habegger, Harry Henderson, Howard Horsford, Amy Kaplan, Mordecai Marcus, Wayne Miller, Robert Rechnitz, Eric Solomon ("Henry Fleming, the antihero"), Kermit Vanderbilt and Daniel Weiss, and Charles Walcutt (Fleming is "like a squirrel in a track"). Their arguments do not replicate each other, nor are they uniformly persuasive. Henderson's essay ends in a welter of generality about "the History revered in Everyman's consciousness." Kaplan's essay is indifferent to the historical reality of a regimental flag-bearer and "reduces the novel to a social allegory." But all of these studies can and do account for what happens in the novel with precision and can represent "the narrator's oppositional and ironic voice" with unalloyed, unapologetic accuracy. Horsford's "'He Was a Man'" is an excellent and representative example. "The Henry Fleming that Crane presents" at the end of the novel "stands in contradistinction to the

---

3. Richard Halliburton, *The Color of the Sky: A Study of Stephen Crane*, 124; George Monteiro, *Stephen Crane's Blue Badge of Courage*, 131; Linda Davis, *Badge of Courage: The Life of Stephen Crane*, 71.

Fleming many readers have accepted, who take him at his word." Seen accurately, Private Fleming at the end is essentially the same as he was at the beginning: "a figure of rueful absurdity"; "to the very end Crane presents him with wry irony. Fleming may believe, as the Union army retreats from Chancellorsville, that it is 'over.'" But "Would that it were so—for him—for every young man." Horsford's argument is eloquent and persuasive. It is limited only, as are almost all these "negative" arguments, by giving little if any attention to the curious fact that the book nonetheless, and obviously, does mislead all those "many readers," who "take him at his word."[4]

—⁜—

As noted above, those scholars and critics who are undertaking wide-ranging studies and give relatively brief consideration to Private Fleming's career tend to accept the "positive" or "affirmative" position. Thus, in setting up his study of World War I and the American novel, Cooperman (see Chapter 5) briskly says, "Henry Fleming becomes a man through confrontation, fear, cowardice, resignation, and courage" because, before 1914–1918, "War, for all Crane's irony, is still the magnificent proving ground." In The Living Novel, V. S. Pritchett says that "the purpose" of The Red Badge of Courage "is to show the phases by which a green young recruit loses his romantic illusions and his innocence in battle, and acquires a new identity, a hardened virtue."[5]

This is the case as well in some book-length studies specifically devoted to Stephen Crane's life or work. In his elegantly brief overview, Edwin Cady says that "Crane's irony bites only at [Fleming's] past delusions. He has become entitled to 'images' of flowery peace." Two late biographies of Crane likewise present Private Fleming's transformation in unequivocal terms. According to Bettina Knapp, the "episodes" in the book "may be viewed as testing stages in" Fleming's "psychological evolution" as he passes "from dreamy-eyed youth to

4. John Berryman, "Stephen Crane: The Red Badge of Courage," 281; Jean Cazemajou, "The Red Badge of Courage: The 'Religion of Peace' and the War Archetype," 149; James Cox, "On Stephen Crane's Red Badge of Courage," 61; William Dillingham, "Insensibility in The Red Badge of Courage," 268; Habegger, "Fighting Words" 231; Harry Henderson, "The Red Badge of Courage: The Search for Historical Identity," 237, 243; Amy Kaplan, "The Spectacle of War in Crane's Revision of History," 101–2; Mordecai Marcus, "The Unity of The Red Badge of Courage," 237; Wayne Miller, An Armed America, Its Face in Fiction: A History of the American Military Novel, 79–81; Robert Rechnitz, "Depersonalization and Dream in The Red Badge of Courage," 162; Eric Solomon, "A Definition of the War Novel," 162; Kermit Vanderbilt and Daniel Weiss, "From Rifleman to Flagbearer: Henry Fleming's Separate Peace in The Red Badge of Courage," 293–94; Charles Walcutt, "[Stephen Crane, Naturalist]," 211; Howard Horsford, "'He Was a Man,'" 126–27.

5. Cooperman, World War I, 47; V. S. Pritchett, "[Crane's Gift for Raising the Veil]," 234.

manhood." According to Christopher Benfy, "The plot of the book is deceptively simple, consisting of two days in the life of the new recruit—episodes ranging from tedium to terror, after which Fleming is changed forever." According to James Nagel, "The drama of the novel is epistemological, a matter of perception, distortion, and realization which finally culminates in Chapter 18 with Henry's epiphany."[6]

Patrick Dooley's *The Pluralistic Philosophy of Stephen Crane* is perhaps the most significant recent monograph on Crane and belongs in this second category. Its argument for Fleming's growth is painstakingly thoughtful. "His growth to adulthood is not due to battlefield heroics and public deeds. Rather, his quiet manhood is the fruit of three separate moral realizations: his confrontation with a serious ethical choice, his acknowledgement that he had failed to respond morally, and his most difficult and humbling experience, the decision to forgive and accept himself." This statement is achieved toward the end of four densely argued chapters. It is supplemented by a footnote of six paragraphs, which constitutes a profound survey of the major scholarship on this subject. And it is embedded in a general (entirely persuasive) argument that "Fleming does what all humans do—he seeks meaning and he struggles to affect outcomes. What Fleming cannot do is to render the world static, make it fully comprehensible or undo the past."[7]

Two oft-cited studies from the 1950s sought to take him "at his word." James Colvert said that when Fleming "throws himself into battle, blind with rage and despair, he symbolically accepts the world for what it is and tries to come to terms with it." Thereby Fleming "undergoes a change," experiencing for the first time, as he says, a "'sublime absence of selfishness,'" and emerging with "a truer measure of his personal insignificance." On the other hand, Eric Solomon said that Private Fleming "has become a new man who views life in a fresh framework, aimed not toward glory but a job to be done." The problems with both these graceful readings are immediately apparent: far from showing any awareness of his "personal insignificance" at the end of the novel, Fleming is "smiling" because of his belief that "the world was a world for him"; and far from being now braced for some "job to be done," he is anticipating "an existence of soft and eternal peace" (RBC 233).[8]

---

6. Edwin Cady, *Stephen Crane: Revised Edition*, 143; Bettina Knapp, *Stephen Crane*, 59, 63; Christopher Benfy, *The Double Life of Stephen Crane*, 106–7; James Nagel, *Stephen Crane and Literary Impressionism*, 59.

7. Patrick Dooley, *The Pluralistic Philosophy of Stephen Crane*, 89, 167–69, 140.

8. James B. Colvert, "Structure and Theme in Crane's Fiction," 341; Eric Solomon, "The Structure of *The Red Badge of Courage*," 336.

J. C. Levenson's later reading is far more cautious and nuanced: Crane's "theoretical inventiveness depended on his having an entirely plausible narrative which could support more than one reading." The thoughtful subtlety of this reading makes it one of the most significant of those that still, more or less, "take Private Fleming at his word." Levenson argues that Fleming's "learning to live with and put" his sin "at a distance" and his discovery about "the great death" are "touchstones of his coming to manhood." The shape of the narrative affirms, he says, that Private Fleming has outgrown "'the brass and bombast of his earlier gospels.'"[9]

In famously incautious contrast, R. W. Stallman argues that Private Fleming's story is entirely one of Christian redemption. This is evidenced in the famous image of "the red sun" being "pasted in the sky like a wafer" and in the initials of the dead Private Conklin. In radical contrast to this Christian reading, John Hart believes Private Fleming's story obviously evokes pagan rites of passage. Rather than find a significant pattern of Christian imagery in the novel, Hart produces a catalog containing "The whole paraphernalia of myth-religious and sacrificial rites." In reductive contrast to both Stallman and Hart, John Fraser claims that Private Fleming matures because he rejects any sense of a "supernaturally penetrated universe" and has *"earned"* his mature status by having existentially "exposed himself to the tumults of existence." James T. Cox agrees, but then he uses exactly Stallman's own catalog of Christian allusions to argue a point exactly opposite: "that in this red world Jesus Christ is a grim joke" and that Fleming's maturity comes about when he manages to shed the consequences of his "religious education." "Awareness—the ability to perceive truthfully the nature of this symbolically revealed, hostile universe—alone confers this new quiet, this new dignity."[10]

John Rathbun argues that Private Fleming's transformation is brought about by his "refusing to brood" upon moral issues and by his learning that, "For all his vaunted reason, man best meets the conditions of life when he does not think on them but trusts instead to his irrational self." For Marston LaFrance, on the other hand, the substance of Fleming's maturity is exactly the opposite to this. It is instead located in his learning "authentic self-knowledge" and learning "to accept the characteristic position of the mature

9. Levenson, "Introduction," li, liv.

10. R. W. Stallman, "Notes toward an Analysis of *The Red Badge of Courage*," 251–53; John E. Hart, "*The Red Badge of Courage* as Myth and Symbol," 196; John Fraser, "Crime and Forgiveness: *The Red Badge* in Time of War," 221–22; James T. Cox, "The Imagery of *The Red Badge of Courage*," 322.

man[,] that his own inner view of himself is vastly more important than the external opinion of others."[11]

In James Nagel's argument, Private Fleming's "significant development" occurs "in visual terms." It is that "he has relinquished his dreams" and his " 'red' " images of "fear, . . . in favor of a more mature and balanced picture of himself as part of humanity." Andrew Delbanco, on the other hand, argues that what Fleming had to "shed" was exactly his "symbol-making imagination," which had been generated in him by the "controlling assumptions" he inherited from his family and his culture. Shedding these, he is then able to achieve a successful "reeducation into a kind of epistemological purity."[12]

Not only are these "positive" readings wildly divergent, they are all pretty clearly swimming against the facts and patterns of the text. They often challenge and sometimes discomfit a reader's judgment. For three decades, Stallman's radical Christian surgery upon the text of the novel has been lambasted. Hart seems equally guilty of ignoring the narrative context for almost all the mythic "paraphernalia" he locates. Consider Levenson: "putting away" sin is not easily considered a "touchstone of maturity," is it? Private Fleming carrying the praise of his fellows as well as their regimental flag, it can be argued, is as prone to bombastic self-assessment as ever.[13]

In Fraser's argument, the pivotal moment in the novel is when Private Fleming "is overwhelmed by the fleeing men," late in the afternoon of the first day. It is then that "he is shocked out of his sense of the fixity of the battle lines and of his own uniqueness in running." This does not reflect, though, what was going through Fleming's mind, up to the twilight moment when he encounters those fleeing men. The blow with the musket butt that one of them applies to Fleming's head, does this not almost shock him out of his senses altogether? In Private (soon to be Color Sergeant) Fleming's last musings, the world seems as "penetrated" with "supernatural" presences as ever ("the world was a world for him"), although these presences are now providentially, mistily, entirely benign.[14]

In seeking to show how Private Fleming has learned not to "be paralyzed by the knowledge of sin" and to look "to the future," Rathbun—in the absence of any concrete evidence—is reduced to pure speculation. "Presumably," he writes,

11. John Rathbun, "Structure and Meaning in *The Red Badge of Courage*," 331–32; Marston LaFrance, "Private Fleming: His Various Battles," 344, 348.

12. Nagel, *Impressionism*, 54–57; Andrew Delbanco, "The American Stephen Crane: The Context of *The Red Badge of Courage*," 72.

13. Levenson, "Introduction," li, liv.

14. Fraser, "Crime and Forgiveness," 221.

Private Wilson has learned to "refuse to brood" upon past sins (there is no evidence in the novel to support this), and "When Fleming pushes aside the memory of his wrong, I think he might well be following a similar course." About Rathbun's general point: at the end of the novel, is Fleming not engaged—exactly, and very happily—in "thinking on the conditions of life"?[15]

In seeking to discern a path toward "authentic self-knowledge" in Private Fleming's various wanderings, LaFrance makes over the literal and historical Wilderness of Virginia (through whose dense terrain we have been tracing Fleming's movements on this afternoon of May 2, 1863) into a metaphorical "thicket of cowardice, selfishness, and immaturity," out of which he must seek "a way." "The first tentative step towards emerging from the forest is consciously determined," LaFrance says, "but he now wants 'to come to the edge of the forest that he might peer out.'" At this point in the novel, however, Fleming is explicitly not at all concerned with escaping from the forest but, rather, with satisfying his curiosity about a sudden and "tremendous" new eruption of battle (RBC 82–83). To consider LaFrance's general point: Is the final "self-knowledge" Fleming displays indeed "authentic" ("He knew that he would no more quail"), as he marches in the ranks of the 304th New York? And, carrying its flag and basking in the esteem of his fellows, has he really learned to discount "the external opinion of others"?[16]

As profound as is Nagel's study of impressionism in the novel, his argument that Private Fleming has experienced an "epiphany" does not locate any actual occasion. More confounding, Nagel's crucial sentence—"The drama of the novel is epistemological, a matter of perception, distortion, and realization which finally culminates in Chapter 18 with Henry's epiphany"—comes immediately after a sentence acknowledging that the novel "consists of the sensations and thoughts of a private engaged in a battle he does not comprehend and cannot even clearly see." To address the substance of Nagel's argument: Are the "visual terms" surrounding or credited to a character entirely equivalent to the moral terms in which he envisions himself, or the moral terms in which a reader should envision him? Even granting that such may possibly be the case, consider one of the last "visual terms" in which Fleming conceives himself: "he saw that the world was a world for him, though many discovered it to be made of oaths and walking sticks" (RBC 232). Does this in any way constitute "a more mature and balanced picture of himself as part of humanity"?[17]

15. Rathbun, "Structure and Meaning," 331.
16. LaFrance, "Private Fleming," 340–41.
17. Nagel, Impressionism, 59.

Let us look at Delbanco. If Private Fleming's experiences have happily divested him of much of his "symbol-making imagination," why is it still so active ("he knew that he would no more quail before his guides") at the end of the novel? If he has been reeducated into "epistemological purity," why are his thoughts ("red sickness," "sultry nightmare," "tranquil skies, fresh meadows, cool brooks") so trite and hackneyed (*RBC* 232–33)?[18]

Let us return finally to Dooley's argument, which argues that Private Fleming's "growth to adulthood is not due to battlefield heroics and public deeds. Rather, his quiet manhood is the fruit of three separate moral realizations: his confrontation with a serious ethical choice, his acknowledgement that he had failed to respond morally, and his most difficult and humbling experience, the decision to forgive and accept himself." I can find no evidence in the text itself to support either the first or the last of these claims. Nothing in the work indicates that Fleming ever conceived of himself during his encounter with the tattered soldier as being involved in a "confrontation with a serious ethical choice." His brutal behavior was dictated entirely by a thoughtless sequence of egocentrically ugly emotions. Nor does Fleming's final ability "to put the sin at a distance" constitute anything approaching a "decision to forgive and accept himself." This newly mustered ability to distance sin was based entirely upon the fact that his "vivid error" remained undetected. "He took no share in the chatter of his comrades, nor did he look at them or know them, save when he felt sudden suspicion that they were seeing his thoughts and scrutinizing each detail of the scene with the tattered soldier" (*RBC* 231). They are not seeing and cannot "see his thoughts." Yet suppose one of them were to say "By th' way, Henry, I met a feller from the 124th New York who ses he thinks he saw yeh abandon one of his mates yestirday, in a field off the Plank Road. What was you doin', way back there, anyhow, and why didn't yeh take keer a' th' feller?" In this—altogether unlikely—circumstance, would Fleming still be able to muster the "force to put the sin at a distance"?[19]

The scholars whose responses belong in this second, the "positive," category, are more than aware of these problems. Fraser acknowledges: "That Henry, apparently in a complete impasse after Jim Conklin's death, with every mental escape route blocked by his own arguings, is able to awake the following day a completely free man is certainly the strangest thing in the novel." After presenting the best he can muster by way of affirming Fleming's positive claims, Levenson spends twenty pages not in amplification but in melioration: "For readers

18. Delbanco, "The American," 72.
19. Dooley, *Pluralistic Philosophy*, 89.

who want Fleming transformed by his two days' seasoning, his dream of soft and eternal peace seems to undercut everything. For Crane it was only a sign that the mind is as various as the changeable world to which it instinctively turns for moral reinforcement."[20] Dooley's entire book is shaped by addressing the problems inherent in seeking to secure an affirmative reading of Private Fleming's story.

—ᴍ—

The third category consists of critical responses that seek to account for the presence of the two such radically contradictory "voices" in *The Red Badge of Courage*. Some arguments find that the novel is elementally flawed because it does not manage to achieve a plausibly "comprehensive account" of Private Fleming's experience, such as the one advanced by Colvert in 1967, while others find that its unique greatness lies in its profound understanding that "comprehensive accounts" are themselves snares and delusions, such as the one advanced by Colvert in 1990.[21] In the earlier of these two essays, Colvert says that, by seeming to confirm Fleming's affirmations of growth at the end of the novel, Crane "throws away . . . the richest theme in the story." In the later essay, Colvert acknowledges that his own understanding has undergone a profound shift. Having earlier "often supposed" that "the ethical implications of the state of Henry's mind at the end of the book is what matters most of all for Crane's art," he now sees quite differently: "Crane's genius was for capturing the poignant feeling of the instability and uncertainty of things." The novel depicts Crane's "burgeoning distrust of simplistic assumptions about human character." This last essay, "Crane, Hitchcock, and the Binder Edition," is invaluable for its wide-ranging, deeply considered, and to me finally incontrovertible resolution of the textual controversy that has bedeviled the study of the novel since the mid-1970s and the appearance of the Parker-Binder claimant. Colvert's compelling argument on behalf of the Appleton edition is based upon a great deal of deeply pursued, widely considered research. Insofar as Fleming's career is concerned, the essay falls squarely in the third category: Crane's final excisions, it illustrates, are exactly to the point of "sharpening the ambivalence of Henry's moral development."[22]

Stanley Greenfield's early essay on "The Unmistakable Stephen Crane" is

---

20. Fraser, "Crime and Forgiveness," 221; Levenson, "Introduction," lxxvi.
21. James Colvert, "Stephen Crane's Magic Mountain"; Colvert, "Binder Edition."
22. Colvert, "Magic Mountain," 303; Colvert, "Binder Edition," 258–59.

mordantly insightful about imprecise readings, and it is compelling in its own conclusions. It drifts toward much the same final point: the novel "is infused with an irony which neatly balances two major views of human life," the "ethical" and the "deterministic and naturalistic." Donald Gibson, painstakingly and in prose so limpid it can be undervalued, develops a book-length argument on exactly these lines: "Crane by virtue of presenting . . . opposing perspectives does not signal that he perceives them as possessing equal value. Though he presents the traditional view, it is clear that the non-traditional view is the more authoritative." But if "he presents finally a perspective that is more sympathetic toward the naturalistic perspective," the book is "not entirely free from the influence of more traditional views." He concludes that "Crane's mind is a complex one," and the novel "reflects that complexity in its most brilliant manifestation."[23]

Michael Fried in his generally (and bizarrely) postmodern *Realism, Writing, Disfiguration* finds a different way into this third category. Crane's short story "The Veteran" is certainly a sequel of sorts to *The Red Badge of Courage*: its central character is named "Henry Fleming" and he mentions his experiences at Chancellorsville and his late friend Jim Conklin. But Fried says, persuasively, that the seeming "answers" therein to the issue of Private Fleming's development "can't unproblematically be read back into *The Red Badge of Courage*," because in this story "Crane emerges as the first . . . of his totalizing readers, who traditionally have felt compelled to subsume" the issue of Fleming's growth "under a univocal moral and/or psychological interpretation."[24] My own concern herein is to explore the creative, imaginative, and historical impulses that led to Crane's brilliant novel, in order to illuminate it further. "The Veteran" came after the novel's success had won Crane international renown, and it comes from entirely different impulses. Nor does it seem, in general, a good idea to read initial works of literature in terms of works sequential to them: for example, "The Appendix" to *The Sound and the Fury* is a wonderful, evocative work on its own, but it distracts from rather than amplifies the patterns, characterizations, and emphases of Faulkner's initial story of how the Compsons variously experience Easter week.

23. Stanley B. Greenfield, "The Unmistakable Stephen Crane," 309; Donald Gibson, *The Red Badge of Courage: Redefining the Hero*, 99.
24. Michael Fried, *Realism, Writing, Disfiguration: On Thomas Eakins and Stephen Crane*, 160. The postmodern theoretical basis of this book renders it, to me, not only uncongenial but bewildering (a similar response, it seems, to that of many Crane scholars). But this point, teased out of its dense stylistic and theoretical matrix, seems quite cogent and persuasive.

This third category has been articulated with the greatest power by Donald Pizer. "In its events and much of its symbolism, the novel is a story of the coming of age of a young man through the initiatory experience of battle. But our principal confirmation of Henry's experiences as initiation myth is Henry himself, and Crane casts doubt—through his ironic narrative voice—on the truth and value of Henry's estimation of his adventures. And so a vital [and the modifier "vital" is crucial] ambiguity exists." In the novel's last passages, those eventuating in Private Fleming's belief that "the world was a world for him," Pizer says that the characteristic "fatuousness of Henry's conception" of himself is still paramount. But before we can therefore assume "that Crane wishes us . . . to reject completely the validity of [Fleming's] initiation experience," we have to reckon with, or digest, the last sentence: "Over the river a golden ray of sun came through the hosts of leaden rain clouds." This image is "not attributed to Henry," so "the narrative voice wishes us to be left, as a final word, with the sense that life is truly ambivalent—that there are rain clouds and that there is the sun." This is compelling stuff, developed with a well-warranted authority and a rhetorical grace to which justice cannot be done through picking out (as I have just done) selected gobbets.[25]

—m—

I do not think, however, that it tallies with the experience of reading, rereading, or re-rereading, the novel. My experience of almost forty years of teaching the novel to college students has been that the response of the overwhelming majority of intelligent people on a first or (more generally) second reading corresponds exactly to the responses seen in the second category of critical responses surveyed above. They, too, "take Private Fleming at his word," and they, too, agree with the "voice" in the novel that "expresses Henry Fleming's affirmations of growth." Thus persuaded, they are capable of extraordinarily able responses, seeking (as did the critics evidenced above) to explain the sources of his "growth," or—increasingly—demurring, sometimes powerfully, from what they take to be the "martial" or "masculine virtues" they think Crane is promulgating.

Then, persuaded to register instead that "oppositional voice," persuaded to trace out "the narrator's undercutting and ironic commentary," on subsequent readings they become entirely committed to that ironic reading. Their work thereafter quite closely and often quite intelligently parallels the arguments evidenced in the first category above. The fact that James Colvert's own career more

25. Donald Pizer, "*The Red Badge of Courage*: Text, Theme, and Form," 262, 264.

or less replicates this sequence convinces me that it is a true account of most readers' experience with the book. As limned above, Colvert's initial response (in 1959) produced an intelligent and eminently valuable appraisal of the way in which Private Fleming learned "to see the world in its true light." Then (in 1976) he produced an intelligent and equally valuable criticism of the novel, based upon what he took to be Crane's failure to sustain its undercutting irony. Then (in 1990) he produced his powerful (and immensely valuable) affirmation of Pizer's point.[26]

But what Pizer's reading would have a reader do is something that seems almost impossible: to sever the last sentence of the novel from the experience of the sentences preceding it, and to give it equal weight. For those convinced that Private Fleming has significantly developed, of course, this is not only impossible but unnecessary—the sentence would seem (with perhaps unfortunate obviousness) to affirm this fact. For those persuaded that Private Fleming has not developed, the description of the sun bursting through seems altogether of a piece with other instances of the sheer, ghastly (or demoralizing, or hilarious) indifference of the natural world. "So," the irony-dominated reader thinks, "Henry, in his fatuousness, will read it as if it is affirming the benignity of the universe. He'll have forgotten that rotting corpse, just as he has just now managed to forget the tattered man." In her popularly intended biography of Crane, Linda Davis did not even think it necessary to explain why the "last line" is "ironic."[27]

Nor do I think that the responses I have placed above in the second, the "positive," category are substantially (or wilfully, or ignorantly) inappropriate to Crane's ultimate intentions. In Pizer's words: "A sizable number of critics have had the 'felt response' that Crane wishes to affirm some aspect of experience in his depiction of Henry and they have struggled manfully in order to define the nature of this theme." Most of those critics are arrayed in the second category above, and among them are some of the most subtle, imaginative, learned, and most deeply and widely read students of American literature.[28]

Both those who read the novel quickly (including V. S. Prichett) and those who, despite the manifest difficulty of the task, seek "manfully" to establish the argument that Private Fleming did indeed have a life-changing epiphany share alike in "feeling" a "response" that Crane designedly elicited. Far from

26. Colvert, "Structure and Theme" (1959), 339. The other two essays are Colvert, "Magic Mountain," and Colvert, "Binder Edition."
27. Davis, *Badge of Courage*, 71.
28. Donald Pizer, "[Crane and *The Red Badge of Courage*: A Guide to Criticism]," 136.

"misreading" Crane's novel, they are reading it absolutely as he intended (and the purposes behind that intention I will try to set forth in my concluding two chapters). This "felt response" is largely attributable to Crane's having based his novel upon that most paradigmatic of all narrative patterns—the one set forth in the first portion of this chapter. Recall that this pattern presents a central figure who experiences failure and its consequences, and then achieves a moment of redemption. Recall that this narrative pattern encompasses—as one Russian babushka doll encompasses another, and then another—a basic "psychological" pattern from which the significance of the story depends. At the outset of the narrative, the hero is possessed by some sort of illusion; failure leads to a shattering moment of disillusioned recognition; after suffering or sacrifice, the hero will at last achieve "success," but a "success" established on the basis of this new, more profound comprehension of reality. The mark of the hero's new wisdom is that this ultimate success will be altogether different from that which he (or far more rarely, she) first sought to achieve.

This most familiar of all narrative patterns corresponds exactly to the story of Private Henry Fleming's experience at the battle of Chancellorsville: the narrative pattern is the template framing and shaping the story. Readers' lifelong experience with countless versions of this narrative pattern ensures that they will confidently and all but subconsciously expect that Fleming's story will reaffirm the various moral truths that seem implicit in the pattern: among them, that the world will shatter vainglorious illusions, that achieving public esteem and reputation is far less satisfying than achieving private magnanimity of character, that failure and suffering lead to moral and spiritual growth, that experiencing the brutality of the world will lead to wisdom and maturity. In Crane's particular version of this narrative pattern, though, as it closely follows the experience of this particular private soldier during the hours between late afternoon on May 2, 1863, and noon the next day, those familiar expectations will frequently collide with specific facts, some of them historical. The questions emerging from those collisions will occupy most of the rest of this study. First, though, we will consider those collisions in detail.

—◊—

There is surely no question that illusion is at the very center of Private Fleming's abject failure on the afternoon of May 2, 1863, and that it is a monstrous illusion caused by his monstrous self-absorption. The passage with which this chapter began, wherein Fleming "had believed that he must be a hero" (*RBC* 11), is not exactly irrelevant to his subsequent failure, for it displays his illusory sense that human psychology consists of clear and immutable categories. But during the days immediately preceding the battle, Private Fleming was no longer confident at all about "the heroism" of his own potential conduct; nor was he even thinking of himself in such conventional terms. He was as blind as a child to the grim reality of what he was about to face; he was in the grasp of a solipsistic self-absorption that we also identify with childhood. He had thus come (unconsciously, but all the more powerfully) into the gargantuan illusion that circumambient reality was arranging itself so as to confront him with one "supreme trial," which, if he passed, would prove he was "magnificent," "a fine fellow," and "even with those ideals which he had considered as far beyond him" (*RBC* 64). When General Lafayette McLaws's rebels attacked the Second Corps positions again, this huge illusion was shattered, and he broke in "blind" panic (69). He will never again approach combat in the same blind, illusioned way. But will he come to recognize (as King Lear did) the extraordinary quality of his solipsism, which produced this first, monstrous illusion?

Well, one aspect of an answer to this question is indeed certain: if Private Fleming does have such a traditional recognition, the tradition dictates that it should occur sometime between the moment when he flees from the ranks of the 304th New York in the midafternoon of May 2, and sometime around seven-thirty that evening. And it should occur somewhere in the Wilderness of Spotsylvania north of or just adjacent to the Old Orange Pike, where that road joins the Orange Plank Road in the mile and a half between the Chancellorsville crossroads and Dowdall's Tavern. Crane's fusion of this literary tradition with the historical details of the battle of Chancellorsville enables us to fix the window of opportunity in which Fleming may have come to such a recognition, at exactly these four hours, and within exactly this square mile.

This period of Private Fleming's personal crisis probably constitutes the low point of the novel for most readers. Fleming's self-centered, self-pitying, uncertain mental condition, never producing anything in the way of action, makes him very uncongenial company. But as a moment of crisis tending toward a recognition, it is rich indeed in circumstances traditional to such. Private Fleming is alone as he wrestles with the crisis to which he has been brought: so too were Achilles, Lear (for all practical purposes), Pip in *Great Expectations*, Arthur Dimmesdale in *The Scarlet Letter*, Ahab in *Moby-Dick*, Lambert Strether in *The Ambassadors*, Kurtz in *Heart of Darkness*, Lily Bart in *The House of Mirth*, Gatsby in the novel bearing his name, Frederic Henry in *A Farewell to Arms*, Quentin Compson in *The Sound and the Fury*, and Charles Smithson in *The French Lieutenant's Woman*. Fleming is in the raw natural world, thereby possibly more in contact with elemental truth and less distracted by illusory human institutions: so too were Lear on the heath, Prospero on his island, Arthur Dimmesdale and Hester Prynne in the New England forest, Frederic Henry on the bank of the Tagliamento, Quentin Compson in the Massachusetts countryside, and Charles Smithson on Ware Common. He witnesses extraordinary things, which could help recast his own perception: so too did Lear "I' th' storm," Hamlet (evidently) at sea, Ahab as the Pequod sinks, Strether in the French countryside, and Quentin Compson on the day he is preparing to commit suicide. The hours of the crisis extend for him into the evening, as they did for Lear, Lambert Strether, Lily Bart, Kurtz and Marlowe, Quentin Compson, and Gatsby and Carraway.[29]

In this portion of *The Red Badge of Courage*, both the landscape through which Private Fleming wanders and the things he sees are drawn from a detailed knowledge of the historical record: his general journey can be plotted in both time and space. Although Crane continues faithful to historical realities and logical probabilities, however, he does depart twice from such faithfulness during this portion. Both cases are in order to provide Fleming with dramatic, unmistakable challenges to his pervasive solipsism.

Although in his initial panic, Private Fleming "lost the direction of safety," he nonetheless instinctively heads for "the rear" (*RBC* 69), which means he is fleeing westward. The seventy-three thousand men of the Army of the Potomac under Hooker's direct command at Chancellorsville were aligned in a great saucepan shape curving from northeast to west-northwest, where the Eleventh Corps formed the handle of the pan. The Second Corps was facing the rebels to the east and so it was deployed in the center-left of the Federal position. This is, as we look down envisioning it, to us the right-hand side of the bowl of the saucepan. The depiction of the terrain through which Fleming flees accords so closely with that which lay behind the Second Corps's position that afternoon, as suggested by detailed maps, that Crane probably composed this section—for all its seemingly offhanded impressionism—with just such a map before him.

It is a landscape of "wee hills" and "hillocks" (*RBC* 71). A rebel battery is firing from one, and the advantage Lee's artillery took of such slight elevations

---

29. William Shakespeare, "The Tragedy of King Lear"; Charles Dickens, *Great Expectations*; Nathaniel Hawthorne, *The Scarlet Letter: A Romance*; Melville, *Moby-Dick*; Henry James, *The Ambassadors*; Joseph Conrad, *Heart of Darkness*; Edith Wharton, *The House of Mirth*; F. Scott Fitzgerald, *The Great Gatsby*; Hemingway, *A Farewell to Arms*; William Faulkner, *The Sound and the Fury*; John Fowles, *The French Lieutenant's Woman*; Shakespeare, "The Tempest" (Prospero), and Shakespeare, "Hamlet."

throughout the course of the battle was a major factor in his victory. In the first, most panic-stricken moments of Private Fleming's flight, he must have crossed the road running north from the Chancellorsville crossroads, for the Second Corps reserves were formed immediately east of that road. So now he is in the small brush-dotted fields that abut the western side of the road and that are now under rebel artillery fire (*RBC* 70). This terrain is sufficiently open to permit a Union brigade to keep "formation" (71) as it advances eastward into support. His panic somewhat abating and his characteristic visual interest engaged once more, Fleming watches this infantry, and then an artillery battery redeploying. His pace "moderating," a little "later" and somewhat further to the west, he comes upon a "general of division" controlling his part of the battle from this relatively open area (72). Tree lines and copses obscure some of the combat to the east (75), but, mounted, the general is able to see well enough to follow the flow of the battle, and from his reactions, Fleming discovers that his comrades in the Second Corps "had won after all!" (75).

Crushed by the news, Private Fleming goes "from the fields into a thick woods, as if resolved to bury himself" (*RBC* 77). Now he is going westward once again, away from the small fields near the road and into the dense second-growth woodland notoriously characteristic of the Wilderness. "The ground was cluttered with vines and bushes, and the trees grew close and spread out like bouquets. He was obliged to force his way with much noise. The creepers, catching against his legs, cried out harshly as their sprays were torn from the barks of trees. The swishing saplings tried to make known his presence to the world" (77). Witnesses to the battle of Chancellorsville recorded the unusual way in which this terrain baffled and blocked noise of the battle in unexpected ways (*OR* 5), and Fleming soon finds that "Off was the rumble of death"; he can hear insects and the chattering of a squirrel (*RBC* 78). This particular part of the battlefield is also entangled with creeks and marshes that feed southward into Scott's Run, and Fleming "found himself almost into a swamp. He was obliged to walk upon bog tufts and watch his feet to keep from the oily mire" (79).

Until he discovers that the "imbecile line" from which he has fled has "remained and become victors" (*RBC* 75), Private Fleming has faced no crisis at all. His impressions have run the gamut from raw panic to sorrow for, bewilderment about, and then anger toward others who are going about their duties. Now, although he cringes "as if discovered in a crime" (75), his mental responses are much the same as possessed him before and then during combat earlier that afternoon. He still conceives of his situation in childish terms. Just as he feared shame earlier but with no real conception of injury or death, now he is unaware of the realities, legal and military, of his plight but worries instead about "what" his fellow soldiers "would remark when later he appeared in camp." He feels the same personal helplessness and self-pity at having been "betrayed" as he felt on the way into battle that morning: then he was trapped in the "iron laws of tradition and law" (35); now he is "trodden beneath the feet of an iron injustice" (76).

There is one manifest difference, however. Now he is separated from rather than trapped within the ranks of the 304th New York Volunteer Infantry Regiment. So his mind justifies his isolation on the basis of his obvious superiority to his fellows. He believes he is "the enlightened man . . . of superior perceptions and knowledge," who has been "betrayed" by the "blind ignorance and stupidity" of the "fools" who are his "comrades" (*RBC* 76). His self-pity, his "agony and despair" and "the expression" in his eyes "of a criminal who thinks his guilt and his punishment great" (77) all develop from the belief in his superior "enlightenment" and from the fact that its claims are hardly self-evident in his current, his "ill used" situation.

—⁓—

Buried away from the battle in the "thick woods" of the Wilderness north of the Orange Plank Road, Private Fleming finds "assurance" in the natural "landscape" itself. "It was the religion of peace"; "He conceived Nature to be a woman with a deep aversion to tragedy." He throws a pine cone at a squirrel, and it runs away. "The youth felt triumphant at this exhibition. There was the law, he said. Nature had given him a sign" (*RBC* 77–78). Recall that Fleming was initially surprised, upon emerging from his first firefight, to find that "Nature had gone tranquilly on with her golden process in the midst of so much devilment" (63). But needing some confirmation of his own superior rectitude at this moment, his mind now enlists "Nature" in its (in "her") entirety. "The youth wended, feeling that Nature," preferring peace to war and gracing him with that "sign" that life is to be chosen over stolidly doing one's duty even to the death, "was of his mind" (79). Please note: it is not that he has had to learn any of this from Nature, but that "She *re-enforced his* argument with proofs that lived where the sun shone" (79; my italics). The credit he implicitly gives himself in this moment, the especial favor he believes Nature itself (herself) sent him: this kind of mental reaction shows that, at this point, his solipsism is as active as ever and continues to supply him with monstrous illusions about himself and his situation.

This particular illusion is so very monstrous that Crane, in order to challenge it instantly and unmistakably, abandons at this moment two of the most successful and sustaining features of *The Red Badge of Courage*. The randomness of his narrative has been one of the most forward-looking and significant of its qualities: the randomness of modern battle will not allow Achilles to face Hector in single combat, nor Macduff to encounter Macbeth, nor the black knight to prove to be Richard the Lionheart, nor *The Spy's* master to be George Washington. *The Red Badge of Courage* shares this refutation of coincidence with the post–World War I narratives. Likewise, it has been a central thesis of this study that *The Red Badge of Courage* is closely based upon the historical details of the battle of Chancellorsville. But Private Fleming's illusion about "Nature" is, according to Crane's profoundest Naturalistic understanding, so untrue as to be obscene. Crane's literary imagination had been educated in the school of Naturalism (see Chapter 11), and although his impressionistic style sets his work apart from the work of Frank Norris and Theodore Dreiser and other Naturalistic novelists, he completely accepted its central tenet. "Nature," according to that tenet, was not only completely indifferent to the fate of the individual, but it—never "She"—was also completely indifferent to the fate of the human species. Fleming's fatuous ignorance provides the perfect occasion to drive this lesson home, so at this moment Crane introduces both a rank coincidence and a detail that does not seem to conform to the historical record.

In the "greater obscurity" of the Wilderness amid the northeastern branches of Scott's Run, Private Fleming finds a natural "chapel" of "high, arching boughs," "green doors," and "a gentle brown carpet" of "Pine needles." Crane's images here, making over natural details into details of religious architecture, promise that this place will present whatever ultimate "religious" truths can be seen in raw "Nature." And, in its "religious half light," Fleming is indeed "given a sign"—a real one, this time, demonstrating the real truth of the relationship between "Nature" and the individual. He is "horror-stricken" at it (*RBC* 79).

> He was being looked at by a dead man who was seated with his back against a columnlike tree. The corpse was dressed in a uniform that once had been blue, but was now faded to a melancholy shade of green. The eyes, staring at the youth, had changed to the dull hue to be seen on the side of a dead fish. The mouth was open. Its red had changed to an appalling yellow. Over the grey skin of the face ran little ants. One was trundling some sort of a bundle along the upper lip. (79–80)

This ghastly spectacle is the most perfect possible refutation of Private Fleming's new illusion that "Nature" is "a woman with a deep aversion to tragedy" and all the sentimental rest thereof. Nature's callous indifference to the fate of the individual is apparent in gruesome detail. To make the lesson unmistakable, the corpse before Fleming is of a Union soldier such as himself, so this destiny is not a matter of dialect, or diet (southern pork, say, rather than midwestern beef), or belief, all possible rationalizations that might arise in Fleming's mind were this the corpse of a dead rebel. And to insist upon the reality that each and every individual will be eventually annihilated in nature's inevitable embrace, the feature of this figure that connotes the broadest, simplest fact of his human history—the blue uniform testifying that he was a soldier for the Union—is being erased into nature's universal green.

The abrupt randomness seemingly so characteristic of the novel—the battle beginning abruptly "One grey dawn," Private Fleming's company commander slain without prelude in the first exchange, his own sudden flight, and so on—renders most readers oblivious to the extraordinarily instantaneous collision here between illusion and refutation. But this manifestation, this particular "sight" located in this particular circumstance at this particular moment in the narrative, is preternaturally coincidental. And Crane's commitment to his theme at this point seems to have outweighed his commitment to his historical sources. It is hard to find a plausible historical action or event that could have deposited such a corpse, so uniformed, in this place in the wilderness northwest of the Chancellorsville crossroads on the afternoon of May 2.

The problem is not with the corpse itself. Crane needs a body upon which nature has had a chance to operate, so a recent fatality—a soldier from "Saunders' brigade," say, who took a mortal wound and stumbled off to this isolated location—would not do. But those ants are key, and in reasonably warm weather such scavenging can begin within hours of death. The corpse's "grey skin" indicates pretty clearly that it is around twelve hours old: much beyond that period in such weather, the face would turn black and the entire corpse would become bloated with expanding gasses. The dull dead-fish hue of the eyes is likewise consistent with a body of that vintage, though the mouth turning "yellow" is a less certain development. The mucus membranes would more probably turn an ashen color—could hemolysis explain the yellow? Given the location, this soldier was most likely a victim of rebel artillery fire: elements of both the Second and the Third Corps had endured shellfire in this general area during the preceding twenty-four hours (OR 78, 114). But the soldier could have taken a mortal wound during infantry skirmishing anywhere on this southeastern quadrant of the army's front and then found his way here before dying.[30]

---

30. The medical analysis here is generously and expertly provided by Dr. Robert E. Rodstrom, of Mount Vernon, Ohio.

Whatever the condition of the corpse, however, it is inconceivable that a blue uniform would have "faded to a melancholy shade of green" after only twelve hours of exposure to spring weather. Nor for that matter would twenty-four, forty-eight, or even a hundred and fifty hours (the length of the entire campaign so far for the most strenuously engaged of the Union infantry) have effected such a change in color. The dead man is surely wearing a woolen sack coat, called the "fatigue" or "service blouse," the uniform coat in which we pictured Private Henry Fleming in Chapter 1. Union soldiers were issued white flannel pull-over shirts to be worn beneath their service blouses, but the only other Federal-issue outerwear was a bulky overcoat of kersey, light blue in color, for wintertime wear and of course colorfast. This overcoat, if issued at all, was typically shed early in any springtime campaign.[31]

The sack coats, ubiquitous in any photograph or correspondent's sketch of Union soldiers on campaign, were intended to serve as outer garments in any kind of weather, and to retain their distinguishing blue color even with long wear. Early in the war, unscrupulous contractors supplied the Federal armies with uniforms of such poor quality that the term "shoddy" ceased to mean a woollen yarn made with a large percentage of reused rag material and came exclusively to mean "what is worthless and pretentious in art, manufacture, ideas," and so on. The earliest example of this new meaning in the OED is, significantly, from an American source in 1862. Nonetheless, I am unaware of any complaint that even such shoddy early issue faded to green with outdoor wear. And after the first year of the war, Union soldiers were receiving issue clothing of consistently reliable quality.

In fact, the battle of the Wilderness would begin in exactly this same place exactly one year later. Union soldiers would then find many skeletons of soldiers whose bodies had gone unburied the previous year: "We wandered to and fro, looking at the gleaming skulls and whitish bones, and examining the exposed clothing of the dead to see if they had been Union or Confederate soldiers." So even the passage of a full year would not leach the identifying blue color from these fatigue blouses.[32]

Crane is so precise in his historical detail that it is tempting to try to find a historical warrant for his portraying a uniform jacket in a "shade of green." In fact, two regiments in the Army of the Potomac were wearing green uniforms

---

31. Stackpole, *Chancellorsville*, 73; Robertson, *Tenting Tonight*, 72–76; Haythornthwaite, *Uniforms*, notes to plates 3 and 15.
32. Gregory Jaynes et al., *The Killing Ground: Wilderness to Cold Harbor*, 63.

during the battle of Chancellorsville: the First and Second U.S. Sharpshooters (mentioned above in Chapter 1), who comprised Colonel Hiram Berdan's Third Brigade in the Third Division of the Third Corps. They were posted in this general area during the night of May 1–2 and left from there on an offensive operation against the rebels on the morning of the 2nd. Though their losses that morning were "trifling," they did take casualties (OR 166), and the table of Union casualties for the campaign lists a dozen enlisted men "captured or missing" from the two regiments (OR 4). But the passage is, alas, specific: this "uniform that once had been blue, but was now faded." Nor is there any rhetorical warrant for wresting the authority for this apparition away from the narrative voice and for attributing it instead to the imagination of a panicked Private Fleming.[33]

So, in order to set this unmistakable object lesson before his hero, Crane departed both from the randomness of his narrative and from the details of Civil War history, two of the most compelling, persuasive qualities of *The Red Badge of Courage*. I do not mean to imply that this constitutes a weak moment in the novel. Crane develops it with deftness. The effect of the moment is enhanced and its uncertain historical (or logical) provenance is elided by the familiarly childish cast of mind that characterizes Private Fleming's panicked reaction. He is "horror-stricken," and "for moments turned to stone," as if in a scene from a child's nightmare. "He feared that if he turned his back the body might spring up and stealthily pursue him." But as he backs away, his childish curiosity tempts him "to touch the corpse," though "as he thought of his hand upon it he shuddered profoundly." Breaking free of this mesmerized state, he runs away "unheeding the underbrush," just as he had crashed blindly into a tree in his earlier flight from the line of battle. "After a time he paused, and, breathless and panting, listened. He imagined some strange voice would come from the dead throat and squawk after him in horrible menaces" (RBC 80–81). Although these reactions are the stuff of nightmare, because of their childishness they are quite familiar and palpable to readers. As with Fleming's earlier reactions to the prospect of battle, to combat itself, and to the unexpected renewal of the rebel assault, readers may so submerge themselves in Fleming's mind they may even assume his reactions are typical of those of combat soldiers encountering corpses. But published memoirs suggest quite otherwise: even relatively inexperienced soldiers report retreating in gagging disgust from such spectacles, not fleeing in terror. In fact, the moment may be so persuasive as an evocation of a

33. Katcher, *Potomac*, plate D3 and notes; Haythornthwaite, *Uniforms*, plate 27.

"typical" soldier's experience that readers may themselves miss the profound lesson implicit in that "religious half light"—just as Private Fleming does.

For this last is the point of my inquiry: the extraordinary lengths to which Crane has gone to present Private Fleming with this lesson make all the more extraordinary Fleming's failure to recognize anything whatsoever—about the natural world, or about his own insignificance therein—from it. Far from any sort of significant recognition, Fleming exhibits here in the wilderness north of the Orange Plank Road exactly those same particular mental characteristics that he exhibited in the fields northeast of the Chancellorsville crossroads in his first experience of battle. These are the same mental characteristics he exhibited back in camp at Falmouth when the campaign began: self-absorption; a grandiose sense of his own importance; an ignorance about certain ineluctable realities, including those of his own mortality; a vivid imagination; a recurrence in patterns of thinking to images and experiences of childhood. And along with these childish characteristics, this young private soldier also has a child's extraordinary mental resilience.

Private Fleming's unreasoning panic at the spectacle in the "chapel" dissipates as quickly as it arose. He becomes absorbed in the descent of "twilight" upon the wilderness around him. His mind imposes upon this natural phenomenon exactly the same quasi-religious impressions—suffused with yet another half-glimpsed principle of universal peace—that it produced before he stumbled upon the corpse. Trees "sing a hymn" and chant a "chorus"; the sun sinks deliberately; "there was a lull in the noises of insects as if they had bowed their beaks and were making a devotional pause" (*RBC* 82). The break between the novel's chapters 7 and 8 may tend to mask the fact, but Fleming's mind has reverted entirely to his earlier perceptions. He has utterly failed to recognize the harsh truth implicit in that corpse.

Once again, Private Fleming's pastoral revery is challenged, this time not by a historically improbable corpse but by the most massive, most electrifying moment of the historical campaign: General T. J. Jackson's surprise descent, with twenty-six thousand rebel soldiers, upon the exposed right wing of the Army of the Potomac. "Then, upon this stillness, there suddenly broke a tremendous clangor of sounds. A crimson roar came from the distance" (*RBC* 82). This transmogrifying attack was led off by Brigadier General R. E. Rodes: "At 5.15 p.m. the word was given [by Jackson himself] to move forward" (*OR* 363).

Private Fleming at first is "transfixed" by this. "It was as if," to his imagination, "worlds were being rended." His own "mind flew in all directions," but his child's vivid curiosity once again takes control of his willpower. He sees that it is "an ironical thing for him to be running thus toward that which he had been at such pains to avoid." He says to himself "that if the earth and the moon were about to clash, many persons would doubtless plan to get upon the roofs to witness the collision" (*RBC* 82–83).

"This uproar," "a celestial battle" in its magnitude, dwarfs "the late encounter" he and "his fellows" have had with the rebels. "They had taken themselves and the enemy very seriously and had imagined that they were deciding the war." In the nanosecond signified by this punctuating period, Fleming's ego then elevates himself above the ruck of such deluded "fellows," about whom he himself, in his superior wisdom, can only speculate. "Individuals must have supposed that they were cutting the letters of their names deep into everlasting tablets of brass, or enshrining their reputations forever in the hearts of their countrymen." Private Fleming knows better. In "fact," the "affair" upon which they have been engaged "would appear in printed reports under a meek and immaterial title." But he recognizes that it is "good" that such ignorant delusion possesses the great majority of his fellows, since without it "every one would surely [as he had] run" (*RBC* 83–84).

Private Fleming, at this point in the novel, is working his way through the thick "brambles" and "trees" of the wilderness to the north of the Orange Plank Road. He reaches a vantage point from which he can see "long gray walls of vapor" to the west "where lay battle lines." He continues on toward the "battle" and climbs a fence. "On the far side, the ground was littered with clothes and guns. A newspaper, folded up, lay in the dirt." There is a single dead soldier there, and then "a group of four or five corpses." He thinks, "A hot sun had blazed upon the spot"; the dead are "swollen." Fleming is now emerging from dense woods and entering an area of partially cleared fields and country lanes on the northern side of the Plank Road. For the past twenty-four hours, various elements of the Third Corps had occupied this area, under sporadic, sometimes "well-directed" and "heavy" rebel artillery fire (*OR* 108, 110, 112, 118). The grouping of the bodies and the litter suggest that the dead in this "forgotten part of the battle ground" are Third Corps victims of that fire, slain while in bivouac or reserve. Their caps would be marked with diamond-shaped badges (*RBC* 84–85).

"He came finally to a road from which he could see in the distance dark and agitated bodies of troops, smoke-fringed" (*RBC* 85). Private Fleming is standing beside the Orange Plank Road or the Old Orange Turnpike: the two were conjoined here. This was the only east–west road through the Wilderness between

Chancellorsville crossroads to the east, behind him, and the open areas around Wilderness Church and Dowdall's Tavern to the west. It was thus the only road offering such a vision of the fighting on the right or western flank of the Union army. The combat he is watching is about three-quarters of a mile away. The road there rises westward past Dowdall's Tavern to Talley's Hill, which the rebels have captured, so the rising terrain and the open roadway enable Fleming to secure this view of the battle.

Those "dark and agitated bodies of troops" trying to block Jackson's advance were mostly from General Carl Schurz's Third Division of the Eleventh Corps. Devens's First Division, the westernmost of this corps, was destroyed in the first rebel onslaught, which fell upon them in unexpected strength from unexpected directions. Steinwehr's Second Division, which had earlier supplied half its strength to a Third Corps offensive thrust southward, was likewise in no position to offer resistance. The time is now toward six o'clock (OR 252). Throughout the rest of this twilight portion of the narrative, Private Fleming will remain beside the Orange Plank Road. Generally, he will be working his way east, along with the wreckage channeled into this road from the army's ruined right flank.

First among the refugees are the wounded: "In the lane was a blood-stained crowd streaming to the rear" (RBC 85). A few of these might be casualties from the Eleventh Corps, but the rebels are advancing with such speed that most of the Eleventh's casualties will have fallen into rebel hands. The majority of these wounded men in the Plank Road are soldiers wounded earlier in the battle, compelled to retreat from the field hospitals. Most of these are from the Third Corps, since this section of the Orange Plank Road lay to the immediate rear of that corps's general position during most of May 2. The one soldier in this throng with whom Private Fleming will have any significant exchange is a lean man wounded in the head and the arm (88). Both the tattered condition of his uniform (87) and the general cast of his conversation (88, 102–3) indicate he was in action most of the early afternoon. His satisfaction with the conduct of the "fight" of his "feller" soldiers shows they were successfully engaged in offensive operations against the enemy. He is from Birney's First Division of the Third Corps (their diamond badges are red), which, since noon and alone among the divisions of the Army of the Potomac, have been on the offensive this day, attacking the flank and rear of Jackson's corps in its passage across the southern front of Hooker's army (OR 108, 112). The field hospital for the First Division of the Third Corps was established that morning "on the Plank Road one mile west" of the Chancellorsville crossroads (OR 110), which would be very near where Private Fleming is standing now.

"One of" the wounded "was swearing that he had been shot in the arm through the commanding general's mismanagement of the army." Paranoid perhaps, but astute enough, given that Hooker's cravenness on May 1 and his careless deployment of his army's right flank on May 2 caused this debacle. "Another had the gray seal of death already upon his face" (*RBC* 86). This man, in Crane's second departure from the randomness of the narrative, will turn out to be Private Jim Conklin (92), and the ensuing encounter between the two of them will receive close attention below.

"Orderlies and couriers" gallop down the turnpike, carrying reports and pleas from the collapsing front and "scattering wounded men right and left" in their passage. But of far more danger to these walking wounded are the artillery "batteries that came swinging and thumping down upon them, the officers shouting orders to clear the way" (*RBC* 87). Sometimes massed batteries alone could blunt ill-handled infantry assaults, and something of this sort is soon to happen at Hazel Grove, about a mile due south of this part of the turnpike (*BL* 3:181). But the plight of artillery in this new day of the rifled musket meant that artillery batteries distributed in support of infantry units were certainly at immediate risk if those units gave way. So remnants of batteries of Eleventh Corps artillery are fleeing post haste down the Plank Road.

Civil War artillery pieces were drawn by teams of six horses, harnessed in pairs, with a driver mounted on the left-hand horse of each pair. These teams were yoked to a two-wheeled "limber," which carried an ammunition chest, and to which the trail of the gun was hooked. Each gun was accompanied by an additional team and limber, towing a caisson, which was another, larger, two-wheeled cart carrying two more ammunition chests. Each artillery piece thus went into action immediately provided with four chests full of powder charges and projectiles. Empty chests weighed 200 pounds; when full, they weighed over 550 pounds. At times when rapid movement was necessary (exactly the sort of moment Private Fleming is witnessing at this twilight hour), the nine-man gun crews rode on the ammunition chests. A twelve-pounder cannon and limber assembly weighed two tons; fully loaded caissons with their limbers weighed close to three tons. Batteries in the Army of the Potomac in the spring of 1863 generally had six artillery pieces, each piece with its own caisson team, and in addition six more caisson teams with reserve ammunition, a traveling forge, and a supply wagon. So down a single country lane, a battery in rapid retreat could hurl twenty teams comprising 120 horses and sixty wheeled vehicles comprising fifty tons of wood and iron.[34]

34. Coggins, *Arms and Equipment*, 62–73; Nosworthy, *Crucible*, 456–57.

These batteries could deploy (or flee) much more rapidly than the wagons, ambulances, and the like that made up an army corps's supply trains, because their teams were larger and were whipped into action by three drivers each. They could obviously outpace infantry. So these batteries fleeing "helitywhoop down th' road" (*RBC* 95) are the first units fleeing from the catastrophe to appear in the Plank Road. Private Conklin, reduced to a "stalking specter" (94) by his wounds, is particularly afraid he will "fall down" and "them damned artillery wagons" will run over him (93).

The rebel attack continues to press eastward, bringing closer "the furnace roar of the battle" and clouds of gun smoke. "The woods filtered men," and "the fields became dotted" with the detritus of shattered Eleventh Corps formations. A "crying mass of wagons, teams, and men" jams the Orange Plank Road, comprised of supply columns from that corps desperate to extricate themselves, their panic-stricken drivers lashing at their "mules" and "teams" (*RBC* 107).

Not only were the army's horse- and mule-drawn elements channeled down the Plank Road. So also were those Union formations deploying or redeploying westward to meet the rebel advance. Private Fleming sees "a forward-going column of infantry" forcing its way through the "dense mass" of the Eleventh Corps's mule teams, wagons, and teamsters. He is impressed by their pride, discipline, and stern demeanor. This was the Second Brigade of General Hiram Berry's Second Division (white diamond-shaped badges) of the Third Army Corps (*OR* 140). General Berry's division was advancing westward through the hysteria on the Plank Road to establish a defensive position to the north of it. Its Second Brigade was the "Excelsior Brigade," raised at the outbreak of the war by Daniel Sickles, now commander of the Third Corps. The brigade originally consisted of five New York regiments, the Seventieth through the Seventy-fourth, and during the winter it had been reinforced by another New York regiment. Its composition was unusual in an army that had a policy of forming brigades out of regiments from various states. It drew its proud nickname from the New York State motto, and it was as close to an "elite" formation as could be found in this almost entirely volunteer army. Looking on, Private Fleming feels "that he was regarding a procession of chosen beings" (*RBC* 108–9).

This formation moving so handsomely against the flow of the retreat generates in Fleming's ever-active imagination a sequence of "debates." "He saw a picture of himself, dust-stained, haggard, panting, flying to the front at the proper moment to seize and throttle the dark, leering witch of calamity." So he "started forward slowly." But equally vivid to him are images of possible personal catastrophe. "He stepped as if he expected to tread upon some explosive thing. Doubts and he were struggling." Then, "he said that his tireless fate would bring forth, when the strife lulled for a moment, a man to ask of him an explanation. In imagination he felt the scrutiny of his companion as he painfully labored through some lies." The routed or retreating soldiers considerably outnumber the advancing formations from the Third Corps, so eventually, "his courage expended itself" and it becomes "almost impossible for him to see himself in a heroic light" (*RBC* 110–11).

Note that over and again during this portion of the novel, Private Fleming's internal imagination responds and corresponds precisely to whatever external spectacle he is witnessing. When he first heard the noise of Jackson's assault, it sounded "as if worlds were being rended," and his own mind thus "flew in all directions" (*RBC* 82). The same correspondence obtains repeatedly, as Fleming wanders without any regimental discipline to focus his characteristically "busy" imagination, and without a true understanding of himself and the world around him to act as ballast.

Just some minutes after the passage of the Excelsior Brigade toward the new front, "dark waves of men come sweeping out of the woods and down through the fields," shedding their equipment and fleeing "like terrified buffaloes" (*RBC* 118). Most of these are infantrymen from Schurz's Third Division of the Eleventh Corps (their crescent-shaped corps badges are blue). Of the three divisions in the Eleventh Corps, only the Third made any concerted resistance, and they too have now been swept into the general rout. Eleventh Corps soldiers who fled earlier could "filter" through the woods and fields (*RBC* 107), but it is now "dusk" (after six-thirty, or later), and as the Third Division tries to withdraw through the darkened wilderness, they find themselves "helpless in the matted thickets and blinded by the over-hanging night." Confusion and panic overtake them (*OR* 252). These soldiers are frantically trying to find the road that will lead them to the rear and safety. The Eleventh Corps contains a high percentage of German immigrants and soldiers of German ancestry: one in "pain and dismay" near Private Fleming is asking "'Say, where de plank road? Where de plank road?'" (*RBC* 119). Even in the best of times, this German soldier's confusion would be understandable, since the road beside him is known as both "the Orange Plank Road" and "the Old Orange Turnpike."

Finding himself in the midst of these terrified men, Private Fleming is "horrorstricken" (*RBC* 118). But "within him something bade to cry out." His impulse is to "make a rallying speech" or "to sing a battle hymn," but he can only manage to produce "incoherent questions" corresponding—again—to the "thousand wild questions" and "insane" gabbling of the routed Eleventh Corps soldiers (119–20).

The Federal "artillery booming, forward, rearward, and on the flanks" adds to Private Fleming's disorientation (*RBC* 119). Batteries on the Plank Road itself, given time to redeploy, are shelling the rebel advance (portrayed in *BL* 3:166). Artillery from the Twelfth Corps in position at Fairview just south of the Plank Road can also bring their cannon to bear upon the oncoming rebel infantry, as Jackson's attack breaks through the Eleventh Corps's last positions (*BL* 3:201). Union commanders have also managed to assemble a score of field guns, mostly from the Third Corps, on the ridge at Hazel Grove, due south of the area where Fleming is encountering these routed soldiers (*BL* 3:179). Jackson recognizes the value of this elevated position and swings an axis of his attack south toward it. Other batteries are being sent into action north of the road. Fleming is surrounded by Union artillery, and the concussive impacts of twelve-pound powder charges can stun a bystander.

In fact, in the dusk, this massed Union artillery is just beginning to dominate the battlefield. The rebel assault has so far been completely successful, but with that success, and given the tangled terrain through which they have advanced, their formations are jumbled and confused. And, on the march since daybreak, the rebel infantrymen are exhausted. Soon the artillery will begin to wreck them (*BL* 3:181).

Private Fleming has no awareness of this. Bewildered, still seeking to put "stuttered" and incoherent questions to the fleeing soldiers, he clutches one "by the arm." The man slams the butt of his rifle against Fleming's head (*RBC* 120). Thus does Private Fleming receive the titular "red badge of courage"; and if the irony of its narrative context is manifest, so too is the irony of its historical context, in this campaign in which cap badges were used for the first time to create esprit de corps by identifying the divisions to which individual soldiers belonged. Although the blow will prove fortuitous, at the moment it is "numbing" (121).

He manages to get to his feet and lurch away toward the rear. Despite his "dulled senses" (*RBC* 121) and confusion, he still witnesses details of the action along the Plank Road. Batteries of Union artillery continue to sweep past him toward the front, "assembling as if for a conference." Then "into the unspeakable jumble in the roadway rode a squadron of cavalry. The faded yellow of their facings shone bravely" (122). In the Federal service (and the Confederate), the distinguishing color of the cavalry branch was yellow. The "facings" are the piping and the two long button-loops on the stand-up collar and the piping on the jacket's edges, seams, and cuffs. All marks of rank including chevrons, trouser stripes, and officers' shoulder straps were likewise yellow.[35]

This is the First Squadron of the Eighth Pennsylvania Cavalry Regiment. Hooker had sent most of his cavalry on a raid to the west (see Chapter 1), but a few regiments were retained to scout for his infantry divisions. The Eighth Pennsylvania had been operating with the Third Corps. At about six-thirty, General Alfred Pleasonton, trying to check the rebels until he could assemble artillery on the ridge at Hazel Grove, ordered this regiment to advance to support General Howard (OR 304, 306; BL 3:179). These cavalrymen, it seems, were ignorant of the suicidal nature of the task they had been set. Many toward the rear of their column were unaware they were about to enter battle. They were advancing by twos down a narrow lane through the wilderness terrain, horses at a walk and sabers still in their scabbards (BL 3:186–88).

When Private Fleming sees them, the head of their column is turning north and west into the Plank Road—and right into the full face of Rodes's division leading the rebel assault. The "mighty altercation" greeting them will kill their commanding officer (there will be fifteen separate wounds in his body) and shatter the regiment (BL 3:183–88). This brief episode will subsequently receive considerable attention: a surviving officer from the regiment will even claim (without justification) that General T. J. Jackson was mortally wounded in this encounter (OR 306). What prompts such interest is that this is one of the very few occasions during the Civil War in which a cavalry formation was engaged in a central action on a major battlefield. Its fate therein reiterates the plight of cavalry in the age of the rifled infantry weapon.

Private Fleming himself continues eastward. Just behind him, the "assembled" artillery of the Union army opens a "tremendous" fire upon the "opposing infantry," which replies with the "shattering peal" of rifle fire. But in the "shadowy" closing of the day the rebel attack has lost its cohesion. There is no effective control at brigade or regimental level. Rather than bringing all this unsupported Union artillery under rifle fire, exhausted rebel soldiers surge forward shoulder to shoulder, and "heaving masses" of them try to press ahead through sheer weight of numbers: a perfect target for the Union cannoneers, who will batter them to a halt along this front. Fleming hurries "on in the dusk," passing the "lifeless" litter, dead horses, wrecked vehicles, of the panic (RBC 123).

The pain of his wound subsides, but he is beset by anxiety and fear and drifts

35. Katcher, Potomac, plates 4 and 5; Haythornthwaite, Uniforms, plate 27.

into hallucinations about home life. Just as he is about to succumb to "dragging weariness," he is given a saving "lift" by a soldier from "Ohier" (*RBC* 125). The man finds out Private Fleming's regiment and corps, observes (correctly) that "they're way over in th' center," and says he did not think they were engaged "t'day" (126). This is a reasonable surmise, given the light action that in fact took place on the Second Corps's front that afternoon.

In his dazed condition, Private Fleming never even sees the face of this soldier who not only leads him back all the way to the campfires of the 304th New York but also handles encounters with "'provost-guards'" with "the valor of a gamin" (*RBC* 126–27), assuring that Fleming returns to physical security with his afternoon desertion undetected. This faceless man cannot be placed at all: he is a long way from his own regiment (126). His anecdotes about the day's battle—confusion surrounding the ranks of his regiment, "Johnnies comin' through th' woods" at them, and a man asking directions to "th' road t' th' river" (127)—could reflect action from virtually any part of the Union army's lines in the Wilderness on May 2. There were over a dozen Ohio infantry regiments with Hooker that afternoon.

It is obviously ironic that this man who does Private Fleming the greatest service of all remains an absolute stranger to him, but given the major theme of the novel it is also mordantly appropriate. Without the assistance of this Ohioan during the time of his greatest weakness and disorientation, Fleming quite likely would have been killed or captured. If during that bewildered time he had somehow managed to make it back to safety on his own, his criminal desertion could well have been discovered. The Good Samaritan is the paradigm, and it is a popular tradition that such an experience teaches of the "importance of other people" and the like. But Fleming's solipsism remains impervious. It will occur to him only that he "had not once seen" this man's face (*RBC* 128). In the course of the novel down to and including his great satisfaction with himself at its end, as he surveys his personal conduct during the battle, Fleming will never think of this man again.

"Sinking" though "his forces" are, when he is returned to his regiment, Private Fleming produces "his tale": "I got separated from th' reg'ment. Over on th' right, I got shot. In th' head" (*RBC* 130). Thanks to the skill of the unknown soldier who led him back and thanks to the blow from the musket butt he did receive, this lie proves sufficient to deflect or allay any further questioning. "A shot in th' head ain't foolin' business" (136) in any army. Private Wilson who is on sentinel duty and Corporal Simpson who commands the night watch are both instantly solicitous, and Fleming is reabsorbed safely into the ranks of the

304th. Wilson treats his "wound" and gives him cold coffee and his own blankets, into which Fleming snuggles into profound sleep.

After breakfast the next morning, secure in his lie and physically contented, Fleming's "self-pride" is "now entirely restored" (*RBC* 149). By midmorning (162) he has won the praise of Lieutenant Hasbrouck and is on his way to achieving "public deeds" of "great and shining prominence" (229). The trajectory of Private Fleming's career from the moment he receives assistance from that unknown Ohio soldier is simply traced: he is no longer alone, and he rises from one public success to another.

Private Fleming and Private Conklin: "That other one"

To return to the issue beginning this chapter, recall that, according to the literary tradition into which *The Red Badge of Courage* seems to fit so precisely, the nexus between illusion and success involves "some moment of disillusioned or unillusioned recognition" and before, during, or after this moment, suffering or sacrifice of some sort. This tradition also dictates that any such recognition must precede the hero's success. So if it indeed comes, his moment of "recognition" must come at some point before Private Fleming receives his head wound, which renders him incapable of any "recognition" of any sort and leads him into the ministrations of his unknown benefactor. Crane interrupted both the historical precision and the characteristic randomness of his narrative in order to provide Private Fleming with that green-coated corpse, perfectly placed and perfectly decomposed so as to provide the most dramatic possible object lesson to refute Fleming's monstrous illusions about his own importance to the natural world, and to illustrate the reality of its callous indifference to him. But Fleming, in his panic-stricken, childish, and unreflective reaction, never recognized anything at all from the encounter.

There is a second such interruption. Crane overrules historical probability with an implausible coincidence, this time in order to challenge the solipsistic, self-serving cast of Private Fleming's mind as it reacts to his fellow human beings. *The Iliad* provides the paradigm, wherein the death of Achilles' friend Patroclus leads the hero to a shattering recognition of what his self-centered behavior has achieved. So in the crowd of wounded men on the Plank Road, Fleming finds himself side by side with his hut-mate Private Jim Conklin, who has been severely, indeed mortally wounded.

After three hours of sometimes aimless, sometimes curiosity-inspired wanderings across the length of the Union army's front, Private Fleming just happens to find himself alongside the same man from whose side he had fled three hours back. Out of all this great Federal host (there were seventy-three thousand Union soldiers in the Wilderness of Virginia that afternoon) and amid that "crowd," that "mob" or "procession" of wounded men randomly drawn from a completely different front of the battle, it is his own hut-mate Private Conklin who appears beside him in the Plank Road. In fact, this is vastly more improbable than was the earlier incident involving the corpse in the "green" uniform, but even the coincidence itself probably goes unremarked by most readers. As in the incident involving the corpse, a combat-befogged randomness so obviously seems the principle shaping (so to speak) the story that a reader is just not alert to possible coincidences. (Contrast, for example, a reader's warranted wariness about improbable coincidences while working through a novel by Dickens.)

The starkness of the coincidence is also masked by most readers' ignorance of the historical details, both large and small, that surround Crane's "Episode of the American Civil War." To place this coincidence in its historical matrix actually enhances the evocativeness of the novel. The various wandering motivations that eventually led Private Fleming to that place on the Orange Plank Road at some time toward six o'clock on the afternoon of May 2, 1863, have absorbed the reader ever since Fleming's desertion from the 304th New York Regiment. But how on earth did Private Jim Conklin get there?

After Conklin succumbs to his wounds, Fleming himself poses this question to the tattered man from the Third Corps, who has also witnessed Conklin's last moments. "'I wonder where he came from. I left him over there.'" He points due east. "'And now I find 'im here. And he was coming from over there, too.' He indicated a new direction," which is due west. "They both turned toward the body as if to ask of it a question," but of course there is no longer any use "'tryin' to ask him anything'" (*RBC* 101).

Given Private Conklin's phlegmatic, stoic personality, it seems highly unlikely he was a victim of the same sort of panic that swept Private Fleming from the firing line. Even if he had indeed also panicked (he had said earlier that "if a whole lot of boys started and run, why, I s'pose I'd start and run" [*RBC* 17]), those same character traits make it implausible that the curiosity which eventually attracted Private Fleming all the way to the western side of the battlefield would also have brought Private Conklin there. The wounds he suffered (his "side looked as if it had been chewed by wolves" [99]) had fatally damaged his lungs, while causing massive traumatic shock to his entire system. So thus condemned to death by "gradual strangulation" (97), Private Conklin must have roamed in delirium, "stonily" (94), "with mysterious purpose" (95) and "waxlike features" (92), behind the Union lines. He must have been carried on by extra-ordinary reserves of raw energy and strength—" 'he was reg'lar jim-dandy fer nerve'" (100) until "the moment when he should pitch headlong" (86).

So, provided anew with an even more startling opportunity to recognize some basic truths about himself and his fellows, an opportunity virtually man-dated by the literary tradition in which his story seems set, how does Private Fleming respond this time? The most striking initial aspect of this response is that, for "some time" (*RBC* 88), he does not recognize Private Conklin at all. When Fleming first sees Conklin, he is only a nameless man among the "blood-stained crowd," a nameless man who happens to be obviously dying, just as an-other soldier happens to have "a shoeful of blood," another happens to be cursing General Hooker, and another happens to be "marching with an air imi-tative of some sublime drum major" (85–86). Private Fleming's attention then strays to other things: a wounded officer being carried to the rear, couriers, bat-teries of artillery disturbing the column of wounded. He even (though against his will) becomes engaged in conversation with that "tattered man" from the Third Corps, a conversation lasting long enough to reveal a fair amount of this man's military history. Then this tattered man starts asking questions about Private Fleming's own wound. Guiltily unwounded himself, Private Fleming shrinks "back in the procession until the tattered soldier [is] not in sight." Newly absorbed in a self-conscious awareness of his own difference from these wounded men who are legitimately fleeing from the battle, Private Fleming re-gards "the wounded soldiers in an envious way. He conceive[s] persons with torn bodies to be peculiarly happy." All this while his own hut-mate, unrecog-nized, is "at his side like a stalking reproach" (91).

When Private Fleming first glimpsed Private Conklin in the crowd on the Plank Road, Private Conklin "stalked like the specter of a soldier" (*RBC* 86), and his "spectral" nature is reiterated (87, 94). He is Private Fleming's Doppelganger, his ghostly, stalking twin. Conklin constitutes an implicit, gruesome, brutally critical commentary upon Fleming's self-pitying self-absorption during the hours of his wandering. Any moment of Fleming's ruminations during his drift west-ward becomes instantly more self-incriminating when measured against what his hut-mate must have endured during his ghastly parallel journey. For in-stance, believing himself "ill-used," or "trodden beneath the feet of an iron injustice," his "wisdom" and "righteous motives" "frustrated by hateful circum-stances," Private Fleming "shambled along with bowed head, his brain in a tumult of agony and despair" (76–77). Against this, measure the savage "use" that flying chunks of real rebel "iron" (or lead) have made upon Conklin's literal body; the absolutely fatal and "hateful circumstances" under which Conklin is staggering, the unimaginable physical "agony" driving him on in the same direction at the same time, and the desperation, bewilderment, and fear clouding his more limited "brain." An awareness of these two soldiers' bizarrely parallel courses throws Fleming's vanity, self-pity, and blind ignorance into the most monstrous relief.

Fleming's initial failure to recognize Private Conklin ("Patroclus . . . who? Oh, *that* Patroclus") forecasts Private Fleming's subsequent failure to recognize anything of either figurative or general significance from this encounter with his dying friend. The traits of Fleming's personality remain unchanged: his childish curiosity, his desire "to witness" (*RBC* 83) things himself, his infantile self-absorption, particularly his fear that "his shame could be viewed" by others (91). When "something in the gesture of the man" causes Fleming to recognize Conklin, he is stunned and horrified (92). He tries "to assist him" (93), though he is "aghast" at the "spectacle" (96–97) of the goriness of Conklin's wounds, his "waxlike features" (92), his helpless terror. Yet again responding in kind to the external spectacle, Fleming alternates between hysteria and dazed inarticulateness, just as Conklin lurches between "piteous anxiety" and "mysterious purpose," between terrified pleas for help and demands to "Leave me be, can't yeh?" (94–96).

Fleming "sobs" in "anguish" (*RBC* 94) for Conklin. Watching him die, Fleming's own "face had been twisted into an expression of every agony he had imagined for his friend" (98–99). But the phrasing of this last description reveals the truth of the matter. It is preeminently the spectacle that absorbs his active imagination and calls forth his response, not any real concern for the hideous suffering death of Private Jim Conklin of the 304th New York Volunteer Infantry Regiment. Seeing for the first time the severity of his dead friend's wounds, Fleming "turned, with sudden, livid rage, toward the battlefield," shook his fist, and "seemed about to deliver a philippic" (99). But he has nothing of genuine outrage, regret, or anger to express. The moment is purely histrionic. He has nothing to express because his friend's death means nothing "real" to him. As with a child leaving the theater after watching a horror film, the spectacle that had engaged his imagination is now over. Some curiosity over the "plot" of the thing remains, as he wonders (at last) how Private Conklin came to be there. He steals "softly" (101) away, for the corpse (like the posters advertising the movie) can still generate a frisson of fear. Within a very few minutes, however, Private Jim Conklin is no more to him than a show that is over: explicitly so.

Were Private Fleming to have learned anything about compassion or concern for others from Private Conklin's death, Crane provides him someone he could have visited it upon: the "tattered" soldier from the Third Corps. This stranger, a man of limited intelligence but profound compassion, accompanies Private

Fleming as they follow the dying Conklin into the brush-choked fields beside the Plank Road. Now, with only Private Fleming to offer any assistance, this tattered man's own wounds begin to claim him. "I'm commencin' t' feel pretty damn' bad," he says. "O Lord!" the youth replies, groaning. He has had his fill of this kind of show: "He wondered if he was to be the tortured witness of another grim encounter" (*RBC* 102).

As the "tattered man" sinks toward delirium, he asks again about Fleming's "wound": "Where is it located?" (*RBC* 103). The shame Fleming felt when he was in the midst of a crowd of wounded, now that he is alone with this single, faltering, wounded man, turns to anger. "He was enraged against the tattered man, and could have strangled him. His companions seemed ever to play intolerable parts. They were ever upraising the ghost of shame on the stick of their curiosity" (104).

In a "hard voice," he says goodbye to the tattered man and abandons him, leaving him in helpless bewilderment—"Why—why, pardner, where yeh goin'?"— to a lonely, unmarked death, doubtless to become one of those many nameless unburied corpses that soldiers from the Army of the Potomac would find on their spring campaign next year. Private Fleming, "looking at him, could see that he, too, like that other one, was beginning to act dumb and animal-like" (*RBC* 104). Thus the epitaph his invincible solipsism fashions for his hut-mate and "good friend" (94). Private Jim Conklin is "that other one."

So Crane's narrative presents Private Fleming with two dramatic moments, both historically implausible and both altogether untypical of the rest of the novel, that could conceivably lead him to recognize his monstrous illusions about himself. In each instance, he completely fails to achieve any such recognition. The decomposing corpse does not challenge his illusions about his own paramount importance to the natural world. The death of his "friend" and hutmate does not challenge his illusions about his own radical centrality to the human relationships around him—a centrality beside which his fellow soldiers are only "players," phenomena that can excite his imagination but that have no essential existence, and thus no purchase in his heart or mind. His solipsism is invincible.

If we are trying to place Private Fleming in the pantheon of typical heroes, or in the typical pattern through which they move, this has to be baffling. But Private Fleming's failure to respond to either of these stark, profound, almost cosmically engineered lessons is completely characteristic of his mentality throughout the novel. His imaginative responses rarely do more than mirror the physical spectacle before him. His responses are vivid, but superficial; his essential underlying solipsism never changes. Without any profound comprehension of the reality of the people and events surrounding him, he surrenders himself as a child watching a show, to each passing scene.

His first fears upon learning that the lines behind him have held are (again) of the schoolyard stripe: "His mind heard howls of derision" (*RBC* 76). Of courts martial and the like he has no notion, nor of having failed in his sworn duty to his country or to his comrades. His childish fear of being shamed before his fellows remains uppermost: "Because of the tattered soldier's questions he now felt that his shame could be viewed" (91); "His companions . . . were ever upraising the ghost of shame on the stick of their curiosity" (104); "In imagination he felt the scrutiny of his companions as he painfully labored through some lies" (111); "He imagined the whole regiment saying: 'Where's Henry Fleming? He run, didn't 'e? Oh, my!'" (116). His worst nightmare is to imagine he had become "a slang phrase" (117). It may seem illogical that an imagination in the grip of such impervious solipsism, to whom other people do not really exist, nevertheless might have such an overwhelming concern for public reputation. But childish vanity, self-conceit, and self-centeredness can obviously create a solipsistic imagination and, simultaneously, a thirst for public esteem. This is the psychological context for his seemingly crucial recognition that he needed "A moral vindication." Look at the passage in its entirety: "Without salve, he could not, he thought, wear the sore badge of his dishonor through life. With his heart continually assuring him that he was despicable, he could not exist without making it, through his actions, apparent to all men" (114). Even here, it was not with genuine morality but with public repute, and this only, that he is concerned.

Physical wounds continue to have no reality in his childish imagination. "At times he regarded the wounded soldiers in an envious way. He conceived persons with torn bodies to be peculiarly happy" (*RBC* 91). Nor does death itself: "he envied those men whose bodies lay strewn over the grass of the fields and on the fallen leaves of the forest" (105); "he envied a corpse. Thinking of the slain, he achieved a great contempt for some of them, as if they were guilty for thus becoming lifeless. They might have been killed by lucky chances, he said, before they had had opportunities to flee or before they had been really tested" (115).

A reader may yet incline to sympathize wholeheartedly with Private Fleming in these matters, so skillfully does Crane draw us into his psychology. Above all, during Fleming's hegira through this afternoon and evening, Crane surrounds him with all the circumstances established by literary tradition as most favorable for coming to some more accurate recognition of reality. Crane lavishes upon him immediate evidence of his failures of anticipation and perception, dramatic evidence of his personal failure in measuring up in combat, then periods of that loneliness and twilight traditionally conducive to self-examination. Crane graces him with the generosity of nameless people (recall Kent in *King Lear*, rendered nameless by the necessity to disguise himself) and limited people (recall the Fool). Crane also presents Fleming with two extraordinarily delivered lessons: a stunning instance of the naked truth about the natural world, then the ago-nized, agonizing death of one of his two closest companions. All this surely must jar him out of his illusions, for this is how the dominant paradigm of our culture works. There is no wonder at all that, as Pizer said, "A sizable number of critics have had the 'felt response' that Crane wishes to affirm some aspect of ex-perience in his depiction of Henry."[36] Anyone steeped in the fictions of the Western canon must indeed "feel such a response."

But reading or (more likely) rereading the novel closely just does not yield evi-dence to affirm any such positive development in Private Fleming's personality. Private Fleming does not change at all during the afternoon and evening of May 2, 1863.

It is his other hut-mate, Private John Wilson, who seems to have come to some new understandings through his experience in battle, and to have had a "remarkable change" of personality. Wilson seems to have matured; at least the terms Fleming credits to Wilson are those associated with masculine maturity. Wilson is no longer "furious at small words that pricked his conceits"; he is "no more a loud young soldier." Wilson now possesses a "fine reliance" and a "quiet belief" in himself (*RBC* 142). Private Fleming credits him accordingly: "Appar-ently" Wilson "had now climbed a peak of wisdom from which he could per-ceive himself as a very wee thing" (143). This, Fleming thinks, is an accurate self-assessment for Wilson to have achieved. But for himself, on this new morn-ing of May 3, "His self-pride was now entirely restored" (149). His illusions about his own significance in fact have become even more gigantic: "how could they kill him who was the chosen of gods and doomed to greatness?" (151). So by the end of Private Fleming's hegira, he at least (but also at most) has a "red badge" to replace the corps badge he lost when he lost his cap and to mask the "sore badge of his dishonor." The "regimental drums" of the 304th New York Volun-teer Infantry Regiment have sounded the roll for assembly (140). Their second day of battle—May 3, 1863, the final day of the battle of Chancellorsville—is about to begin.

36. Pizer, "[A Guide to Criticism]," 136.

Chapter 7

Private Fleming and
Major General Hooker

Private Henry Fleming's triumphant conduct on the morning of May 3—which earns Lieutenant Hasbrouck's praise, the "awe-struck" regard of his fellow soldiers, and his own belief that he is now "a hero" and "a knight"—is principally enabled by the fact that he is now acclimated to the phenomena of infantry combat. His unfocused nervous energy of May 2, which generated self-pitying paranoia, disorganized his perceptions, and from which his imagination produced pursuing "dragons," shells with "cruel teeth," and hateful "little gods and big gods," he is now able to bring into proper focus. Now this energy generates in him a "wild hate" toward the rebel infantrymen advancing upon the position held by the 304th New York (*RBC* 164). He crouches behind a tree, armed once more with a rifle (165), awaiting them. But it is his "self-pride" that brings him to the literal place and moment where his experience can focus his energy; his "self-pride" has been "entirely restored" (149). The process of this restoration is consistent with the impenetrable solipsism of his character. This process and what follows from it are richly and doubly ironic: ironic in the context of the developing narrative and ironic in the context of the military history from which the narrative, with consistent precision, is drawn.

Awaiting Private Wilson's return from sentry duty the night before, Private Fleming's "senses" were still somewhat "deadened" from the blow he had taken, and his perceptions of the sleeping men of the 304th were ghastly in their inappropriateness. His fellows then appeared to him "like men drunk with wine" after "some frightful debauch." A sleeping officer, clasping "his sword in his arms," looked like a "toddy-stricken grandfather in a chimney corner," "the picture of an exhausted soldier after a feast of war" (*RBC* 132–34). Thereafter, his thirst quenched by Wilson's coffee, his wound bandaged in Wilson's water-soaked handkerchief, stretched out on Wilson's rubber sheet, and wrapped in Wilson's woolen blanket, Fleming went to sleep despite "a splatter of musketry from the distance" (138), where formations from the Third and the Twelfth corps were engaged in confused night action with the rebels near Hazel Grove.

The next morning Private Fleming awakens before the drums and bugles sound reveille, and the carapace of his illusions is not yet formed. To his momentarily naked perception, the "quaint light at the dawning" seems to dress "the skin of the [sleeping] men in corpselike hues," to make their "tangled limbs appear pulseless and dead." Fleming's "disordered mind" interprets "the hall of the forest as a charnel place." He believes "for an instant that he was in the house of the dead, and he did not dare to move lest these corpses start up, squalling and squawking." This perception is as ghastly as the one of the night before, but this time the ghastliness lies in its appropriateness, which, as he recovers "his proper mind," registers momentarily: "this somber picture was not a fact of the present, but a [and here his awareness flinches and supplies a deflating modifier] mere prophecy" (*RBC* 139–40).

Regimental activity distracts him. By the third of his querulous awakening expostulations, he is undertaking the recovery of his self-pride: "Gosh-dern it!" he says to Private Wilson, who is checking his wound, "you're the hangdest man I ever saw! You wear muffs on your hands. Why in good thunderation can't you be more easy?" (*RBC* 141–42). Wilson's kindly efforts afford Fleming the opportunity to castigate his "friend." The pattern of Fleming's recovery of self-confidence nestles further ironies one within the next.

This recovery begins with Fleming's burgeoning feeling that, whatever else, he is "immensely superior to his friend" Private Wilson (*RBC* 149). The overall irony is hugely apparent: it is Wilson who stood to his duty the previous afternoon, and Fleming who fled "like a proverbial chicken" (68–69). If the experience of combat has the capacity to bring maturity to callow young men, it is Wilson who has thus been transformed. "Yer changed a good bit," Fleming observes, after Wilson has made peace between two fellow soldiers (146). Fleming himself, despite having enjoyed all the circumstances denominated by literary tradition as appropriate to a significant transformation, has changed not one iota.

With a further ratchet of the ironic machine in this portion of the novel, Private Wilson's newfound maturity is the very thing that delivers him over to Fleming's "condescension" (*RBC* 149). Fleming does not know "when his comrade had made the great discovery that there were many men who would refuse to be subjected by him," but this discovery suits Fleming very well, as does Wilson's new perception of "himself as a very wee thing" (143). It comforts Fleming and boosts his own self-esteem to find himself in the presence of such a newly diminished man. Since Wilson did remain in the ranks of the 304th New York, his experience of the battle was much more limited than Fleming's own, which advantage Fleming soon plays upon him. When Wilson says that "All th' officers say we've got th' rebs in a pretty tight box," Fleming refutes him because of "What I seen over on th' right," which "looked as if we was gettin' a good poundin' yestirday."

> "D'yeh think so?" inquired the friend. "I thought we handled 'em pretty rough yestirday."
> "Not a bit," said the youth. "Why, lord, man, you didn't see nothing of the fight."

At which point he suddenly recollects Private Conklin's death. Far from being embarrassed that for some hours he had completely forgotten this signal fact about their former tent-mate (and, one would assume, friend), he readily adds the news as further evidence of the insignificance of Wilson's experience in contrast to his own (144).

Happily, too, for Private Fleming, there is the matter of that little "misguided packet" that Wilson "had intrusted to him" yesterday, in the mistaken belief that he was about to be killed. Private Fleming "now rejoiced in the possession of a small weapon with which he could prostrate his comrade at the first signs of a cross-examination." Fleming still fears "questionings" about his own "adventures of the previous day" from "his friend" who stayed the course. But with this "weapon" Private Fleming will always be the "master." Wilson "had, in a weak hour, spoken with sobs of his own death," but then he had made the mistake of not dying, "and thus he had delivered himself into" Fleming's "hands" (*RBC* 148–49). So what is, of course, a matter of supreme good fortune for Wilson—the best conceivable good fortune—is transformed, in Fleming's busy mind, into an actual mischance.

Private Fleming fully intends to make some "remarkable" and withering "comment upon the affair" if Wilson asks for the letters back, but the moment comes, and Fleming can "conjure nothing of sufficient point." No matter: out of his own failure to produce something sufficiently sarcastic, Fleming takes "unto himself considerable credit. It was a generous thing." Wilson's cheeks flush with embarrassment as he asks for the letters back. Fleming "felt his heart grow more strong and stout. He had never been compelled to blush in such manner for his acts; he was an individual of extraordinary virtues" (152).

"After this incident," Private Fleming's sense of superiority to "'the poor devil'" Wilson makes Fleming feel "quite competent to return home and make the hearts of the people glow with stories of war." He imagines "his gaping audience picturing him as the central figure in blazing scenes. And he imagined the consternation and the ejaculations of his mother and the young lady at the seminary as they drank his recitals. Their vague feminine formula for beloved ones doing brave deeds on the field of battle without risk of life would be destroyed" (RBC 153). Given Mrs. Fleming's pitiful, pain-struck reaction to her only son's departure for the army, and given the reiterated instances of Private Fleming's own manifest blindness about the reality of death, this last sentence deserves remarking. The warmly tinted domestic scene he is imagining centers upon self-delusions and transferences worthy of some great tragic figure—Othello, or Lear, or Coriolanus. But since we know that Private Fleming survives, we tend to respond to this moment with a pleased recognition of its psychological accuracy. Suppose, however, one of Melville's "undeceiving" bullets were to offer this young hayseed a speechless, quick, chaotic bundling into eternity before lunchtime this May 3, 1863? How would this passage strike us then?

It is out of these childish comparisons and imaginings that Private Fleming's "self-pride was now entirely restored. In the shade of its flourishing growth he stood with braced and self-confident legs, and since nothing could now be discovered he did not shrink from an encounter with the eyes of judges, and allowed no thoughts of his own to keep him from an attitude of manfulness. He had performed his mistakes in the dark, so he was still a man" (RBC 149–50). "He was a man": the phrase will echo and re-echo throughout his perceptions during the coming hours of battle.

As yet, Private Fleming's self-confidence is (to borrow military terminology) essentially defensive. He believes himself superior in experience and repute to his "friend" Private Wilson, at least. His own "mistakes" have not been discovered, and he possesses weapons, attitudes, and poses with which to keep them hidden. But during this time, while the 304th New York are "standing at order arms at the side of a lane, waiting for the command to march" (*RBC* 148), active, positive certitudes also begin to develop: a new, relaxed anticipation about the immediate future—"the possibilities of the ensuing twenty-four hours"—and a blossoming "faith in himself" (151). Ironically, these things develop directly from his return to the same monstrous illusions concerning himself and the world that were so ruinous to him the previous afternoon.

That afternoon he was living in a drama produced for him by his solipsistic imagination, which took its essential "plot" from the schoolhouse. He came (clearly without any conscious thought about the matter) to believe that circumambient reality was constructing one "supreme trial" for him, which, once successfully "passed," would confer upon him some permanent status of personal "magnificence," imbued with "ideals" of some "far" superior kind (*RBC* 64). So, after his first experience on the firing line yesterday afternoon, he assumed, unconsciously and thus all the more forcefully, that his private drama had reached its happy conclusion. When the rebels attacked again, this radical failure of circumambient reality to conform to his private "plot," combined with the obvious failure of his initial success to engender within himself any such permanent mental status, sent him speeding "toward the rear in great leaps" (69), and sent him into the various sorts of chaotic experiences—cosmic, martial, moral, mental—he experienced yesterday in the Wilderness thickets and on the Orange Plank Road.

From these experiences (and some of them seemingly set explicitly for the purpose), he might well have learned how completely false was his self-centered fictional drama, to natural, human, and psychological realities. The natural world was demonstrably and brutally indifferent to any given individual. The battle of Chancellorsville proceeded with equally brutal indifference to his own condition and his own comprehension. His own mind, despite his having passed the "supreme trial" of combat, continued to respond haphazardly to each new challenge, steadfast to no newly acquired "ideals" (*RBC* 64) but consistent only in its own rank self-absorption. Further, despite all his dread both before and during these experiences, it turned out that there was absolutely no penalty for his abject failure to "pass" the "supreme trial," while "penalties" of the most appalling sort befell both Private Conklin, despite all his calm soldierly qualities, and the tattered infantryman from the Third Corps, despite all his generous compassion.

Today Private Fleming is indeed aware of at least one lesson implicit in the last: "He had been taught" by his experiences yesterday "that many obligations of a life were easily avoided" (*RBC* 150). His solipsism remains unaffected.

Rather than recognize the raw, horrific randomness of reality that is implicit in all that he experienced, he continues to assume he is caught up in a structured drama in which he is the central—and only—character. He does, however, assume certain changes in the "parts" that others about him are there to "play" (104), and some changes in the nature of the test facing the hero. Private Wilson has become a valuable foil for Fleming's own starring role. More important: "when he remembered his fortunes of yesterday, and looked at them from a distance he began to see something fine there. He had license to be pompous and veteranlike." After all, "he had been out among the dragons" then, "and he assured himself that they were not so hideous as he had imagined them. Also, they were inaccurate; they did not sting with precision. A stout heart often defied, and defying, escaped" (150–51). He had before (all unconsciously) assumed that this "supreme trial" (64) would be set for him by some omniscient power. But now he concludes that the potential cosmic antagonists in his drama are not omnipotent at all but are instead laggardly, blind, and several.

Envisioning his dramatic antagonists in this way changes the nature of the challenge facing the "hero" of the play. The issue is no longer whether he can "pass" some "supreme trial," with everything this implies about moral, even spiritual stakes, but whether he can continue to go "out among those dragons," defy them anew, and escape again. The measure of his heroism becomes not triumph but survival. Not surprisingly, he can "put out of his sight" his "panting agonies of the past," because failures count for nothing so long as the hero escapes the consequences (*RBC* 150). Shame evaporates. Thus, "With these facts before him he did not deem it necessary that he should become feverish over the possibilities of the ensuing twenty-four hours. He could leave much to chance" (151). Again, ironically (or perversely), his abject failure yesterday supplied him with grounds for today's superior self-confidence: only through such failure could he have discovered the true nature of the antagonists in the play. So "a little flower of confidence" was "growing within him. He was now a man of experience," knowing what to make of those "dragons," and demonstrably capable of defying them and surviving. And this little flower takes only three sentences, two of them very short, to reach a startlingly full bloom: "And, furthermore, how could they kill him who was the chosen of gods and doomed to greatness?" (151).

Could *Paradise Lost* have influenced Crane here? The difference in register between the two works makes this hard to imagine, but Satan's seduction of Eve parallels precisely what Private Fleming's own mind achieves here. Satan also reworks the cast of cosmic characters so that, to Eve's imagination, an omnipotent

"God" becomes an array of "gods," beings merely more privileged than humanity, and similarly deserving of defiance. Satan's ultimate appeal is likewise to "experience" and the lessons it seemingly teaches. And Satan concludes his appeal by envisioning a similarly immortal future awaiting Eve. Eve will shortly discover the brutal answer: Private (soon to be Color Sergeant) Henry Fleming will be preserved in his happy ignorance ("how could they kill him who was the chosen of gods and doomed to greatness?") for the rest of *The Red Badge of Courage*. But there will be other battles ahead, and "What like a bullet can undeceive!"[1]

Crane's novel and *Paradise Lost* are so different, and Crane's education was so indifferent, that direct influence is not plausible, but these works resemble each other at these moments because both illustrate how the human tendency toward thoughtless solipsism can be engaged—and the monstrous reaches this tendency can achieve. The constituent elements of this human tendency are immutable: an unwillingness to acknowledge any reality that does not center upon one's own self, an unflagging belief in the supremacy of one's own experience, and an utter ignorance of one's own mortality. Private Fleming now believes that the triumphant climax of his play is certain—and note that this confidence has been occasioned by an almost bewildering entanglement of ironies. His new confidence is based upon things that happened (or failed to happen) to him yesterday, when yesterday afternoon he ran "like a proverbial chicken" (*RBC* 68-69). That poultry-like panic descended upon him because he was at that point possessed by a similar but far less solipsistically monstrous illusion: "the man who had fought thus was magnificent" (64).

Despite Private Fleming's certainties about his own greatness, the 304th New York Volunteer Infantry Regiment, pressed steadily by the rebels, retires from one defensive position to another during the course of this early morning on May 3. Private Fleming's "self-pride" and new certitude lead him into some declamations that are quite extraordinary, given his personal record. "Well, don't we fight like the devil? Don't we do all that men can?" (*RBC* 157). A sarcastic rejoinder—"Mebbe yeh think yeh fit th' hull battle yestirday, Fleming"—to one such remark reduces him "to an abject pulp," and for a few minutes he becomes "suddenly a modest person" (158–59). But despite this reverse, his solipsism remains invulnerable: "There was a maddening quality in this seeming resolution of the foe to give him no rest, to give him no time to sit down and think." This is how Private Fleming conceives of the operational plans of General R. E. Lee and his field commanders, pressing their attack against the Army of the Potomac.

1. Melville, "Shiloh. A Requiem," line 16.

"For to-day he felt that he had earned opportunities for contemplative repose. He could have enjoyed portraying to uninitiated listeners various scenes at which he had been a witness or ably discussing the processes of war with other [*sic*] proved men. Too it was important that he should have time for physical recuperation" (163). These angry feelings are at once plausible and yet hilariously blind to elemental realities. They are exactly of a piece with his thoughtless assumption of the previous afternoon that the second rebel attack "was all a mistake" (66). But it is—and yet again, ironically—from these very idiocies that his "wild hate" will arise (164) that will be supremely essential to his accession to knighthood and repute.

Beside him is Private Wilson, whose own (dutiful) experience of battle the previous afternoon has rendered him "weary." Wilson is "trudging along with stooped shoulders and shifting eyes like a man who has been caned and kicked" (*RBC* 157); he is "jaded," though still capable of "calm confidence" (161). Obviously he is, a mature man, altogether beyond Fleming's idiotic self-centeredness and the "great hatred" (164) it will promote. But so, in turn, Private Fleming's sudden display of wild unconsciousness, indifference to pain (166), and complete commitment to combat (167) will be altogether beyond Wilson's capacity to match or even comprehend. The regiment "at last halted" (159) in a small clearing, as the pressure of the rebel advance develops around them, and their lines shift "a trifle" in anticipation of an assault coming through the thickets on their front (162). At this dire moment, Private Fleming "had not deemed it possible that his army could that day succeed," and for a mature, reflective mind such as Wilson's this would surely be reason for personal hesitation and reluctance: who wants to risk his life without any prospect of his army's success? But Fleming instead, still personalizing the battle of Chancellorsville and still ignorant of his own mortality, develops from this general despair a childishly defiant "ability to fight harder": he becomes blindly, ferociously "engrossed" in the morning's first actual combat (166–67). Witnessing Fleming's conduct, Wilson can only respond afterward in bewilderment: "Do yeh feel all right? There ain't nothin' th' matter with yeh, Henry, is there?" It is to Private Fleming, not the newly matured Private Wilson, that Lieutenant Hasbrouck, himself "drunk with fighting," has already "called out": "By heavens, if I had ten thousand wild cats like you I could tear th' stomach outa this war in less'n a week!" (168).

In the "lull" in the action on the regiment's immediate front (*RBC* 167), Private Fleming sprawls on the ground and gropes for his canteen while his comrades look upon him, with attitudes ranging from awe and amazement to concern and contempt, as "a war devil" (168). And he ponders: "he saw that" his unusual, awe-inspiring behavior had been "fine, wild, and, in some ways, easy. He had been a tremendous figure, no doubt," and "he was now what he called a hero. And he had not been aware of the process" (169).

Crane's close description of Fleming's psychology shows, however, that this "process" whereby Private Fleming "had slept, and awakening, found himself a knight," a "hero" (*RBC* 169) has been (yet again) utterly ironic, in detail and in sum. In instance after instance, he has been propelled into the mental states necessary for this process—into forgetting his "past agonies," into new "self-pride" and a new "faith in himself," into a new belief in his own "greatness," and finally into a "wild hate" for the Confederate infantry coming toward him—by facts, memories, situations, and illusions that ought really to have accomplished an exactly opposite end. Some of these very things led to his panic yesterday; and in any rational sequence, they ought to have had the same disastrous effect upon him on this morning of May 3, 1863. So, when considered in detail and then taken in sum, the narrative shows a nonsensical pattern: out of the reasons for yesterday's record of blind panic, groveling fear, puling self-pity, and disloyalty toward both cause and comrades has arisen this morning's courageous, selfless, glorious conduct.

All of which illustrates Crane's profound conception of the ultimate truth in the human situation: namely, that "reality" is random, and utterly without either rational sequences or sensible patterns. This is where *The Red Badge of Courage* differs so critically from the mass of modern-war fictions and the stereotypical plot underlying them (see Chapter 5, and below). In a malign universe, Fleming's first failure and disillusionment necessarily would continue (in *A Farewell to Arms*, for example, Tenente Henry's loss of his command during the retreat from Caporetto prefigures his loss of Catherine during childbirth). Only in an utterly chaotic, utterly random world could a hero's failure reverse of its own momentum and surge, on the morrow, into glorious success.

In an utterly random world, the play of (or outcome of) Private Fleming's blind solipsism may lead to a "knight's" heroic success as easily as it may lead to the panic of the "proverbial chicken." Giving as it does self-confidence (however unbased in reality) and direction (however meaningless in fact), such solipsism may actually produce an excellent and exemplary combat soldier, while a truer sense of reality may produce the weary tone and the stooped, nervous carriage of "a man who has been caned and kicked" (*RBC* 157). It is obvious that Private Wilson's "quiet belief" and "inward confidence" (142) are more mature than Private Fleming's belief that he is "doomed to greatness" (151). It is absolutely certain that Fleming's solipsism will prevent him from any genuine concern or compassion for his fellows: it is Wilson, not Fleming, who binds wounds, shares blankets, and makes peace among his fellow soldiers in the 304th New York. But a random universe cannot be counted upon to reward either maturity or compassion; and in such a universe Private Fleming must be a far better color-bearer for the 304th New York than Private Wilson. In the long run, a regiment that receives swift, decisive direction in combat will take fewer casualties than one that falters or becomes paralyzed. The less time soldiers remain exposed to the hail of rebel shell, solid shot, canister, and .577 caliber minié balls, the better. And however random the universe may be, Confederate riflemen have already shown (witness the early deaths of Brigadier Henderson and of Fleming's company commander) a disconcerting ability to achieve considerable precision.

—⁓—

Studying this part of *The Red Badge of Courage* in its precise historical context reveals even more ironic depth and significance. There is, throughout, the greatest imaginable discrepancy—yet again, a radical absence of rational sequence or sensible pattern—between Private Fleming's personal history and what was happening all around him. The upsurge of his own morale that begins in this part of the novel will continue unbroken through the book's final paragraphs. Meanwhile, the Army of the Potomac was suffering its most demoralizing defeat of the entire war. The historical battle of Chancellorsville is a brilliant setting, both perfectly appropriate and mordantly ironic, for the novel's depiction of the plight of the human mind in an utterly random universe.

Remember Private Wilson's comments at breakfast this morning about the army's "chances" for walloping the rebels today. "All th' officers say we've got th' rebs in a pretty tight box. They all seem t' think we've got 'em jest where we want 'em." And Private Fleming derided Wilson's modest reliance upon the opinion of the officer corps. "What I seen over on th' right makes me think it was th' other way about," he said, arrogantly confident in the superior truth of what he himself had experienced. "Why, lord, man, you didn't see nothing of the fight" (*RBC* 144).

For all Private Fleming's bluster, however, Private Wilson was right. On this morning of May 3, 1863, "th' rebs" were indeed "in a pretty tight box," both strategically and tactically. General Hooker's initial strategy made the most brilliant use of the Army of the Potomac's huge numerical superiority that the war had yet seen, or would see: his adroitness threw into radical contrast the operational weakness of every other commander—McClellan's timidity, Burnside's incompetence, Meade's inertia, Grant's brutality. At the beginning of the campaign, Lee's army had already been reduced by two divisions, Longstreet's thirteen thousand men, absent on a complex assignment from which an early return could not be expected. Hooker thus had over a 130,000 soldiers confronting Lee, who had less than half that number. Hooker's brilliantly conceived, meticulously calculated turning maneuver, which sent three full corps west and then south, completely outflanked Lee's lines facing east across the Rappahannock at Fredericksburg, and the Fredericksburg area became Lee's rear. Hooker rapidly added two additional corps to his deployment, while Lee still had to protect Fredericksburg against General Sedgwick's forty thousand Union soldiers remaining opposite. Lee was compelled to leave another ten thousand soldiers behind at Fredericksburg as he moved the Army of Northern Virginia westward against Hooker's main force. So, facing over seventy thousand Federal soldiers on this new front in the Wilderness area, Lee himself now had less than fifty thousand in hand. Hooker's plan of campaign forced him to choose between abandoning the critical Rappahannock position altogether (the logical course), or somehow driving Hooker away.

Lee's decision two days ago had been, characteristically, to attack. But a frontal assault against such numbers was out of the question, so he had determined to try a turning maneuver of his own against Hooker, which compelled him to divide his far smaller army yet once more. Jackson's forces, for all the success of their assault yesterday afternoon, had not yet managed this morning to reunite with those under Lee's direct command. So advantages from Hooker's brilliant strategy continued to accrue to his Army of the Potomac. This morning the rebels' strategic plight—that is to say, the way in which the respective forces were distributed across the map—was in fact even worse than it had been twenty-four hours ago. Then, the Union army had been divided into two main chunks, whereas Lee's army (counting Longstreet's large detachment) had been divided into three. Now Lee's army was divided into four parts: Longstreet was still absent; Jubal Early's ten thousand were entrenched at Fredericksburg, protecting what was now Lee's rear; Jackson's twenty-six-thousand-strong "strike force" was now immured in the Wilderness to the west, minus its excellent commanding officer; and the remaining seventeen thousand rebels under Lee's immediate direction were still east of the Chancellorsville crossroads.

Furthermore, Sedgwick over to the east on the Fredericksburg front was at last beginning offensive operations, with the twenty-eight thousand men remaining under his command. At worst these would pin the ten thousand rebels there in place, at best penetrate their thin lines and menace the rear of Lee's forces in the Wilderness. Reynolds's First Corps of seventeen thousand men had marched from Fredericksburg to Chancellorsville during the night, giving Hooker a current numerical superiority, in the Wilderness area alone, of two to one: eighty-six thousand men poised united and solid between Lee's divided force of around forty-three thousand.

The rebels' tactical situation—that is to say, how and where they were in contact with the Union army—was fully as dire as their strategic situation. Keep in mind that yesterday it had taken Jackson from dawn until dusk to move west from Lee's position to the position from which he launched his assault at twilight. This assault shattered two divisions of the Eleventh Corps and produced some of the war's most memorable scenes of rout: but what then?

With its high percentage of German immigrants ("Dutchies" and "foreigners"), the Eleventh Corps had always been something of a pariah. It had been used negligently, or given out-of-the-way postings (as its deployment yesterday was to have been). In point of fact, of the five Federal corps in the Wilderness yesterday, by this early morning hour only the Eleventh and two-thirds of the Third had been fully engaged. Despite Crane's account of what befell the fictional Saunders's brigade, the Second, Fifth, and one third of the Twelfth corps had hardly been in action at all. Well over half of Hooker's seventy-thousand-man main striking force had spent May 2 just standing in their field fortifications. With the arrival of Reynolds's First Corps, that main force was stronger by another seventeen thousand men than it had been the day before.

Nor had Jackson's assault achieved any significant topographical or geographical success. It had not gained any critically important ground. The gap it momentarily opened in the Union right flank along the Orange Plank Road had been plugged (as Private Fleming witnessed) by confident infantry of the Third and Twelfth corps, and by masses of Federal artillery superior in quality and quantity to anything the rebels could bring against it.

How could the rebels genuinely exploit their successful surprise attack? Concerned with this very question, Jackson had been on a personal reconnaissance last evening when he was severely wounded by a volley from a North Carolina regiment. A. P. Hill, the senior major general in Jackson's corps, was wounded by Federal artillery just after he saw to his wounded commander's removal to the rear. Along with the death of Jackson's engineer officer in the same shell burst, this brought to a halt whatever further plans Jackson may have intended to put into effect. R. E. Rodes was the senior of the remaining division commanders, but he was not a major general. So command passed to Major General J. E. B. Stuart, the commander of Lee's cavalry, who was unfamiliar with the situation but at least widely known throughout the army.

This morning, the rebel soldiers on this part of the field were exhausted after a day on the march and in the attack. Their formations were disorganized after a sequence of headlong assaults through the Wilderness terrain. With the disorganization in the command structure above them, their attack had stalled, while the Union army still controlled Hazel Grove, which had become the key to the battle. It was the only ground on the battlefield suitable for massing artillery: a cleared area about a quarter of a mile in extent, on a plateau that dominated the land south of the Orange Plank Road and shielded the Union positions at Fairview and Chancellorsville. Those positions in turn blocked the Orange Plank Road, and this bastion at Hazel Grove blocked the single forest road tangential to it. So, as long as the Union army held Hazel Grove it blocked the only two roads through the Wilderness by which Lee's army could be immediately reunited. Rebel infantry had been hustled into an attack at Hazel Grove late in the evening (see Chapter 6), and massed Union artillery, without much infantry support, had sufficed to blast them to a halt. Immediately thereafter, Sickles had invested the area with his Third Corps, and confused action thereabouts during the night of May 2–3 changed nothing. Shortly before daylight, Hooker himself visited the Hazel Grove position.

So the rebel situation at dawn on May 3 was acute indeed. The rebels had suffered the wastage of a day of battle, while the largely untouched Union army at the critical part of the battlefield had been reinforced with fresh troops. The major portions of the rebels' main force remained separated by a day's march via circuitous roads, whereas the Union army had become more effectively consolidated. The Confederates at all costs had to consolidate their own forces or risk having each separate part crushed, yet in order to reunite they must either continue to press their attack or retreat far enough to enable them to regroup. Neither choice was at all appealing. Keep in mind that it has always been dangerous to attack veteran troops in prepared defenses and that, thanks to the prevalence of the rifle, this prospect had become downright suicidal. On the other hand, it was frighteningly risky to try to disengage from a rested, superior enemy force (Clausewitz explicitly warns against it).[2] Put in perhaps not unfamiliar terms, Hooker was still reaping the rewards of being the first to get his army there (at Hazel Grove, Fairview, and Chancellorsville), of having (by a two-to-one ratio) the most men, and of having twice as much artillery.

The rebel forces remained in disarray. Their best corps commander was wounded (mortally, it turned out) and had been replaced by a cavalryman

2. Carl von Clausewitz, *On War*, 322–23.

unfamiliar with the front or with infantry operations in wooded terrain. The heaviest concentration of their soldiery, upon whom the resumption of the attack must rest, was the weariest and had been without reinforcement or resupply for two days. In the event, throughout the upcoming day, their attacking formations, overextended and overspent, would often collapse in the face of vigorous local counterattack. Whatever the overall outcome, the Union army was going to enjoy a harvest of prisoners and rebel battle flags all along the western face of the battlefield.

If, then, the rebels are not "jest where we want 'em" (*RBC* 144), it is hard to imagine what more the Union command could have desired. In mature postwar consideration, Private Fleming's corps commander would write that "The situation of Jackson's corps"—comprising three-quarters of the rebels' main force—"on the morning of May 3rd was a desperate one"; "It only required that Hooker . . . take a reasonable, common-sense view of the state of things," and "the success gained by Jackson should have been turned into an overwhelming defeat" (*BL* 3:164). In a similar reconsideration, General Pleasonton, whose massed guns had blunted Jackson's evening assault against Hazel Grove, wrote that "the 3rd of May" should have been "a complete success" for the Army of the Potomac. It was a "golden opportunity" (*BL* 3:182).

It was arguably the best single opportunity to destroy the Army of Northern Virginia that the Army of the Potomac ever had, down to the very end of the war. The previous September, General McClellan had squandered a famous chance at Antietam because he did not coordinate his huge army's assaults. But McClellan had been in the grip of one of his paranoid overestimations of the size of his enemy's force (he put them at almost ten times their real number), and Union success depended upon successful attack. Here, on this morning, Hooker enjoyed accurate information about the size of the rebel army, and he had no need to attack at all; all he had to do was reinforce the Hazel Grove position and sit still. The rebels were in exactly the situation most to be dreaded in this new day of the rifled infantry weapon: they had no real choice but to attack the Union forces straight ahead of them.

To this end, even as Private Fleming was groggily viewing his fellow soldiers of the 304th New York in the light of the new dawn, General J. E. B. Stuart was deploying his three divisions in three waves three hundred yards apart. He was about to commit them to a straightforward assault, without subtlety, deception, coordination, or any attention to either the flanks of the Union position or the flanks of his own lines. It is hard to imagine such an attack succeeding; whether it succeeded or not, there must be great slaughter of rebel infantry.

If Hooker did indeed choose to strike at Stuart's corps, his prospects were excellent and several. The Union defensive line overlapped both flanks of the on-coming rebel assault. Hooker could put in an attack by thirty thousand men (Meade's Fifth Corps and Reynolds's completely fresh First Corps) upon Stuart's exposed left flank, and Stuart's entire command did not number thirty thousand. Stuart could be decisively crushed. Whether or not Hooker attacked on this flank the morning must see the decimation of Stuart's part of the Army of Northern Virginia. This would leave Lee with the remaining rump of seventeen thousand men, trapped between Sedgwick's oncoming attack, which would soon breach the rebel lines at Fredericksburg, and Hooker's main force. The eastward-facing entrenchments of Hooker's main force, upon which those hapless seventeen thousand rebels would be hammered by Sedgwick's assault, were held by two virtually unused Federal corps, which just by themselves outnumbered the soldiers Lee himself commanded.

May 3, 1863, may not see the end of the southern Confederacy nor even the end of the Army of Northern Virginia (the stopping power of the rifle was such that a devastating pursuit of a beaten foe was rare). But it would surely see the end of General R. E. Lee as commander of that army. His characteristic aggressiveness had achieved one outright victory, at the Second Battle of Manassas; but it was obviously not the quality best suited to an army always numerically inferior to its enemy, which suffered chronic logistical problems at every level from division up to the War Cabinet itself, and whose general officers tended toward undisciplined impetuosity. The rebels' catastrophic situation at Chancellorsville showed Lee's faults at their worst. He would be permitted to retire into history and the company of kindred spirits such as Prince Rupert of the Rhine, Prince Charles Edward Stuart, Charles XII of Sweden, Auguste Marmont, John Bell Hood, Conrad von Hotzendorf, and Renya Mutaguchi, thrusters all, whose over-ambitious plans led to unmitigated catastrophe for their outnumbered forces.[3]

Except that none of this happened. At the dawn hour when it is occurring to

---

3. Prince Rupert led the Royalist cavalry to its destruction in the English Civil War. Charles XII of Sweden gratuitously sought a war with Russia, got crushed at Pultowa in 1709, and reduced his nation to minor-league status. Charles Edward Stuart ("Bonnie Prince Charlie") led the Jacobite forces to total defeat at Culloden Moor in 1746. Marshal Auguste Marmont held Lord Wellington and his Anglo-Portuguese army in contemptuous disdain long enough to accomplish the virtual destruction of his own French forces in the Peninsular War. The "Gallant Hood of Texas" destroyed the Confederate Army of Tennessee (see Chapter 2). In the opening years of World War I, the disastrously brilliant von Hotzendorf directed the Austro-Hungarian armies to defeats so catastrophic that they doomed the Dual Monarchy and the House of Habsburg. Renya Mutaguchi was so confident of victory over the despised Anglo-Indian army in Burma that he did not provide supplies for his forces in their "march on Delhi" in 1944, since they would be able to feed themselves from captured enemy stores. He thereby achieved the greatest catastrophe ever suffered by Japanese land armies.

the temporarily illusion-less Private Fleming that he is in "a charnel place" (*RBC* 140), Confederate Major General James Ewell Brown Stuart was organizing—if that is the right word—his exhausted rebel infantry for a desperate, almost surely foredoomed assault. At just that hour, Major General Joseph Hooker issued orders to all the Federal forces at Hazel Grove, including those artillery batteries that had dominated the closing hours of battle the previous evening, to withdraw.

Stuart's attacking rebels struck the Third Corps while it was withdrawing and succeeded handsomely despite themselves. It never occurred to them that Hooker could be withdrawing. Their subsequent official reports assumed their arms had achieved an unprecedented success. For instance, the report of General Heth, commanding the division that captured the position: "General Archer advanced with his brigade. Conforming his line of battle to that of the enemy, he charged the works in his front, and, without the least halt or hesitation, carried them, driving the enemy before him, who outnumbered him five to one" (*OR* 339). Forty years later, General E. P. Alexander, whose artillery had supported that assault and soon replaced the Union guns on Hazel Grove, saw the truth of the matter: "The battle was still Hooker's, had he fought where he stood. But about dawn he made the fatal mistake of recalling Sickles from the Hazel Grove position. . . . There has rarely been a more gratuitous gift of a battle-field" (*OR* 339).[4] In no objective category does Hooker's decision make any sense.

But it did in Hooker's mind. That is to say, it made perfect sense in the "plot" or story by which Hooker himself was understanding and conducting his life during the night of May 2–3, 1863. Remember that when Lee struck Hooker's columns as they advanced eastward beyond the Wilderness on May 1, Hooker had illogically recoiled and pulled his advancing divisions back into a defensive array. This had been his instinctive reaction to the discovery that there was indeed "someone else out there" after all (General R. E. Lee) who was not just a pawn in the grandly unfolding pattern his own intellect had fashioned.

Hooker's self-confidence soon reasserted itself, and with it, his complete self-absorption. Mark the first-person pronouns in his statement to his senior corps commander: "'I have got Lee just where I want him; he must fight me on my own ground" (*BL* 3:161). The resilient "plot" in Hooker's mind whereby he understood himself and the world about him had been one in which, thanks to the brilliance of the army's operations under his leadership, "our enemy must

4. Luvaas and Nelson, *War College Guide*, 255.

either ingloriously fly, or come out from behind his defenses and give us battle on our own ground, where certain destruction awaits him"—this, his public proclamation to his army on April 30, 1863 (*OR* 171). To his officers he boasted repeatedly (with only the degree of profanity varying) that "God Almighty will not be able to prevent the destruction of the rebel army!"[5]

Yesterday Jackson's columns on their long march across Hooker's front and toward his exposed right flank had been observed from Hazel Grove. Those columns had been brought under artillery fire, and Sickles's Third Corps had developed attacks against them. Scattered reports of rebel activity on his army's right flank had been arriving at Hooker's headquarters throughout the day. But General Hooker determined from all this evidence that Lee was in retreat, a determination that is "unfathomable" in objective terms, but which makes perfect sense according to Hooker's personal plot: Lee was not attacking "on our own ground" along the fortified left flank where Hooker expected him, so the rebels must be in "inglorious flight."[6]

Then the rebels struck yesterday afternoon, providing apocalyptic proof that the mind (or force or whatever) opposing him was no mere chimera, supplying a pleasant tension to his "story," but real—and that it had overmatched him. In the solipsistic mentality, overweening self-conceit and overmastering self-pity are complementary states. Disconnected as these both are from the steadying flywheel of reality, either one can swiftly replace the other (we have seen this amply demonstrated in Private Fleming). So after Jackson struck the right wing of his army with such savage surprise, another "plot" rapidly generated itself. In this plot, Joe Hooker is a general beaten by brutal circumstance. Before this, the circumambient reality had been plastic in the service of the "plot" in which he figured as the conquering hero; now, the entire circumambient world was obviously against him. Still the story's hero but now a tragic and victimized hero, he must bend all his efforts to save his army. Hence appeared the new "plot" and the task to which he was committed ever since the wreckage of his right flank came pouring down the Orange Plank Road past the porch of his headquarters at the Chancellor House yesterday afternoon. Early this morning he visited Hazel Grove to see for himself not how potentially strong but how potentially precarious was the Union position there. Since the story in which he now found himself involved saving his army rather than defeating the rebels, he had

---

5. Stackpole, *Chancellorsville*, 147; Catton, *Glory Road*, 187. For a vivid and insightful presentation of Hooker's personality, see Longacre, *Commanders of Chancellorsville*, especially 72–127.
   6. Esposito et al., *West Point Atlas*, 1:87.

no intention of sending more men off into an exposed position in the now menacing Wilderness. Instead he commanded Sickles to withdraw his Third Corps into closer, more symmetrical defensive positions around Fairview.

Given Crane's own fundamental concern with solipsism in *The Red Badge of Courage*, what drew him to the battle of Chancellorsville must be apparent. Hooker's conduct, rendered above in the terms we have been applying to Crane's novel, has been the subject of a great deal of military, historical, biographical, and psychological speculation, for it holds the key to the most startling Union defeat of the war. Throughout his military career, Joseph Hooker had shown himself to be imaginative, self-dramatizing, self-seeking, and self-absorbed. When he became the commander of the Army of the Potomac, where his word defined reality and his desire became fact, the further development of a profoundly solipsistic cast of mind is hardly surprising. General Hooker had personally witnessed the wreckage of his right wing on May 2. He had been filtering reports, casualty figures, messages, requests, and pleas ever since. As incomplete and inaccurate as the evidence may have been that his army had been signally defeated, this evidence was far more compelling than the evidence upon which Private Fleming was, at this same hour, basing his belief that he himself was "doomed to greatness" (*RBC* 151).

If the rebels massed their own artillery at Hazel Grove when Hooker abandoned it to them, his position at Fairview would become virtually untenable, and whatever Stuart's shortcomings he had always appreciated good artillerists. In short order he had six batteries there. Thereafter, the previously promising compactness of the Union army's position became a liability. Rebel artillery was able to play upon it from three sides, and most devastatingly from the splendid new firebase at Hazel Grove, which overshadowed both Fairview and the Chancellorsville crossroads beyond. The terrain put Union artillery at an impossible disadvantage, and so the rebel artillery was unchallenged by counterbattery fire.[7]

At about nine o'clock Hooker himself was concussed by a solid shot that struck a pillar of the Chancellor House against which he was leaning. His staff revived him with brandy—just in time, for he arose from his blanket just as another cannonball shredded it. He was hardly fit to continue in command, yet neither was he disabled. His stunned physical condition was a perfect outward, visible sign for the stunned mental condition with which he had been commanding the Army of the Potomac since twilight the day before. The rout in-

7. Luvaas and Nelson, *War College Guide*, 256.

flicted then upon its Eleventh Corps was the most dramatic incident of the battle, but it was on this day, May 3, 1863, that this army was defeated. General Pleasonton wrote that "the unfortunate circumstances that contracted the lines of our army enabled the rebels to inflict the severest punishment upon all the troops that were engaged," and "the greatest injury was inflicted on the 3rd of May" (BL 3:182).

Stuart's rebels opened their assault at dawn that morning with demonstrations all around the perimeter of the Union lines, and their main attack drove against the right-center of the Union army's position. Within ninety minutes, they secured Hazel Grove and began massing artillery upon it. Stuart's attack then initially developed to the north of the Orange Plank Road, against Fairview and the Union lines there, which were principally held by Berry's division of the Twelfth Corps. Divisions of the Third and Twelfth corps were involved in heavy fighting during these early morning hours. The rebel attacks were put in piecemeal: many of his regiments were exhausted from their exertions yesterday, up and down his formations new officers had to replace those wounded and slain, and the Wilderness offered few features by which attacking formations could guide. Despite the disadvantage at which Hooker had placed his soldiers at Fairview, they resisted with determination. One rebel brigade went to ground and could not be persuaded to advance further. Stuart's leading brigades were drawn increasingly into the fighting south of the Orange Plank Road, and Union forces were able to press sharply against the left flank of his advance north of it. Stuart committed all the reinforcements he could to his left, his three battle lines became entangled there in the forests with further loss of order and control, and some of his regiments were running out of ammunition (OR 338). His attack was everywhere confused and in some places faltering.

Hooker neither significantly reinforced his own engaged divisions nor ordered counterattacks elsewhere; quite the opposite. The weight of rebel artillery fire from Hazel Grove proved decisive against the Federal forces at Fairview, and across the battlefield generally. Confederate gunners, enjoying an unobstructed field of fire from the Hazel Grove position, rained shell and solid shot everywhere upon Union formations trying to deploy against rebel infantry. This then was a rare instance of the decisive use of artillery in an offensive operation. General Berry, the commander of the division holding the Federal front north of the Orange Plank Road, was killed just as the position there began to unravel. By ten o'clock the Union positions that blocked the Orange Plank Road were overmastered, and the Army of the Potomac began to retire all along its line, to a tighter defensive arc shielding the pontoon bridges at United States Ford by which they could cross the Rappahannock River to safety.

Stuart's corps reestablished contact with Lee and by ten o'clock had cleared the length of the Orange Plank Road. His men shifted their axis of attack from east to north and advanced all along the line. The battle on this front being completely under control, Lee himself directed Anderson's and McLaws's divisions eastward to meet the threat from Sedgwick at Fredericksburg. So as May 3 developed past the noon hour in the Wilderness, Stuart's twenty-five thousand rebel soldiers (all of them exhausted) were chivvying seventy-five thousand Yankees (over half of them quite fresh) back upon their bridgehead at United States Ford.[8]

This is the historical context into which Crane placed, with well-researched precision, the 304th New York Volunteer Infantry Regiment and Henderson's brigade of the Second Corps. The increasing conventionality of Private Fleming's metaphors through the course of the novel (see Chapter 5) reflects the increasing clarity and "ordinariness" of his perceptions. Acclimated as he has now become to the phenomena of combat, on this second day the details of the battle emerge sporadically but with clarity and historical accuracy.

The advancing rebel soldiers no longer impress Private Fleming as "machines of steel" (*RBC* 67) or "the red and green monster" (68). At the outset of the regiment's second engagement on the morning of May 3, he will note "the clannish yell" (180) of the Confederate infantry: "their peculiar yell" (*OR* 79), the high-pitched rebel yell, "shrill and exultant" (*RBC* 156), here put into a category perfectly appropriate to the Scots-Irish or Border heritage of a high percentage of the rebel army. During this same action, Fleming will remark the appearance of the Confederates opposite as "a brown mass of troops" following a "fierce-hued flag" (192–93): again, a perfect depiction of the rebels' ubiquitous butternut-brown homespun clothing, and their battle flag in which red is much more dominant than in the Federal flag. Shortly thereafter, when a rebel formation amid the fog of battle stumbles upon the 304th New York, Private Fleming perceives "that their uniforms were rather gay in effect, being light gray, accented with a brilliant-hued facing." It also strikes Fleming that "the clothes seemed new" (195). So this rebel formation, probably a single regiment, is clothed in "official" gray because it has received a new issue of clothing from the haphazard

---

8. Catton, *Glory Road*, 217.

Confederate logistical command. Confederate gray did indeed appear as a "gay" color in contrast to the somber browns of their home-dyed uniforms, and to the dark blue of the Federal uniforms. As in the Federal service, the distinguishing color of Confederate infantry was sky-blue, which appeared on cap band, collar, cuff, and piping; hence the "facing" Fleming will see as "brilliant-hued."[9]

Likewise, the strategic situation endured by the divisions in the center of the Army of the Potomac on the morning of May 3, 1863, is rendered with complete accuracy. From the beginning (*RBC* 156) to the end of this portion of the novel (227–28, 232), the army is retreating. Whatever modest local successes they might achieve, soldiers on the line of battle everywhere are facing victorious, advancing rebel infantry (156, 159, 174, 203, 209, 214, 227) and are frequently under rebel cannonade (155, 162, 173, 180–81, 209, 227). One of the rare vistas afforded by the Wilderness shows Private Fleming a distant road "crowded with retreating" Union "infantry" (173). Finally, the 304th New York themselves are ordered back from the battle line as Henderson's brigade is reformed. They leave the battlefront and rejoin their division in a road. Thence the division itself marches "away from the field" of battle and go "winding off in the direction of the river" (228) as the constituent parts of the Army of the Potomac retreat back across the Rappahannock.

The attitude of the men in the lower ranks during this morning of withdrawal is absolutely plausible, given the historical situation. The exhilarated temper generated by combat and the elation of local success yield moments of pride and excitement, but their initial discourse is one of disheartened frustration (*RBC* 156), to which some of them return during their final withdrawal (231). They know where they are: "If they keep on chasing us, by Gawd, they'd better watch out," Private Fleming says. Private Wilson answers, "If they keep on a'chasin' us they'll drive us all inteh th' river" (164), that is, the Rappahannock. They sense that something has gone terribly amiss in the high command, which explains their plight: "Now," Private Fleming says, "I'd like to know what the eternal thunders we was marched into these woods for anyhow, unless it was to give the rebs a regular pot shot at us. We came in here and got our legs all tangled up in these cussed briers, and then we begin to fight and the rebs had an easy time of it. Don't tell me it's just luck!" (160–61). Hooker's failure to advance his army clear of the Wilderness two days earlier, his defensive passivity yesterday, his numbed retreat today—President Abraham Lincoln himself will like to know the reasons once this disastrous and disappointing campaign is over.

9. Haythornthwaite, *Uniforms*, plates 44–46.

Chapter 8

Private Fleming and the 304th
New York on May 3, 1863

Teased out of the welter of emotions dominating Private Fleming's mind, the experiences of the 304th New York Volunteer Infantry Regiment in *The Red Badge of Courage* correspond precisely to the experiences such a regiment would have endured if the fictional Henderson's brigade had been under General William H. French's command on the morning of Sunday, May 3, 1863.[1] Conceive of the Army of the Potomac around the Chancellorsville crossroads at six A.M. on May 3 as if it were splayed out upon a giant compass face. Due north on the face before us, just below the letter "N," is Chandler's farmhouse, which Hooker is about to designate as the southernmost and central point of a great shallow chevron-shaped defensive deployment into which he decides to retire his army. The lines of this deployment extend far off the compass face toward the northwest and the northeast; Hooker regroups his divisions into or behind this position, holding there, but intent above all else on preserving for his army the option of a staged withdrawal back across the Rappahannock via the United States Ford. Insofar as this morning's action is involved: the Old Orange Plank Road (it could also be called the Turnpike, or "Pike," since the two roads join as

---

1. In addition to the *Official Records* as listed throughout, this account is shaped by Luvaas and Nelson, *War College Guide*, 256–70, in particular.

they pass through the heart of the Wilderness) bisects the compass face, entering at due west and exiting at about east-southeast where the Chancellor house and the Chancellorsville crossroads lie. The north–south road between Chandler's farm and the Chancellorsville crossroads runs just inside the eastern (or right-hand) edge of the face, closely following the arc between north-northeast and east-southeast.

The Second Corps remains posted in an array of defensive lines east of and parallel to that north–south road. French's Third Division of the Second Corps is still in its position in the reserve lines of that array: this is the position it held yesterday afternoon and continued to occupy through the night of May 2–3. Yesterday afternoon, one of French's three brigades was removed from his division and dispatched westward to join the forces assembling to face Jackson's onslaught. Now, at six-thirty in the morning and with commendable independence and foresight (French's shortcomings lay in his administrative capacities, not in his understanding of combat), he recognizes that the front before him poses no threat, and that the main rebel assault continues to drive upon the Federal position behind him to the west. He begins to redeploy his formations accordingly.

The main rebel assaults are coming in between south-southwest on our imaginary compass face and west-northwest, and all along this chord the Federals are embroiled in difficulty. The extraordinarily valuable Hazel Grove position is at the edge of the compass face at south-southwest, and Fairview is a nondescript geographical feature above it that has temporarily become a bastion of sorts for the Union forces hereabouts. They are heavily engaged with rebel infantry, and rebel artillery is beginning to dominate this quadrant of the field. With the death of General Berry and the discomfiture of his division, the Federal forces in the area just below the "W" on the dial are beginning to collapse. Stuart's rebel regiments, opposite, are likewise experiencing difficulties: the fire of massed numbers of rifled muskets was so destructive that it was not unusual for two opposing formations on a Civil War battlefield to be, simultaneously, dissolving under shattering losses.

"Taking the discretionary power" given him by his corps commander, General Couch (OR 93), General French withdraws four of the six regiments of Carroll's brigade and all three regiments of Albright's brigade from their rifle pits facing east, marches them a short way down that north–south road and then west into the fields above the Orange Plank Road: he thus deploys them a little above the center of the compass face. French at first faces his regiments south toward the Orange Plank Road; then discerning more clearly the direction of the rebel assault, pivots them clockwise, so that his division faces west, between the "W" and west-northwest. Carroll's brigade is left, Albright's right. Their regiments are now mostly in fields, but they are facing thick woods through which the rebels are attacking. Bear in mind that these rebel and Federal forces will generally be trying to operate in dense, hampering woodland, where vision is exceedingly limited and sound becomes distorted.

General Hooker, finding these regiments to hand thanks to French's foresight, makes his one positive contribution to his army's predicament along the Plank Road: "about 8 a.m., the general commanding the army, who had arrived on the left of my line a short time previous and noticed my dispositions, directed me, through a staff officer, to move forward with my division, attack the enemy, and drive him through the woods" (OR 93). Such a counterattack is the standard textbook employment of a reserve formation in an army whose main lines are under attack. Hooker's failure to employ more than this portion of French's single division in such counterattack amplifies his supine abandonment of the Hazel Grove position. All morning long, he keeps two full fresh corps in reserve positions extending way off the northern edges of the battlefield. To keep reserve formations in reserve is obviously of no use to formations who are being sorely pressed. (Such undue conservatism could conceivably enable the enemy to attack those reserves in their turn, thus inviting the piecemeal destruction of your forces—although so exigent are the rebels' own circumstances this morning that this is hardly an issue.) But more: throughout military history, enemy forces committed to straightforward tactical assault have always been promising targets for counterattacks. From Patroclus's counterattack against the Trojans at the Achaean beachhead down to Lee's welterweight ripostes to McClellan's heavyweight lunges during the battle of Antietam last autumn, such counterattacks are the very stuff of successful defensive battle. If the attacking troops are being stubbornly resisted, they are rapidly wearing themselves down; if they are succeeding, their advancing lines are probably in confusion and disarray.

The situation on French's left is especially promising for such counterattack, because both conditions obtain. Since dawn Stuart's rebels have been heavily engaged with the Federal infantry and artillery at Fairview at the southwest mark on our compass. As Berry's division begins to give way, Stuart's formations coming east along the Plank Road are lured out of their proper axis of attack. Rebel regiments that should be shouldering through the woods straight toward French swivel off southward instead, and their left flanks are open for his thrust. French's counterattack goes in about eight A.M. (OR 93, 94, 98). Taken in the flank, the rebels break back, exposing the flanks of formations beyond. Carroll's four regiments capture nearly two hundred prisoners (including one major), two stands of colors, and liberate a captured regiment of Federal Zouaves. They cross the Plank Road, driving the rebels back half a mile.

French's own embarrassment lies to his right. This portion of the compass is loosely the responsibility of General Meade's Fifth Corps, but the only orders issued by Hooker call for that corps to remain in reserve, forming a defensive line running northwest from Chandler's house, which line Hooker is busily extending even further to the northwest with Reynolds's First Corps. His orders remove these two corps completely from both the compass face and the battle. So there is little other coordinated Federal resistance to Stuart in this area, and French can see that the rebels are threatening to overlap his right flank and bring his soldiers under enfilading fire. This is a potentially catastrophic situation because rebel rifle balls missing men at the end of French's battle lines will have densely ample opportunities to find purchase deeper down the line. And if battle lines of soldiers under enfilading fire present extraordinarily rich targets, battle lines of soldiers who find enemy forces in their rear will almost invariably dissolve.

French sends back for the two remaining regiments of Carroll's brigade and, despite the fact that they will be widely separated from the rest of their brigade, posts them to the right of Albright's brigade to lengthen the right of his line. As his attack proceeds, he continues to plead for more support for his right flank, and finally receives Tyler's brigade from the Fifth Corps (they will be wearing blue Maltese-cross cap badges). His "left," Carroll's force of four regiments, is "now free to act" for a time, and continues "to break and drive the enemy" (OR 93).

The situation on his right remains the problem. Albright's brigade finds itself too small to plug the widening gap between Carroll's attacking regiments on their left and the two regiments from Carroll's brigade that are sent forward to extend the Federal line on their right. Albright is losing contact with friendly forces on both flanks; the rebels are in the woods all around him and in increasing numbers. He deems it prudent to retire, has his brigade fall back about a hundred yards and form a new battle line, and then soon receives a "furious charge" (OR 107).

Carroll's two detached regiments on Albright's right are staggered by rebel attacks as they try to advance into the woods. Even with Tyler's brigade forming there, the enemy lines still extend beyond the right flank of the Federal forces on this part of the field and they are continuing to press. Tyler's regiments are "scarcely in position" when the rebels hit them (OR 201). The 129th Pennsylvania of Tyler's brigade is isolated and driven in; behind it, the Twenty-fourth

New Jersey of Carroll's brigade also breaks (OR 96). The thinness of the Federal forces on this ground is brutally exposed as rebel attacks drive in Federal units, or as they lose contact with each other as they try to cover the woods to their right. Tyler runs out of ammunition, which French cannot supply and Tyler's own divisional commander will not (evidently; the murkiness of Federal command this morning extends even to this detail, and even to Tyler's own official report). Tyler withdraws after about two hours (OR 201, 202). Albright's right is then completely exposed and outflanked. His right-hand regiment narrowly manages to extricate itself from a rebel assault (OR 107). Thus the right of French's lines have been turned for good, and he must abandon his counterattack.

Meanwhile, without reinforcements, Carroll's four regiments are brought to a standstill. Heavy columns of rebel infantry press on their front and flank; rebel artillery enfilades them, firing grape and canister that drive them back from the Plank Road (OR 98, 100), then bringing them under shellfire as they withdraw further. They fall back to the edge of the woods, hold there unmolested (the rebels having achieved their immediate objective of clearing the Plank Road) for about an hour, and then withdraw with the rest of French's division sometime after 11 A.M. (OR 94, 95).

French reassembles his division around noon, and they spend much of the afternoon digging themselves in to positions to the northeast of Chandler's house along the Mine Run Road, in those lines into which Hooker will place his defeated army pending their eventual withdrawal back across the Rappahannock (OR 93, 94, 107, etc.). From this summary of the *Official Records* bearing upon French's battle on the morning of May 3, one signal fact emerges: French's laudable initiative to restore the western front of the Federal position was hampered and finally frustrated by the limited forces he could commit to his own right flank. If he had still had his Third Brigade, the one dispatched from his Third Division during the emergency of the previous afternoon, he obviously would have sent it to his right flank. This would have enabled him to post Tyler's brigade even further to his right, thus extending the flank that was never long enough or strong enough to keep Stuart's rebels from turning it.

—⁂—

Stephen Crane thrusts his fictional Henderson's brigade, containing the 304th New York, into this confused, fragmented, gradually degenerating portion of the Federal endeavor on the morning of May 3, 1863, and his characters experience the battle accordingly. The account of their experience in *The Red Badge of Courage* on this second day of what we know as the battle of Chancellorsville is an amalgam of what men in the various regiments and brigades under French's authority experienced that morning. At dawn the 304th New York is still in the position it held yesterday afternoon. The fact that the man from Ohio could find the 304th New York during the preceding night is based upon a fact confirmed by their current situation this morning: they remain where they had fought yesterday, in reserve behind the eastern section of the army's Wilderness deployment. This is a now quiescent section, but the "distance was splintering and blaring with the noise of fighting" (*RBC* 139) as Stuart's forces on the opposite, western side of the battlefield launch their dawn assaults.

After breakfast, "The regiment was standing at order arms at the side of a lane, waiting for the command to march." Private Wilson is "thoughtfully staring down the road" (*RBC* 148), as well he might. This road is the one running from Chandler's farm down to the Chancellorsville crossroads. They are not under attack themselves, but they are just about to be redeployed, and they know that most likely they will be marched down that road to reach the morning's fighting. The two brigades remaining in French's division fit this situation precisely, which is true of no other formation in the Army of the Potomac at the post-breakfast hour on May 3, 1863.

"A sputtering of musketry was always to be heard. Later, the cannon had entered the dispute" (*RBC* 154): this is the artillery that the rebels are concentrating at their newly secured firebase at Hazel Grove. "The youth's regiment was marched to relieve a command that had lain long in some damp trenches. The men took positions behind a curving line of rifle pits that had been turned up, like a large furrow, along the line of woods. Before them was a level stretch, peopled with short, deformed stumps. From the woods beyond came the dull popping of the skirmishers and pickets, firing in the fog. From the right came the noise of a terrific fracas" (*RBC* 154). The trenches or rifle pits they encounter are of uncertain identity, as is the command that they relieved. Field fortifications were to be found throughout the area after three days of maneuver and battle, and French's entire intention was to provide reinforcement—"relief"—to the Federal forces that were heavily engaged in this quadrant. In any case, these rifle pits will not figure at all in the 304th New York's experience of combat this morning, for the regiment is redeployed away from them before their part of the battle begins.

With this description of the terrain facing the 304th New York while in this position, compare for instance the "Report of Lieut. Col. Jonathan Lockwood," commanding the Seventh West Virginia Regiment in French's division: "On the 3rd instance, at about 7 a.m., we were ordered to form in line of battle, which we did in an open field fronting the wood that lay between us and the enemy" (*OR* 100). Stuart himself remarks the early fog or "mist that shrouded the field" (*OR* 338). French says that he deployed his soldiers initially "in line of battle on the plain, and facing the direction of the Plank Road" (*OR* 93)–facing south, in other words, which would mean that the "terrific" main action was indeed taking place to their right, although the sounds of skirmishing would have come from all along their front.

As they wait here, "the noise of skirmishers came from the woods on the front and left, and the din on the right had grown to frightful proportions. The guns [that is, the artillery] were roaring without an instant's pause for breath. It seemed that the cannon had come from all parts and were engaged in a stupendous wrangle" (*RBC* 155). Stuart's gunners have concentrated all the cannon they can at Hazel Grove, and they are being countered by all the Federal cannon that the Federal corps commanders on this part of the field–Slocum and Sickles–can assemble at Fairview to oppose them. Fairview is unfortunately a lesser and easily dominated position.

"But at last the guns stopped," and the "din of musketry on the right, growing like a released genie of sound, expressed and emphasized the army's plight" (*RBC* 156). Once the Union artillery at Fairview has been overmastered, the Confederate attack begins to succeed. Crane's description corresponds exactly to the way the sequence of battle would have sounded to soldiers in the positions in which French had first deployed his formations, and the soldiers of the 304th New York understand what is happening. "Among the men in the rifle pits rumors again flew" (155). "Tales of hesitation and uncertainty on the part of those high in place and responsibility came to their ears. Stories of disaster were borne into their minds with many proofs" (156).

—⚬⚬—

There is no transition to their next tactical situation. In one paragraph the soldiers of the 304th New York, lying in those "curving rifle pits," are disheartened and bewildered by the "alleged news" and the prospect of "defeat": the next, "the regiment" is "marching in a spread column that" is "retiring carefully through the woods" (*RBC* 156). Crane's narrative remains immersed in Private Fleming's mental state, which concerns itself entirely with matters of personal prestige. Now that battle, or defeat, is descending upon himself personally, Private Fleming takes little cognizance of the way in which they are being maneuvered. Neither does the novel. But the regiment has obviously been moved out of those field fortifications and into the woods, which is consistent with what ordinary soldiers in formations on the right flank of French's division would have experienced: they were "put on the right" of his attack, "to cover that flank," "where the enemy continued to fill the woods" (OR 93).

It is likewise clear that, after they have been deployed forward into those woods, intense enemy pressure is forcing them to withdraw: "The disordered, hurrying lines of the enemy could somtimes [sic] be seen down through the groves and little fields. They were yelling, shrill and exultant" (RBC 156), and the "noise of firing dogged" the regiment's "footsteps" (159). Similarly, Albright's brigade was compelled to fall back under enemy pressure after their initial fighting advance into those woods (OR 107), which was also the experience of Carroll's two detached regiments and of Tyler's brigade: indeed it was the experience of all the Federal formations engaged along this front at this hour (OR 97, 98, 201). Crane's one description of their rebel opponents is exactly consistent with the historical record of Stuart's attack. The rebel battle lines were indeed "disordered and hurrying" (OR 338–96).

All of this takes place "Before the gray mists had been totally obliterated by the sun rays" (RBC 156). Then "in a clear space," the thinly wooded fringe (164, 166) of the denser forests, "the troops were at last halted. Regiments and brigades, broken and detached through their encounters with thickets, grew together again and lines were faced toward the pursuing bark of the enemy's infantry," which sounded "like the yellings of eager, metallic hounds" (159). This gives fictional embodiment to the inability of Federal soldiers on French's right to maintain their lines of battle in the wilderness. Under enemy pressure, regiments (OR 96) and brigades (OR 107) fell back out of the dense woods in order to reform.

"I was willin' t' bet they'd attack as soon as th' sun got fairly up," Lieutenant Hasbrouck says (RBC 160). "A battery had trundled into position in the rear and was thoughtfully shelling the distance" (160) while Henderson's reformed brigade steels itself to receive the enemy attack. The sunlight becomes full, the Union front shifts slightly as the sound of battle sweeps down toward it, and then "a single" rebel "rifle flashed in a thicket before the regiment" (162). Although Crane's discontinuous prose follows Private Fleming's discontinuity of thought and response, the rebel attack reaches them and they engage it with massed rifle fire (165).

Compare Albright's record of the action of his brigade, which would have been in the same line of battle and just to the left of Private Fleming and his comrades. After they had fallen back and reformed, "A furious charge was then made on our line," and while his brigade was "repelling this attack, the batteries in our rear were throwing shells which exploded directly over my line" (OR 107). This initial rebel assault fell sometime after the eight o'clock hour (OR 93, 94, etc.). One report (OR 107) puts it closer to ten o'clock, though no other records agree with such a late time; one report (OR 201) puts it at nine. Personal time-pieces were still rare in the mid-nineteenth century and they were never syn-chronized, so a reader always finds a wide variation among the times cited in these accounts. But an early morning hour is perfectly consistent with the "full radiance" of the sun soaking the forest just before the 304th New York engaged (RBC 162), and then with the fact that, as Fleming and his comrades subse-quently celebrate their repulse of the rebels, the "sun [is] now bright and gay in the blue, enameled sky" (170).

After this initial rebel assault has been checked, the forest ahead of the 304th New York still bears "its burden of clamor," and "Each distant thicket seemed a strange porcupine with quills of flame": an odd metaphor, but apt, both in the developing array of animal imagery throughout the novel and as a description of the confused fighting all along the western flank of the Federal position. "A cloud of dark smoke, as from smoldering ruins" rises into the sky (RBC 170)—houses are very few in the Wilderness, and this smoke is surely from fires started by muzzle flashes and shell bursts in the thickets and undergrowth. Confederate General Lane, whose brigade was also engaged just to the north of the Plank Road this Sunday morning, reported that, at about this hour, "The woods which we entered were on fire; the heat was excessive; the smoke arising from burning blankets, oil-cloths, etc, very offensive. The dead and dying of the enemy could be seen on all sides enveloped in flames" (OR 353). These fires, hideously dis-tinctive of both this battle and the one fought on this same terrain the following spring, transformed portions of the battlefield into hell for hundreds of the wounded of both sides (BL 3:202).[2]

Unaware of this horror and hesitant to look too closely at a badly wounded comrade named Rogers "thrashing about in the grass," the soldiers are by now in pain from thirst. Private Wilson "had a geographical illusion concerning a stream" and obtains "permission to go for some water" (RBC 171–72). Fleming accompanies him, but ironically (given that they are in the same general area where Private Fleming found that decaying corpse amid waterlogged terrain yes-terday), they cannot find any. "They turned without delay and began to retrace their steps." The narrative then offers one of its two fairly detached perspectives upon this morning's battle:

> From their position as they again faced toward the place of the fighting,
> they could of course comprehend a greater amount of the battle than when

2. Stackpole, *Chancellorsville*, 303–4.

their visions had been blurred by the hurling smoke of the line. They could see dark stretches winding along the land, and on one cleared space there was a row of guns making gray clouds, which were filled with large flashes of orange-colored flame. Over some foliage they could see the roof of a house. One window, glowing a deep murder red, shone squarely through the leaves. From the edifice a tall leaning tower of smoke went far into the sky.

Looking over their own troops, they saw mixed masses slowly getting into regular form. The sunlight made twinkling points of the bright steel. To the rear there was a glimpse of a distant roadway as it curved over a slope. It was crowded with retreating infantry. From all the interwoven forest arose the smoke and bluster of the battle. The air was always occupied by a blaring.

Near where they stood shells were flip-flapping and hooting. Occasional bullets buzzed in the air and spanged into tree trunks. Wounded men and other stragglers were slinking through the woods. (*RBC* 172–73)

The "wounded" and "other stragglers" in the last sentence, the detritus of combat seeking the shortest way to safety, confirm that their search for water led them to the immediate rearward of the Federal battle line on this front.

"As they again faced toward the place of the fighting," they are looking west and south, toward the face of the oncoming rebel attack. Those "dark stretches winding along the land" are lines of rebel infantry beginning to emerge in the fields adjacent to the Plank Road, and perhaps a half-mile to the southwest of their vantage. The "one cleared space" is Hazel Grove, and the "row of guns" there is the massed rebel artillery. The "orange-colored flashes" the two privates see are so prominent because the weapons are being discharged in their general direction, making the muzzle-flashes much more apparent to their vision. They are in an area that is under rebel shellfire.

Remember that houses were few in the Wilderness, so few as to figure prominently in records and historical accounts of the battle. The house they can see "Over some foliage" is on ground now occupied by the rebels. The houses on what remains of the Union part of the field are either to the soldiers' left rear (the Chancellor house and its outbuildings, which Private Fleming will notice later), or out of sight to their right rear (the Chandler farm's buildings, which Private Fleming will see when their division retreats). So this house is probably the tumbled-down old house at Fairview. It is on an elevation ("over some foliage"), half a mile or so from where the two New York soldiers are standing, and on ground just now falling into rebel hands.

The house they are looking at, having a "window," however, seems to be fairly solid (not the case with the shack at Fairview), and it also seems to be burning, and the old Fairview structure survived the battle to collapse in decay some years later. So this might be the Van Wert house instead, evidently also called "the Old School," on the Plank Road: about a mile from the two soldiers, near the spot where Private Fleming was struck and where the Eighth Pennsylvania Cavalry made their attack. But the woods of the Wilderness would probably have blocked that house from their view, and it, too, survived the battle unburnt. A third possibility: could this be a house on Hazel Grove itself? General Alpheus Williams, commanding the First Division of the Twelfth Corps in the forefront of the fighting at Fairview, reported that there was "a farm-house on elevated ground, not over 600 yards distant" (OR 260) from his lines at Fairview, which would place it on or near Hazel Grove. But no maps show any such a structure, nor does the Park Service at Chancellorsville Battlefield. Most probably Crane had in mind the ruin at Fairview. It would show as ruined on the maps he was using, which, in the context of the report of the fires that destroyed the Chancellor house complex, he could have taken to mean that it too burned in the battle.

Then "looking over their own troops, they saw mixed masses slowly getting into regular form." These are those Federal formations under French's command, realigning themselves after their bruising combat in the woods or aligning themselves in preparation to enter it, always under the unremitting pressure of the rebel assault. The "distant roadway" curving "over a slope" and "crowded with retreating infantry" is the road between the Chancellor house and Chandler's. The "slope" was a gentle one, a brief incline just visible through a clearing a half-mile to the right rear of the two New Yorkers' vantage. This road is the one down which the 304th was deployed earlier in the morning, the one along which scores of scattered or retreating Union formations are now being reformed (OR 68, 103, 140, etc.), and the one up which many of them are then being directed, as Hooker's army retreats into its defensive lines centered upon the Chandler farm.

—⁓—

Then, "Looking down an aisle of the grove, the youth and his companion saw a jangling general and his staff" (RBC 173). The scene that follows is as crucial as any in the novel, as a mark of the way The Red Badge of Courage completely reverses the usual fictional portrayal of war. The officers significantly fail to adopt conventional, histrionic poses ("The general . . . looked at the other officer and spoke coolly, as if he were criticizing his clothes") or rhetorical styles ("'Get 'em ready, then'"). Even more striking, the novel's hero fails to be called from obscurity into greatness, quite the opposite: "the most startling thing was to learn suddenly that he was very insignificant" (174–75). The moment is also important in placing *The Red Badge of Courage* in its precise historical context, in order to understand exactly what the 304th New York Volunteer Infantry Regiment will shortly be called upon to do. The two New York privates know that the general officer is "the commander of their division," General William French. The other officer is unknown to them: all they remark is his horsemanship (174). He is the new commander of their—"Henderson's"—brigade.

A short but event-filled time later, Private Fleming will say that "It's a pity old Grandpa Henderson got killed yestirday—he'd have known that we did our best and fought good" (*RBC* 205). The nickname "Grandpa" reflects their affection for an officer who concerned himself with his soldiers' self-esteem. Earlier that morning, well before this moment in which Fleming and Wilson are overhearing this exchange between the two officers, the 304th New York had been retreating through the woods in growing frustration and dismay, and Private Fleming had repeated "a statement he had heard going from group to group at the camp that morning. 'The brigadier said he never saw a new reg'ment fight the way we fought yestirday, didn't he? And we didn't do better than many another reg'ment, did we? Well, then, you can't say it's th' army's fault, can you?'" (157–58). There is no way of knowing whether Henderson actually said this, but such a statement must have been consistent with what they knew of their brigadier. But then, sometime after the regiment's first action yesterday, Henderson had "got killed."

It is no surprise that the two privates do not recognize the new commander of their brigade. He would be the senior colonel of the regiments comprising it. Given the 304th New York's newness, Colonel MacChesnay is probably the least senior, and in an army in which five or six regiments normally comprised a brigade, it is quite plausible that private soldiers from a regiment brand new to it would not recognize one of the colonels of the veteran regiments. And that they would not even recognize the man who is now in control of their private destinies is altogether appropriate to Crane's Naturalistic and mordant portrayal of the true "relationship" between the sapient individual and the brutally indifferent world. Willy-nilly and unwittingly, they have been passed from "Grandpa's" kindly dominion to that of "another officer" who rides "with the skillful abandon of a cowboy" (*RBC* 174).

What General French discusses with this new brigade commander makes perfect sense in the context of the battle on this part of the Federal front at this morning hour on May 3. On his own left, his counterattack is still proceeding well. Straight ahead of him, one of his brigades—"Whiterside's"—is holding, although under increasing pressure. But to his right, everything is up in the air, the rebels there are growing stronger, and all he can do is continue to plead for reinforcements to put in against them. If he does not get them, so be it, and he will have to withdraw, but things have not come to that yet. What he can work on, himself, is Whiterside's predicament: "Th' enemy's formin' over there for another charge. It'll be directed against Whiterside, an' I fear they'll break through there unless we work like thunder t' stop them" (*RBC* 174). The longer he holds this part of the line, the longer his regiments on the left can continue their counterattack across the Plank Road. So he elects to send in one of Henderson's regiments in "'a diversion in favor of Whiterside'" (203), a counterattack through the woods on Whiterside's right; a "diversionary" attack not intended to determine this part of the battle by itself but to enable Whiterside's brigade to continue sustaining its line. Such an attack might just catch the rebels unprepared while they are "forming" their own ranks, or it might hit the left flank of the rebels' attack and fold it up. But in any case, such an attack ought to distract the rebels sufficiently to relieve the pressure on Whiterside.

French asks the brigade commander which regiment he can "spare," and the colonel says, "I had to order in th' 12th to help th' 76th"—one regiment of the brigade moving forward to support another—"an' I haven't really got any. But there's th' 304th. They fight like a lot 'a mule drivers. I can spare them best of any." His term of opprobrium reflects something more than the normal contempt of the line soldier for the soldier of the supply echelon. Drovers and drivers of teams in Civil War armies were most often civilians hired for the task, drawn from the poorest elements of the social order and men notoriously (if understandably) panicked at any prospect of coming under fire. In this tense moment, the colonel's rhetoric is probably influenced by the spectacle of rout on the Plank Road the previous evening.[3]

This will be a risky and probably expensive proposition for the 304th New York, which French acknowledges. But it is a tactical chance worth taking, and

---

3. Details of the personnel serving the Federal supply trains prove, to this student, hard to locate readily. Governments contracted with civilian companies to equip, feed, and resupply their armies, and contractors in turn furnished teams and teamsters. For lengthy attention to this aspect of American military history in a pre–Civil War instance, see Alan D. Gaff, *Bayonets in the Wilderness: Anthony Wayne's Legion in the Old Northwest.* Napoleon created a uniformed service that drove his trains, prefiguring the practice in modern armies, but this seems to have been a revolutionary idea in the early nineteenth century. Even he was still generally in thrall to the age-old practice of relying upon civilian services for most of his supply, and hence upon civilian drivers for the supply trains for his armies: Elting, *Swords around a Throne,* 557ff. It is interesting that until Napoleon's time even drivers for artillery teams were often civilian: *Swords around a Throne,* 254–55.

if the 304th New York is the newest regiment in the brigade (surely the case), this means that it is also the largest. Timing will be absolutely critical in any case, if this counterattack is to succeed. If the brigade goes in too early, before the rebels are committed to their own assault, it will be exposed to the undistracted attention of superior numbers of enemy soldiers. If it goes in too late, after Whiterside has begun withdrawing, the attack will be pointless and will complicate matters when Whiterside falls back. French says, "Get 'em ready, then. I'll watch developments from here, an' send you word when t' start them. It'll happen in five minutes" (*RBC* 175). From all the subsequent evidence, French's timing will be right on the mark.

The counterattack then follows. As before in the novel, the narrative buries the reader in—rather than reports upon—the perceptions and emotions of battle. But Private Fleming's newfound prestige gives him sufficient self-confidence to identify himself with the regiment, so the novel's point of view expands spasmodically to encompass the range of the regiment's emotions and perceptions as well as Fleming's own. Again, the patterns of combat can be worked free of the welter of confusion and emotion embedding them, and the regiment's counterattack can be assessed quite simply: despite the perfect timing with which the attack went in, the 304th New York Volunteers faltered and then, when their color sergeant was killed (*RBC* 188–89), fell back in retreat.

Crane built this part of his novel upon the experiences of the formations under French's command that morning, as reflected in their after-action reports in the *Official Records*. Consider how the experience of the 304th New York Volunteers might be rendered in a much abbreviated (fictional) version, "Colonel MacChesnay's official report":

> *May 3rd*: At about 9 A.M. Col. _____, commanding the brigade after the unfortunate death of General Henderson, ordered the regiment to advance into the woods ahead, in support of Whiterside's brigade on the left. Enemy musketry opened upon the regiment as soon as it approached the woods (*RBC* 180), and it had to endure enemy shellfire and canister throughout (180–81, 183). In the densely wooded terrain, it proved difficult to keep formation (180), and heavy enemy forces could be discerned to the regiment's right (184), where the flank was unsupported. The Three Hundred and Fourth New York Volunteers nonetheless persevered gallantly in its attack until overwhelming enemy numbers and the absence of support compelled it to withdraw some distance in order to reform (194). A line of rebel infantry assaulted the regiment furiously, but was completely routed (195–96), whereafter the regiment withdrew to its original lines (199).

The discerning reader may note a marked difference between the brief objective assessment of the regiment's performance in the paragraph above, and this "Official Report" as its colonel would most likely draft it. But each significant aspect of the 304th New York's experience is based upon specific details to be found in the after-action official reports of the regiments under French's command that morning.

If the "factual" pattern underlying Crane's account is based solidly upon the specific historical record, the pattern within his account presents an interesting understanding of military history and human psychology. It displays in intelligent detail the difficulties of undertaking offensive action in the Civil War in thickly wooded terrain. And it also displays the difficulties of undertaking such operations when using second-rate soldiers.

The terrain, first: either from his conversation with veterans or more likely from his own imaginative conjecture, Crane shows a shrewd understanding of the problems a thickly forested landscape presents to an attacking formation. There is no topographical detail—no stone wall or Dunker Church or Cemetery Ridge or the like—toward which the soldiers can be directed. All Private Fleming sees are "foliages," so as the attack begins, he understandably and instinctively chooses his own objective: "he fixed his eye upon a distant and prominent clump of trees where he had concluded the enemy were to be met, and he ran toward it as toward a goal" (*RBC* 179), and he continues to guide himself thereby (180). This is persuasive, and it seems logical to assume that other individuals along the regimental front similarly select their own objectives. Herein lies an immediate problem. That regimental front is almost two hundred yards long (assuming the men are formed in two ranks, and there are between five and six hundred of them), and the objectives toward which individuals are aiming must be many in number. No wonder that "the right wing swung forward; it in turn was surpassed by the left." No wonder that the regiment almost instantly loses its cohesion, which is further broken by "the bushes, trees, and uneven places" that "split the command and scattered it into detached clusters" (180).

Further, "objectives" consisting of prominent stands of trees become, when they are attained, both shelters and, hence, traps. The regiment's initial surge carries them across one "cleared space" (*RBC* 180), but now that they find themselves in some sort of shelter, their attack instinctively goes to ground. As their energies dissipate under the "windlike effect" of enemy rifle fire, that once "distant and prominent clump of trees" (179) now appears to them comfortingly, protectively "stolid"; the attack begins "to falter and hesitate" (182). Forgetting their initial motivation, men huddle "like sheep" (184). Such paralysis is fatal for the attack and for the soldiers themselves. The protection afforded by thickets and trees is mostly illusory; to falter so close to a veteran enemy equipped with rifles and smoothbore cannon is to invite terrific punishment. And this is exactly what happens to the 304th.[4]

They are finally "belabored" into motion again but come to a second "open space" (*RBC* 184–85), which, despite Private Fleming's paroxysms of enthusiasm and heroism, they never do cross (188–89). Their color sergeant dies in that space, and the attack of the 304th New York Volunteer Infantry Regiment dies there as well. They fall "back to the stolid trees," pause there "a moment" to return fire, and then—finished as an attacking formation, serving no good use in this advanced position, and with an "ominous demonstration" off to their own right flank (184)—retreat back into that "first open space" (190).

—◊—

So, then, "second-rate soldiers"? Is that a fair summary of the 304th New York Volunteers? The focus of the novel is judgmental: its artistic strategies conspire not to render the face of battle for a reader, but to compel a reader to judge first Private Henry Fleming and thereafter the 304th New York Volunteer Infantry Regiment. Private Fleming's inexperienced belief "that he must be a hero" (*RBC* 10) by and of itself demands a reader's assessing response (see Chapter 6). We see him, this morning, come to the belief that he is "the chosen of gods and doomed to greatness" (151). At the end of this morning's experience, he will conclude "He was a man" (232). The terms of his own self-appraisal are changing, and so is the nature of his performance. Are we as readers supposed just to accept the third claim, even though we clearly were supposed to reject the first and the second?

So with the 304th New York: at the end of this abortive counterattack, they will gaze "about them with looks of uplifted pride" and will bestow upon themselves that same masculine sobriquet, that "they" collectively are "men" (*RBC* 198). For an unreflecting reader, these two laconic final claims of manhood-achieved may seem the standard fare of American fiction (especially of the film variety), but the novel itself immediately challenges the regiment's claim. For a close reader, the issue is not closed, but posed: is such self-esteem (in either case) deserved?

What then should we make of the regiment? Thanks to privates Wilson and Fleming, they have some forewarning of what they will be called upon to do.

4. Griffith, *Battle Tactics*, 138.

Lieutenant Hasbrouck is eager for some "real fightin'" (*RBC* 176), but as the men are being formed, they seem anything but ardent (177). When the attack begins, "The line fell slowly forward like a toppling wall, and, with a convulsive gasp that was intended for a cheer, the regiment began its journey" (179).

During this "journey," one fact is confirmed about the 304th New York: the regiment is very badly officered. This was intimated the previous afternoon, when Captain Carrott, the commander of G Company, took himself out of the upcoming battle with the excuse that he was sick. His men threatened to desert rather than serve under him again (*RBC* 47). As the rebel attack came on against them that previous afternoon, Colonel MacChesnay could be seen regarding his own men "as if he regretted above everything his association with them" (55). In preparation for today's counterattack the company officers bustle "like critical shepherds struggling with sheep" (177), hardly figures of inspiration or military competence.

Lieutenant Hasbrouck is the exception that proves the unfortunate rule. When the attack falters in those "stolid trees" and the men become "dazed and stupid," "paralyzed," and "overcome" by the "spectacle" into which they have stumbled, "above the sounds of the outside commotion, arose the roar of the lieutenant. He strode suddenly forth, his infantile features black with rage" (*RBC* 183). The heretofore inconsequential Private Wilson is "aroused" and fires his rifle, and the regiment, "Belabored by their officers," begins to move forward again; but it is a false start. Lieutenant Hasbrouck yet again comes to the fore, this time grabbing Private Fleming by the arm—a wise choice, given Fleming's overweening concern with his private prestige, which he is now identifying with the prestige of the regiment, and his sense of personal invulnerability. Lieutenant Hasbrouck and privates Fleming and Wilson gallop "together down the regimental front" and gesticulate "in front of the colors" (186). This produces the regiment's final forward surge; but here, let us pause to consider what we are seeing.

We know little about Lieutenant Hasbrouck except for his youth (*RBC* 40) and his appetite for battle (160), and seeing him thrust suddenly forward in this way is, granted, to see the mystery of human heroism, which always interested Crane.[5] Setting such a mystery aside, consider what is clear enough about this incident. Lieutenant Hasbrouck is a very junior officer. He is only one of the 304th's ten company commanders, and that for less than a day. He really belongs in a hospital this morning; he had been shot in the hand yesterday after-

---

5. Crane wrote a short story entitled "A Mystery of Heroism" in the spring of 1895, before *The Red Badge of Courage* was published: Wertheim, *Encyclopedia*, 233.

noon. What is he doing—along with these two private soldiers—encouraging a regiment? Given the qualities that are now so apparent in this officer, why did he enter the battle as the second officer of a company, while Carrott commanded G Company until his own manifest cowardice removed him on the eve of combat? What does this reveal about the colonel commanding the regiment?

Speaking of which, where at this critical moment is Colonel MacChesnay? Tactical doctrines codified as military regulations stipulate that the colonel should lead the regiment and remain in proximity to the colors in order to do just that; in order to do exactly what, in his evident absence, one of his most junior officers is doing. After this action, it will develop that Colonel MacChesnay was indeed close enough to the front of his regiment to see and appreciate that a new color-bearer "kep' th' flag 'way t' th' front"—but not close enough to see how Fleming and Wilson were "at th' head 'a th' charge, an' howlin' like Indians all th' time," nor to recognize who those two soldiers were. It may be too much to expect that a regimental commander might recognize two of his private soldiers on sight, but, for whatever reason, it happened that MacChesnay did know these two men by name and face: "My sakes! Well, well, well, those two babies?" (RBC 207). Had he been close enough to the colors to see the two privates, he would have recognized them himself. Why—given that a Civil War regiment was organized specifically as "the largest body of troops that can be directly commanded by a single leader"—was the colonel of the 304th New York Volunteers not within twenty-five yards of his regimental front during this crucial phase of its assault? MacChesnay would later say that Private Fleming and Private Wilson deserved to be major generals (207). Does he himself deserve to be a colonel?[6]

To return to this critical moment, where, for that matter, are the regiment's senior captains? Setting Hasbrouck aside (as he deserves to be, in this consideration), what do we make of the officers of the regiment generally? When the regiment's color sergeant is killed, their attack falls apart completely, despite the fact that, "in an instant of time" (RBC 188), another man comes forward to continue carrying the national flag. Upon such a single casualty their attack founders, although the historical record clearly shows that first-rate regiments in both armies continued attacking behind sequences of self-sacrificing men willing to seize fallen colors and press forward.[7] As the 304th New York begins to fall back, their officers become hysterical: "their voices keyed to screams." A red-bearded

6. Coggins, *Arms and Equipment*, 21 (quote); Griffith, *Battle in the Civil War*, 32.

7. For example, Trudeau, *Bloody Roads*, 298. For a fascinating study of a color-bearer in action, see Gordon C. Rhea, *Carrying the Flag: The Story of Private Charles Whilden, the Confederacy's Most Unlikely Hero*.

officer is shouting in mindless rage, "Shoot into 'em, Gawd damn their souls!" Hasbrouck, in contrast, tries sarcasm: "Where in hell yeh goin'?" (189). As they fall back into the first open space, the men are glaring "dangerously" at their own officers, the red-bearded one in particular (190).

The discipline of this badly led regiment cracks completely during these last moments of their retreat. Individuals "slipping with speed back to the lines" undermine the confidence of those who remain. Most shameful of all, "Wounded men were left crying on this black journey." Crane reiterates "smoke fringes and flames" in the next sentence (*RBC* 192). This may refer to rebel rifle fire, but if the 304th is falling back through one of the areas of the battlefield where brush fires are beginning to establish themselves, the abandonment of these wounded men will doom them to an unspeakable death.

Soldiers become disoriented; the retreat becomes a "wild procession"; "hysterical fear and dismay beset the troops" (193); "Men ran hither and thither"; they are a "mob" (194). Many in the 304th New York go to ground, literally, curling into "depressions" in the ground, while "officers labored like politicians to beat the mass into a proper circle to face" the enemy. Private Wilson, despite or perhaps even because of the chastened maturity he gleaned from yesterday's combat, succumbs and says to Private Fleming, "I guess this is good-by'" (194). "Oh, shut up, you damned fool!" answers Fleming. However ironical the ways and means by which he has come to possess them, Fleming has qualities appropriate to the moment. He and Lieutenant Hasbrouck, almost alone, have been offering genuine leadership during these awful minutes of collapse (190–91, 192, 194).

It is Lieutenant Hasbrouck who enables the regiment to achieve its one moment of modest success during this debacle. Despite the chaos around him, the blur of battle, and the collapse of the regiment, he spots an oncoming rebel battle line (this is the formation in new "light gray" uniforms) and gives those New Yorkers just the fragment of warning and advantage they need. Hasbrouck "had discovered them." These rebels "had been unaware of the proximity of their dark-suited foes or had mistaken the direction." The unsuspected "volley" from the 304th New York staggers them. At first, the two formations seem evenly matched, "a pair of boxers" (*RBC* 195–96), but the 304th New York sustains its advantage in the ensuing close-range firefight and drives them off. The stress in the passage is upon Lieutenant Hasbrouck's individual alertness, initiative, and leadership.

After this last exchange, and looking upon the "tableau" before them of "a ground vacant of" rebel soldiers, "many of the men" spring "from behind their covers and [make] an ungainly dance of joy" (*RBC* 197). Because of this incident, "They gazed about them with looks of uplifted pride, feeling new trust in the grim, always confident weapons in their hands. And they were men" (198). But their return to their own lines is also a return to reality. A veteran regiment ridicules them in contemptuous terms quite apposite to that last fatuous claim:

> "Where th' hell yeh been?"
> "What yeh comin' back fer?"
> "Why didn't yeh stay there?"
> "Was it warm out there, sonny?"
> "Goin' home now, boys?"
> One shouted in taunting mimicry: "Oh, mother, come quick an' look at th' sojers!" (200)

Private Fleming himself is "smitten with a large astonishment." The distances involved in their abortive attack "as compared with the brilliant measurings in his mind, were trivial and ridiculous. The stolid trees" now seem "incredibly near. The time, too, now that he reflected, he saw to have been short." Private Fleming acknowledges "that there was bitter justice in the speeches of the gaunt and bronzed veterans." He looks with "disdain at his fellows" (201).

Despite the fact that Fleming has been carrying the colors during much of the engagement, Colonel MacChesnay now appears for the first time in Fleming's field of vision. He is in the process of receiving an authoritative assessment from the brigade commander who ordered the assault: "Oh, thunder, MacChesnay, what an awful bull you made of this thing!" (*RBC* 202). Crane strikes the perfect note in this tirade delivered by a man who was, yesterday, one of MacChesnay's fellow regimental commanders. "What an awful mess you made! Good Lord, man, you stopped about a hundred feet this side of a very pretty success! If your men had gone a hundred feet farther"—to the other side of that second open space?—"you would have made a great charge, but as it is—what a lot of mud diggers you've got anyway!" (203).

MacChesnay, floundering for a response, unthinkingly gives this "cowboy officer" the rank of general: "Oh, well, general, we went as far as we could" (*RBC* 203). The error may be Crane's own, but it would have been not only unusual and unnecessary but administratively quite difficult for a new brigadier general to have been secured and placed in command of the dead Henderson's brigade, all in the span of a few hours. "'Well, that wasn't very far, was it?'" the brigade commander responds with "cold contempt. 'You were intended to make a diversion in favor of Whiterside. How well you succeeded your own ears can now tell you.'" Proof of their failure comes from "the jarring noises of an engagement in the woods to the left" (203).

The soldiers' reactions are various, but the evidence at hand proves the truth of the brigade commander's accusation. Distances and times were indeed small, and Whiterside is indeed being savaged. Furthermore, the single success the 304th New York enjoyed is proof that the attack was sent in at an appropriate time. At least one of the rebel formations in those woods was surprised and driven off. So the 304th seems to have had, and to have squandered, a chance to do some real damage to the rebel attack on this front.

—⁓—

Now "erect and tranquil," carrying the regiment's colors rather than a rifle and self-confident after having been praised by his colonel and his company commander, Private Fleming observes the battle. He is satisfying his strong visual imagination to the full, and what he sees fits exactly with the historical accounts of the chaotic fighting along this line at this time on this Sunday morning. French's formations—there were too few of them to achieve any sort of redemption of Hooker's fortunes on this front without support—were under severe rebel pressure and had lost their cohesion, although some were still full of fight: "We met Caldwell's brigade going to the front as we were emerging from the woods, retiring" (OR 94, also 96, 97, 100, 201, 202, etc.). Stuart's rebel regiments were sorely bereft of overall leadership, and some of them were at the end of their tether, but they were still advancing (OR 378, 379, 381): "As in the fight of the 2d, so in this of May 3, it is impossible to say what were the separate results" (390, 391, etc.).

So Private Fleming sees "dark-hued masses" of drably clothed rebel infantry (RBC 209) continuing to press assaults against the Union lines, which curve among small hills and thickets. He witnesses the battle degenerating, in the absence of effective command hereabouts on either side, into "separate battles," "incredibly fierce" contests between individual formations "apparently . . . oblivious of all larger purposes of war," "detached" and fighting "little separate battles" amid the dense "wood" and the few "cleared spaces" (209–10). The rebels are everywhere on the offensive, but Union formations enjoy moments of vivid success (211). From his vantage, the rebels seem to him "lighter-hued," in the main (211, 212), in contrast to the Union soldiers in dark blue.

However chaotic this morning battle, certain features of it are unmistakable. "On a slope to the left" of Private Fleming's position "there was a long row of"

Union guns, in the rear of which "stood a house, calm and white, amid bursting shells. A congregation of horses, tied to a long railing, were tugging frenziedly at their bridles. Men were running hither and thither" (*RBC* 210). This is the Chancellor house, just where it would have appeared to a soldier withdrawn back from the woods where most of French's counterattack took place. That "congregation of horses" is there because the house was serving as headquarters for Hooker and for some of his corps commanders. The horses were the mounts for the staff officers and messengers attached to the various headquarters, the men "running hither and thither." It is not yet ten o'clock, because by that hour the Federals would have abandoned both the house and the fields immediately surrounding it. The Chancellor house was in its last moments of service as Union headquarters. Very soon the building itself was set afire by those rebel shells bursting around it, and it burned to the ground. The Union artillery arrayed before it was attempting to delay the final rebel assaults, which very shortly swept across all this area.

The rebels evidently pause to regroup (*RBC* 211). Stuart's right flank made contact at last with Anderson's left. Then, Stuart coming from the west along the Orange Plank Road and Anderson coming across it from the south, they coordinated their forces and began their final attack upon the Union army's positions around Chancellorsville.

The 304th New York is still in the same line of thin woods it had occupied during its first engagement this morning, and from which it had departed on its abortive counterattack. These final Confederate assaults now bear now upon the "emaciated regiment" (*RBC* 213; for a similar encounter, see *OR* 107). "A formidable line of the enemy came within dangerous range. They could be seen plainly—tall, gaunt men with excited faces running with long strides toward a wandering fence." Despite the "volley" the regiment directs toward them, they "gain the protection" of the fence "and from this position they began briskly to slice up the blue men" (*RBC* 214). However experienced the 304th New York may have become, they have not absorbed the critical lesson of the value of field fortifications; either that or they have not learned how to site whatever protection they did build for themselves.

As the rebels load and shoot, they shout taunts. The 304th New York, stung by previous accusations and uncertain about this challenge, fight in "a stressed silence." They suffer "extravagantly"—the more so since they are on the defensive, and on a battlefield dominated by the infantry rifle, they ought to enjoy the advantage. During this crisis their color-bearer is surely providing the regiment with a sturdy example, but probably too much so: being more the example of a suicidal rather than a practical bent. Private Fleming is still absorbed in an "un-speakable hatred" toward his brigade commander, "the man who had dubbed him wrongly" as "mud digger" and "mule driver." He is obsessed by this insult, rather than observing the details of the firefight around him; he is principally determined to enjoy a "final and absolute revenge" by getting himself killed. "The orderly sergeant [a term peculiar to the Union army of the Civil War era that means the 'first' or senior sergeant] of the youth's company" is "shot through the cheeks." Their own fire begins "to wane and drip" (RBC 215–16).[8]

Under such a galling and effective fire, the regiment's situation is unen-durable. They must either fall back from their position in the defensive line or charge the rebels and drive them off. Colonel MacChesnay and some of his of-ficers try, though with characteristic incompetence, to compel the men to charge: "running along back of the line" rather than leading, and revealing an acute dis-trust in their own men rather than offering inspiration as they shout orders (RBC 217). The regiment's predicament is obvious. The men, stung perhaps by previous criticism, respond.

They fix bayonets, which means they slide the shafts of these long steel blades over the muzzles of their rifles. This was an act hallowed by tradition as prepa-rational to an infantry attack and is, interestingly, something they did not do be-fore undertaking that earlier, abortive "diversion in favor of Whiterside." Did their officers forget to order them to do so then, but remember it on this occa-sion? Or does this action reflect the soldiers' own clear understanding of what they are now to undertake? In any case, the testimony from nineteenth-century military history is quite striking about the bayonet: it was almost worthless as a weapon, since firepower decided the overwhelming majority of infantry com-bats before rival infantrymen came to hand-to-hand fighting (and this will hap-pen shortly, in this instance), but the gleam of the fixed bayonets was of considerable psychological value.[9]

Given the regiment's debilitated condition, the attack is made with surpris-ing "force," perhaps generated by the soldiers' sense of their own fading energy. The attack is "a blind and despairing rush by the collection of men in dusty and tattered blue." Private Fleming leads it, keeping the "colors to the front" (RBC 218) and now believing himself "capable of profound sacrifices, a tremendous death"—an attitude toward death that still displays no comprehension of its true finality, nor of his own true mortality. "He had no time for dissections, but he

8. Katcher, Potomac, 5.
9. Nosworthy, Crucible, 594–608.

knew that he thought of the bullets only as things that could prevent him from reaching the place of his endeavor. There were subtle flashings of joy within him that thus should be his mind" (219). However immature and ignorant such an attitude may be, and however unnecessarily dangerous in many battlefield circumstances, it surely is the most appropriate psychological attitude for a regimental color-bearer leading a rush.

As this "rush" closes upon the enemy force (a single regiment, since only one rebel flag is mentioned), "many" of the Confederate soldiers fall back. And why not? The moment at hand can be identified with some precision from the historical record. It is now around ten o'clock, the rebels are everywhere successful, and the Army of the Potomac is falling back from the woods and fields around Chancellorsville crossroads. The rebel infantry on this front are exhausted, and the end of their endeavor is within sight. The defensive positions occupied by the 304th New York, which they brought under such effective assault, will soon be abandoned. The rebels have already done their job on this part of the field, by pressing their foes so relentlessly all morning. There is no need now for further sacrifice. Some of them are running, most of them are retiring while "stubbornly" still firing. One group of about ten of them, though, including their regimental color guard, the boldest spirited and most "grim and obdurate," remain "settled firmly down behind posts and rails" (RBC 220). They are doomed by their own superior courage and resolution.

Although the ferocity of the New Yorkers in the last few feet of their assault makes it seem as though they are about to "launch themselves as at the throats of those who stood resisting," this is only a metaphorical impression. They actually fight in a fashion characteristic of the Civil War and of warfare more generally in the age of the muzzle-loaded nineteenth-century infantry firearm. They come "to a sudden halt at close and disastrous range" and discharge their weapons in a "swift volley." "Four or five" of the rebels are hit (RBC 220–21), among them the color-bearer. Then another "four" are captured, along with their battle flag (223).

The soldiers of the 304th New York now react as they have always reacted when they achieved any success no matter how modest. "At the place of success there began more wild clamorings of cheers." More? the reference can only be to their earlier moments of jubilation, yesterday afternoon after their first engagement and then earlier this morning, and each of those moments was then undercut by the judgment of more experienced soldiers. "The men gesticulated and bellowed in an ecstacy. When they spoke it was as if they considered their listener to be a mile away. What hats and caps were left to them they often slung high in the air" (RBC 223). Private Wilson has personally captured the rebel flag: now he comes to Private Fleming "jubilant and glorified, holding his treasure with vanity" (225), and the two congratulate each other.

Are these celebrations and congratulations more justified than the earlier ones? At first glance, this would appear to be the case. The 304th New York Volunteer Infantry Regiment now occupies ground that once was occupied by enemy soldiers and from which the 304th forcibly ejected them, and occupying ground is the quintessential function of any infantry of any era. There are enemy casualties "stretched upon" that "ground" (RBC 221); there are enemy captives; there is, above all, that battle flag.

Further, a reader realizes that the novel is nearly over, and the last chapter discloses itself to be recitative and summary in tone. Details and literary tradition conspire: both "the youth" and this young regiment have finally triumphed, completing jointly that most familiar of all literary patterns wherein ultimate and mature success concludes a journey begun in immature illusion and pursued through chastening, disillusioning failure to a happy outcome. To read it thus is to accept these triumphant attitudes of Private Fleming and his regimental comrades at face value—and to reduce The Red Badge of Courage to but one more example of this most elemental plot.

Consider the moment again, however, this time in its military context. The regiment was compelled to undertake this charge—given the numbers and the distances, "rush" (RBC 218) is indeed a better word—in order to sustain their assigned position in the defensive deployment of their brigade. They now occupy no new ground, in fact, but merely enabled themselves to hold the ground they had occupied when the rebel assault first reached them. And one wonders why—given the advantages enjoyed by the defense in the age of the rifled musket, and given the opportunity they had this morning to construct some sort of field fortification for themselves—did they ever find themselves in such a tight situation to begin with?

But what, then, of the undeniable fact that Private Wilson has captured a rebel battle flag? For perhaps three centuries down to this hour, flags (and cannon) have been the most treasured and definitive military trophies. Both the completely disastrous Confederate General Hood and the ultimately victorious Union General Grant concurred exactly, that "Guns and colors are the only unerring indications of victory."[10] Baggage can be sacrificed by a rapidly advancing army as well as abandoned by a rapidly retreating one, and an army can acquire

---

10. Griffith, Battle Tactics, 143, 214.

enemy prisoners through simple desertion, but no infantry regiment in any army ever willingly abandons its battle flag. During the rush that captured this one, Private Fleming believed "Its possession would be high pride. It would express bloody minglings, near blows" (*RBC* 221). More obviously, capturing an enemy regiment's battle flag should "express" the superiority of your own soldierly skills and courage, which enabled you to overmaster an enemy regiment and seize the profoundest symbol of its own pride.

This particular flag was captured, however, because of the enemy's superior soldierly skills and courage. Their assault was delivered with "remarkable celerity," that is, with remarkable quickness, decisiveness, and a superior instinct for terrain. The "wandering line of fence" (*RBC* 214) behind which they took position offered them genuine protection—in contrast to the 304th New York Regiment's earlier blundering amid those "stolid trees"—and gave them a superior position from which to bring the 304th under fire. This fire so discomfited the New Yorkers that it compelled them to leave the (curiously limited) safety of their defensive position and drive the rebels away. The "obdurate" courage of the rebel color party, "sublime" and "daring" to the point of foolhardiness and beyond, kept their flag implanted in that fence line even after most of their regiment had withdrawn: some ten men "disdainfully" challenging hundreds (219–20).

Nor was this one incident at all unique at the battle of Chancellorsville. Throughout the day on this part of the battlefield, weary and outnumbered rebel infantry nonetheless continued to press attacks. These often collapsed in the face of counterattacks, and a number of rebel battle flags, carried forward beyond the ability of their formations to support them, were captured: see the report of the Sixty-fourth New York Volunteers, for instance (*OR* 79), or the summaries of battle flags lost in the reports of rebel divisions (*OR* 339, 368) and brigades (*OR* 394). As in the instance before us, those captures actually reflect the superior offensive spirit that everywhere animated the rebel army, which enabled it to achieve this astonishing victory.

Put simply, the 304th New York captured their trophy because the rebel soldiers' superior skill and courage brought it close enough for them to do so in the one "blind and despairing rush" (*RBC* 218) they did manage to muster. So there is the most radical discrepancy imaginable between what a captured flag should represent and what this one actually does represent. This captured flag—the symbol standing in Private Fleming's imagination "as a craved treasure of mythology" (221), and seemingly so self-evident in what it emblemizes—actually represents a truth so much the reverse as to render the flag altogether void of meaning, or totally ironic in meaning. This again is absolutely consistent with Crane's profoundest conceptions of the human predicament in the universe.

The narrative itself proceeds immediately to undercut the regiment's "wild clamorings of cheers" (*RBC* 223) and the two private soldiers' vainglorious mutual congratulations. Uppermost in the soldiers' comprehension is the fact that the battle on this front is "waning." But the reason for this is that their army is in retreat. "On the crest of a small hill was the thick gleam of many departing muskets," from which Private Wilson correctly divines that "we're goin' t' git along out of this an' back over th' river" (226–27). Part of the power of this novel lies in the discontinuity between large events and the small private affairs of the individuals upon which it concentrates. This discontinuity was stunningly unconventional when *The Red Badge of Courage* was first published, and it is still mesmerizing to a modern reader. But it should not register as sheer irrelevance; this discontinuity should not blind a reader to what can be realized by the juxtaposition of those large events with the beliefs and emotions of the common soldiers. Crane has put his fictional regiment's wild celebration and the "jubilant and glorified" (225) attitudes of his two private soldiers in the context of an absolute Union defeat. Their confident happiness and satisfaction could not be more inappropriate to the reality surrounding them, nor to what this reality implies is yet in store for them in their private experiences. They act as if the war, for them, is over. Given the direction in which they are soon to be marching, it is obvious that nothing could be further from the truth.

The 304th New York Volunteer Infantry Regiment march "back over the field across which they had run in a mad scamper" and continue their march "until [the regiment] had joined its fellows. The reformed brigade, in column, aimed through a wood at the road," up which they march "in a way parallel to the enemy's lines as these had been defined by the previous turmoil" (*RBC* 227). This road is (again) the one running north from the Chancellorsville crossroads past Chandler's farm and on to the fords on the Rappahannock—"the road" rather than "a road" because it is by now long familiar to the soldiers of the regiment. Their reserve position the "previous" afternoon had been along its verge, they had deployed down it this morning, and it did indeed lie parallel to the battlefront upon which they had been engaged in the "previous turmoil." Their deployment exactly accords with the historical record: after this Sunday morning's action, the regiments (*OR* 94, 95, 96, 97, etc.) and brigades (*OR* 107) of French's division retired to their former positions of the afternoon and evening before, and then they marched back northward up this road.

The 304th New York pass "within view of a stolid white house"—Chandler's farmhouse, referred to as the "white house" in the official reports (*OR* 108)—and see "in front of it groups of their comrades lying in wait behind a neat breastwork" (*RBC* 227). Federal formations retiring past the farm were still under artillery fire (*OR* 94, 107), and the house was at the center of the new defensive lines Hooker established for his retreating army. As Henderson's brigade marches past, "A row of guns were booming at a distant enemy. Shells thrown in reply were raising clouds of dust and splinters. Horsemen dashed along the line of intrenchments" (*RBC* 227).

"At this point of its march the division curved away from the field and went winding off in the direction of the river" (*RBC* 228), marching along Mineral Springs Run, a "little branch-hung roadway" (230), to take up new defensive positions in the reserve lines. The conclusion of the novel might suggest that Private Fleming and his fellows actually come within sight of the Rappahannock, a fine way of giving a sense of formal conclusion to a novel about a campaign that, for its central figures, opened when they first crossed it coming south. But Crane's conclusion is deliberately allusive rather than definitive: "Over the river a golden ray of sun came through the hosts of leaden rain clouds" (233). Since these soldiers would clearly know that the Rappahannock lay in a vast arc around them from the north to the east (they had contemplated this topography all winter and spring, and had traversed a large portion of it with their marching feet), they would not have had to see the Rappahannock to recognize that it lay beneath that ray of sun in the eastern sky.

That the sun is indeed in the eastern sky probably surprises most readers even on second, third, or fourth rereadings. The impression generated, and deliberately so, is of an epic struggle lasting for many hours. But the historical record is definitive: orders to retire from the positions around Chancellorsville crossroads and the Plank Road were issued about 10 A.M., and the Army of the Potomac had retired into its new defensive position by the noon hour (*OR* 63, 65, 93, etc.). Nowhere does *The Red Badge of Courage* ever contradict or ever fail to affirm this historical reality in any detail; which gives yet another instance of the distance between Private Fleming's vivid impression of his experience and the actual facts of the matter.

Having passed the "white house" and finding their division "winding off in the direction of the river," Private Fleming takes "a breath of new satisfaction" and says to Wilson, "'Well, it's all over.'" Wilson agrees (*RBC* 228). Yet, even in this instance, their perceptions are incorrect, because they will not actually be finished with this campaign until they recross the Rappahannock on the morning of May 6. Their division was shortly set to work contributing entrenchments to massive defensive lines that Hooker held for two more days, in the hopes that Lee would attack them. But just about the time the temptation to do so overcame the rebel commander's better sense, Hooker's own combativeness gave way completely, and ironically, for such an attack would surely have been disastrous for the Army of Northern Virginia, Hooker ordered his army to retreat across the Rappahannock.

So, in a sense, privates Fleming and Wilson are right after all. This campaign for them is over. But if this is indeed the case, it was the case only because of decisions over which they had absolutely no control, and about which they were totally ignorant, decisions taken by commanding officers so remote from their sphere as to be impersonal agents, yet who nonetheless determined these two New Yorkers' own private destinies; the perfect equivalent in the military sphere, in other words, for those great impersonal forces that drive the lives and control the destinies of the individual soul in Crane's Naturalistic universe.

Chapter 9

"He Was a Man"

"Manhood" in *The Red Badge of Courage*

Our central endeavor in this book has been to study *The Red Badge of Courage* in terms of the historical realities upon which it is based and in which it is set, to the end of seeing it as clearly, fully, and accurately as possible. The last chapter focused upon the events on the morning of the second day of the battle, both as they actually unfolded on the western face of the Union army's deployment in the Wilderness of Virginia on May 3, 1863, and as Crane depicted Private Henry Fleming and his fellow soldiers in the 304th New York experiencing them, showing how these soldiers judged themselves, how others judged them, and how a reader enabled by the historical record could perhaps achieve a sophisticated judgment upon these judgments. *The Red Badge of Courage* then brings us, finally, to two paragraphs showing Private Henry Fleming coming to a profound final judgment of himself.

> Yet gradually he mustered force to put the sin at a distance. And at last his eyes seemed to open to some new ways. He found that he could look back upon the brass and bombast of his earlier gospels and see them truly. He was gleeful when he discovered that he now despised them.
>
> With this conviction came a store of assurance. He felt a quiet manhood, nonassertive but of sturdy and strong blood. He knew that he would

> no more quail before his guides wherever they should point. He had been
> to touch the great death, and found that, after all, it was but the great
> death. He was a man. (*RBC* 231–32)

Yet again, then, and with the end of the book before us, we are confronted with
a compelling self-assessment; the frequency with which such self-assessments appear constitutes one of the most significant strategies in this "Episode of the
American Civil War." Crane's development of these moments is consistent. He
never contradicts or confirms them with overt, direct authorial intrusions. It is
up to the reader to judge whether such self-assessments are accurate. This is the
consistent end of Crane's method. But what follows such moments elsewhere in
the book—what Private Fleming then goes on to do or what superior officers or
experienced witnesses then say—should warn a reader against the error of unre-
flectively accepting such self-assessments as accurate, self-evident, or justified.

Nothing of a similarly "objective" or cautionary quality follows this last self-
assessment. Only three paragraphs remain in the book, and the first two of
them, still set firmly within Private Fleming's thoughts, respond to this critical
moment with lyrical, positive images. The book's final paragraph presents a flat
but seemingly confirmatory meteorological statement. Then the novel ends.
The penultimate paragraphs of any fictional narrative hold a powerful tyranny
over a reader's imagination. These two paragraphs surely seem typical of such
penultimate moments. They surely seem typically right: appropriate, and hence
persuasive. "He was a man": we are powerfully tempted to assign this critical
sentence to the "author," the "book," or the "truth." But there is no compelling
rhetorical reason not to locate it also—if indeed not entirely—in Private Fleming's own conscious perception of himself, at the moment.

The crucial passage consists of four monosyllabic words and is understated in
its simplicity. If we credit this thought to Private Fleming's own conscious perception, its rhetorical quality alone compellingly suggests that the matter of its
essential accuracy is as closed as the book is about to be. Do we not instinctively
assume that the use of understatement is, itself, a sign of maturity?

Because the category of "manhood" implies more at this moment than
virtues involved in infantry combat, the gender exclusivity of the language must
be acknowledged. I wonder, though, if the narrative pattern described in Chapter 6 does not predominately focus upon male characters, and if the conceptions about "reality" and "maturity" we will shortly be considering are not those
especially involved in masculine self-assessment. It is beyond both the scope of
this study and my own capacity to do more than suggest this, but it seems to me

that the great majority of narratives centering upon the disillusionment of a hero are centered upon male heroes. Were Shakespeare's great tragedy the tragedy of Cordelia rather than of Lear, its pattern and its climax and, above all, the psychological trajectory of its central character would be entirely different. Even when a work attends particularly to the disillusionment of a female character, as in the story of Hester Prynne in *The Scarlet Letter*, or of Jane Eyre, or of Dorothea Casaubon in *Middlemarch*, the lines of force do not lead to the moment of disillusionment, but from it and into the ways in which the heroine then deals with life. It is certainly the case that the single female figure of consequence in *The Red Badge of Courage* would find it no consolation at all, in her wise, mature, loving agony of concern for her son, to learn that Private Fleming is now considering himself to be a "man."

To return, though, to Private Fleming's situation at this moment, the stylistic simplicity in this moment of self-assessment does seem to reflect a new maturity. We surely ascribe this style—unconsciously, but correctly: "This is the way the youth himself is thinking, right now"—to the mind that is asserting herein that it is now mature. So the temptation to accept Private Fleming's self-assessment at face value is almost overwhelming. But is this the most insightful and informed response?

The 304th New York: "And They Were Men"

The crucial assertion "He was a man" in this final self-assessment exactly echoes the one, "And they were men," assumed by the 304th New York Volunteer Infantry Regiment at an earlier moment of self-assessment. It was powerfully tempting, then, to assign that assertion to "the author" or to "the truth of the book," and that assertion also consisted of four monosyllabic words. These two assertions of "manhood" are so exactly analogous that the novel teases the attentive reader to recall the first when finally confronting the second, and the first assertion was produced quite some time before the book was to be either literally or figuratively closed.

Having driven off the first rebel advance against them earlier on the morning of May 3, the 304th New York Volunteers had been grimly exultant: "'By thunder, I bet this army'll never see another new reg'ment like us!' 'You bet!'" (*RBC* 169–70). This regimental pride was swiftly undercut for privates Fleming and Wilson and for the reader when their new brigade commander assessed the 304th as "a lot 'a mule drivers" (175). But the two privates did not report this insult (178), so the regiment proceeded into their counterattack unaware of how their previous performance had been assessed professionally, and thus with their illusions intact. The regiment's blundering failure then ensued, but as they fell back from the woods, they vanquished a rebel attacking formation; and they reacted to this minor but unmistakable victory with "joy" and "a hoarse cheer of elation" (197).

The two paragraphs summarizing this portion of the 304th New York's experience that morning are strikingly similar to the two penultimate paragraphs summarizing the entirety of Private Fleming's experience throughout these two days of battle:

> It had begun to seem to them that events were trying to prove that they were impotent. These little battles had evidently endeavored to demonstrate that the men could not fight well. When on the verge of submission to these opinions, the small duel had showed them that the proportions were not impossible, and by it they had revenged themselves upon their misgivings and upon the foe.
>
> The impetus of enthusiasm was theirs again. They gazed about them with looks of uplifted pride, feeling new trust in the grim, always confident weapons in their hands. And they were men. (*RBC* 197–98)

These paragraphs also seemed somehow right, both in the way they addressed the large issues and in the way the rhetoric resolved itself into that short conclusion, so persuasive precisely because so short. Its brevity and understatement also seemed to replicate the quality of "manhood" being ascribed—or rather, self-ascribed—to the regiment: "Yes, that is the way," something urges the reader to acknowledge, "that is just the way 'men' conceive of themselves, once they have genuinely achieved manhood." So "manhood" in this context implies a particular quality, one that has emerged from a particular kind of experience, and we find ourselves caught up in quick agreement. We may or may not agree that "manhood" is indeed a genuine quality, or virtue, but if we disagree, our disagreement is—we viscerally feel, we instantly assume—not with these soldiers' assessment of themselves, but with "Crane," or "the book," or "the patriarchal culture that celebrates such barbarous, or gender-specific, or chauvinistic virtues."

What do these critical paragraphs exactly mean, then? Why have we agreed with them so readily, as summing up a profound truth as the novel understands the truth? What exactly is that truth?

The first critical point that these paragraphs claim is that the soldiers have been through a chastening ordeal, of a specific kind. This ordeal explicitly introduced them to—it was indeed even administered by—the essential hostility of the reality surrounding them: "events were trying to prove" their helplessness, "little battles had evidently endeavored" to demonstrate their weakness; they had been brought to "the verge of submission to these opinions" generated in them by the apparent malevolence of their circumambient world. This experience was emotionally painful; it created profound psychological "misgivings," of course; but it also led them (it is more than suggested) to come to know the painful truth that the universe is actively malevolent and that we will suffer in it. Assuming such a malevolent "reality" is the way we instantly make sense of the claim that, because they won a "small duel," they "had revenged themselves upon their misgivings [that is, they had proved themselves, in some critical way] and upon their foe."

After all, the passage is far too portentous to permit us to think that this "small duel" merely "showed" how the five hundred men of the 304th New York were capable of outshooting the two hundred men of the Twelfth North Carolina Infantry Regiment, say (*OR* 390). It never occurs to a reader to make only this of the experience. You cannot even assume that "the foe" means only the Army of Northern Virginia: to do so would also belie the rhetorical sweep of the paragraph and would be manifestly illogical, because their "small" victory over a rebel unit hardly meant they had "revenged themselves" upon R. E. Lee's entire army (which by the way was still relentlessly attacking their brigade's position).

We understand instead, and instinctively agree, that this "small" victory has much wider significance. We understand that the men demonstrated thereby their ability to face the harsh reality of their existence, to continue to function despite that harsh reality, and even to seize small victories from it. What finally is implicit immediately and persuasively, I think, for most readers is that this "small duel" was a combat against a manifestation of the malevolent structure of the world around them.

Thus, then, their "manhood": it is a "new trust" in their weapons and in their own abilities, and one that will "always" be resident in the weapons in their hands, a self-confidence upon which they know they can always rely, and a new "pride" that is thoroughly warranted, because both the self-confidence and the pride are based upon their sure knowledge that they have faced and overcome the ultimately "grim" truths of the world. "And they were men": at last capable, through the new knowledge garnered through this brutal experience, of facing and dealing with whatever else "reality" may yet have in store for them. And they are modest, to boot, because childish notions based upon delusions of human importance in a felicitous world are firmly and forever shorn from them.

Why does it seem so unnecessary, even so tedious, to offer this exegesis? Even the explanation of what it means to capture an enemy regiment's flag (see Chapter 8) probably seemed less unnecessary and redundant. Why, again, do these paragraphs seem so inherently and immediately right? Why have they brought us to agree so readily with this last assertion, believing without even a moment's reflection that it sums up a profound "truth as the novel understands the truth"?

Do these paragraphs seem so right because of literary tradition? Granted, the exegesis above is in one way a reprise of that most pervasive of all literary patterns (see Chapter 6), wherein a hero such as Achilles or Lear, or a group of people such as Christ's disciples or the "Seven Samurai," possessed by some sort of illusion, undergoes or undergo a shattering disillusionment, and thence, after suffering, achieves or achieve a final triumph that, because of the new wisdom generated thereby, is altogether different from that which was first sought. But while the issue of "manhood," of masculine maturity or of human maturity irrespective of gender, may indeed be a part of this final triumph, it is not necessarily central to the pervasive pattern: "manhood" or "maturity" seems not necessarily or even particularly relevant to the ultimate personal triumphs achieved by Sophocles' Oedipus, or Shakespeare's King Lear, or Duke Prospero in *The Tempest,* or Charlotte Brontë's Jane Eyre in the novel of that name, or Ahab in Melville's *Moby-Dick,* or Hemingway's Tenente Frederic Henry, or the Japanese warriors in "The Seven Samurai," or for that matter even Achilles himself—all of whom entered their shaping experiences with considerable and in some cases even wizened familiarity with the realities of their worlds. The Chorus at the end of "Oedipus the King" would not say "And he was a man," would it?

Do these paragraphs seem so right because of the more recent, post–World War I tradition about literature and war? At first glance, this exegesis may seem something of a reprise of that pattern of literature about war wherein individuals are transformed completely and forever by contact with the random, meaningless obscenity of modern combat (see Chapter 5). But the transformation undergone by the soldiers of the 304th New York is clearly a positive one, no matter how brutal the experience that engendered it or how "grim" the new attitudes characteristic of it. The rudimentary plot device shared by most all of such works is simply not present. There is no single devastating wound shared by the entire regiment, nor are there any wounds administered by soldiers on the same side. Had that red-bearded officer followed through with his cries and managed to have a volley pumped into his own retreating soldiers; failing that, had some of them followed through with their "dangerous" glares and murdered him during their panic-stricken moments in the woods; then we would have had a pivotal moment to place alongside the pivotal moments in *A Farewell to Arms* or *Paths of Glory*, or "Paths of Glory," or "Attack."[1] But no such thing actually occurred.

So we have to look elsewhere, away from these two possibilities, to answer our question. It is worth rephrasing the question here. Why does it make such instant sense, why does the meaning of it seem beyond doubt when, at the end of their abortive counterattack, it is written "And they were men"?

When the claim about the regiment's "manhood" was made, the novel was not yet nearing its end. So let us put it back in the context of the moment of its utterance, and remark what then followed (see Chapter 8). Whatever the phrase meant to the soldiers of the 304th New York Volunteer Infantry Regiment and whatever a reader may assume it means more generally, it meant nothing at all to the "gaunt and bronzed" soldiers of the "veteran" regiments who witnessed the New Yorkers' performance and who mocked them in terms insisting upon their callowness: "Was it warm out there, sonny?" (*RBC* 200). The claim meant nothing to their new color-bearer, perhaps the best individual private soldier in their ranks, who, given the chance to reflect, looked at his fellows with veiled "disdain." And the claim obviously would mean less than nothing, would be utterly ridiculous, to the commander of their brigade (no "Grandpa" Henderson he) who upbraided them publicly in terms that remind a reader—as "mule drivers" now became "mud diggers" in his stuttering rage—of his previous estimation of them. Nor did Colonel MacChesnay think to advance this claim on their behalf—"Well at least, Sir, they are now men."

Crucial to this claim "And they were men"—again, it seems rather silly to spell this out—is the understanding that they were now at last capable of effectively dealing with "reality" no matter how it would challenge them. The claim implies that they now know the true nature of "reality," and the truth of their own abilities. But, thinking again about the analysis of their final actions on May 3, 1863, is this the case?

The immediate challenge that "reality" next presented them this morning was one they had faced twice before, viz. a rebel infantry attack of regimental size or less. Their response seems in fact no different—in particular, no more capable—than yesterday afternoon, before their "transformation" into "manhood."

1. Humphrey Cobb, *Paths of Glory*; "Attack" (1956).

At the beginning of this final action, "There had been no order given; the men, upon recognizing the menace, had immediately let drive their flock of bullets without waiting for word of command" (*RBC* 214). This may suggest they have gained a new sense of battlefield reality. But remember that yesterday afternoon Private Fleming himself "got the one glance at the foe-swarming field" and blazed away "before he was ready to begin" and obviously before he was ordered to open fire, and remember too that the regiment joined him instantly (see Chapter 3). The most salient "fact" about their defensive fire then was their lack of poise and a consequent failure to do much damage to the rebels. Their quick response on this third occasion may reveal some new instinct for battle, but the result was the same and "their flock of bullets" did not at all arrest the rebel rush. Yesterday afternoon they had suffered casualties all out of proportion to their situation, given all the advantages the rifled musket should have bestowed upon them as infantrymen in a defensive posture. They had failed then to provide themselves with effective field fortifications (despite ample opportunity to do so), or to discipline themselves to take advantage of such. This morning, they likewise "bled extravagantly" (*RBC* 216), and were so badly positioned or so ineptly entrenched that they found themselves being "sliced up" by rebel infantrymen who had achieved "the protection of the wandering line of fence"—an obvious feature of the terrain immediately before them that they still had not had the wisdom to recognize as a menace to their own line.

Judging from the officers' conduct on this occasion, nothing in the phrase "and they were men" would seem to apply quite yet to the regimental officers of the 304th New York. There was nothing newly competent or confident in the officers' conduct, either, no matter their experience during the regiment's counterattack. They did order their men to erase the rebels' superior position with a counterattack, but they seemed just as "resentful" and mistrustful of their men as they had been yesterday. Colonel MacChesnay was still leading from the rear (*RBC* 217).

Private Fleming's own response to this predicament may have been his alone, but its placement suggests that it can to some degree be credited to his fellow soldiers. "He saw that to be firm soldiers they must go forward. It would be death to stay in the present place, and with all the circumstances to go backward would be to exalt too many others" (*RBC* 217). Clearly he had in mind the stinging criticisms just visited upon the regiment. But is such motivation a part of what it means to be a "man"? To allow the criticism of others—even in cases where you do not believe it to be true—to direct your own actions even to your own death? Here, as in much else, *A Farewell to Arms* provides an interesting counterpoint: after he has deserted from the Italian army, Frederic Henry, in civilian clothes, is scorned by some aviators: "They avoided looking at me and were very scornful of a civilian my age. I did not feel insulted. In the old days I would have insulted them and picked a fight" (*FTA* 243).

Private Fleming "expected that his companions, weary and stiffened, would have to be driven to this assault, but as he turned toward them he perceived with a certain surprise that they were giving quick and unqualified expressions of assent" (*RBC* 217). Is this response indicative of some new maturity? Perhaps. But in essence they were "assenting" to following the orders they had been given. The further description of their motivation suggests not maturity of some toughened kind but an altogether different psychological state. Their "rush" was explicitly "blind and despairing" at the outset, though as they rush forward, they "were again grown suddenly wild with an enthusiasm of unselfishness." This last, the "unselfishness" bit, has a noble sound, but one that seems rather dissonant with the tone of the assertion ("And they were men") with which we are wrestling. In any case, Crane immediately goes on to stress not the nobility of their effort here, but the frenzy; and to suggest, startlingly, that the main source of their wild emotion, now that they were bodily committed to the attack, might lie in those "vanities" we (and surely they) assumed they had put well behind them in the "grim" process of becoming "men": "they were in a state of frenzy, perhaps because of forgotten vanities, and it made an exhibition of sublime recklessness" (*RBC* 218–19). Blindness, despair, recklessness, frenzy based upon childish vanities—are these constituent, central elements in the state of being "men"? In any case, all these psychological states were surely true of them in their first encounter with the rebels the previous afternoon.

Their responses to their "successes" yesterday and today are similar. Yesterday, when the first rebel probe was blunted, Private Fleming had gone "into an ecstacy of self-satisfaction," and "There were some handshakings and deep speeches with men whose features were familiar, but with whom the youth now felt the bonds of tied hearts" (*RBC* 64–65). Today, after they had successfully driven away this rebel threat, "there began more wild clamorings of cheers. The men gesticulated and bellowed in an ecstasy. When they spoke it was as if they considered their listener to be a mile away." Privates Fleming and Wilson—the latter "jubilant and glorified"—"sat side by side and congratulated each other" (*RBC* 223–25). With their captured rebel soldiers and their captured rebel flag they were (understandably) far more exhilarated this morning. But there is no hint of any more wise, experienced, or chastened awareness in any of this second celebration; the men seem as innocently joyful now as they were then.

It is striking that even their conversation after their "conversion" into "manhood" is identical to their conversation before. As the campaign opened for them, they had argued about whether the Army of the Potomac was being committed to a turning movement against the rebels (*RBC* 2). In the battle line they had discussed officers (the lamentable Captain Carrott, at least) knowledgeably enough and talked about the accident that befell Bill Smithers when his hand was crushed by a fellow soldier (*RBC* 47–48). This is exactly the substance of their conversation as they march away from the field at the end:

> "Oh, hush, with your comin' in behint 'em. I've seen all 'a that I wanta. Don't tell me about comin' in behint—"
>
> "Bill Smithers, he ses he'd rather been in ten hundred battles than been in that heluva hospital. He ses they got shootin' in th' nighttime, an' shells dropped plum among 'em in th' hospital. He ses sech hollerin' he never see."
>
> "Hasbrouck? He's th' best off'cer in this here reg'ment. He's a whale."
>
> "Didn't I tell yeh we'd come aroun' in behint 'em? Didn't I tell yeh so? We—"
>
> "Oh, shet yeh mouth!" (*RBC* 231)

Is this being too critical? After all, the sequence of events seems so clear: they failed, yet established in the process their ability to face "reality"; given a second chance, they succeeded handsomely, capturing a rebel flag in the process. What could be clearer confirmation that they have indeed undergone a significant transformation, one that has rendered them "men"? But refer back to a close consideration of this sequence (see Chapter 8), which reveals that it has no inherent significance at all. Given a chance to achieve something of real tactical importance on this narrow part of the front, they failed, through a lack of leadership, battlefield discipline, experience, and courage. Thereafter the rebels, directed by superior leadership, battlefield discipline, and experience, confronted them with the necessity to secure their own defensive position, at which they succeeded with that "rush"—a success modest enough in itself, and which manifestly had no significance at all, even to this even narrower part of the front. No sooner had they driven the rebels off than they abandoned the position themselves. In this latter process, through an overabundance of courage, the rebels virtually gave them a handful of prisoners and a regimental flag. The sequence itself is ludicrous enough. To find therein a significant confirmation of some quality about the soldiers of the 304th New York Infantry Regiment clearly is an act not of clarification or of analysis, but of imposition.

This is an act most readers automatically make, and this is the key to the nested sequence of questions posed above. This is the human (perhaps particularly the masculine) response to the blank, meaningless chaos of our condition: to impose an imaginary and preconceived order upon it. And when such an imaginary and preconceived order is widely shared within a culture, it is known as a "myth."

Return again to the claim that "they were men," and to its precipitating moment. Their new brigade commander characterized their abortive counterattack as, in general, "an awful mess," which is fair enough. In both military and experiential terms, it was an instance of sheer chaos. Their battle line instantly lost cohesion; the only thing "coherent" about their attack was the "trail of bodies" it left behind; time and distance lost definition, and the landscape seemed "new and unknown"; bewildered emotional states succeeded each other in stupefying sequence, "mad enthusiasm" becoming "dazed and stupid" paralysis, prideful competence becoming abject despair; their flag appeared to be both "hating and loving"; and a dead man "obstinately" fought in "ludicrous and awful ways" for that flag's possession. Then, right at the apex of utter catastrophe, when the soldiers were "panic stricken" and "beset" with "hysterical fear and dismay," they were presented with a neat little victory.

What the 304th New York actually experienced was an extraordinarily heightened instance of the raw, meaningless chaos that, Crane believes, is the ultimate truth of our predicament in the universe. But what they make of the experience is something quite other. They "interpret" it as an example of perhaps the most widely shared and widely held myth of their (and our) culture. Look again at their response: "It had begun to seem to them that events were trying to prove that they were impotent. These little battles had evidently endeavored to demonstrate that the men could not fight well. When on the verge of submission to these opinions, the small duel had showed them that the proportions were not impossible, and by it they had revenged themselves upon their misgivings and upon the foe" (*RBC* 197). They are imposing intentionality, consciousness, perhaps even "opinion," upon what is, in fact, raw chaos. They assume that this intentionality, this consciousness, is malevolent, but compared to the truth of the matter (that we are utterly alone in a flatly indifferent, chaotic universe), there is considerable comfort in a belief that the universe is guided by a principle of active, conscious malevolence.

What such a belief does is to see the world as a kind of cosmic boot camp, wherein benign illusions will inevitably be stripped away by experience, wherein experience itself will inevitably (the adverb is critical) be chastening. Those who endure and survive such experience will be "men," demonstrably proof against the capacity of "reality" to surprise them any more. Their newfound knowledge of the malevolence of the world may be a harsh knowledge, but it is indeed knowledge, and not everyone has it. There are always plenty of "Fresh fish," the "new" boys (*RBC* 16–17) who have not yet learned the truth of reality. Indeed, there are people who never do see the "truth." Such facts actually make it a very pleasant thing, to be burdened with this awful knowledge.

Once again, *A Farewell to Arms* is immediately apposite. Frederic Henry and his friend Rinaldi and his lover Catherine Barkley manifestly "know"—in dramatic contrast to Helen Ferguson, who believes in old verities, and Gino, who is a patriot, and Ettore Moretti, who is "a legitimate hero who bore[s] everyone he [meets]" (*FTA* 124). No matter how ghastly this knowledge, in that novel it surely does enable its holders to consider themselves a veritable aristocracy. They speak to each other with the clipped language of members of an elite club, they are smugly superior to the kinds of mores and enthusiasms that dominate nonmembers, they enjoy lavish personalized service from the lower orders—headwaiters, bartenders, paper-cutters—who recognize their superiority. And if you are interested in further apposite examples, remember Lemuel Gulliver. He manages to readjust his perspective after his first and second voyages, but after his fourth voyage—where he alone among the Yahoos was privileged to benefit from the company of the Houyhnhnms and hence was endowed with a special knowledge that made him superior to all the rest of Yahoo-kind, which is to say, all the rest of humanity—he never recovers: "My horses understand me tolerably well; I converse with them at least four hours every day."[2] To be the one who "knows" the truth, or to be among the select few who "know" the truth—the appeal to one's pride is overwhelming. Yet the very fact that the knowledge is so grim can obscure the truth of that appeal from the possessor. He (or she) may become a monster of vanity while remaining blessedly unaware of the fact. So thus: "And they were men" (*RBC* 198).

The reason my exegesis about this claim probably seemed so unnecessary, so self-evident and redundant, is probably because this myth—that "reality" is malevolent and will inevitably strip away benign illusions through chastening experience, and that the condition of "manhood" awaits the survivors at the end of this process—is so prevalent in the modern world. To put it simply, the myth assumes that the devil exists, but God does not. It is not even Gnostic,

---

2. Jonathan Swift, "A Voyage to the Houyhnhnms," chapter 11, in Swift, *Gulliver's Travels and Other Writings.*

this myth. It is not even new: it is as old as human despair, and Nathaniel Hawthorne's "Young Goodman Brown" is a wonderfully sardonic treatment of it.[3] But the prevalence of the myth (assisted hugely by folding any sense of an afterlife into those illusions that will inevitably be stripped from us by "experience"), and the striking way that this prevalence is so treasured by the modern sophisticated imagination—these seem to me to be the "modern" ramifications of it.

Under its sway, we just assume, we take for granted, that "experience" will sooner or later savage us and strip away our illusions, that this is what it means to "face reality." Hence the happy cynicism so prevalent among American undergraduates, especially undergraduate males. To assume this stance in advance of experience—American undergraduates currently being among the most generously and fortuitously endowed people in the history of the world—is, in a way, a sort of inoculation, and in another way a sort of one-upmanship. Hence the reiterated claim, to be found in most forms of art that seek wide public audience (popular fiction, film, television), that "everybody knows that everything is full of —, that everything is all —— —." And hence, too, the thematic justification for the ritualistic use of such debased, obscene language in such works currently. Such language suggests that the user thereof is one who "knows."

According to Crane's fiction all this is, finally, a myth. A belief about the "universe" that is entirely unsupported by any evidence is assumed to be an immutable and unchallengeable fact. The clearest single point to emerge from Crane's mature fiction is that the "universe" is not hostile—not "cruel," which he puts first in his clearest statement of its reality, "nor beneficent, nor treacherous, nor wise"—but that it is "indifferent, flatly indifferent."[4]

The mythic belief that the universe is malevolent validates certain egocentric attitudes and stances, such as cynicism, and offers us certain genuine comforts: among them, that some category called "manhood" exists, which, once achieved, renders a person invulnerable to further surprise, and confident, competent, and capable to face whatever life may hold. But the history of the 304th New York Infantry Regiment on the morning of May 3, 1863, shows that this, in itself, is an illusion. The history of the 304th New York shows that circumambient reality is utterly chaotic and unpredictable, and that the human mind, a creature of this reality, is likewise chaotic and unpredictable, an organ endlessly capable of reverting back to "forgotten vanities" whatever intervening experience

3. Nathaniel Hawthorne, "Young Goodman Brown," in *Young Goodman Brown and Other Tales*.
4. Stephen Crane, "The Open Boat," in *The Red Badge of Courage and Other Writings*, 309.

may seem to teach or whatever states of supposed maturity may seemingly have been achieved.

This is a myth especially for survivors, it should be noted; it tends to put them in a category superior to those who do not survive. It tends, further, to imply that having survived is somehow a guarantor of further survival. It ignores the raw fact that a chaotic universe distributes death chaotically. The world's great literature has always insisted upon this fact, needless to say: "How dies the wise man? As the fool" (Ecclesiastes 2:16). It rains upon the just and the unjust alike. Death claims Cordelia as well as her two sisters; the sea swallows the hero Ahab and the coward Pip. It follows that devout cynicism is surely no more "effective" or "protective" than devout belief, in facing the ultimate fact of our morality. It follows that the fact that the soldiers of the 304th New York consider themselves to be "men" after their failed counterattack will be of no consequence whatever in the distribution of death along their battle line in any future fighting. Rather than the superior knowledge of themselves and the world that is implicit in this claim, the soldiers of the 304th would have been far better served, in the fighting immediately before them and the campaigns yet to come, had their experience led them instead to some mundane and specific perceptions about the Civil War battlefield: about the way to secure effective field fortifications for themselves, and about the value of disciplined, coolly aimed rifle fire that could take advantage of the new military technology they have in their hands.

"And they were men." By thus ending a two-chapter sequence in which the 304th New York has undergone a brutalizing experience and then enjoyed a modest success, Crane is taking a considerable risk; especially when he then goes on, in an ensuing three-chapter sequence, to "reward" the regiment with that rebel battle flag. The risk is that his readers themselves will see in this sequence just another confirmation of the widespread myth about the universe and human (or at least masculine) experience in it. The reason he takes this risk is that his subject is not, after all, how the experience of combat affects those who undergo it but, rather, how the human mind reacts to the world in which it finds itself. To make his point in a more facile way, to check this perception about "manhood" with an immediate and overt authorial confirmation would not serve his final end, for it would spare the reader the experience of discovering just how much that myth does indeed shape his or her own instinctive, unreflective, immutable, immediate conception of circumambient reality.

My assumption is that most readers' immediate response to this assertion about the regiment's new "manhood" is to agree, simply and quickly (not even pausing to consider its implications), and to move on: making themselves thereby the freshest possible examples of Crane's point. Confronted by a vicarious experience that is utterly chaotic in nature, readers nonetheless instantly seize upon and agree with this imposed mythic interpretation. Crane himself assumed that this would happen, and that reflective readers, pondering the actual details of these chapters more thoughtfully after having themselves submitted momentarily to the myth, would thereby come to understand the subtle, omnipresent, and compelling nature of this human instinct to make over our world into a more comfortable, because a more comprehensible, place, even at the price of assuming that we are surrounded by a consciously malevolent reality.

But the risk would probably not have appeared all that considerable to Crane, at the hour of his writing his novel. He instantly follows this claim with contradictory challenges from veteran soldiers, from his own central figure, and from an experienced superior officer. He displays the 304th New York's next engagement, where they revert to the incompetence they displayed the previous day, and thereafter revert to old "vanities" as they seek to recover the tactical integrity of their position. He displays all their efforts (and all their celebrations) as rendered irrelevant when they are almost immediately withdrawn from the field. He counts upon a reader's general awareness of the actualities of Civil War combat to assess the progress of the regiment's performance and offers the rebels' successes in constant counterpoint to their blunderings. He must have assumed that, however much the broad outlines of his plot would encourage his readers to see this "Episode" (initially) as just another example of a group of raw soldiers achieving "manhood" through toughening "experience," the constant play of such details would compel intelligent readers to ponder the sequence with some attention and finally to come to the conclusion that whatever the readers' first assumptions, this myth is (in this instance at least) ridiculous, given the amassed and amassing contradictions and complexities of the situation. What Crane might not have foreseen is the submerging of his audience's knowledge of the realities of Civil War combat in the gigantic "testimony" of fiction about subsequent wars: how the ridiculous therein becomes the norm, and proof in itself of the malevolence of general reality.

Nothing in *The Red Badge of Courage* is more percipient or more forward-looking than Crane's awareness that this sense of the malevolence of reality would come to dominate the human mind as it sought to make sense of the world in the very late nineteenth and twentieth centuries. I do not have the expertise, resources, time, or space to consider why this has been so, other than to note the obvious fact that religious beliefs gave way during the nineteenth century in much of the Western world—and in particular, in those parts of the world in which Crane would have found his audience—and that "the abdication of belief," as Emily Dickinson put it, not only makes "The behavior small" but surely leads to a profound—even if (especially if) illogical—sense that something horrible has become regnant in the universe. In the Western world, a belief in God came to be replaced by a powerful belief in human existentialist progress, which, when the fruit of that progress proved rancid, generated in its own turn the ominous figure of Kurtz in Joseph Conrad's *Heart of Darkness*. Kurtz can at least say "The horror! The horror!" while Marlow finds himself—as Crane believed that a genuinely insightful hero in the "new ignorance of the grave-edge" would indeed find himself—"with nothing to say" as a summary of our human predicament.[5] Whatever the reason, echoes of this myth, that "manhood" involves a brutalizing and transforming experience with the malevolence of the universe, can be found in writers of the time as distinct as Twain and Kipling, and this myth comes into its post-World War I own with Fitzgerald and Hemingway.

A close reading of *The Red Badge of Courage* reveals that there is a quality within this myth that is profoundly dehumanizing. Not to look too closely, to discipline oneself not to look too closely, at the horror that this myth posits as lying at the center of human existence is one thing. Both Frederic Henry in *A Farewell to Arms* and Nick Carraway in *The Great Gatsby* have absorbed this well. But there is also a tendency for the myth's adherents to look upon those who are not of this particular "elect"—to look upon those who are not burdened with this knowledge and who do not belong among the people who "know"—with indifference, if not contempt. This is always the problem with any "elect," Calvinist, Communist, or any other individual or group that believes it enjoys a particular status or a particular knowledge making it superior to other people. Kurtz's notorious last injunction to "exterminate all the brutes" is finally not so different in kind from Frederic Henry's gust of contempt for Helen Ferguson; or from Nick Carraway's admiration for Jay Gatsby, which forgives—thanks to Gatsby's "dream" and his final awakening therefrom—the brutal fact that Gatsby established himself in business "'gonnegion'" with Wolfsheim by employing on the whilom home front his experience as a machine-gun officer in World War I.[6] This dehumanizing quality, this sense of a great personal superiority, in these works becomes surprisingly explicit. It is even more so in the popular fic-

---

5. Emily Dickinson, "Those—dying, then," in Emily Dickinson, *The Complete Poems of Emily Dickinson*; Joseph Conrad, *Heart of Darkness*, 71–72; Crane, "The Open Boat," *Other Writings*, 309.
    6. Conrad, *Heart of Darkness*, 51; Fitzgerald, *Great Gatsby*, 70, 179.

tions of our current time: think not only of the treatment of all those by-the-book police captains in the thousands of detective films and television shows of today, but also the treatment of those lesser beings who do not share the central figures' ethos in the television series "M*A*S*H."

In *The Red Badge of Courage* this dehumanizing quality lies not so much in the attitudes toward the living that the myth generates in its hero as in his attitudes toward the wounded and the dead. If the assumption is that ultimate knowledge is scarifying and is produced by scarifying experience, the death of others can be considered as just a part of one's own education. The pain that is or should be felt in witnessing their suffering can be felt or registered as the price one pays for one's toughening experience in the world, and thus the raw facts of their individual suffering and extinction can be ignored. Private Fleming presented a splendid example of this tendency as he witnessed the death of his hut-mate and "friend," Private Conklin. Recall that his first response was to shake his fist "toward the battlefield" and say "Hell—" (*RBC* 99). This might possibly be an expression of regret for the extraordinary suffering and final death of a friend, but more likely it is his own reaction to a particularly harsh lesson placed before him. Most likely it is a purely histrionic gesture akin to a student's groan when the subject of the final examination is announced. Within a few short minutes, as the tattered soldier from the Third Corps was entering his own death agonies, Jim Conklin was already reduced in Private Fleming's mind to "that other one," just another "part player" (104) in the process whereby Private Henry Fleming was destined to become a "man."

We know nothing equivalent about how the minds of other soldiers in the regiment worked, as they noticed or ignored their unfortunate fellow soldiers being transformed from "men" into "bundles of blue" (*RBC* 216). From the moment the 304th New York Volunteers were committed to their final "rush" through to its successful completion and thence on to the end of the novel, not much attention is given any additional casualties the regiment must have taken when they exposed themselves fully to the rebel rifle fire (218). But then, this portion of the novel is attributed almost completely to Private Fleming's mind. With the prestige of his regiment uppermost in his mind, and the "craved treasure" (221) of that rebel battle flag before him as a target and then as a possession, at this point in the novel we are hardly surprised at Private Fleming's utter lack of interest in his slain or wounded comrades.

Considering their corporate claim that they were "men" and in light of the casualties suffered by the 304th New York Infantry down to that moment, we have to recognize that their claim is based upon a colossal self-absorption. Do they really mean that the captain of Private Fleming's company was not a man because he was killed at the outset, before he could partake of this valuably chastening experience? What of Private Conklin, with his unspeakable agonies of the previous afternoon? Did he die not yet a man? What of Private Jimmie Rogers, "shot through the body" during their first exchange this morning? He did not experience their abortive counterattack either—is he likewise not yet a man, for all the suffering his (doubtless mortal) wound causes to him in his single human (and mortal) existence? Again, this is a myth that particularly celebrates survivors. If these New Yorkers' corporate claim about themselves is correct, the logic that must follow concerning all these casualties is inescapable: they were all less than "men" because they did not survive until the end of the lesson. And as with Private Fleming, so with the 304th New York: does their corporate happy discovery of their own manhood mean that those dead and wounded—including those "Wounded men" they "left crying" behind them in the fire-stung wilderness during their panicked retreat—are finally to be registered as instances, objects, integers essential to the education of the survivors?

Private Henry Fleming: "He Was a Man"

Needless to say, it seems to me that this consideration of the implications of the regiment's belief that "they were men" bears directly upon Private Fleming's ultimate belief that "He was a man." If it seems unwise to accept the former without question, why would it be wise to so accept the latter? The risk Crane runs (see the beginning of this chapter)—that this final claim will nonetheless be taken at face value—is immeasurably greater than the risk he ran in presenting, unchallenged by any authorial comment, the regiment's own assertion of their manhood. So one of the ways Crane cautions a reader against understanding this to be the final and only "truth" of his novel is to present the regiment's claim first and to proceed immediately to assert a sequence of challenges to it; then to present Fleming's claim in exactly the same language and exactly the same rhetorical posture (at the end of a very portentous-seeming paragraph).

There is a second way the reader has been warned—and repeatedly. This claim that Private Fleming "was a man" is the last in a sequence of similar self-assertions, at least three of which a reader has been compelled to decide were untrue. Perhaps the earliest: "On the way to Washington his spirit had soared. The regiment was fed and caressed at station after station until the youth had believed that he must be a hero" (*RBC* 10). Literary tradition itself, indeed the entire narrative tradition of Western culture, precludes us from accepting this moment at face value (see Chapter 6). But since we are considering the novel here in light of a current mythology that informs no small part of our current literature and our current narrative tradition, we can here add yet another reason this first moment all but defies us to believe in its validity. The very use of the word "hero" renders it invalid. Modern heroes, given (or "cursed with") the knowledge of the malevolence of the circumambient world, consciously avoid using the word to refer to themselves, because to use it suggests a naivete about reality. There are surely figures in Western culture to whom the nonliterary version of the term has been applied fully and without irony. Such are the historic heroes in the pantheons of nations, who have generally died in inspirationally heroic ways, such as Nathan Hale or Horatio Nelson, or the fictional heroes enshrined in the heroic songs and tales of Western culture, such as Galahad or Roland or William Tell. Such are more modern heroes who have been elevated to that status because of nobility or intrepidity, such as the arctic explorer Robert Scott who sacrificed himself to try to spare his companions, or Charles Lindbergh or Amelia Earhart. The category is amorphous, but these are all figures whose heroism is regularly introduced into the instruction of a nation's children, and who seem to us to have been innocent about the horrific truth of human existence. These were heroes who permitted others to celebrate their victories over mundane foes such as enemy warriors, the weather at the polar extremities of the globe, the reaches of the North Atlantic while flying solo across it in a small monoplane, or who occasioned others to celebrate their heroic deaths, but who never came face-to-face with what is truly horrific according to the dominant mythology of our day; who never came face-to-face with the true malevolence of the universe. There may indeed be a prudential quality in consciously refusing the term "hero." Given a consciously malevolent universe, the first people it would seek to destroy would be those who thrust themselves forward as "heroes," of the very race that is its primary prey. (Think here of the inevitable quick doom that befalls any character in a popular film who proclaims "the bullet with my number on it hasn't been made yet," or the like.)

See again *A Farewell to Arms* for a classic treatment of such a hero according to the current mythology. Tenente Ettore Moretti has in fact been wounded three times, and one wound, suffered in close combat, refuses to heal. His enthusiastic belief in old military verities—in the significance of wound stripes, medals, and rank, in the respect due to officers of field grade, and in the shibboleths important to soldiers in the line—culminates in the application of the word "hero" to him, which accolade he seems to accept, and happily. This warrants contemptuous dismissal of him by those (including Tenente Frederic Henry, wounded by a trench mortar while eating pasta and cheese) who truly "know." Moretti is the "legitimate hero who bored everyone he met," and so the wound in his foot that steadily extrudes rotten bone is a source of aesthetic revulsion rather than common compassion (FTA 124). This is not, though, to suggest that the central figure in the novel is an "anti-hero," quite the opposite. Frederic Henry is obviously to be admired throughout the course of the novel, most especially for his escape from a Carabiniere firing squad on the banks of the Tagliamento, for declaring his own "separate peace" when he deserts from the Italian army, and for his feat in small-boat navigation when he rows his pregnant mistress from Stresa up Lake Garda to the safety of neutral Switzerland during a late autumn night. Above all, he is to be admired for knowing the malevolent truth about the universe—"But they killed you in the end. You could count on that. Stay around and they would kill you" (FTA 327)—and yet still knowing how to live, for instance, how to order beer ("A light demi") in a café in Lausanne while his mistress is enduring protracted labor in the hospital. Frederic Henry is indeed a hero because he will not be called one. Real heroes do not call themselves heroes. It is a matter of style ("they're much quieter," says Catherine) and terminology (FTA 124).

And so it is with readers following the experience of Private Henry Fleming of the 304th New York Volunteer Infantry Regiment. We, too, await the moment when Fleming will finally adopt the style and terminology our myth teaches us is "true." When Tenente Ettore Moretti touches his officer's collar badges at the mention of his getting killed, it seems to us a groundless and ludicrous gesture, because we do not share the myth that produces it. But when we instantly and unquestioningly accept Private Fleming's claim that "he is a man," is it not because we do unquestioningly accept the myth, without even recognizing it is a myth (but then, this is Crane's whole point), in which such terminology and, above all, such understatement validate the true heroism of the person (the man?) who utters it?

Private Fleming's next happy understanding of his own condition came immediately after the regiment's initiation into combat, after they had resisted that initial rebel probe: "He perceived that the man who had fought thus [he himself] was magnificent. He felt that he was a fine fellow. He saw himself even with those ideals which he had considered as far beyond him" (RBC 64). This claim is instantly undone by the behavior that almost immediately followed it, when he fled "like a proverbial chicken" from the rebels' second probe. But still, such rhetoric strikes a reader as inappropriate: true heroes eschew applying words to themselves such as "magnificent" for the same reasons they eschew the word "hero"; even "fine fellow" seems a little arcane ("fine boy" would pass Cath-erine Barkley's muster, though). True heroes know that in a malevolent universe "ideals" are ridiculous. There may be things worth cherishing—love, friendship, the taste of red wine with cheese and apples even during a major military disas-ter—but the term "ideals" implies that there is some system of nonmaterialistic value that the cosmos will validate; a ludicrous notion in a world where in fact "they will kill you in the end."

After he had been safely returned (though not through his own exertions) to his regiment, Private Fleming began to reassemble his vanity and self-esteem and in the process fumbled his way into the first explicit use of the formula that confronts us so imperiously at the end: "His self-pride was now entirely re-stored. In the shade of its flourishing growth he stood with braced and self-confident legs, and since nothing could now be discovered he did not shrink from an encounter with the eyes of judges, and allowed no thoughts of his own to keep him from an attitude of manfulness. He had performed his mistakes in the dark, so he was still a man" (*RBC* 149–50). A reader surely shrinks from ac-cepting this claim at face value. Private Fleming has (as yet) demonstrated no ca-pacity for facing a renewal of combat, so in terms of the narrative itself the confidence this reveals is ludicrous enough. But worse: the myth of manhood achieved through illusion-shattering experience is a myth that insists upon a process of internal, interior growth. Fleming's claim implicitly refutes this myth: it obviously argues that being a "man" has to do completely with one's standing in the "eyes of judges" in the surrounding world. It cannot be, we think, that the novel or the author could possibly be affirming Private Fleming in this ludi-crous belief that he is still "a man" because his mistakes were not observed.

But in dumbfounding fact, this positive self-assessment may actually be more plausible than the one Private Fleming will reach at the end of the novel. The issue of whether Private Fleming has finally developed in some crucially "mature" way at the end of the battle of Chancellorsville is very much open to doubt, but that he does still enjoy the respect of his fellows at this moment early on the morn-ing of May 3, 1863, is obviously true. In their eyes, sure enough, "he was a man," in the sense that he was not categorized in any other way—as a coward or a "chicken" or a "boy" or a "mother's boy" or someone who deserves to be called "sonny" (*RBC* 200). That this is true is of crucial importance in this volatile mixture of self-delusion and self-confidence that motivates him to perform with unques-tionable heroism—combat-influencing, unit-leading, reputation-winning hero-ism—when the rebels close in upon the 304th New York a short while later.

Consider the self-assessment that follows this moment (it is even presented as a separate paragraph): "And, furthermore, how could they kill him who was the chosen of gods and doomed to greatness?" (*RBC* 151). Fleming's belief here seems manifestly ridiculous, and so much so it cannot be taken seriously. If a reader notes this paragraph at all, it is probably with a whimsical glance: "There goes that youth again, can you believe it?" or the like.

Why, though, is the claim at the end of the novel—that "he was a man"—any more necessarily or self-evidently true than the claim here that "he was chosen of the gods and doomed to greatness"? As the critical record reveals (see Chapter 6), the question of whether Fleming develops in any significant way is far from closed, while a surprisingly strong case can be made for his belief that he is "doomed to greatness." Private Fleming's failures have been miraculously masked from his immediate comrades and superiors, he will be rocketed upward in their esteem without conscious intention or even awareness, and by the end of the book he will have made it untouched through two engagements as color-bearer of his regiment.

His next self-assertion is likewise problematic for those who believe in the myth of cosmic malevolence and all that this entails, or it would be problematic except this instance carries its own scarcely veiled disclaimers. After they repulsed the first rebel assault of the morning and Private Fleming garnered the praise of Lieutenant Hasbrouck, he mused: "He had fought like a pagan who defends his religion. Regarding it, he saw that it was fine, wild, and, in some ways, easy. He had been a tremendous figure, no doubt. By this struggle he had overcome obstacles which he had admitted to be mountains. They had fallen like paper peaks, and he was now what he called a hero. And he had not been aware of the process. He had slept and, awakening, found himself a knight" (*RBC* 169). To the troublesome term "hero" has been added the antiquated term "knight"— neither at all appropriate according to the myth that Crane is enticing his readers to project upon this fundamentally chaotic episode of the American Civil War. The ease of their achievement implicitly loosens the appropriateness of such terms: "fine, wild, and, in some ways easy"; "paper peaks"; "he had slept." These terms confirm what is implied by the rhetorical patterns—"tremendous figure, *no doubt*"; "what *he called* a hero"—that these terms are rendered meaningless because they were earned by worthless conduct. Seeing these unfashionable terms swathed in faintly ludicrous contexts and aware that the novel still has some pages to run, a reader assumes that the "hero," Private Fleming, will see his way (with more experience) to something more true.

While our myth of the malevolent universe may have rendered "hero" and "knight" unfashionable, is it necessarily the case that they are somehow less "true" about Private Henry Fleming than the ultimate word "man"? Is it truly the case that it is inappropriate for Fleming to conceive of himself in these ways? Some associations clustered around the image of the "knight" may be archaic in themselves and so may tinge the knight image with an implication of innocence concerning the nature of reality, an innocence that no self-respecting believer in the myth would ever wish to be accused of. But when the term does appear in popular culture, it is typically applied to people—such as Richard Boone's Paladin in "Have Gun Will Travel" or Joseph Wambaugh's burned-out policemen—who are devoid of chivalric optimism. The image of the knight is not exactly ironic nowadays, but it seems safely remote from romantic or traditional connotations and hence such innocence. Insofar as it implies merely a warrior who has at last proved his capacity for combat, it seems appropriate for Private Fleming to apply it to himself.

Private Henry Fleming is, beyond question, a "hero." During the course of the morning of May 3, 1863, he proved himself completely fearless in combat and ferocious on the firing line, earning the praise of his company commander. At a moment of crisis, he stepped forward from the enlisted ranks to join Lieutenant Hasbrouck in providing exemplary leadership—an amazing act for a young private soldier. When the regiment's color sergeant was slain, he unhesitatingly seized the colors and thereafter kept them steadily to the front, showing again his fearlessness. These qualities brought him to the attention of his regimental commander, who praised him lavishly. His example and his leadership evidently played a major part in the action when the 304th New York captured a rebel banner. Such behavior on a field of battle surely qualifies as "heroic" by any standards of any age.

Yet most readers probably do not assess him thus and are vaguely surprised to see the claim thus validated. Again, several reasons probably conspire. The strong tendency to see Private Fleming as "Everysoldier" masks the outstanding nature of his performance for many initial readers of the novel (see Chapter 5). So too does the portrayal of the experiences of central figures in the overwhelming majority of subsequent post–World War I fiction, where martial heroism at once both conventional and triumphant never appears anymore, so readers are not prepared to see it or register it in *The Red Badge of Courage*. The myth under which we mostly live and move and have our being nowadays ridicules exactly this kind of heroism. The myth teaches us to expect that characters endowed with this type of heroism will get blown away instantly, or will be figures of ridicule (see Tenente Moretti) to those who really know the score. Insofar as the vividness of *The Red Badge of Courage* and the plausibility of

Private Fleming's character draw us to him, we discount this moment, assuming that he will come to see things more accurately by the end—indeed, that this process of discovery will actually constitute the end and his coming into his true "manhood," which at first glance seems to be the case.

But there is a final twist. Even readers cautioned by the constant play of the novel, and who believe that no such process of discovery has taken place, even readers who do not believe he is at last "a man," are often surprised to discover that Private Fleming must nonetheless be recognized as an authentic "hero." How can someone who so consistently fails to recognize the truth about himself or the reality surrounding him become, or be called, a "hero"? But then, also, why not?

What we actually see in the novel is a central character who tries on a number of titles, as if they were various items in a wardrobe. With splendid and mordant irony the titles we tend to ridicule, ignore, or discount are in fact the ones most applicable, whereas the title we tend to accept and rest happiest with—that at last "he was a man"—is, of all, the least accurate. In this process we ourselves replicate Crane's central thesis, the profound, unreflecting, elementally self-deceptive human tendency to impose a myth upon the chaos of human experience.

Our steady close consideration of Private Fleming has revealed that he undergoes no essential transformation at all in the course of these two days. The same characteristics that marked him at the beginning of the campaign mark him at the end: a vivid visual imagination, devoid of sympathy for others; an absolute and impenetrable solipsism; a profound ignorance concerning mortality, and his own mortal condition in particular. Given every opportunity hallowed by literary convention to achieve a fundamental recognition concerning himself, he never does so. Given extraordinary, even cataclysmic object lessons about reality, he easily ignores their implications.

This is not at all to say that his responses to various challenges are coherent or consistent. His unchanging personal characteristics shield him from any genuine contact with elemental factual realities and thus cause him to respond to events with quite extraordinary (although quite "believable") conceptions about how they may affect him, and with quite extraordinary swings of emotion. The actual conduct of General Hooker, commanding the Army of the Potomac during those days in the Wilderness, provides a historical correlative to Crane's psychological portrait of his hero.[7] So those characteristics at first work to plunge

---

7. For an absolutely contrary example, consider how Benjamin Franklin shaped his *Autobiography* to persuade people against such solipsistic behavior, to the end of achieving what Private Fleming never does: a "uniform rectitude of conduct." Benjamin Franklin, *Autobiography and Other Writings*, 75.

him into panic; subsequently, they conspire to propel him into glorious success, and by the novel's end, they have convinced him he has achieved the status of manhood.

—⁓—

Reconsider, in light of this study, the last pages of the novel. As they withdraw from the Chancellorsville vicinity into the new defensive lines shielding the army's remaining Rappahannock bridgehead at the United States Ford, Private Fleming's mind "was undergoing a subtle change," casting "off its battleful ways" and resuming "its accustomed course of thought." With the distorted emotions of combat behind him, "at last he was enabled to more closely comprehend himself and circumstance" (*RBC* 228). This sounds promising, and quite in keeping with our most elemental narrative tradition: only a few pages are left, the action is over, we (supposedly) will see that our hero is at last "enabled" to "comprehend himself and circumstance" somewhat "more closely" (228).

His first new "comprehension" could not possibly be wider of the mark, however. "He understood then that the existence of shot and counter-shot was in the past. He had dwelt in a land of strange, squalling upheavals and had come forth. He had been where there was red of blood and black of passion, and he was escaped. His first thoughts were given to rejoicings at this fact" (*RBC* 229). The most immediately apparent objective fact is that the Army of the Potomac is retiring, it had been defeated; there is no suggestion that the war is any closer to its conclusion than before. Rather than a "closer comprehension of himself and circumstances," he is displaying that same solipsistic tendency to conceive of himself as at the center of the world and the only "real" thing in it. His language betrays his colossal illusion: phenomena of battle are not, in his current imagination, things to which as an enlisted soldier he must become wearily inured but, rather, bizarrely disembodied sensations produced by a "strange" unreal land from which he has permanently emerged. Since he has passed the test and has profited by the experience, he cannot conceive that it is not altogether concluded, that the circus tent or house of horrors is not gone for good. He is back exactly where he was at the end of his first experience of combat the previous afternoon: "So it was all over at last! The supreme trial had been passed," and so on (*RBC* 64). The raw fact is that these experiences are not at all "in the past," nor has he "come forth" or "escaped" from them: they await him and his fellows at a small Pennsylvania town just two months hence. If he survives that (no sure thing at all), he will return to exactly this same landscape next year at this time, for a campaign of unparalleled slaughter.

Reflection upon his past actions then follows: "he began to study his deeds, his failures, and his achievements," using the relative tranquillity of the moment to "marshal all his acts" for review. "At last they marched before him clearly. From this present view point he was enabled to look upon them in spectator fashion and to criticise them with some correctness, for his new condition had already defeated certain sympathies" (*RBC* 228–29). As with that "closer comprehension" three paragraphs earlier, so here: another last-chapter paragraph with portentous claims. As in the previous paragraph, Private Fleming is crediting himself with having achieved a "new condition." Now he believes he is no longer infected by "certain sympathies" (presumably immature passions, beliefs, and the like that experience has stripped from him) so that he is now capable of criticizing himself and his past actions correctly. There is no doubt that Private Fleming has been through an altogether extraordinary and cataclysmic two days of battle, exactly such an experience—the myth assures him (and us)—as will strip a "youth" of immature "sympathies" and enable him to understand himself and the world more accurately.

Crane knows how exhilarating it is to believe we have undergone this transformation and are not as we were before, and Private Fleming is "gleeful" as he brings his "new" and more correct judgment to bear upon his past conduct. A moment earlier, however, Fleming's belief that his "brain" was no longer "clogged" was immediately undercut by the inaccuracy of his assessment of his future. The same undercutting pattern obtains again, as he assesses his past. The assessment itself reveals that, despite his belief that he has been stripped of illusions, his mind is in fact unchanged, or if it has changed at all, it has in fact become more infatuated with immature "sympathies" than it was before. "Regarding his procession of memory he felt gleeful and unregretting, for in it his public deeds were paraded in great and shining prominence. Those performances which had been witnessed by his fellows marched now in wide purple and gold, having various deflections. They went gayly with music. It was pleasure to watch these things. He spent delightful minutes viewing the gilded images of memory" (*RBC* 229). The controlling image is that of the most conventional martial pomp and ceremony: a victorious military march-past complete with bands and outfitted in the specific colors (purple dyes being rare and expensive in the classical Mediterranean world) of Greco-Roman triumph. Those classical references to purple, gold, and "gilded images" suggest those "old ideas" Fleming used to hold, before his enlistment and subsequent experiences (supposedly) outfitted him with this "new condition," which he assumes is maturely purged of "certain sympathies." Back then, he at least believed that "Greeklike struggles would be no more. Men were better, or more timid" (11). Now his imagination is no longer constrained by such precocious cynicism.

What we come to realize is that now, thanks to his belief that he has achieved some mature "new condition" of understanding, he is completely free to apply the most immature, conventional, traditional, and heroic terminology to himself and his conduct. Now that he is a "man," he obviously can no longer believe in childish things. Thus if he now believes he is a hero in the classical mold, it must be true. (If you believe in the modern myth, you cannot be mistaken even if you apply chunks of other myths to yourself.) Indeed, "He saw that he was good. He recalled with a thrill of joy the respectful comments of his fellows upon his conduct" (*RBC* 229).

Then "the ghost of his flight from the first engagement appeared to him and danced," and "For a moment he blushed, and the light of his soul flickered with shame" (*RBC* 229). Yet again, we encounter what the narrative tradition in our world teaches us to expect to encounter: a hero's ultimate confrontation with his own past failures, and some placing of them in the context of his current situation. Private Fleming then goes on to remember what most readers (appropriately) find far more damning in his conduct than his panic-stricken flight: he is suddenly beset by "A specter of reproach," the "dogging memory of the tattered soldier" who "had loaned his last of strength and intellect for the tall soldier" and who, "blind with weariness and pain, had been deserted in the field" (*RBC* 229–30).

These are certainly appropriate occasions for shame and regret. But something about the language in which they are cast is not quite right. In both cases, Private Fleming evidently conceives of these occasions as personified, slightly unreal figures—"ghost" and "specter"—who seem mostly intent upon embarrassing him. He does not remember them as occasions in which he committed acts of treachery with consequences for other real human beings, actions requiring some kind of sincere penitence or expiation. Note the passive construction with which his recollection of the tattered soldier is brought to its conclusion: who "had been deserted," not whom "he had deserted."

The profoundly immature, self-centered quality of his seeming "shame" and self-reproach is confirmed in the very next sentence: "For an instant a wretched chill of sweat was upon him at the thought that he might be detected in the thing" (*RBC* 230). We are reminded of Twain's mordant comment in "The Man That Corrupted Hadleyburg": "a sin takes on new and real terrors when there seems a chance that it is going to be found out."[8] Even more are we reminded of Private Fleming's concern of the previous afternoon, when another seemingly promising moment of self-reproach turned out in fact to be only a concern for his personal prestige among his fellows: "A moral vindication was regarded by the youth as a very important thing. Without salve, he could not, he thought, wear the sore badge of his dishonor through life. With his heart continually assuring him that he was despicable, he could not exist without making it, through his actions, apparent to all men" (*RBC* 114). As he now stands "persistently" before this "vision" of shameful acts that could just possibly cost him all his public adulation, he reacts with a spontaneous gesture surely familiar to most of his readers: "he [gives] vent to a cry of sharp irritation and agony," and when Wilson asks him, "What's the matter," he gives "an outburst of crimson oaths" (230). His actions and reactions are utterly typical, enough so (Twain would agree) as to appeal to almost any reader. But the reader must recognize the truth of the matter. Far from a "new" ability to "criticise" his own actions "with some correctness," his "sympathies" (remaining completely, relentlessly only for himself), his concerns, and his attitudes are exactly as they were before.

For some minutes, "this vision" of his own "cruelty brooded over him," because, understanding himself to be at the very center of the world, he feels "sure that" his fellow soldiers "must discern in his face evidences" of "the somber phantom" that is haunting him. Despite the characteristically banal discussion going on in the plodding, "ragged array" around him, he has a "sudden suspicion that they were seeing his thoughts and scrutinizing each detail of the scene with the tattered soldier" (*RBC* 231), so his solipsism remains as complete as ever. "Yet gradually he mustered force to put the sin at a distance" (231–32). His secret, not surprisingly, remains undiscovered. Twain again: our "consciences" readily enough "quiet down," when they become "discouraged."[9]

This, then, is the specific buildup toward those critical paragraphs that will deposit the final claim, "He was a man." The single word "seemed" leaps into enormous significance—"at last his eyes seemed to open to some new ways"—and in fact it is hard to see what "earlier gospels" he now "despises." The current myth teaches him, and us, that our "new manhood" must be "quiet" and "nonassertive," for the myth denies and devalues an overt hero. But the accolades that so confirmed his profound, happy belief in his new manhood were

8. Mark Twain, "The Man That Corrupted Hadleyburg," in *Selected Shorter Writings of Mark Twain*, 286.
9. Ibid.

garnered because he first "bawled," "danced and gyrated" in front of the regiment when its counterattack faltered, and moments later asserted himself by seizing the colors when the bearer was killed. As its color-bearer, he is now the single most prominent enlisted man in the 304th New York Volunteer Infantry Regiment. He is so completely possessed by the myth of his own new "manhood" (exactly as when, on the way to battle, he had been completely possessed by his own new self-pity) that he completely misunderstands and misrepresents his own most recent personal history.

The myth also insists upon his (and our) new capacity to meet any challenge that reality might hit us with; possessing such a new capacity is critical to being "a man." And so with Private Fleming: "He knew that he would no more quail before his guides wherever they should point." But no such confidence is warranted, according to Crane's most basic and consistent vision. The chaotic universe is not at all predictable: the very image of having "guides" to or within it is a product of a monstrous illusion about it. Nor is the human mind predictable. Refer back to privates Wilson and Fleming themselves, after the soldiers of the regiment had found themselves transformed into "men" during the waning moments of their counterattack. Responding to the new brigade commander's violent criticism of their regiment, Wilson angrily criticized the man, but Private Fleming had "developed a tranquil philosophy" that enabled him to respond "soothingly." And then in the length of three paragraphs, that "philosophy" had been replaced in Fleming's mind by "sudden," furious "exasperation" (*RBC* 205–6).

"He had been to touch the great death, and found that, after all, it was but the great death" (*RBC* 232). This is a paradoxical statement but, loosely considered, it seems potentially plausible, and the kind of statement that professors are paid to explain. But when it is closely considered in the context of the novel and we recall Private Fleming's manifest inability to conceive of his own mortal condition, it becomes no longer paradoxical but fatuous. And when we recall Fleming's self-centered reduction of the dead Jim Conklin to "that other one," the statement becomes appalling. It is surely the case, however, that Private Fleming, who has been widely and publicly praised and now finds himself on his way to comfort and rest, is quite comfortable about death because he still has no conception of it as a real fact of human (and his own) existence: he has never in fact "been to touch it" (or been touched by it) at all.

The paragraphs that follow the statement "He was a man" develop a sequence of stereotypical images of peace: "He came from hot plowshares"—his unconscious confusion about the truth of his situation as an enlisted soldier in the Army of the Potomac in May 1863 is reflected in the unconscious confusion of the biblical imagery of swords and plowshares—"to prospects of clover tranquilly [sic], and it was as if hot plowshares were not" (*RBC* 232).[10] These and other images lead to the triumphant last claim that "an existence of soft and eternal peace" extends before Private Fleming (232). This is absolutely contradicted by the most massive and immediate physical evidence before him at this midmorning moment: infantrymen of a defeated army retreating down muddy roads.

Richly contented with himself, publicly praised, with the prospects of camp and rest before him, carrying the regimental colors, it may indeed seem to him "that the world was a world for him" (*RBC* 232). The totality of Crane's fiction and poetry bear witness, however, that absolutely no human claim could be further from the truth. The world is not a world for Private Henry Fleming nor, given its blank indifference toward the creatures that inhabit it and its own inherently chaotic nature, is it a world "for" any human being within it.

These penultimate paragraphs cannot, then, be taken at face value. They are not speaking accurately or truly about his actual circumstances and prospects. How then, can the claim that Private Henry Fleming "was a man" be so taken? If we thus recognize that he has not been transformed into "a man" in any significant or essential way, can we see him in any significant or essential way as a hero?

The word "hero" in literary contexts is a tricky one, implying as it does a figure worthy of respect and emulation on the one hand, and the central figure in a narrative work on the other. For example, how can you call Macbeth a hero? The issue is more complicated here, because Private Fleming's conduct on the morning of May 3, 1863, surely deserves the accolade: he is as much a "hero" as one could expect to find in the enlisted ranks of an army. Yet, unquestionably, his "manhood"—in the sense of admirable full maturity, wisdom, or humanity—is radically deficient. To assume he cannot be a "hero" until he is a "man" is to return again to the imposition of a human mythology upon a chaotic reality; it is to assume that true rewards for valor and the like befall only those who have passed the boot camp run by "reality." But there is no such structure in the universe surrounding us; nor is there any such structure even in our own constantly fluctuating human minds. The universe around us is disjointed and discontinuous—as are, by their very natures, our own minds.

Crane's conception of his hero is even more mordantly good-humored than

---

10. Virtually all other editions give "clover tranquility" instead, which seems far more plausible. See "Textual Notes," in Crane, *Red Badge of Courage* (University of Virginia edition), 277.

is implied here. It is precisely because Private Henry Fleming fails so hugely to acquire anything resembling true "manhood" that he succeeds so hugely as a genuine military hero. The same characteristics that sent him pelting from the battle line on the afternoon of May 2 promoted him to prominence and success on the morning of May 3 (see Chapter 7). Private John Wilson evidently did undergo some kind of transformation, but this transformation seems to have produced in him qualities that led to moments of more rounded and hence less concentrated perception, to moments of hesitation and self-doubt. At that telling moment when the 304th New York was paralyzed with confusion and close to collapse, Wilson joined in the general despair, earning Fleming's contempt ("Oh, shut up, you damned fool!" [*RBC* 194]). And although, before that moment and then especially after it, Private Wilson proved himself a superior soldier in his own right, at each critical moment he followed Private Fleming's spontaneous lead. It is absolutely consistent with Crane's general understanding of the ridiculousness of the human predicament in the universe that Private Fleming's worst qualities and his severest limitations as a human being were the very things that conspired to make him a superb and admired combat soldier during the second day of the battle of Chancellorsville.

Chapter 10

The Red Badge of Courage and War

So Private Fleming's most childish qualities, his deficiencies in those characteristics that we identify with full maturity, are the very things that conspire eventually to make him a superb and admired combat soldier. Does this mean that *The Red Badge of Courage*—perhaps equating martial virtues with human childishness and surely illustrating in this single "Episode" that the latter can produce the former—is an "antiwar" novel? On this issue critical opinion is radically divided. Consider two estimations. From *The Unwritten War* by Daniel Aaron: "*The Red Badge* is usually read as a tale of initiation: a youthful hero, after having been overmastered by fear, regains self-confidence and acquires a juster view of his importance in the cosmos. Less obviously, it is a profane parable against war and against its glorifiers and apologists." From *Male Desire and the Coming of World War I* by Michael C. C. Adams: "Undergraduates regularly describe Stephen Crane's *The Red Badge of Courage* as the first modern antiwar novel in English. Though hallowed by repetition, this opinion misreads the viewpoint underlying the text. It fails to acknowledge that Henry Fleming, the hero, is made a man through war." These conclusions are absolute mirror images one of the other, even in the assumption each makes about the fallacious general consensus against which its own argument is set.[1]

1. Aaron, *Unwritten War*, 215; Michael C. C. Adams, *The Great Adventure: Male Desire and the Coming of World War I*, 47.

Thus we come to a second issue. Why has this novel generated such radically different arguments about such central matters? *The Red Badge of Courage* is probably the most immediately accessible of all the works regularly considered central to American literature. It is hard to think of another that poses fewer problems of either style or subject, for a reader of any level of sophistication. Why has this seemingly so simple novel generated such an array of mutually baffling responses? The next chapter of this study will essay a possible answer to this second question. This chapter will consider *The Red Badge of Courage* as in itself it really is, as a novel set on a battlefield, which thus inevitably implies certain things about the nature of war. These things cannot, I think, be summed as either pro- or antiwar, because the novel's "attitude toward war" is not central to it. Its central "attitude," rather, is concerned with the issue at its core: the human plight in the universe.

Crane's writings, both prose and poetry, are remarkably consistent. The immense issue of our human plight is always central, and his conclusion is always the same. We are self-conscious creatures—the only self-conscious creatures—in a universe that, although it has produced us and given us that self-consciousness, is utterly indifferent to our existence, either as individuals or as a species. The roots of this particularly black flower are obviously "Darwinian," and its most immediate fruit is that Crane believes our situation to be ridiculous, and our predicament absurd.

Crane's reputation will never rest, I believe, upon his poetry. His conception of the human plight is too rigidly reductive to encourage the free play of creative delight or joy in the details of existence, so his poems close in upon themselves rather than expanding in our imaginations. But they do present this vision with unmistakable clarity, and one of them famously so:

> A man said to the universe:
> "Sir, I exist!"
> "However," replied the universe,
> "The fact has not created in me
> "A sense of obligation."[2]

For people alive to our plight in such a universe, self-consciousness is a burden; to be aware of ourselves is to be aware of the ridiculousness of our circumstance and aware of the final extinction of the self. Self-consciousness immerses such

---

2. Stephen Crane, "A man said to the universe," *Other Writings*, 388.

people psychologically in the situation in which the black cabin-boy Pip finds himself literally immersed, in our literature's finest brief evocation of this plight, "The Castaway" chapter in *Moby-Dick*. He is lost overboard, with no ship or human figure in view. Even though he is eventually rescued, the experience drives him insane. "The intense concentration of self in the middle of such a heartless immensity, my God!, who can tell it?"[3]

Even for people unaware of the awful truth of our circumstance, Crane believes, self-consciousness is no especial advantage and can be a detriment. Crane is hardly a professional student of evolution or of the human mind, quite the contrary, but the question of why and how this trait of self-consciousness came to be established during the process of evolution is a question that has challenged the best students of both subjects: for example, Julian Jaynes.[4] The squirrel at which Private Fleming threw that pine cone during his wandering in the Wilderness is more at home in, less estranged from, the chaotic reality of the natural world than Fleming is. Were Fleming not a self-conscious creature, were he a mere creature of pure instinct, he would not have produced that fantastic, solipsistic array of "plots" about himself, which, ever distorting reality, sent him first into panic-stricken flight, then into violent combat, and ultimately into that suicidal impulse to seize his regiment's flag. Compared to the squirrel's simple instinct for self-preservation, Fleming's motivations as a self-conscious creature seem bizarre, both crazed and self-destructive. But, fortunate so far in his military career, to this point in his life he has never had to pay any price for that self-consciousness. His solipsism and essential immaturity have so far kept him from recognizing the truth of his existence, so he is unaware of the crushing psychological burden that self-consciousness can suddenly—witness Pip—impose.

In light of these raw facts, war does offer some positive things to the human soul. In the first place, conventional illusions about military glory and the like— illusions of the kind held by Tenente Ettore Moretti in A *Farewell to Arms*—do constitute a structure of beliefs that can be tested in the unquestionably real experience of combat. Combat in turn does unquestionably evoke some of the most elemental and "real" human emotions, as evidenced by the emotions that surged through Private Fleming during his first experience of combat: panic, loyalty, brotherhood, rage, love, ecstasy. Combat does confront the individual with unquestionably real facts of raw physical pain and death. The outcome of combat can often be unquestionably real: victory, or defeat. For many (perhaps somewhat limited) young men, then, this conventional set of beliefs seems to

---

3. Melville, *Moby-Dick*, 371.
4. Julian Jaynes, *The Origin of Consciousness in the Breakdown of the Bicameral Mind*.

have an inherent reality and is one in which they can absolutely put their faith. If Moretti survives World War I, he will probably go to his grave believing that his five medals and especially his "'three wound stripes'" were genuinely "'fine to have'" (*FTA* 121), and that touching "the stars at his collar with his thumb and forefinger" whenever "'anybody mentions getting killed'" (123) was the thing that kept him alive. He has risen through the ranks to become an officer and has killed at least one man in face-to-face combat. Who is going to try to tell Tenente Moretti that his beliefs are illusory and foolish? Private Henry Fleming himself, with his solipsistic ignorance about the truth of the universe, with his heightened imagination and his ultimately conventional system of values (he "flushes from thrills of pleasure" when he hears that Colonel MacChesnay has praised him [*RBC* 208]), is a superior example of the type. This set of beliefs shields these young men from the far bleaker facts about their existence. All creatures eventually go down to death, but such young men often die in the full flush of happy illusion. I have (perhaps unwisely) opened the subject of Crane's poetry, so I may as well add another. The poem known as "War Is Kind" seems to me to confirm this understanding:

> Do not weep, maiden, for war is kind.
> Because your lover threw wild hands toward the sky
> And the affrighted steed ran on alone,
> Do not weep.
> War is kind.
>> Hoarse, booming drums of the regiment,
>> Little souls who thirst for fight,
>> These men were born to drill and die.
>> The unexplained glory flies above them,
>> Great is the battle-god, great, and his kingdom—
>> A field where a thousand corpses lie.

Taken often as an example of verbal irony (that is, "No poet could possibly mean that 'war is kind'"), this seems to me, rather, an example of cosmic irony. (See also the poem "A youth in apparel that glittered.") For those men of limited awareness who luckily emerge alive and with some measure of self-satisfaction at the end, their happy illusions may be sufficiently strengthened to protect them for a lifetime from the truth of their situation: "he saw that the world was a world for him, though many discovered it to be made of oaths and walking sticks" (*RBC* 232).[5]

5. Stephen Crane, "War Is Kind," *Other Writings*, 385–86, and "A youth in apparel," ibid., 383.

Such illusions are not accessible to those who know the truth of the human condition. To such intelligence, Private Fleming may seem fortunate, but he will also seem foolish, a case study in our human tendency to delude ourselves about the truth of our existence. There is a severe aesthetic, even a logical problem for the novelist laboring under this vision of reality, because characters who are obviously less intelligent than the reader are advanced nonetheless as "typical" of the human condition. This problem is manifest in the Naturalistic fiction of the period, especially in the most celebrated: Theodore Dreiser's *Sister Carrie*, Frank Norris's *McTeague* and *The Octopus*. But I think that *The Red Badge of Courage* is unique in avoiding this problem because of its unusual narrative strategy (see Chapter 11).

Concerning the novel's "attitude" toward war, a good deal of what has been "positive" in Private Fleming's experience of battle strikes a sophisticated reader as based upon this particular soldier's naivete and self-delusion. But perhaps war can offer something of value to even an informed and knowledgeable mind: rare moments of experience so heightened, so outwardly directed, so selflessly committed, that self-consciousness becomes not a burden but a source of delight; moments when the self-absorption inherent in self-consciousness is replaced by absorption in something else. During Fleming's first moments on the battle line, "He suddenly lost concern for himself, and forgot to look at a menacing fate. He became not a man but a member. . . . There was a consciousness always of the presence of his comrades about him. He felt the subtle battle brotherhood more potent even than the cause for which they were fighting" (*RBC* 56). Such experience tends toward exactly that kind of selfless (so to speak) self-consciousness. But Fleming's first combat experience is altogether incoherent, and this instance is itself fragmented and incomplete (see Chapter 4). Nor does it last: during the first exchange the next morning, utterly self-centered, self-regarding hatred for the enemy absorbs him completely.

Then, during the first stages of their abortive counterattack on the second day, "There was the delirium that encounters despair and death, and is heedless and blind to the odds. It is a temporary but sublime absence of selfishness. And because it was of this order was the reason, perhaps, why the youth wondered, afterward, what reasons he could have had for being there" (*RBC* 182). During the "rush" that dislodged the last rebel thrust, "they were in a state of frenzy, perhaps because of forgotten vanities, and it made an exhibition of sublime recklessness" (*RBC* 218–19). Private Fleming "himself felt the daring spirit of a savage religion mad. He was capable of profound sacrifices, a tremendous death," and "There were subtle flashings of joy within him that thus should be his mind" (219). Such "sublime" moments can be found in combat; they are far different from and far superior to the ordinary course of our experience and are to be treasured.

They are also manifestly transient, the product of moments when "delirium" or "frenzy" overtake us; they are purchased at great cost in human life, and they form no basis at all for any philosophy of ordinary human conduct. In the case of the private soldier central to this novel, they are readily forgotten when he has the opportunity to gorge his self-consciousness with recollections of his own personal accomplishments, thoughts of the esteem he now enjoys, and contemplations of his own "golden" private future. The "celebration" of these selfless experiences in the long run seems hardly "pro-war" so much as "anti-cosmos" or the like; benchmarks, so to speak, that reveal the desperation of our plight through the desperate mental states necessary to achieve some fleeting experience of "sublimity."

On the other, the "anti-war" hand: pulling together those aspects of The Red Badge of Courage that can be catalogued as "antiwar" reveals that Crane's underlying, unwavering conception of our plight in the universe produces a far more critical and damaging attack on war as a significant human experience than can be found in celebrated works that are declaratively "antiwar," such as the novels A Farewell to Arms, All Quiet on the Western Front, The Naked and the Dead, The Thin Red Line, Catch-22, or the movies "All Quiet on the Western Front," "Apocalypse Now," "Full Metal Jacket."[6] Implicit in such works is the myth that war is, finally, significant, though hideously so. It is this myth that still attracts, even in a world whose serious fictions have been purged of conventional conceptions of "glory" (if such ever, in fact, had much appeal to the masculine mind) for over a century.

—⁂—

Let us begin with obvious things: how Crane's novel deals with immediately familiar assumptions and perceptions about warfare. Military service is traditionally associated with training in certain particular, interrelated human virtues such as discipline, or loyalty to something larger than oneself (a nation, a cause, a unit, and so on), or—supremely—comradeship. It could be logically assumed that any private soldier who succeeds heroically in combat would possess these virtues, that his conduct would demonstrate their worth.

6. Hemingway, *A Farewell to Arms*; Remarque, *All Quiet on the Western Front*; Mailer, *The Naked and the Dead*; Jones, *Thin Red Line*; Heller, *Catch-22*.

Private Fleming evinces none of these. Despite all those winter months of drill and review (*RBC* 11), basic discipline—even discipline of a grudging but self-denying sort—plays no part in his constitution. On his way into battle, military discipline is a "box" completely external to himself, compelling him forward with "iron laws of tradition and law" (35). His first act in combat is to ignore his company commander's express order not to "shoot till I tell you" and instead to fire "a first wild shot" (55–56). His training has obviously not instilled sufficient discipline in him to overmaster his panic, nor does discipline compel him back to the firing line thereafter. A certain "creed of soldiers" has been impressed upon him: "His education had been that success for that mighty blue machine was certain" and he "discarded all his speculations" (*RBC* 115) about the happy possibility of a Union defeat that would vindicate his conduct. Just before receiving the blow to his head, Crane says Fleming had "returned" to that "creed" (116). But this is a "return" only in his thinking: this "creed" does nothing thereafter to discipline his own conduct.

In fact each of "Those performances which had been witnessed by his fellows" (*RBC* 229) and had made him a hero results from spontaneous, self-absorbed, and undisciplined moments. Completely absorbed in his personal early morning combat with the rebels, he continued firing even after "there ain't anything t' shoot at" (*RBC* 167), presumably even after an order to cease fire. When he joined Lieutenant Hasbrouck in trying to inspire the 304th New York as they faltered in their counterattack, it is a specifically undisciplined action (as a private soldier, his place is in the ranks, not "gyrating" in front of the regiment's colors), inspired by "a sudden unspeakable indignation against his officer" (186). During this counterattack, finding himself near the colors, he was seized by a sudden "love," powerful but lurid, for the thing: "It was a creation of beauty and invulnerability" (187). This is an emotion bereft of any sense of the value of the flag to his regiment. His springing to grasp it is an instinctive, boldly self-assertive action; his keeping the flag boldly to the front is a compound of his personal infatuation with the symbol and his desire for "a fine revenge upon the officer who had referred to him and his fellows as mule drivers" (191). His final action as flag-bearer is of a piece with these others: motivated by the still-rankling damage to his own self-esteem (217), by thoughtless impulse (219), by a vainglorious desire to capture that rebel flag (221). None of this is to suggest that Fleming is an isolated instance in the ranks of the 304th New York Volunteer Infantry Regiment: endemic problems with its discipline appear both early and late (see Chapter 8). But note that, in his case, both his abject failures and his subsequent successes occur not because he has absorbed military discipline, but because he has not.

The dearth of any concern whatsoever for the causes of the Civil War is one of the novel's most famous attributes. Private Fleming is not necessarily bereft of loyalty to the Union cause or to the cause of freedom for the slave, but if he does feel any, it never surfaces in his mind and is not significant enough to motivate him. At that instant during his first engagement when he was dimly aware he had become "not a man but a member," he was even more dimly aware of feeling loyal to something larger than "concern for himself" at this moment: "He felt that something of which he was a part—a regiment, an army, a cause, or a country—was in a crisis" (*RBC* 56). His inability to define the object of his loyalty confirms that it is no such thing but, rather, a sort of back-construction. Soldiers go into combat (he assumes) because they are loyal to something greater than their own self-interest; he is in combat and is not as self-absorbed as he was; thus he must be being loyal to *something*, even if he is not sure just what it is (note the implication of the conjunction "or" in the phrase "or a country"). He is, shortly, willing to sacrifice any of these—his regiment, then his army, cause, and country—if such would assuage the wound to his self-esteem inflicted by his panicked flight. When he learned that the line from which he fled had "held 'im" after all, he cringed "as if discovered in a crime." The 304th New York became to him that "imbecile line" that held because of its "blind ignorance and stupidity." He wished instead that the regiment had been shattered, "every little piece" in it "rescuing itself if possible," because then his own flight would be vindicated. He felt "a great anger against his comrades" and "ill used" (74–76). As he later watched the panic-stricken retreat of the Eleventh Corps, he was "comforted in a measure by this sight"—the sight, that is, of the single greatest catastrophe to befall a corps of the Army of the Potomac during the course of the Civil War. "There was an amount of pleasure to him in watching the wild march of this vindication" (108). Though his thinking during these minutes did waver, "yet, he said, in a half-apologetic manner to his conscience, he could not but know that a defeat for the army this time might mean many favorable things for him" (112). And "he said, as if in excuse for this hope, that previously the army had encountered great defeats and in a few months had shaken off all blood and tradition of them, emerging as bright and valiant as a new one; thrusting out of sight the memory of disaster, and appearing with the valor and confidence of unconquered legions" (113).

It is at once both hilarious and appalling to see a private soldier rationalizing so readily his private "hope" that his army's present campaign would end in another "great defeat." To fulfill this "hope," Fleming "felt no compunctions for proposing a general as a sacrifice," even if the public outrage might "hit the wrong man" (*RBC* 113). Although Fleming would have no way of knowing this, it was probably beyond the power of the outnumbered rebels to inflict such a "great defeat" upon the Army of the Potomac. But had they been able to do so and had that army collapsed, more than a single general would have been sacrificed. So too, most likely, would have been the "cause" and the "country" for which it had assembled.

In point of historical fact, for the third spring in a row, the major Federal army in the east had marched southward full of confidence only to find itself in extremely short order fighting for its very survival. To this general experience add one total defeat at the Second Battle of Bull Run, a stalemate at Antietam in the bloodiest single day in American military history, and all the utterly vain sacrifice in blundering assaults against the rebel lines at Fredericksburg the previous winter. A catastrophic disaster could now quite likely have overwhelmed the Federal army's powers of resilience: even the humiliating moral defeat that ensued all but destroyed its confidence. That the Army of the Potomac did manage to forge ahead until final victory owed a great deal to its victory later this summer at Gettysburg (a virtual gift from General R. E. Lee, accomplished after three days of severe slaughter), and even more to the institution of national conscription. The latter, though bitterly resented and opposed, refilled with drafted men divisions depleted by bloodshed, defeat, and the consequent collapse of active support for the war—the kind of support that previously had supplied hundreds of regiments of willing volunteers (such as the 304th New York) to the Union armies. Fleming finally "discarded all his speculations" in this "direction," and "returned to the creed of soldiers." But this is specifically not because of any resurgent loyalty. Rather, it is because "it was useless to think of such a possibility. His education had been that success for that mighty blue machine was certain; that it would make victories as a contrivance turns out buttons" (*RBC* 115–16), which in itself is an interesting example of the victory of preconceived "truth" over manifest reality.

Neither does his triumphant conduct on the second day of the battle reflect a resurgent loyalty. Far from losing "concern for himself," or becoming "not a man but a member," his private urgencies constantly impelled him to set himself apart from the body of the regiment, both physically and mentally. Thus his " 'wild cat' " conduct in the first action (*RBC* 168), his assertion of himself alongside Lieutenant Hasbrouck in front of the regiment's colors, and his seizing the flag. As their attack faltered and they began to retreat, he was mortified, enraged that his hope for "a fine revenge upon the officer who had referred to him and his fellows as mule drivers" could not "come to pass." It is not a baffled loyalty to the regiment that is uppermost in his mind. His "blackened face was held toward the enemy, but his greater hatred was riveted upon the man, who, not knowing him, had called him a mule driver" (191). When he recognized the "bitter justice" in the taunts from the "veterans" that witnessed the regiment's failure, "He veiled a glance of disdain at his fellows" (201). He was stung anew by the brigade commander's public criticism of the regiment; but when word came to Private Fleming that he and Private Wilson had been singled out for praise by Colonel MacChesnay, he "speedily forgot many things. The past held no pictures of error and disappointment" (208).

Private Fleming's penultimate delight was entirely concentrated upon himself: upon his "deeds" and "performances," and the "respectful comments" he had won from his fellow soldiers (*RBC* 229). There is no suggestion he took any pride in the regiment's accomplishments or felt any particular loyalty toward its future—despite the public role he was going to play in that future as its color sergeant. When he did look "at his companions," he did so "stealthily," and with "suspicion" that they might see into his darker secrets: he was redeemed from his anxiety by the dull-witted mediocrity of the dialog surrounding him (230-31). His final satisfaction and contentment was completely personal, set explicitly against what had befallen the army: "The procession of weary soldiers became a bedraggled train, despondent and muttering, marching with churning effort in a trough of liquid brown mud under a low, wretched sky. Yet the youth smiled, for he saw that the world was a world for him, though many discovered it to be made of oaths and walking sticks" (232). His personal contentment was at odds with, was in point of fact disloyal to, the army in this hour of its disheartening defeat, disloyal as well to the cause and country depending upon that army.

In thus refuting conventional (or what are often assumed to be conventional) attitudes concerning the valuable lessons in discipline and loyalty that are instilled by warfare and military service, *The Red Badge of Courage* is similar to a great body of specifically "antiwar" fictional narratives. Military discipline itself becomes the enemy in such fictions as *The Enormous Room* and such films as "The Hill." Its brutalizing rather than redemptive quality is the subject of "Full Metal Jacket." The full fury of *All Quiet on the Western Front* is focused upon the authority figures who instilled martial and patriotic loyalties in innocent schoolboys.[7]

In Crane's novel, it is the way in which these attitudes are refuted that is atypical. Military discipline is not characterized by brutal monsters or by monstrous

7. Cummings, *The Enormous Room*; Remarque, *All Quiet on the Western Front*.

injustices. Discipline is simply nonexistent—and with interestingly various consequences. It is the same with loyalty to cause or country: rather than proving empty or obscenely misleading, to this novel's hero it is just nonexistent. Nonetheless in these two matters Crane's novel does not depart (so to speak, since again it actually precedes the post–World War I tradition) in substance from the tradition of the antiwar fictional narrative.

—⁓—

Not so in its depiction of the value of war in instilling the virtues of comradeship, friendship, and love. The celebration of these virtues is a theme so prevalent in the post–World War I tradition of literature about war that it has generated several by now hoary stereotypes. To affirm the significance, even the miraculousness of these virtues, the tradition inevitably presents them as growing to embrace people from radically different backgrounds: for example, *All Quiet on the Western Front,* or *A Farewell to Arms* (where the two lovers come from completely different worlds).[8] To enforce this argument, often two characters who initially despise each other grow to be best friends: see, for example, *Goodbye, Mickey Mouse, Piece of Cake,* or "Hamburger Hill."[9] This theme is then typically developed to reinforce the larger portrait of war-as-obscene-because-meaningless, because the same catastrophe that produces such rare and precious human relationships proceeds to destroy them. These fictions often develop into another stereotype, in which the ultimate action finds a hero giving his utmost—performing an almost superhuman act of endurance or daring or intelligence—in an inevitably doomed effort to save his beloved friend: consider in this light the radical similarity between such dissimilar acts as Paul Baumer carrying (the already dead) Kat to an aide-post in *All Quiet on the Western Front* and Frederic Henry rowing (the already doomed) Catherine Barkley to Switzerland.[10]

Private Fleming is as incapable of or as impervious to comradeship as he is to loyalty. Immured in his solipsism, utterly childish in his concern with his self-esteem and his public repute, he has great visual curiosity but no compassionate imagination. Other people just do not exist except as figures that are "ever to play . . . parts" (*RBC* 104) in the drama of his own personal existence. The new commander of Henderson's brigade, for example, is above all else "the man

8. See also Werfel, *Forty Days of Musa Dagh;* Ernest Hemingway, *For Whom the Bell Tolls;* Zweig, *Education before Verdun;* John Hersey, *The War Lover;* McDonald, *1915;* Sebastian Faulkes, *Birdsong.*

9. Deighton, *Goodbye, Mickey Mouse;* Robinson, *Piece of Cake.*

10. The device appears in one form or another in, for example, Zweig, *Education before Verdun;* "Dawn Patrol"; "Gallipoli"; and Watkins, *Night over Day over Night.*

who, not knowing him, had called him a mule driver"—and Fleming accordingly "riveted" a "greater hatred" (191) upon him than upon the rebel soldiers concurrently decimating his regiment. When those parts become "intolerable," the people playing them lose their essential human identity altogether. When the tattered soldier continued to pester him after Private Conklin's death, Private Fleming, "looking at him, could see that he, too, like that other one," that is, his hut-mate and whilom friend Jim Conklin, "was beginning to act dumb and animal-like" (104). The film versions of *The Red Badge of Courage* by John Huston and by Lee Philips both accepted the conventional attitude that combat affirms the critical value of comradeship, and both found Jim Conklin's death to be the perfect catalyst for Fleming's courageous decision to return to combat. In the novel, it is anything but that.

When on the other hand their actions, situations, or personalities are such that they fit into his private drama in some fashion that feeds his vanity and self-esteem, he thus, and only thus, registers their existence. Colonel MacChesnay demonstrated little capacity for leadership, and the 304th New York suffered disproportionate casualties under his command; Private Fleming, carrying the regimental colors, demonstrated that he was one of the superior enlisted men in the regiment and leapfrogged its entire noncommissioned officer structure, to become, as color-bearer, one of its authentic and recognized leaders. As such, one could assume he would be concerned with what MacChesnay's performance on this battlefield portended for the regiment's experience on future battlefields; nothing of the sort. When he heard secondhand that MacChesnay had praised him, "the past held no pictures of error and disappointment." His heart "swelled with grateful affection for the colonel" (*RBC* 208).

Consider then the way in which his other hut-mate and "friend," Private John Wilson, registers with Private Fleming. The experience of combat on the afternoon of May 2 did indeed have a significant effect upon Wilson, which Fleming recognized—because it serves his private drama quite well (see Chapter 7). Before, Wilson had appeared to him "as a blatant child with an audacity grown from his inexperience, thoughtless, headstrong, jealous, and filled with a tinsel courage." But "Apparently" Wilson "had now climbed a peak of wisdom from which he could perceive himself as a very wee thing" (*RBC* 143). There is of course that packet of letters, concrete evidence of Wilson's prebattle jitters. Nothing of the sort existed evidencing Fleming's own actual capital-offense-warranting behavior. The diminishment of Wilson's self-esteem was exactly the tonic Fleming needed as his imagination and his vanity set about recovering his own self-esteem. The true comradeship Wilson displayed toward him, true concern for Fleming's physical comfort and health, went completely forgotten. Private Wilson was not important to Private Fleming as another person, but only as the "player" he needed in his monstrous—and monstrously private— drama. Wilson is a foil for Fleming not only in his own drama but in the novel itself, because it is Wilson and not Fleming who evinces true comradeship: "Are yeh all right, Fleming? Do yeh feel all right? There ain't nothin' th' matter with yeh, Henry, is there?" (168). Pathetically, Wilson evidently thinks that Fleming is indeed a friend and a comrade. It is to Fleming that he turned to offer a last formal farewell when he thought they were doomed: "Well, Henry, I guess this is good-by—John" (194).

Private Wilson is the one who has absorbed whatever "lessons" combat is supposed to teach, those lessons that some readers such as Michael Adams believe Private Fleming learned by way of becoming "a man." In Fleming's own perception, Wilson "had made the great discovery that there were many men who would refuse to be subjected by him," Wilson who had "now climbed a peak of wisdom from which he would perceive himself as a very wee thing." Fleming saw "that ever after it would be easier to live in" Wilson's "neighborhood." Fleming himself could only "wonder where had been born" Wilson's "new eyes." Look again at Fleming's conception of his "friend" Wilson before the battle: Fleming "had been used to regarding his comrade as a blatant child with an audacity grown from his inexperience, thoughtless, headstrong, jealous, and filled with a tinsel courage" (143). This seems to me to be an excellent description of Fleming himself after the battle, as we see him marching amid his fellows in that "trough of liquid mud." His courage may be something better than "tinsel"—but otherwise, what would be inaccurate in this description?

Crane deliberately contrasts these two characters and, with equal deliberation, focuses upon Fleming, not because Fleming is "more typical" or because Fleming's atypicality produces a superior soldierly "machine" or the like but because Crane believes and aims to convince a reader that Private Fleming's reaction to military service and combat is, in everything, as plausible as Private Wilson's. Crane does this because the myth of our time—the myth that is so widespread and deep-seated that we do not even understand it to be a myth (it seems to us instead just an ineluctable, perhaps even the ineluctable, fact of our existence)—prepares us for the story of Wilson. To challenge that myth, Crane makes Fleming's absolutely contrary psychological reaction to his experience of combat believable and plausible.

—m—

At that last, Crane may have succeeded too well, given that Fleming is generally assumed to be "typical" (an assumption challenged in Chapter 5). Recall that the myth assumes the universe has a shape, albeit a malevolent one; likewise then that human life will have a shape; and likewise then that the human mind, if "fortunate," can achieve a permanent status called manhood. A true "man" is one whose life has taught him these malevolent realities, and who is as a result capable of facing up to them (see Chapter 9). The myth exists as well in a specifically military version, which has always had a powerful purchase in the (masculine) imagination. This military version holds that military life and the experience of combat offers a full, toughening plunge into these harsh realities of our existence. To seek such experience is to be an active, conscious hunter rather than an unwitting, passive victim. To have experienced military combat is the surest way to establish that one is a "man," both in the estimation of others and in one's own self-esteem. This is a crude summary of the myth, but there is no denying its ubiquity or its elemental appeal. For powerfully eloquent versions, see almost any of Hemingway's significant fictions, including *A Farewell to Arms* and *For Whom the Bell Tolls*.

This elemental appeal is the reason so many deliberately "antiwar" fictions—in their valiant efforts to characterize the combat experience as obscene and repellent—actually become counterproductive.[11] In each case, the sincere determination to present combat as the ultimate horror unwittingly makes the corollary argument that not to have experienced this ultimate horror is to be incomplete and immature, given a universe that has such horror in store for everyone. The same even obtains for those fictional narratives that establish their antiwar argument upon the basis not of blunt realism but of absurdity.[12] To have supped full of such absurdity is to be assuredly shriven of one's immature illusions that life has any redeeming purpose or hope. Not to have experienced such absurdity is to be still (suspiciously) inexperienced, and hence immature, vaguely aware that some absurdly horrific catastrophe is in store, and thus always whistling nervously through the graveyard of life, rather than limping through it with grizzled, wizened confidence.

As in much else, Hemingway's fiction gives these issues their best and most

---

11. See, for example, Hemingway, *A Farewell to Arms*; Remarque, *All Quiet on the Western Front*; Manning, *The Middle Parts of Fortune*; Yeates, *Winged Victory*; Sherriff, "Journey's End"; "Dawn Patrol"; Wagner, *Sands of Valor*; Shepard, *Paper Doll*; Watkins, *Night over Day over Night*; Derek Robinson, *A Good Clean Fight*; Jones, *Thin Red Line*; "Hamburger Hill"; "Full Metal Jacket."

12. See, for example, Hasek, *Soldier Schweik*; "Oh What a Lovely War!"; Heller, *Catch-22*; "How I Won the War"; "Catch-22."

succinct expression. Thus the famous objective correlative for all Frederic
Henry has experienced in *A Farewell to Arms*, as he learns his child has been born
dead and he senses that Catherine too will die:

> But they killed you in the end. You could count on that. Stay around
> and they would kill you.
>   Once in camp I put a log on top of the fire and it was full of ants. As it
> commenced to burn, the ants swarmed out and went first toward the cen-
> tre where the fire was; then turned back and ran toward the end. When
> there were enough on the end they fell off into the fire. Some got out, their
> bodies burnt and flattened, and went off not knowing where they were
> going. But most of them went toward the fire and then back toward the
> end and swarmed on the cool end and finally fell off into the fire. I re-
> member thinking at the time that it was the end of the world and a splen-
> did chance to be a messiah and lift the log off the fire and throw it out
> where the ants could get off onto the ground. But I did not do anything
> but throw a tin cup of water on the log, so that I would have the cup empty
> to put whiskey in before I added water to it. I think the cup of water on the
> burning log only steamed the ants. (*FTA* 327–28)

Horrific and apocalyptic, to be sure, but given such a vision of the world who
would prefer to be a healthy inexperienced ant nesting in an as yet unburned
log to being one of those ants with the burnt and flattened bodies who have had
the experience?

—m—

The military version of the myth is appealing in yet another manner. An interrelated presupposition of fictions based upon the myth is that its heroes are
cursed with some kind of war experience that is more horrific than any preceding it. Post–World War I narrative fictions tend to imply that modern war is especially or unusually brutal. Thus they add another stratum (consisting of most
past generations of fighting men) to the class that includes the "fresh fish" of
untested Union regiments, Nurse Helen Ferguson and Tenente Ettore Moretti
from *Farewell to Arms*, Squadron Leader Rex from *Piece of Cake*, and Major
Frank Burns from "M*A*S*H"—the invaluable class, that is, of those who do
not "know" and whose existence is thus critically important to the self-esteem of
those who do. These fresh fish form the bourgeois against which the aristocracy
of savaged savants can measure its own superiority. Hemingway yet again estab-
lishes this sense with masterful brevity. Tenente Frederic Henry outfits himself
for his return to the army:

"Have you any need for a sword?" she asked. "I have some used swords very cheap."

"I'm going to the front," I said.

"Oh yes, then you won't need a sword," she said. (*FTA* 149)

Similar passages accrue throughout this novel—how Catherine Barkley antici- pated that her English fiancé might be wounded ("with a sabre cut") as opposed to what actually happened ("They blew him all to bits"); Frederic Henry's expe- rience with "the words sacred, glorious, and sacrifice and the expression in vain," and so on. Equivalences can be found in a good deal of post–World War I fiction. Antique romantic or chivalric notions about war are imported into the present, and the measure of the hero's growth lies in his coming to contemn them.[13] Sometimes novels more substantially contrast a past world in which meaningful sacrifice was possible with the (often unprecedentedly) horrific pre- sent.[14] The burden is almost always the same, however—that past generations were innocent of what current heroes must endure. Hence these present heroes are more genuinely in touch with the harsh reality of existence; they suffer more and are thus more to be admired and pitied than martial figures of the past. As with raw recruits and military zealots, so too with past generations: all of them alike are loosely assumed to believe in an effortlessly achieved conventional mili- tary glory, whereas the true "glory" lies in knowing the "reality," and enduring it.

That this is the strict truth of the matter, that all the warrior generations be- fore the late nineteenth century were besotted with illusions of glory and were innocent of the "truth" of human existence, is surely open to question. Rudyard Kipling's writings (which may come as a surprise to those who think of him only as a propagandist for Empire) suggest far otherwise, both in his presenting com- bat as a dirty, thirsty business ("But when it comes to slaughter, / You will do your work on water") offering essentially the same "rewards" as those that ac- crue to Hemingway's combatants, and in his claiming that it was ever thus, even for "The Men That Fought at Minden," and even when "'Omer Smote 'is Bloomin' Lyre." (Kipling's only full-scale depiction of battle turns upon the humiliating rout of a British regiment.) Y. N. Harari finds precious little ini- tial "illusion" of any sort in the "Renaissance" texts that constitute the earlier portion of his brilliant study of "Martial Illusions: War and Disillusionment in Twentieth-Century and Renaissance Military Memoirs." When, in 1778, Samuel

13. Remarque, *All Quiet on the Western Front*; Siegfried Sassoon, *Memoirs of George Sherston*; Phillip Rock, *The Passing Bells*; Robinson, *Goshawk Squadron*; Wagner, *Sands of Valor*.

14. Sassoon, *George Sherston*; Ford, *Parade's End*; Waugh, *Sword of Honour*; Deighton, *Bomber*; Evan Hunter, *Sons*.

Johnson said, "Every man thinks meanly of himself for not having been a soldier," he went on to add, "or having been to sea"; and it is the context of the latter, the sampling of the worst that life can offer rather than the glorious best,
that the remark is set. Shakespeare's portrayal of one of the greatest military victories in English history works against an audience's expectations and, instead
of martial glory, focuses mostly upon the brutality necessary to enforce military
discipline; the duplicity inherent in the wielding of political power; and the
squalid compromises that are implicit when a family's dynastic interests seem to
coincide with those of a nation. The only thing Shakespeare shows Henry V
doing during the combat phase of the battle of Agincourt is ordering the (probably necessary) killing of French prisoners.[15]

Rather than work back so incrementally, the literary imagination could also
leap all the way back to *The Iliad*. Glory and honor and the like therein constitute no icing on any cake, no added enhancement to a rich, warm, or god-
sheltered existence, but quite the opposite. See the exchange between the Trojan
allies Sarpedon and Glaucos in book 12: so short, brutal, and barren is human
existence that military glory and consequent public adulation are the only
things giving it any significance at all. But these "significant things" consist of
pathetically trite rewards such as "precedence at table" and grants of farmland,
which transitory things are to be gambled for by repeatedly risking life itself, in
a world that conceives of death as a shadowy gibbering vampire state to which
all humans are consigned. This seems a bleaker vision than anything obtaining
in Hemingway. The presupposition, then, that the current experience of war is
far worse than any preceding it—a presupposition embracing works as distinct as
A Farewell to Arms and *Gravity's Rainbow* or "All Quiet on the Western Front"
and "Apocalypse Now"—is itself mythic, another example of the tendency of the
human imagination to refashion the world in ways that give it particular, even if
morbid, satisfaction. Recall again *The Iliad*: the background to that story, set in
the ninth year of a war of pointless slaughter, offers tales of past battles, generally sharp, successful, and always involving heroes (Heracles, Meleager, or
Nestor in his salad days) superior in kind to any of the present day—heroes immune to and hence ignorant "back then" of the kind of suffering and anguish
Homer's characters are enduring on the plains of Troy. That this "generational"

15. Rudyard Kipling, "Gunga Din," in *Rudyard Kipling's Verse: Inclusive Edition, 1885–1926*, 465;
"The Men That Fought at Minden," ibid., 501; "When 'Omer," ibid., 403. The story of the
British rout is "The Drums of the Fore and Aft," in *A Kipling Pageant*, 100–133. Harari, "Martial
Illusions"; Samuel Johnson, quoted from Boswell's *Life*, secured at http://www.samueljohnson
.com/soldiers.html#267; William Shakespeare, "King Henry V," 4.6.

presupposition is itself a myth of considerable antiquity should caution us against accepting as necessarily "true" the larger myth about combat and "manhood" of which it is such a significant part.[16]

—⟋ɯ—

The particular, even peculiar, brilliance of *The Red Badge of Courage* is in how it confronts this myth of combat experience as the myth is configured in the modern world. Alone among modern works about war, as far as I know, this work accepts the myth at face value. This is to say that the novel allows its hero to accept the myth at face value and to prosper, in order the better to show that it is indeed a myth, rather than a fact of masculine life, and in order the best to show how pervasive and persuasive the myth nonetheless is. Many things in Crane's creative impulse may have contributed to the unusual way his novel functions: perhaps a tendency to denigrate the significance of an experience he had been denied; more likely, an understandable decision to fashion his novel around the experience of an atypically obtuse private soldier, in order to deflect possible challenges from veterans about the accuracy of Fleming's responses (there is ample evidence that Crane need not have been concerned about this). But Crane's absurdist conception of our plight in the universe is right at the heart of his mordant, sardonic treatment of this particularly potent myth in his most brilliant of fictions.

Private Fleming's history surely seems to touch all bases. He is outfitted at several early stages with the language of immaturity: he believes himself a "hero," then "magnificent," then a "knight." A contrast is drawn between battles of the classical past and those of the present world: "Greeklike struggles would be no more." He finds himself robbed of individual liberty by the rigors of an "iron" military discipline. Amid a scene of carnage, he fails completely the test of combat, which in turn leads to a long period of self-recrimination, during which he has unusual experiences replete with instructive lessons about himself and the world. One of the men closest to him is inexplicably killed. He himself is wounded in a way that seems sacramental, or baptismal, or of the chivalric tradition—in a way, in any case, that suggests he has been profoundly changed. He returns to his regiment and reenters combat; he is surrounded anew by savage random slaughter, but now he is capable of facing his foes and fighting well. At a crucial moment he transcends all that he has been and becomes the reverse: the (very) private soldier becomes the regimental flag-bearer, the alienated individual

16. Homer, *The Iliad*, 12.360ff.

becomes the cynosure. Thereafter he leads his comrades to their moment of un-qualified success. In the aftermath of this experience, he studies "his deeds, his failures, and his achievements." He looks "back upon the brass and bombast of his earlier gospels" (evidently the initial language in which he conceived of him-self, and of combat) and "now despises them." Thus, we come to the envoi—per-fect alike, so it seems, to the traditional story of the youth who is stripped of his illusions and achieves manhood, and to the overlapping and equally traditional story of the young soldier whose experience of military life and combat has ma-tured him: "He was a man."

At no point, however, is the former traditional story genuinely true in the case of Private Fleming and his illusions, and neither is the latter, the military version. It is as though a sequence of extension cords led from a socket to a neon sign proclaiming "manhood." Plugged in, the sign for a second flickers, but sparks cascade from each connection between the cords, and there is the stench of burning. The narrative could not run truer to the tradition, but no single portion of it is inherently true. Fleming's combat experience has not given him a full, toughening plunge into the harsh realities of our existence, far from it.

In the first place, rather than exposing him to a sequence of events reflecting the trustworthily certain malevolence of the universe, combat has exposed to him a sequence of events that are utterly chaotic in substance. Crane uses a se-quence of bizarre ironies to insist that human experience, even the heightened experience of combat, has no inherent or inevitable shape. Fleming's crimes go unpunished because unperceived; his wounding is the most fortuitous thing that could have happened; he is led back to his regiment by a man whose face he never sees. Because Private Wilson did his duty where Fleming failed to do his, Fleming enjoys a crucial sense of moral superiority over his "friend." The same emotions and attitudes that led to his panic on the afternoon of May 2 lead to his "sublime" heroism on the morning of May 3. The capture of a rebel flag il-lustrates absolutely the reverse of what it should (the supremacy of the rebels' skills as combat infantrymen, and the superiority of their courage and elan). Private Fleming achieves his apotheosis of self-satisfaction and self-esteem in a battle in which his own army suffers an unsurpassed humiliation. More largely, this is set in a battle in which the Union army could not lose, but did; and in which the rebel army could not win, but did—yet in so winning it lost more than it could afford (because, recall, rebel soldiers mortally wounded their own best corps commander) and hence "really" lost.

In the second place, just as the events are, in substance, chaotic rather than malevolent, so the experience for Private Fleming has not been unrelievedly hideous nor has its trajectory spiraled consistently downward. Enduring long hours of self-doubt and consequent agony, he actually suffers more before the combat even begins than he does later. When the battle breaks upon him, he is plunged into an extraordinary sequence of emotions including both hate and love, climaxing in "the most delightful sensations of his life" (*RBC* 64). His subsequent panic plunges him into a moment of nightmarish fear; and during his wanderings behind the lines he has moments of abject self-pity, even moments when he envies corpses, but he also has moments of quite lively curiosity and is privileged to witness some extraordinary things. Upon his return to the regiment, not only is he unpunished for his desertion, he actually returns to a far more pleasant condition than the one he left. Gone now are the experiences of unrelieved anxiety and isolating self-doubt. Even before the action begins on the morning of May 3, he enjoys a self-confidence quite unlike anything he has felt previously during the campaign—and all this, largely, because he did panic the day before. This new (and altogether unwarranted) self-confident spirit is then confirmed, of all things, by his subsequent actions. After these actions are underway, he has moments of intense hatred not always focused appropriately upon the rebel soldiers opposite him; but he also "basked" in pleasure at his conduct during the rebels' first probe, feels a "sublime absence of selfishness" during his regiment's counterattack, is "very happy" when praised by his officers, is self-confident and smilingly "tranquil" when the action is renewed, and concludes the whole experience in a rapture of personal pride, confidence, and contentment.

In the third place, no matter what Private Fleming thinks, his illusions, "the brass and bombast of his earlier gospels," have not been stripped from him. Instead, they have become plated over with a new and even more impenetrable set of illusions, rendering them now impervious to assaults of even the most obvious kinds. Witness how now he can believe that "an existence of soft and eternal peace" is ahead of him, despite the tactile, logical evidence on all sides: when he is surrounded by "despondent and muttering" soldiers retreating down a "trough of liquid brown mud" toward "the river" they crossed at the beginning of the campaign and hence is indisputably a member of a defeated army with a good deal of "the red sickness of battle" yet ahead. The experience of combat has in fact "toughened" Fleming, but not by compelling him to face the naked truth; rather, by strengthening his illusions about himself and the world.

How Private Fleming has been brought to this final moment still encumbered—more than ever encumbered—by his illusions has absorbed a good deal of our attention in this study of the novel. His solipsism, his childish vanities, his vivid visual imagination, his lack of human sympathy or compassion, all these have consistently shielded him from learning the lessons that are there for him to learn. These characteristics have steadily enabled him to revise the facts of his history and his situation so that they feed into rather than interrupt the narrative of the play in which he is the (inevitable) hero. Believing himself "doomed to greatness" even before he has proved he can stand up to the test of the battle line, he has thereafter gone on to prove that he is "great," at least in the not-so-small theater of the 304th New York Volunteer Infantry Regiment.

What we saw in terms of the myth of "manhood" (see Chapter 9) is reiterated in terms of the myth of the significance of combat experience. Both myths culminate in the same claim: that having survived two days of battle, "He was a man." Private Fleming obviously believes in both myths. He surely makes no discrimination between them. But for the purposes of the discussion here, he obviously believes that combat constitutes a profound "test": he has so conceived of it from the outset, believing, in the banal terms of an experiment in chemistry, that he is "proving himself" by "going into the blaze" (*RBC* 18–19). Hence the military myth: that the experience of combat will be a toughening plunge into "reality," and if he emerges from it, he will have established some profound truth about himself. The vagaries of the ensuing days cause his imagination to spew forth various titles, ranks, and estimations that he thinks apposite to himself at various moments. But at the end, having been through the experience and now calmly (albeit hugely) self-contented where before he had been wrenched by spasms of self-doubt and anxiety, his imagination finds itself happiest by applying to himself full-bore the "military experience myth." According to the myth, the experience of combat plunges soldiers into contact with the reality of existence, and this makes them men. He has been in combat, thus he must have been plunged into the reality of existence. Just as earlier he assumed that, since he is on the firing line, he must be being loyal to something, so here: "He had been to touch the great death," he tells himself, thus fulfilling the terms of the myth (with phrases just as empty as those he supplied earlier to explain his unwonted loyalty), "and found that, after all, it was but the great death." Now he believes that the battle, so far as he himself is concerned, is over. So both those spasms of self-doubt and those phantasmagoric images of military glory now seem part of "the sultry nightmare" through which he has proved himself. How pleasant it now is, instead and in contrast, to relish the simple, understated conception of himself as merely a "man." But this conception of himself is educed in the context of his sure knowledge that his comrades, his company commander, and his colonel hardly think of him as "merely a 'man'": to them, he is "a war devil," a " 'wild cat,' " " 'a very good man t' have,' " and " 'a good 'un.' "

The fact that he believes in this new illusion—that he has experienced reality and that he is a man—enables him to reaffirm with an entirely free hand his earlier illusions about his personal greatness in and his centrality to the world. No experienced soldier could be mistaken about his status in the universe. Fleming is an experienced soldier, thus he could not be mistaken in the "gleeful pleasure" he takes in the "great and shining prominence" of his recent actions. He could not be mistaken in his confidence that "he will no more quail" no matter what challenges he will face in the future. He surely could not be mistaken in his new certainty "that the world was a world for him."

Crane's great novel is then "antiwar" in a unique and a profound way. Rather than inadvertently reinforcing the myth that combat is an introduction to "reality" and thus a sure way to achieve a chastened but genuinely informed maturity or "manhood," *The Red Badge of Courage* purchases the myth, sets it into motion, and then dismantles it. It purchases it by replicating the full pattern of the thing. Its hero is not deflected from a full experience of combat into some rear echelon or some peculiar sideshow. He is not distracted from combat by a brutal or insane commanding officer. His experience of combat is not supplanted by some bizarre mischancing of military justice, or by having punishment officially appropriate to his dereliction of duty visited upon him. He is not killed at the outset and does not suffer some gruesome although relatively unusual wound. The maldistribution of rewards does not become an issue.[17]

The Red Badge of Courage presents the purest possible situation in which the myth can develop. It develops the narrative exactly according to the basic "story" in the myth: an inexperienced young soldier enters combat, suffers, emerges transcendent from his suffering, and finds himself a "man" at the end of the process. But, throughout, Crane offers sequences of events, motivations, and psychologies that are, in each instance, absolutely different from those supposedly inevitable to the myth. And despite the great variety of critical assessments visited upon the novel, no one has challenged the plausibility of these sequences. Indeed readers tend to identify with him completely ("Yes, that's probably what I would have felt, had I been in his place"). Most readers so readily understand the sequences of Private Fleming's thinking—his various self-justifications and

---

17. For the rear echelon, see "Mister Roberts"; for some peculiar sideshow, see "King of Hearts" or Waugh, *Sword of Honour*. For a brutal or insane commanding officer, see Wouk, *The Caine Mutiny*; Smith, *A Killing for the Hawks*; or "Platoon." For some bizarre mischancing of military justice, see Cummings, *The Enormous Room*; Cobb, *Paths of Glory*; "Paths of Glory" (1957). For appropriate punishment, see "King and Country"; for death at the outset, see Roth, *Radetzky March*; for some gruesome unusual wound, see Trumbo, *Johnny Got His Gun*; for the maldistribution of rewards, see Ford, *Parade's End*.

the like—and find them so persuasive that he is typically regarded as "typical," as a sort of "Everysoldier" (see Chapter 5).

It is true that we do not follow him very far. We do not see what other results might follow from another year or more of experience. But Private Fleming certainly seems to have had more experience of actual combat in these two days than did Tenente Frederic Henry in his two years in the Italian motor-ambulance service. Implicit in the myth about the particular "value" of the experience of combat is that it is a particularly swift way to be plunged into the hideous reality of the world. The putatively inoculating power of the experience should not, surely, be a matter of the length of one's exposure to it.

Further, implicit in the myth about the particular "value" of this experience is that it is not only a very swift but also a very certain way of plunging into the hideous reality of the world. Private Fleming's experience of combat on the afternoon of May 2 is, however, radically different from his experience of it on the morning of May 3: compare "On his face was all the horror of those things which he imagined" (*RBC* 69) with "the youth felt serene self-confidence" (209). I cannot think of any other fiction in which the hero's first taste of combat is so substantially different in kind from that which succeeded it. Such is not the case in *All Quiet on the Western Front,* or *Look Down in Mercy,* or *The Thin Red Line,* or *Goodbye to Some,* or "Hamburger Hill"; or, for that matter, in *The Iliad.* Here, too, in the simple plausibility of Fleming's psychology, the "military myth" is undermined.[18]

Basic to Crane's challenge to the "military myth" (the myth that combat leads inevitably to the experiencing of the world's hideous reality, and thence to maturity) is his refusal to accept the myth that underlies it. He denies the "cosmic boot camp" mythology, the myth that the universe is guided by a principle of active, conscious malevolence (see Chapter 9). Crane is sardonically aware of the comfort, even pleasure, to be derived from believing in this myth. He refutes it because, in his understanding, our plight is far worse. The universe does not make any "sense" at all, not even "sense" of this malevolent, frightening kind. "But they killed you in the end," says Frederic Henry. "You could count on that. Stay around and they would kill you." There is a crude sort of basic truth in this, since all living things do eventually die. But in a world where one male creature was born dead while another "was living to be a hundred years old and played a smoothly fluent game of billiards" at ninety-four (*FTA* 260), is it not fi-

---

18. Remarque, *All Quiet on the Western Front;* Baxter, *Look Down in Mercy;* Jones, *Thin Red Line;* Gordon Forbes, *Goodbye to Some.*

nally ludicrous to claim that "you can count upon" finding a universal pattern imposed upon all human experience by some band of shadowy cosmic antagonists?

The novel acknowledges that there is an extraordinary "reality" to combat: that it does confront participants with elemental realities (among them, pain and death) in an urgent, concentrated fashion, and that it does evoke displays of heightened, most elemental emotions. The "reality" encountered by Private Fleming during these two days of combat, however, has been not so much malevolent as purely chaotic. The events in this "Episode" have not proceeded ineluctably to some final, paradigmatic, confirming horror, such as Catherine Barkley dying in childbirth, Paul Baumer getting killed on a day when the "Western Front" is reported as "All Quiet," Captain Tony Kent in the British edition of *Look Down in Mercy* committing suicide in the safety of Delhi after having miraculously survived the retreat from Burma, or Mr. Roberts killed while drinking coffee in the wardroom of his destroyer. Rather, Fleming's actual "career" during these two days—as opposed to his "experience" of it—has been utterly chaotic. Actions proceed without logical sequence or consequence (witness how his act of desertion eventually produces in him a conception of his own "greatness"), which events then illogically, perhaps even outrageously, proceed to confirm. Thus, although his myth-making propensity is too strong for him to see the truth, combat actually has introduced him to "reality."

If the reality of our situation is finally chaotic, it means that our individual lives are destined no more necessarily for catastrophe than for happiness or for triumph. Is every log containing an ant colony "destined" to be placed upon a campfire? People who await some sort of personal apocalypse are no more certain to be "rewarded" with one than are people who believe in quite other destinies, though the former will surely be more miserable throughout the course of their lives. People who consciously seek scarifying or brutalizing experiences are no more to be admired than people who seek serenity and security. Indeed, in light of Crane's belief concerning the absurdity of our situation in the universe, the apocalypse-believers seem curiously bent on gratuitous self-mutilation.

Neither does combat inevitably offer, in the "Episode" at hand, a useful disciplining or chastening of the emotions. Granted, after a single day of battle, Private Wilson is quieter, less pompous, more thoughtful than he was before. But a chaotic world will produce a chaos of emotional reactions. It is equally plausible that, at the end of combat, a private soldier (Henry Fleming, for instance) could be more conceited, more pompous, and less knowledgeable about himself and the world than he was before.

Combat is just as liable to reinforce—and reinforce virtually beyond redemption—illusory beliefs about the world and our status in it as it is to strip such illusory beliefs from us. Seen in a sort of long view, or squint, *The Red Badge of Courage* offers a reiterated pattern: characters (most often Private Fleming, but once at least the 304th New York as a whole) struggle, writhe, or squish through an experience; confidently assert thereafter that they have been transformed into "hero," "knight," "man," or the like; then blunder into another experience that proves they are no such thing; emerge therefrom nowise daunted; proceed to yet another confident self-assertion; blunder anew into another refutation; and so on. In Crane's vision, what is radically untrue is to believe that there exist any permanent "ranks," "categories," or "classes" bespeaking some permanent accommodation between the individual and the world. Through the responses it elicits from its readers, even in the process of demonstrating this dour truth, Crane's fiction also demonstrates—mordantly, hilariously, perhaps even optimistically—that the human capacity to believe in such things is ineradicable.

Chapter 11

Literature as Mousetrap

The Reader Caught

The Red Badge of Courage mounts an unusual and profound challenge to the enduring myth of the "value" of combat experience. The overwhelming majority of its mature readers are people concerned with the issue of warfare and steeped in the post–World War I literary response, which is almost entirely "antiwar." Why, then, is Crane's novel so rarely understood in this way?

Although overwritten at times, Crane's novel is the most stylistically accessible of all the novels traditionally considered "canonical" in American literature. Its study of human psychology is so plausible, clear, and persuasive as to be enthralling to most readers. Whether it is admired or not, that the novel portrays comprehensible and typical states of mind in its characters is not an issue but a given. Its themes are among the most common and elemental treated in literature; its narrative follows the single most pervasive structure found in the literature of the Western world. Why then has it generated such a bewildering array of different critical responses, many of the most thoughtful of which are in radical opposition to each other?

In order to address this issue and to summarize what Chapter 10 sought to establish, let us consider a short story by Stephen Crane that is widely read but, in point of fact, not very good. "The Blue Hotel" moves with the unsubtle directness of Crane's poems to its central point, when the character known as the Swede makes his way through a winter storm into Fort Romper, Nebraska:

> He might have been in a deserted village. We picture the world as thick with conquering and elate humanity, but here, with the bugles of the tempest pealing, it was hard to image a peopled earth. One viewed the existence of man then as a marvel, and conceded a glamor of wonder to these lice which were caused to cling to a whirling, fire-smote, ice-locked, disease-stricken, space-lost bulb. The conceit of man was explained by this storm to be the very engine of life. One was a coxcomb not to die in it. However, the Swede found a saloon.[1]

Such "conceits" most pointedly include the sorts of egocentric myths the dismantling of which forms the substance of *The Red Badge of Courage*; the sorts of myths that so shield Private Henry Fleming from the gaping reality of human existence. "The Blue Hotel," with a vengeance, validates the truth of this stark portrayal. The Swede has arrived in Fort Romper steeped in a myth derived from the pulp fictions and lurid gazettes of his day, a myth that conceives the "West" to be bloody and lawless. In the overheated common room of the small, seedily respectable Palace Hotel he blurts out, apropos of nothing, "I suppose there have been a good many men killed in this room." But then it is surely more comforting to believe you are in the "hellish" world of Billy the Kid and the Dalton Gang than that you are "clinging to a whirling, fire-smote, ice-locked, disease-stricken, space-lost bulb." Strong drink allays his fears; he accuses the proprietor's son of cheating at cards and thrashes him in a fight. And so a second myth, one of his own cosmic invincibility, succeeds the first: of the near-blizzard outside, he tells the proprietor, "Yes, I like this weather. It suits me." Drunkenly pressing himself upon the town's professional gambler, he gets himself stabbed dead. His corpse, "alone in the saloon, had its eyes fixed upon a dreadful legend that dwelt atop of the cash-machine: 'This registers the amount of your purchase.'"[2]

"The Blue Hotel" depicts, with merciless clarity, our human predicament as self-conscious creatures in a brutally indifferent universe, and our consequent tendency to generate and to live (and die) by egocentric myths. It thus depicts the Naturalistic understanding of the human condition that is obviously central to *The Red Badge of Courage*, but which is worked out there with far greater complexity. The stark clarity of the story makes it particularly useful at this point in our study of Private Fleming, but that clarity is also the reason it seems unsuc-

---

1. Stephen Crane, "The Blue Hotel," *Other Writings*, 273.
2. Ibid., 254, 274, 277.

cessful as a work of fiction. It is a good example of how most Naturalistic fiction is beset with logical and aesthetic problems.

Literary Naturalism was generated by the impact of Darwinism in the last half of the nineteenth century, and it held that human beings are essentially no different from any other species. Human beings are far more complex animals than laboratory rats—or well-meaning cows (*RBC* 57) or jaded horses (68) or proverbial chickens (69)—but human nature is finally shaped by and human behavior inevitably reflects the same brutally indifferent evolutionary forces as govern all species. Literary Naturalists believed that the only true representations of human nature and of human behavior were ones that demonstrated the play of these forces, and that the most enlightened writers would thus consider themselves as scientists of a kind. Crane's impressionistic style set his work apart from that of the rest of the Naturalists, who aspired to the flat style of scientific investigation, but most of his fictions (including *The Red Badge of Courage*) were otherwise completely shaped by literary Naturalism. Naturalistic works were centrally committed to displaying how blind forces and raw facts, such as the crudest animal instincts, inherited traits of character, social conditioning, and fortuitous or ghastly accidents, concatenated in entirely dominating—and entirely explaining—the lives of suitably selected human specimens.

In selecting such specimens, though, crippling logical and aesthetic problems arise for the fictions produced by the Naturalist movement. Heroes in Naturalistic fictions have to be blind to the reality of their situation. They might otherwise rebel or behave in desperately atypical ways. Herman Melville's "Bartleby" perfectly exemplifies the danger that would accrue in selecting a hero who is even moderately aware of his plight. Stunned into an awareness that he is entrapped in a blindly indifferent universe, Bartleby just refuses to play his part: he "would prefer not" to go on acting, or living, at all.[3] His awareness of the human predicament in a Naturalistic world makes Bartleby a spectacularly unsuitable candidate for the starring role in a Naturalistic story, which illustrates the logical problem inherent in literary Naturalism. In Naturalistic fictions, central characters who are necessarily less intelligent than their authors and their readers are nonetheless advanced as illustrative of the human condition. Crane clearly intends for "The Blue Hotel" to be understood by a wide readership, but if the supposedly typical, myth-besotted Swede had understood what Crane intends for his readers to understand, he would never have gotten himself into such a pickle.

3. Herman Melville, "Bartleby," in *Billy Budd, Sailor, and Other Stories*, 25.

This logical problem is even more apparent in longer works, novels that, through a single and tyrannical pattern of symbolism and through frequent dictatorial explanations, insist upon the universality of the Naturalistic truth upon which they are built. But if it is a universal truth, why does it not apply to the book's author, or to its readers? The only fully fledged and stylistically typical Naturalistic novel that seems to me to escape this problem is Richard Wright's *Native Son*, in which most of its characters are less able to comprehend their plight than are most of its readers because of racist barriers that keep them in an inferior condition. But for the rest, even the most famous Naturalistic fictions— Theodore Dreiser's *Sister Carrie* or *An American Tragedy*, Frank Norris's *The Octopus* or *MacTeague*, James Farrell's *Studs Lonigan* trilogy—all seem to me to wreck themselves on this reef.

This logical problem is inevitably compounded by a severe aesthetic problem. The Naturalistic author observes his characters (the appeal of the Naturalistic thesis seems quite gender specific) and invites us to observe them as though they were beneath a pane of glass. At best, Hurstwood in *Sister Carrie* or even Bigger Thomas in Richard Wright's *Native Son* may prompt some feelings of pity: they are incapable of evoking a more profound response. They are (designedly) specimens, intended to evoke not sympathy but rational evaluation; the author's constant tapping of the pointer on the pane of glass reminds us of that. In "The Blue Hotel," Crane, exactly like a professor rushing to add one more point just as the period ends, adds a gratuitous concluding scene that makes the remaining characters even more remote, even more unsympathetic than they were before. The cowboy evinces even more stupidity, the "Easterner" confesses to having been a coward. All this turns upon a fact—that the proprietor's son actually was cheating at cards—of mind-numbing inconsequence, which had nonetheless been kept from the reader until this last post-bell moment. The characters' limitations are always so obvious in these fictions. Rather than being drawn imaginatively into their world we are relieved to find ourselves above it. Even as we watch the events unfold in "The Blue Hotel" with a morbid fascination, we are profoundly grateful not to be sharing that overheated parlor and the embarrassingly lower-class fellowship within it. For all its self-conscious concern with issues of social justice and with introducing its readers to the "realities" of modern life, Naturalistic fiction actually encourages, it seems, a grateful sense of aristocratic superiority in its readers, as in "The poor old Swede doesn't have a clue, does he?"

As a result, the forces, fictions, and circumstances that dominate the characters in Naturalistic fiction finally seem pretty remote from a reader's own experience ("I would never act the way the Swede does. I would go to my room, lock the door, and read Henry James for the rest of the night"). The result is fiction of a vivid, dramatic, but ultimately sterile, even distasteful sort. Contrast, for instance, "The Blue Hotel" to James Joyce's "Counterparts." Farrington in Joyce's story is a brutal man and an alcoholic, but rather than inviting us to observe him from a superior vantage, Joyce plunges us imaginatively and immediately into his world. We are seduced into sympathy, and at the climax of the story, when Farrington takes out his frustrations by beating his innocent child with a walking stick, we are emotionally stunned rather than coolly enlightened.[4]

In *The Red Badge of Courage* Crane's understanding of the human situation is very largely a Naturalistic one, but he is concentrating upon a specific aspect of that situation, which is present in but rarely central to most Naturalistic fiction. To reiterate: this novel is not a study of "the mind of a soldier in combat" but, rather, a study of the universal human tendency toward solipsism, toward perceiving the world in some congenial because comprehensible fashion, toward myth-making. This is a tendency that embraces everyone, novelists as well as their characters, and commanding generals of armies ("Fighting Joe" Hooker) as well as private soldiers. "The conceit of man" is, in Crane's vision, humanity's most distinctive attribute. We even find ourselves evaluating his characters according to an implicit, half-glimpsed scale based upon the "quality" of the myths pervading their lives. The appalling tawdriness of the Swede's mythic conception of the "West," cobbled together out of the most ignorant kinds of pulp fiction, is one of the most off-putting things about him. In contrast, Private Fleming's myths seem positively noble. They are utterly conventional; but they are derived from conceptions of heroism and the like that have obsessed humanity for centuries, and which have produced some of the greatest works of the human imagination. Recall too, in this context, how the "correspondent" in "The Open Boat" finds his mind returning repeatedly to the image of "the soldier of the Legion" who "lay dying in Algiers," a poetic shard recollected from the melancholy romantic myths of his childhood, the reappearance of which may be inexplicable and ironic, but by no means ignoble or pitiable.[5]

—⁂—

So, then, this "myth-making" (to summarize the above, clumsily) is an understandable human tendency that Crane knows we all share. His intention in *The*

4. James Joyce, "Counterparts," in *Dubliners*, 82–94.
5. Crane, "The Open Boat," *Other Writings*, 306–7.

Red Badge of Courage is focused not so much upon establishing the central Naturalistic "truth" that human beings are just unusually complex animals but, rather, upon exploring this central tendency that makes us so complex. Rather than showing human beings scurrying about like rats in an experiment (the substance of "The Blue Hotel" and most other Naturalistic fiction), he is focusing instead upon the unique attribute that sets this "animal" apart from all others.

Crane above all intends to demonstrate how powerful, pervasive, and universal is this solipsistic myth-making tendency. To this end, his novel is set to trap his reader into complicity with the myth-making tendency of his characters. We have seen the result throughout this study: witness how often I have suggested or made an informed guess about "the immediate response that most readers have" to a given situation—in order to differentiate that response from the reality of the situation itself; in order, in turn, to show that most readers' responses will ignore that reality; and to show that this is indeed the end to which Crane's strategy intentionally works. His strategy is a difficult thing to define crisply, and my powers of definition can do no better. For simplicity's sake, let us call this novel one of the rare instances of the "narrative as mousetrap."

The art of "trapping" a reader—into erroneous, confused, puzzled, or most often unfulfilled responses, through withholding information for a while—is not merely a part of the narrative art, it *is* the narrative art. It is crucial to sustaining a reader's active curiosity and interest. This is true whether we are considering O'Henry's "The Gift of the Magi" or James Joyce's "The Dead"; Agatha Christie's *The Murder of Roger Ackroyd* or Faulkner's *Absalom, Absalom!*; "Gone with the Wind" or "The Godfather"; "The Sound of Music" or Shakespeare's *Othello*. We know that Desdemona is innocent and we surmise that she will nonetheless be killed, but this remains only a surmise until the action is completed. Nor do we know until that moment the setting, the tone, the circumstances, or the last gestures and pleadings circumambient to her death; all things of great interest and moment that are withheld from us until the exact moment appropriate to their revelation.

None of these fictions is finally a mousetrap. By the end of each, the cage door is opened: the truth revealed, the moral pointed, the reader liberated into full realization. And we, as readers, have counted upon just this. We have suspended not our disbelief so much as our insistence upon certainty (in every form of narrative except live drama, it is always possible to flip or "fast-forward" to the end). We have played a game in which we have pitted our intellect against the pattern of the fiction, consciously or unconsciously trying to determine ahead of the ultimate moment itself what that moment will reveal to be the "truth," whether factual, moral, or even spiritual (as in *Moby-Dick*, for instance). To the extent that this final moment of revelation is, in retrospect, congruent with what has preceded it, we finally enjoy and admire the work. I say "in retrospect" because if the final moment has been too apparent beforehand, if not enough has been withheld, we find the narrative "too obvious," boring, or the like. Narrative fictions too committed to displaying single truths—whether they are spiritual or Naturalistic or "of the heartland"—seem to fail for just this reason.[6] I say "congruent" because if the final moment is not coherent with what has preceded it, if too much has been withheld until the end, we feel irate, somehow cheated.[7] The perfect timing of the crucial revelation in Book Eleventh of Henry James's *The Ambassadors*—which brings to culmination a dozen subtle patterns of themes and images preceding it, enjoyed with a consequent shock of recognition at the moment and then relished in retrospect—makes that novel a brilliant success.

The Red Badge of Courage is not a fiction of this most typical sort, though it seems to be: this is necessary to its strategy. It does indeed seem to lead us to final revelations about Private Fleming's destiny, which we have indeed anticipated. Thus, to many readers, the second half of the novel evidently seems "too obvious" even to repay close attention. The novel's real intention is to evoke these very anticipations, with the purpose of making us reconsider them, and by extension ourselves: to think finally not about the destiny of Fleming, but about why we ourselves brought that particular set of anticipations to bear, why we applied them despite all kinds of evidence that they are not really applicable, and why we held to them so steadfastly despite the fact that they were proving ever more inappropriate as the novel develops.

This is not a matter of misleading readers by withholding crucial information until well after their anticipations have apparently been fulfilled, which is quite within a narrator's power. See its frequent use in modern horror films, where the monster shudders back to life after the hero and heroine stagger off screen, just before the credits roll. This relatively cheap device is used especially when authors seem unsure as to whether their fiction at last "signifies" (if you are afraid

6. For spiritual truths, see Nathaniel Hawthorne, "The Birthmark"; for Naturalistic truths, see Stephen Crane, *Maggie, a Girl of the Streets*; for truths "of the heartland," see "Hoosiers."

7. Nathaniel Hawthorne's determination to wrench a positive ending out of the tragic matrix of *The House of the Seven Gables* seems an example of this. So too does Alice Walker's *The Color Purple*. See also the positive ending of the American edition of Baxter, *Look Down in Mercy*.

it may not, then add some gratuitous, complicating, ironic last "fact"). But it produces dissatisfying fiction. It is, after all, essentially an attenuation of the tendency in some fictions to withhold too much for too long. One of the basic problems with "The Blue Hotel" can be seen as an example of the inherent weakness of this clumsy narrative strategy. To a story already problematic in the matter of its basic appeal, Crane has added a gratuitous, complicating, ironic "last fact."[8]

Fiction of the "mousetrap" kind (that is, fiction that does not actually use the "trap" but that ultimately is itself the trap) works in exactly the opposite way. Throughout its length, not only intimations and foreshadowings but raw facts are presented in such a way as to direct a reader's responses into courses that are different from those which—directed instead by anticipations and presuppositions that override or ignore those facts—they nonetheless follow. Rather than pointing the moral at the end, rather than finally disclosing some crucial but heretofore hidden fact, the author leaves the reader's anticipations, and the responses produced, alone on the field.

An example of this extraordinary kind of fiction is (in its own way) as brief and as brusquely to the point as "The Blue Hotel." This is Flannery O'Connor's "A Good Man Is Hard to Find."[9] At the very place where our lifelong familiarity with printed fiction has taught us to look for "the meaning"—in the penultimate paragraphs of the story (recall how Crane's "He was a man" falls exactly there)—we are confronted with the following earnestly delivered speech from a character called the Misfit: "Jesus was the only One that ever raised the dead, and He shouldn't have done it. He thown everything off balance. If He did what He said, then it's nothing for you to do but thow away everything and follow Him, and if He didn't, then it's nothing for you to do but enjoy the few minutes you got left the best way you can." The colloquial "thown" and the grammatical infelicities may deflect a reader a bit, but the ultimate appeal of this as a profound statement of the vexing truth of Christianity is unmistakable. It seems so "right," falling exactly where we expect a statement of profundity, that its position alone probably carries a reader past the Misfit's actual definition of how to enjoy oneself in this brief sparrow's flight of life—"by killing somebody or burning down his house or doing some other meanness to him"— to the next statement, a *cri de coeur* that appeals to our yearning for certitude, for the knowledge that can come only through personal experience, for cosmic fair-

---

8. For a more puzzling instance, and one that troubled the author enough to send him back years later to try (unsuccessfully) to repair it, see the ending of Allen Tate's *The Fathers*.

9. Flannery O'Connor, *A Good Man Is Hard to Find: Ten Memorable Short Stories*.

ness: "I wasn't there so I can't say He didn't [raise the dead]. I wisht I had of
been there. It ain't right I wasn't there because if I had of been there I would of
known. Listen lady, if I had of been there I would of known and I wouldn't be
like I am now."[10] And we think, "Of course!" How can it be "right" or fair that
the miraculous dispensation we identify with Jesus Christ is something immured in history? Why does Doubting Thomas have the truth proffered to him
alone, out of the billions of people who would indeed have reformed their lives
if they could have "been there" and thus "known"?

What the Misfit says at this sacrosanct place in the story speaks not only to
us, in bracingly succinct phrases, but for us, as well. Thoughtful readers brought
unprepared to this moment surely think "Yes, we are all misfits," terminology
that five decades of Existentialist fiction (such as Albert Camus's *The Stranger*,
André Malraux's *Man's Fate*, or Samuel Beckett's "Waiting for Godot") have assured us is exactly appropriate for human beings cursed with independent and
rational minds. Two short paragraphs follow this, and then five short sentences
of dialog, the last so clearly confirming the existentialist truth of the Misfit's argument that (again) just listing Existentialist titles (Jean-Paul Sartre's "No Exit"
and *Nausea*, or Albert Camus's *The Plague*) suffices to confirm its significance:
"It's no real pleasure in life." Nothing in the conclusion, no turn of plot, no authorial intrusion keeps us from a full identification with the Misfit's spiritual
frustration and consequent alienation from life.

Nothing, that is, but a thoughtful review of who it is, exactly, that we are so
persuaded to identify ourselves with. Even as we watched, the Misfit has just directed the cold-blooded murder of a family of five: father, son, mother, daughter, and finally the grandmother, which last he performs himself. These five are
unquestionably unpleasant people, representatives of the spiritually and cultur-
ally inert bourgeoisie at their worst. This very inertness makes their deaths finally not completely gratuitous, just as it probably contributes to our relative
indifference to their fate and enables us to find the Misfit a sort of touchstone
of honesty or the like. But the fact remains that an insane serial killer has become a spokesman, if not a hero—for us. We also have to face the fact that there
is indeed a subsequent logic, which follows upon the Misfit's argument. If we accept his argument as the ultimate reality in the world, we have to accept that
logic. There is "No pleasure but meanness": if someone so honest and earnest
in his existentialism believes this, and if we have identified this existentialism as
our own, we have nothing besides purely personal preference with which to
challenge him: "Maybe that's how you feel, but that's not the way I feel. I myself

10. Ibid., 27–29.

take pleasure in sunsets, puppies, and the Boston Red Sox." That does not quite get the job done, does it?

Thus we find ourselves trapped. Returning with even more ferocious attention to the story itself does not help, since we read it closely to begin with, and with a full and sophisticated awareness of general literary tradition and an eager alertness to the specific allusions within it. So what the story finally makes us do is to reevaluate the very reason we agreed with such a monster in the first place. The story makes us reflect upon the unreflective presuppositions about ourselves and the world we brought to bear from the outset. Here, as in virtually all of O'Connor's most compelling fiction, we are brought face-to-face with the consequences of a set of beliefs that are so basic to our natures as to be almost instinctive: a belief in the supremacy of pure rationality among human capacities; a belief in the critical importance of personal experience in knowing the truth about ourselves and our world; a consequent disdain for "authority" and for "blind" faith. This set of beliefs that seemed so benign, bland, and humane actually constitutes a monstrous egocentricity; they reveal the nexus between the old Protestant demand to "know God" for ourselves in our own personal terms, and modern self-centered existentialism. So when our culture becomes only nominally "Protestant," and its conscious theology decays into those unexamined and unconscious mental tendencies, we are betrayed into the worldview of the Misfit.

O'Connor obviously believes these habits of thought are genuinely baneful. Why does she not make her belief explicit? Why does she not, so to speak, open the door of the trap herself, through some device of plot or characterization? Why does she instead run the demonstrable risk of leaving a proportion, perhaps a great proportion, of her readers inside the mousetrap, that is, in the grip of the erroneous belief that her story confirms the spiritual attitudes of Kafka and the Existentialists?

She avoids taking these explicit steps not because she is indifferent about whether her work is understood but precisely because she is so committed to its ultimate effect. She believes these habits of thought are baneful exactly because they are so deep-rooted and because they constitute the unreflective attitudes with which most of her readers approach the world. She recognizes how limited is the hortatory style—the imposed argument, the sermon, the exemplum reinforced with taps of the pointer upon the blackboard—in compelling anyone to come to any fundamental personal realization. Any "truth" that is put in some easy, direct way immediately loses its plangency; it can be, with equal facility, ignored. Made immediate and obvious (as in "Protestantism and existentialism alike lead to egocentricity, which is a bad thing; here is the heart of this story"), this truth can then be readily discounted, as not at all personally applicable ("I get the point of the story now, and I've even known some people like the ones in it. But I have always known that egocentricity is a bad thing. And although my own parents were Baptists, I don't really believe in anything myself. So I'm sure I'm not a bad person"). When confronted with any general truth or fact, we always assume ourselves to be an exception: this is why historical accounts of the total annihilation of a garrison or of a ship's company or the like register with so much more horror in our imagination than accounts of events wherein even one person survives.

Conversely, to have to come to understand, by myself, what it was in my own system of perception and belief that led me to such an appalling conclusion is to recognize, to be brought fully face-to-face with the degree to which I myself share in such a general truth. Granted, some may (no! some inevitably will) never come to such a recognition. If a person's imagination is so stunted as to find that the Misfit is indeed a sufficient personal "representative" of his or her own spiritual malaise, stunted by being steeped in works that can make a hero of a man who starves himself to death (as in Franz Kafka's "Hunger Artist"), for example, or another who murders an Algerian because the noonday North African sun is oppressive (as in Camus's *The Stranger*), then arguably no approach, no matter how brutally direct, could be redemptive.

It is in this fashion, as a "mousetrap" for the reader's individual response, that most of O'Connor's short stories work. They repeatedly confront us with characters whose claims or arguments seem utterly plausible, yet these characters or claims are finally utterly repellent. For example, see Manley Pointer's brutal confirmation of Hulga (Joy) Hopewell's nihilism in "Good Country People"; Julian Chestny's politically correct challenge to his mother's racism in "Everything That Rises Must Converge"; and conversely, Mr. Head's grace-through-racism with his grandson in "The Artificial Nigger." Again and again her stories end with climactic moments in which we find ourselves shocked by the consequences of what we have steadily been beguiled into affirming. One of the few avatars she gives us is Father Flanagan, in "An Enduring Chill," but the "hero" Asbury Porter Fox has been given such a complete arsenal of modernly appropriate attitudes and enthusiasms that, by any reach of usual persuasiveness or logic, Flanagan is completely outmatched.[11]

Having mentioned Father Flanagan, let me immediately confess: a wide variety

---

11. "Good Country People" and "The Artificial Nigger," in *A Good Man Is Hard to Find*. "Everything that Rises Must Converge" and "The Enduring Chill," in *Three by Flannery O'Connor: Wise Blood, The Violent Bear It Away, Everything that Rises Must Converge*.

of other examples would make me more confident that I am indeed defining a certain recognizable type of literature. The category of literary criticism that is inevitably elicited by this kind of fiction is readily named: "reader response" criticism, which is brilliantly exemplified in Stanley Fish's study of *Paradise Lost*. But this type of literature itself is hard to specify, and harder to exemplify. Milton's reader may remain obdurately convinced that Satan is the "real hero" of *Paradise Lost*, but this will be despite both the brilliant subtleties undercutting Satan throughout the epic, and everything that is overtly, directly, and unambiguously shown and declaimed about him after line 999 of book 9.[12] *Paradise Lost* is hardly an example, then, and although I can make a stab at claiming that some of Mark Twain's fictions are, candor finally compels me to drop them from the (very limited) roster. I can finally think of only one other example of great fiction that operates in this unusual way, and this is Herman Melville's darkly brilliant *Benito Cereno*.[13]

Benito Cereno offers an array of significances, some profoundly in keeping with those established by Melville in *Moby-Dick*: the impenetrable "blankness" (rendered here as "gray," though, rather than "white") of the world around us and of human experience in it; the corresponding irrelevance of conventional systems of human virtue or intelligence in safe-guarding ourselves; the unyielding inhumanity of the natural world; the no less impenetrable power of such a seemingly transient thing as individual human temperament, which means that some bruises can never be soothed while some obtusenesses will never be penetrated; the catastrophic power of darkness. So it is quite possible to read the story with full intellectual satisfaction while remaining utterly oblivious to having fallen into the trap, at its center, that captures us because of our unconscious racial attitudes. Indeed it is quite possible to believe that the story reveals—has trapped for the witness of futurity—Melville's own virulent racism.

Then it is also quite possible to read the story as just a hugely enjoyable detective story and to be completely satisfied with finding out at last "the truth" of the situation aboard the *San Dominick* into which, "In the year 1799, Captain Amasa Delano, of Duxbury, in Massachusetts, commanding a large sealer and general trader," finds himself plunged (*BC* 166). Delano is a liberal and genial

---

12. Stanley Fish, *Surprised by Sin: The Reader in Paradise Lost*. For the significance of line 999, book 9, see Galbraith Crump, *The Mystical Design of Paradise Lost*.

13. Herman Melville, *Benito Cereno*, in *Billy Budd and Other Stories*, 166. Further references to this work will be given parenthetically in the text as *BC*.

man of a liberal, genial, and generous racism: "like most men of a good, blithe heart, Captain Delano took to negroes, not philanthropically, but genially, just as other men to Newfoundland dogs" (*BC* 213). The constant play of Delano's racism throughout the first gray-shrouded and mystifying portions of the story continually invites a reader's bemused contempt. Delano especially admires Babo, "a black of small stature," who is Captain Benito Cereno's personal servant. In Babo's "rude face, as occasionally, like a shepherd's dog, he mutely turned it up into the Spaniard's," Delano sees "sorrow and affection . . . equally blended" (167). Delano's liberal but racist imagination repeatedly compares blacks to animals—dogs, deer, leopardesses, doves. It "credits" them with loving faithfulness to their white masters, general irresponsibility, a love of gay colors, "the unaspiring contentment of a limited mind," a fondness for holidays, the barbers' trade, and music (212–14). It also continually invites a reader to admire his or her own freedom from any such prejudice.

Yet, infuriatingly, it is the constant play of Delano's racism that alone saves the captain's life. The truth is that the cargo of slaves aboard the *San Dominick*, under Babo's leadership and taking advantage of the benign trust their owner had reposed in them, have seized control of the vessel and have slain a number of the white officers, crew, and passengers including their owner, whose skeleton they have preserved at the bow of the ship to terrify the remaining whites into obedience. Storms have since battered the undermanned ship. When Delano first sights it, it is short of water and provisions and is barely seaworthy. When he comes aboard, they perpetrate a masquerade upon him, pretending that Captain Benito Cereno and the white crew are still in command.

It is a haphazard masquerade at best, shot through with discordant notes, warning hints, conscious acts of defiant contempt once the depths of Delano's ignorance have been sounded (Babo uses the Spanish royal flag as a barber's apron), even a display of outright piratical curiosity about Delano's own ship, the *Bachelor's Delight*. But Delano rejects all such; compelling himself (it is a fascinating study in deliberately obtuse optimism of a peculiarly Protestant and American sort) to remain oblivious. Almost all of his stillborn fears and suspicions have to do with the peculiar behavior of the Spanish captain (faltering and incoherent as it is, given the pressure the man is under). At one moment it does occur to Delano that there may be some malevolent secrecy afoot among the blacks under Cereno's direction: "could then Don Benito be in any way in complicity with the blacks?" He dismisses this thought, though, with a racial assessment so speedily produced it obviously is less a thought than an instinctive assumption: "But they were too stupid" (*BC* 201). Again, this obtuseness, grounded so completely in Delano's racism, is what (maddeningly) saves him. Had he ever revealed any "understanding," Cereno assures him after the event is over, "death, explosive death" would have ensued (256). Insofar as a reader's typical experience with any display of racism in narrative fiction is concerned, this is a richly disturbing turn of events in itself.

Delano's consciousness is almost always at the center of the story (there are only one or two sentences from a perspective beyond his own), and the reader is in the same fog of uncertainty that engulfs Delano for much of the story's length. But at last the climactic, declarative action comes. Frantic to warn this generous, well-meaning American of the danger he is in, Cereno risks his life by throwing himself into Delano's whale boat as it pulls away from the side of the *San Dominick*. Babo leaps after Cereno and tries to stab him; Delano at last understands the situation. The first-time reader as well is exhilarated at finally understanding things and completely accepts Delano's own rapidly expanding comprehension. Ask any group (a classroom, say) of intelligent readers to identify the moment when Delano at last "sees the truth," and at least nineteen out of twenty will produce that moment in the whale boat: "Captain Delano, now with scales dropped from his eyes, saw the negroes, not in misrule, not in tumult, not as if frantically concerned for Don Benito, but with mask torn away, flourishing hatchets and knives, in ferocious piratical revolt" (*BC* 233).

Delano has heretofore credited the blacks, especially Babo, with an array of positive virtues—loyalty, innocence, patience—while harboring deep suspicions about the whites, and a reader has been more or less dragged along with these suppositions. Just as the reader at last recognizes that authority and power aboard the *San Dominick* have been the reverse of what Captain Delano assumed, so too the reader now agrees with Delano that the moral equation is also the reverse: actually the whites are the innocent victims, and the blacks are "dervishes," "cawing crows escaped from the hand of the fowler," figures of brutal, "malign," and barbarous evil; Babo's head, "fixed on a pole in the Plaza" of Lima after his execution, is called "that hive of subtlety" (*BC* 258). Ask the same classroom of readers if the story finally does provide an example of that which Captain Delano with his "singularly undistrustful" American "good nature" can hardly believe in at its beginning—"malign evil in man"—and at least nine out of ten will say that it surely does, in the figure of Babo (162). Yet again, for a reader's literary imagination steeped in our popular culture's typically hamfisted approach to racism wherein the black is almost always portrayed as misunderstood but noble, this moral revelation is startling enough.

These final moral assessments are confirmed by a process in which the (typically white, Western-educated) reader is likely to repose ultimate confidence: a formal, official "investigation" of the "whole affair" in the law courts of Lima. The narrative itself now devolves into "extracts" from a "document selected from many others" presented in "the case." The major document is Benito Cereno's own officially notarized deposition explaining "the true history of the *San Dominick's* voyage" to the investigating tribunal. The legal language and the public forum of its presentation, so rock solid in contrast to that world of "shadows" that preceded it, assure, at least to the reader's (Western) imagination, that we are seeing the "truth" upon which civilized justice can now be established. The "atrocities" of the blacks are publicly attested in this court of law, their criminality dispassionately proved, and following full corroboration from "subsequent depositions of the surviving sailors," the "tribunal," soberly mindful of its "duty," passes "its capital sentences" (*BC* 239f).

Broken by his "'memory'" of this experience and unable to live much longer in the "'shadow'" of "'The negro,'" Benito Cereno is sadly impervious to the fatuous blandishments of Amasa Delano; "three months after being dismissed by the court," he dies. This last development invites a reader to consider profound issues: that of the plight of human consciousness—"memory"—amid a brightly indifferent natural world (Crane everywhere offers the best gloss upon Melville to be found in our literature), and that of the presence of "malign evil" (in Spanish *negro* means "blackness") and its impact upon that consciousness (*BC* 256–58). Left then with much to ponder, a typical first-time reader is nonetheless also profoundly satisfied to have come to see the truth at last. The story *Benito Cereno* obviously rewards rereading. The typical reader can relish the mordantly hilarious play of irony throughout, knowing at last the truth of the situation aboard the *San Dominick*. For example: "Marking the noisy indocility of the blacks in general, as well as what seemed the sullen inefficiency of the whites it was not without humane satisfaction that Captain Delano witnessed the steady good conduct of Babo" (169). He calls Babo a "Faithful fellow!" and says, "Don Benito, I envy you such a friend; slave I cannot call him" (176). Readers reading it a second time can enjoy disentangling the interlocked ironies: it is true that Babo "cannot" be called a "slave," he has liberated himself; but for "steady good conduct" a reader can supply exactly the opposite; and for "faithful fellow," read "faithless enemy."

Whether satisfied just to have come to see "the truth" at last or rereading the story and supplying such "informed" interpretations, typical readers thus fall into the trap, revealing thereby their own altogether unsuspected and unconscious racism. Melville's assumption is simple, and accurate: confronted with this situation, most white readers (perhaps, persuaded by the "legality" of the last "deposition" portion, most Western readers) will identify with the whites. But when Amasa Delano, "scales dropped from his eyes," sees the blacks "in ferocious piratical revolt," he is not seeing the "truth," but only a "truth" that a white ship's captain would indeed see. The blacks are unmistakably in "ferocious revolt," but the piracy is only incidental to it. To acquire the *San Dominick* was not their intention but, instead, the means to their intention since they are seeking "their liberty," however pathetic their chances of achieving it. Their act of "piracy" pales in contrast to the sanctioned "piracy" of racial slavery, of which they are the victims. Seen in this light (though it is a light that pervades the narrative only after most readers have been caught, and well caught, in the trap), Babo is in fact heroic in his fidelity to his people and his cause. He is self-sacrificial and faithful to the end. Seen in this light, his "conduct" is not so much "steadily good" as "steadily heroic."

Given (finally) such a light, heretofore minor details take on altogether new significance. The "investigation" of the "affair" takes place in "the vice-regal courts" of a Spanish colony wherein racial slavery is legal. The deposition is notarized by a member of the Spanish Inquisition ("the Holy Crusade of this Bishopric"). The legal authority of such a court and such a judicatory system may be absolute but its moral authority, as it "assembles the data whereon to found the criminal sentences," is no better than that under which the blacks dispensed brutal disciplinary justice when they controlled the *San Dominick*. Indeed, given that the white courts seek to sustain slavery while the blacks are seeking liberty, the moral authority of the former is virtually nonexistent. Other details register for the first time: the crude warning ("Follow your leader") chalked below the owner's skeleton is exactly the mate's cry as he leads the American sailors to recapture the *San Dominick* (BC 234–37). Those sailors, saviors of the situation in most readers' first response to the story, are encouraged by the prospect of prize money, whereas the blacks, whom most readers are at first happy to see overpowered, are fighting for their freedom. The murderous brutality visited upon the helpless white crew when the ship was first seized is repaid exactly in kind once the blacks have been recaptured and are in shackles. Indeed, the total casualty lists for the whites on the one hand and the blacks on the other are remarkably similar, perhaps even identical. The most barbarous act perpetrated by the blacks, rendering the skeleton from the corpse of their murdered owner (done "in a way the negroes afterward told the deponent, but which he, so long as reason is left to him, can never divulge") is copied, and for exactly the same ends of terrifying an enslaved people, by the "vice-regal court," which fixes Babo's head "on a pole in the Plaza" for "many days" (251, 258). How many first readers are as appalled by the second act as by the first? How many of them initially perceive the court's action as anything other than just?

The characterization of Amasa Delano's genial racism is perfect for the final springing of the trap. The slaveholding Spaniards are obviously racist, but they belong to another, easily condemned culture. In contrast, Delano from Dux-bury invites a reader's amused contempt: "He's basically a good man, but he should know better." He should, in sum, be like the readers: capable of recog-nizing racism, because they are personally untainted by it. So when—and if—readers ever recognize the racism they have unconsciously applied with marvelous con-sistency to the story, they cannot help but judge themselves by the same stan-dards whereby Delano was judged. Perhaps they can at last understand that racism is not an attitude consciously adopted by depraved or evil people, for some ulterior motive (garnering more votes, for instance, in an election in a southern state); nor even something that affects only people who are deficient in intelligence or upbringing. Readers will understand what an instinctive, en-demic, and thus pernicious thing racism really is, because they have just pro-vided a living example of it.

It is sorely tempting to add a couple of Mark Twain's novels to this category of "mousetrap" fiction. It is tempting to think that, in *Pudd'nhead Wilson*, when Wilson declaims "Valet de Chambre, Negro and slave—falsely called Thomas a Becket Driscoll—make upon the window the fingerprints that will hang you!" the fact that even an astute and reflecting reader will on a first reading find this a cause for unalloyed satisfaction is the moment when a deliberately fashioned trap snaps shut.[14] The "real" Valet is so Caucasian as to have misled the "real" Tom Driscoll's own father and to have had himself raised, educated, and un-questioningly accepted as a member of the slave-owning aristocracy. This fact is proof positive, it would seem, that the category "Negro" is a "fiction" based upon a monstrous, omnipresent, racist belief that "blood" predetermines ca-pacity and predestines character. To apply it to the "real" Valet is ludicrous; to apply it at all is contrary to all the evidence of the novel. Were this then an ex-ample of a fictional mousetrap, on a second or third reading our readers would recognize how their initial satisfaction reveals their atavistic proclivity to accept racist categorizations if they are promoted by the metaphorically one-eyed liberal

14. Mark Twain, *Pudd'nhead Wilson*, 164.

(with whom the reader has been steadily identifying) in this benighted kingdom of the slaveholding blind. The reader would then have to go on and recognize that Wilson himself, for all of his "State of New York" background, has been absorbed by the racial codes of Dawson's Landing, Missouri. But I think that the moral and intellectual authority of Pudd'nhead Wilson is too thoroughly established in the novel for this climax to be read as anything other than Wilson's own triumphant vindication. This climax does not entrap but rather (supposedly) rewards a reader's expectations. The lines of force and the lines of emotional authority in the novel just do not intimate or even permit the kind of startling revision (or re-vision) that a newly aware reader is impelled into through reading these fictions of O'Connor, Melville, and Crane. To review (or re-view) Pudd'nhead Wilson is possible, it goes without saying; but to do so diminishes rather than increases our respect for the author's endeavor.

Let us glance at Adventures of Huckleberry Finn, and the way in which almost all first- or second-time readers get caught up in the rich, wildly variegated humor of Tom Sawyer's crack-brained "evasion" whereby the (already-free) Jim will be liberated. The last fifth of the novel almost always entraps unwary readers, who have been contemptuously confident about their vast superiority to the white racists populating the novel, but who have therein been trapped into demonstrably, instinctively identifying with the (white) Huck and Tom rather than the (black) Jim. They have thus not clearly realized that Jim has been kept in slavery in order to satisfy Tom's yearning for adventure. Again, while this aspect of this great novel is there to be (finally) seen, the circumambient patterns finally dissuade me from confidently adding Huck Finn to this collection.

—⁂—

The mousetrap strategy central to Benito Cereno and the fictions of O'Connor seems to me to be clearly and crucially central to The Red Badge of Courage. In Crane's novel, rather than being trapped by their unwitting existentialist egocentricity or by their unconscious racism, readers are trapped by their unthinking belief in the same myths whereby Private Henry Fleming and his fellows in the 304th New York Volunteer Infantry Regiment understand themselves. Crane's work differs in tone from those of O'Connor or Melville, for those are attentive to attitudes and systems of belief that are pernicious, both evil in themselves and productive of evil in the world around them. Crane's strategy is intended to display a universal human tendency. This tendency may inevitably be mistaken, but inherently it is neither "good" nor "evil."

The two principal myths addressed by his fiction are so overlapping that they both can be summarized by the same phrase: "manhood achieved." The second myth (concerning the value of combat experience) depends in modern times upon the first (that the world is consciously malevolent toward humanity). I have sought to show how Crane counts upon his readers to anticipate the same myth, of the "boot-camp" nature of the world, that drives his characters, and to replicate it as they read the novel (see Chapter 9). Crane is confident that most of his readers will do this despite the continually accruing evidence, which denies that this myth has any validity whatsoever in the experiences of Private Fleming or of the 304th New York Volunteer Infantry Regiment during the battle of Chancellorsville. Nonetheless, Fleming and his regimental comrades, and typically those reading about them, persevere doggedly down to and through a conclusion in which the myth sweeps to a triumphant conclusion, despite the most basic and immediate facts of the book.

The same strategy is also at work concerning the second myth (the value of experiencing combat). The fact of the matter is that combat does not necessarily plunge a soldier into the harsh realities of our existence (see Chapter 10). It does not inevitably transform a person at all, and it certainly does not inevitably transform a "callow youth" into a "man." Combat does not necessarily purge a soldier of his immature illusions; it can instead reinforce those illusions. Combat can just as well "transform" a soldier into a "man" of arrogant, "heroic" self-delusion as change him into a man of cynical stoicism or wise maturity. This last sentence is a synopsis of what happens to Private Fleming at the battle of Chancellorsville.

Yet much critical study of the novel begins (or ends) with the assumption that Henry Fleming has matured in some crucial way. This assumption is implicit or explicit in many of the scholarly responses (see Chapter 6). Daniel Aaron and Michael C. C. Adams are both thoughtful, ambitious, widely read cultural historians, and they radically disagree about the novel itself, even about how the majority of its readers are likely to experience it. Yet, that "the youth" has undergone a profound transformation of some sort is central to each man's study of *The Red Badge of Courage*. This proves the enduring pervasiveness of those myths that Crane's novel was designed to "entrap" us into realizing we also share.

Is it indeed possible that a young man whose habits of thought and response strike us as realistic and familiar—as typical of our own habits, and even as sympathetic (no Tenente Moretti, in other words)—could go through two days of combat, witnessing the death of officers and close comrades on every hand, fleeing in terror at one point and compelled to face the fact of his own cowardice, fortuitously reprieved from the consequences of this, but thrust immediately back into the furnace of battle, and not be matured by the experience? Is it indeed possible that this young man could go through all this and emerge even more self-deluded about himself, about combat, and about the elemental realities of human life than he was before? Put so starkly, it seems incredible. But it seems incredible because of the presuppositions we ourselves, products of a particular time in human history, bring to the contemplation of such circumstances. First among them and dictating the rest is our instinctive (that is, our mythic) sense that there is a single harsh (that is, malevolent) "truth" that any "significant" (that is, any chastening) experience must impose upon any "normally perceptive" person (that is, any person prepared to understand the malevolence of the universe).

Crane has shown us that this entirely opposite result is entirely credible: especially—and paradoxically—if the "young man" involved believes in this very myth, and thoughtlessly and instinctively accepts it as the "truth." The myth itself will insulate him from the facts of his circumstances. It will enable him to translate or transmute these facts into a pattern, a story, conforming to his unwitting assumption that he is the central figure in the world. It will cause him to believe that the world itself is conforming to his understanding of it—that is, to this myth. Crane demonstrates that our own presuppositions are based, not upon immutable facts about "reality" and human nature, but upon myths; and that the only "immutable fact about human nature" is that it will generate all but impermeable myths about itself and its relationship to surrounding reality.

It seems to me that a typical reader's experience of *The Red Badge of Courage* is much like that of the characters in the novel (see the end of Chapter 10)—and designedly so. Crane's novel offers a reiterated pattern: characters and readers alike struggle through a battlefield ordeal; confidently believe thereafter they have witnessed some critical psychological or moral transformation; undergo another ordeal, which proves that no such thing took place in the first place; emerge therefrom nowise daunted; proceed to yet another confident assertion of belief; are led anew into another refutation; and so on. In Crane's vision, what is radically untrue is the very belief that permanent transformations bespeaking some permanent accommodation between individual and world actually take place. Yet what is profoundly true is the human tendency to put faith in such a belief.

By its very nature, literature of this sort (the sort I have called "mousetrap" literature, though the term seems embarrassingly shallow) is very daring. Eschewing the tyrannical powers inherent in literary closure whereby his or her "real meaning" can be riveted into place, the author risks being utterly misread.

And since the very intention of this kind of literature is to challenge omnipresent "misreadings" of the world, the risk is great indeed. The author crafts the fiction knowing full well that very many of its readers will be predisposed toward misreading it, because they are already predisposed toward misreading the world.

This misreading is the author's target, but to attack it in this daring way is to play with fire. There is no way of knowing how many readers of *Benito Cereno* have found it to be a confirmation of their own instinctive attitudes about the inherent savagery and brutality of the black race; but the critical imagination, misunderstanding Melville's story from the opposite pole, has sometimes found the story itself to be racist (see Sidney Kaplan's essay "Herman Melville and the American National Sin"). And in his eloquent, sophisticated 1988 essay in the *New Yorker* celebrating the Library of America's publication of Flannery O'Connor's collected works, Brad Leithauser takes at face value the crack-brained "communion" achieved between Mr. Head and his grandson Nelson as they are transfixed by "The Artificial Nigger." In his understanding, O'Connor's work concurs that this "communion" is indeed to be seen as "a state of holy grace," which response, completely missing the story's satire upon backwoods Southern Protestantism, necessitates two tortured paragraphs of justification.[15]

—⚅—

To return at last to the inquiry at the heart of this chapter: this mousetrap technique upon which *The Red Badge of Courage* is based is manifestly the reason it has evoked such an inconsistent, baffling, and variegated array of critical responses. The novel deliberately generates conventional and powerful anticipations and seems to fulfill them, and with them, whatever surmises about human significance underlie them. And these surmises are never explicitly contradicted. Yet most mature readers are aware of a curious dichotomy between the completely familiar direction in which the novel has seemed to unfold and many of its actual details; that the general "end" of the novel is in some way not consistent with specific facts.

Awareness of some of those facts, this study has consistently argued, has been submerged by post–World War I fiction and a corresponding lapse of knowledge about the actual nature of battle in the Civil War. Some of those "facts"— the warning signs, the cautionary notes, available during the first reading of the

15. Sidney Kaplan, "Herman Melville and the American National Sin: The Meaning of 'Benito Cereno'"; Brad Leithauser, "A Nasty Dose of Orthodoxy."

novel, then to be reconsidered or given new credence as a reader's confident first response begins to unravel and he or she reviews Private Henry Fleming's story anew—have thus become misunderstood or lost. Both professional students of the novel and its "ordinary" readers, not surprisingly, have often floundered off in quite different directions, directions set by their own individual presuppositions about issues of morality, warfare, and the like. To repair or recover the facts of the Civil War pertinent to an imaginative, rich, and sophisticated response to *The Red Badge of Courage* has been the central endeavor of this volume.

Conclusion

By way of illustrating exactly what Crane's unusual narrative strategy accomplishes, let us measure *The Red Badge of Courage* against another work of fiction depicting combat between Western armies in the mid-nineteenth century, Leo Tolstoy's *The Sebastopol Sketches*. Tolstoy's book presents three fictional "sketches," of short-story or novella length, set in the siege of Sebastopol during the Crimean War. It is, says J. C. Levenson, "The most important book that lies behind *The Red Badge*."[1]

Some of the similarities are immediately apparent. In *Sebastopol* the sun lingers indifferently or rises accusingly, thereby providing raw material for the industry created by R. W. Stallman's famous claim concerning the significance of the last sentence in Chapter 9, "The red sun was pasted in the sky like a wafer" (*RBC* 99).[2] Of more significance, in Tolstoy's sketches, death is distributed just as randomly as it is in *The Red Badge of Courage*. In both works, officers neglect "to stand in picturesque attitudes" (*RBC* 59), though Tolstoy's Russian Imperial officers at least strive to do so and are sometimes embarrassed when they think they have been caught out. In both works, in Levenson's precise phrase, "the controlling purposes of characters do not shape the action," although Crane's American infantrymen do manage to impose their wills upon a part—admittedly, a minute part—of the action on the battlefield of May 3, 1863.[3]

1. Levenson, "Introduction," xl.
2. R. W. Stallman, "Notes toward an Analysis," 251–53.
3. Levenson, "Introduction," xlv.

In an altogether different register of significance, however, the two fictions are strikingly similar. This is in the challenge each work mounts to regnant mythologies about war and about the human condition. Crane's novel profoundly challenges the widespread belief that the experience of combat turns "boys" into "men" (see chapters 10 and 11). Tolstoy's *Sebastopol Sketches* also explicitly and forcefully challenge this belief. At the outset of the sketch "Sebastopol in May," the "down-at-heel" Lieutenant-Captain Mikhailov is a particularly unimpressive, unimaginative, narrowly configured man, who grovels in the presence of both aristocrats and superior officers. Mikhailov then enters a vicious night battle during which his men recover a trench with their bayonets. A fellow officer is slain by a shell that explodes right beside Mikhailov's head yet leaves him untouched. From this experience Mikhailov emerges as a down-at-heel and particularly unimpressive, unimaginative, narrowly configured man who grovels in the presence of both aristocrats and superior officers. Prince Galstin remains a coward, Adjutant Kalugin remains immensely brave but immensely supercilious, Cadet Volunteer Baron Pest (whose bayonet kills a Frenchman) remains a conceited little snot. The single character who is changed by his experience of combat is the toadying, unpopular cavalryman Captain Praskukhin, because he gets himself killed. He accomplishes this by freezing in fear when a shell with a lighted fuse falls spluttering at his feet. Foremost among Captain Praskukhin's last conscious thoughts is that he owes Lieutenant-Captain Mikhailov twelve roubles.[4]

So contentious may be this argument—that combat does not necessarily transform "boys" into "men"—that it is worth remarking that Tolstoy's *Sketches* are based upon his own experience as an ensign in the Eleventh Brigade of the Imperial Russian Artillery during the siege of Sebastopol. Ample evidence exists that, although Captain Oliver Wendell Holmes Jr. of the Twentieth Massachusetts Infantry Regiment may have found his heart had "been touched with fire" during the Civil War, other officers were decidedly not so affected. For example, Herman Melville's cousin Henry Gansevoort, an officer in the Third U.S. Artillery Regiment: before his experience of combat he is a touchy, vain, ambitious, hypocritical, self-centered, and self-pitying man, concerned only with his social standing and constantly petitioning for transfers and promotions. Lieutenant Gansevoort serves with his battery in the thick of the fighting at Antietam— "Artillery Hell," according to the rebel gunners, and the bloodiest single day in

---

4. Leo Tolstoy, *The Sebastopol Sketches*, 62, 96. Further references to this work will be given parenthetically in the text as *SSk*.

American military history. Thereafter, he is a touchy, vain, ambitious, hypocritical, self-centered, and self-pitying man, concerned only with his social standing and constantly petitioning for transfers and promotions. And lest one think (recall Chapter 5) that, while such may have been the case before the day of modern artillery and the machine gun, the experience of modern combat could hardly fail to devastate its participants, recall the paradigm-perplexing statistics cited in Samuel Hynes's *The Soldier's Tale*: "71 percent of the Vietnam veterans polled were glad they went to Vietnam, 74 percent enjoyed their war, and 66 percent would be willing to serve again."[5]

Crane's novel challenges an even more widespread belief, the perhaps gender-specific belief about the malevolence of the universe that is so endemic in the Western world. This belief holds that the universe has a malevolent shape; that if a human being fortunately survives his inevitably bruising encounter with this malevolence, he will thereby achieve a permanent status called "manhood"; and that once this status is achieved, its possessor thereafter will be capable of facing up to whatever this malevolent reality can throw at him—that, as Private Fleming thinks, once you become a "man" you will "no more quail before [your] guides wherever they should point" (*RBC* 232). This, too, *The Sebastopol Sketches* ridicule. In the ranks of the tsar at Sebastopol, there is a very great deal of "quailing," most particularly among those most experienced in the malevolent brutality of combat. A thoroughly experienced company commander gets himself so ferociously drunk before an assault that his colonel has to order him to be quiet (*SSk* 93). The logistical chaos afflicting the Russian army delays an enthusiastic volunteer so long that his courage entirely vanishes: "Had he gone straight from P—— to the bastions, he really would have been a hero" (*Ssk* 123). Thoroughly experienced artillery officers squabble drunkenly in their mess: "Tomorrow, perhaps even this very day, each one of these men will go proudly and cheerfully to his death, and will die with calm and fortitude," but under the attenuated tension of enduring bombardment in a besieged city, this band of brother officers has degenerated into a "deeply depressing scene" (*SSk* 157).

---

5. Stanton Garner, *The Civil War World of Herman Melville*, 159–61, 197–200, 205ff, 217–18, for example; Samuel Hynes, *The Soldier's Tale: Bearing Witness to Modern War*, 222. For yet another example of a soldier who emerged remarkably unchanged from the experience of battle in the latter half of the nineteenth century, see Leonce Patry's *The Reality of War: A Memoir of the Franco-Prussian War and the Paris Commune (1870–1871) by a French Officer.* This book reflects combat in the brave new world created, just five years after the Civil War, by the omnipresence of the breech-loading rifle. But it contains a memorable and detailed account of the experience of leading an infantry assault in the style that would have been familiar to Lord Cornwallis or Archduke Karl or General Pickett.

Above all, there is the fate of the two Kozeltsov brothers: the wizened, experienced, effective, popular Lieutenant Mikhail, returning to his infantry battalion from hospital with his head wound still bandaged, and the dashing, youthful, vivacious, introspective, popular ensign of artillery Vladimir. In a night assault, French rifle bullets quite indifferently and efficiently kill them both.

Central then to the fictions of both Tolstoy and Crane is a compelling challenge to two shaping myths of the Western imagination. But how differently each work compels its reader's response. Tolstoy's point of view is entirely godlike. It ranges widely and magisterially: "Again, as on earlier days, promising joy, love and happiness to the whole of the quickening world, the sun's mighty, resplendent orb arose from the waves" (SSk 102); it can confidently present alternative outcomes; it hovers above the siege of Sebastopol like a hunting hawk, suddenly and inexplicably diving down to seize upon one particular figure out of moiling thousands.

This style is the polar opposite of Crane's style (see Chapter 4). Crane immerses a reader in his characters' imaginations and in the ways that experiences register upon them. When Tolstoy descends to describe an entirely interior moment in a single character's experience (when, for instance, he details what is going on in the mind of Lieutenant Mikhail Kozeltsov at the exact moment of his death), it is not to immerse a reader therein but, rather, to demonstrate his own extraordinary power of artistic detachment. This power can descend even into such secret spaces as the mentality of a single dying man and can then effortlessly elevate itself upward again into another horizon-girdling sweep: "Surging together and ebbing apart like the waves on the sea on this gloomy, swell-rocked night, uneasily shuddering with all its massive volume, swaying out along the bridge and over on the North Side by the bay, the Sebastopol force slowly moved in a dense, impenetrable crush away from the place where it had left behind so many brave men" (SSk 183).

The result is that Tolstoy's challenge to these myths registers with a bemused but distant intellectuality. Readers are at first puzzled by the random distribution of Tolstoy's narrative attention but soon understand that they are to share, and exult in, the range of its power. This intellectual distance and aesthetic exultation is powerfully enhanced by the remarkably unsentimental, unsparingly detailed attention Tolstoy gives to his central characters. We seem to be looking at them under a microscope: "It was a face that would have been handsome had it not been for a certain puffiness and the presence of large, soft wrinkles (not of the kind associated with age) which enlarged his features and made them flow into one another, giving the whole a coarse, unfresh appearance" (SSk 111–12).

It is manifest that Mikhail ("Misha") Kozeltsov would never envision his own face in such coldly dispassionate terms. Contrast the way in which Crane steadily imposes upon the reader Private Fleming's own self-conception of himself as "the youth": so much so that the reader finds it almost impossible not to assume that Fleming is indeed appealingly youthful in comparison to his fellows. To offer parallels from the visual arts, Tolstoy's style is similar to photography; one is reminded that the Crimean War was the first war visited by and rendered permanent through the actions of the photographer. Consider in these terms the surprisingly seedy appearance of elegant British hussars and be-furred and be-kilted Highlanders in Roger Fenton's mercilessly objective photographs.[6] Crane's style, on the other hand, corresponds to that of the impressionist painters of his own time. As Fleming becomes more acclimated to combat, the style moves from the troweled-on desperation of Van Gogh to the precise pointillism of Seurat.

In *Sebastopol Sketches*, then, we assume the same eminence as the author. We look down upon the specimens of humanity Tolstoy has assembled for our attention. The first sketch is embarrassingly patriotic: "We will die, men, rather than surrender Sebastopol"; "We will die! Hurrah!" (*SSk* 57). It thus depressingly prepares us for a volume promising to be entirely remote from our world in the worst of ways, archaic, innocent, conventional, absurd, with an introductory short story promising only tedium in what will follow. When the second sketch dispels much of this claustrophobic material because of the random and sardonic deployments of its narrative, we find ourselves entertained in a fashion pleasantly unanticipated. When, in the third sketch, everything collapses in defeat and confusion and both of our barely known heroes are quite unemotionally shot dead, we are pleasantly surprised. Old Tolstoy seemed such a creature of the benighted nineteenth century, with its devotions and patriotisms and enthusiasms for all the putative martial virtues: how pleasant to discover that old Tolstoy in fact agrees with us, in our altogether different, modern, superior view of reality; how pleasant that the famous old fellow agrees with us about how foolish is all that military nonsense about "honour" and the like. Our response toward his characters is perhaps pitying, more likely disdainful, in any case distant from and steadily superior to the mentalities of the poor creatures on display before—or, rather, below—us. "Yes," a reader thinks, "that is just the way

6. Roger Fenton, *Photographer of the Crimean War: His Photographs and His Letters from the Crimea*, with an essay on his life and work by Helmut and Alison Gersheim. See also Matthew Lalumia, *Realism and Politics in Victorian Art of the Crimean War*.

people in general are. They (present company excepted) really aren't capable of changing, are they? Interesting point." Tolstoy's fiction thus never makes us aware of how fully our own sense of reality is in fact still shaped by that myth about the effect of combat, or by that "anti-myth myth" about the inevitable shape that must be taken by human experience in a reliably malevolent world.

Crane's daring narrative strategy, on the other hand, repeatedly persuades, entices, compels, seduces us into imposing our own versions of these deep-seated, scarcely recognized mythic systems of belief upon his characters; and this despite all of the evidence steadily accumulating before us that those systems are indeed ultimately mythic. A second reading, more cautiously attentive to the actual details of the novel (see chapters 2–3, 6–8), holds up a mirror to our initial response. In this mirror we find ourselves outfitted in ancient, faintly ridiculous heraldic garments blazoned with names such as "hero" or "man," and we are amazed we ever put them on. So we come to realize exactly how literally informed our own minds are by these myths, despite our assumptions concerning our own cool superiority to the world of those common nineteenth-century infantrymen, because our mental reactions to Private Fleming have proved to be entirely, yet unwittingly, dominated by them.

Even the most basic, prevalent, compelling, time-honored, use-honored narrative of the Western world (so Crane's great novel argues), the narrative of the alienated hero, is itself finally mythic. Even this most basic staple in our imaginative appraisal of reality finally bears no more necessary or elemental correspondence to anything either in the circumambient world or in the human mind than does, say, the Christian myth, or the Deistic, or the Romantic or the Transcendental, or even the Existential in its more ponderously mordant forms. There is "no exit"? Says who? It all depends, doesn't it? *The Outsider? Nausea?* Speak for yourself. "A man with a full stomach and the respect of his fellows had no business to scold about anything that he might think to be wrong with the ways of the universe" (*RBC* 150).

Confronting the absolute, almost unendurable chaos of the external physical universe and of the internal mental universe, the human response—generated by its ridiculous, almost unendurable condition as the self-conscious creature—is to impose some, to impose any, shape.

> "Well, it's all over," he said to him.
> His friend gazed backward. "B'Gawd, it is." (*RBC* 228)

In fact, by God, or by General R. E. Lee, or by raw accident, or by sheer contingency, by the active malevolence or rank indifference of the universe, "it" is anything but "all over." On the most basic level, it cannot be "all over" because the army containing Private Wilson and Private (soon to be Color Sergeant) Fleming is retreating, and there will inevitably be future combat. But then, even the Aristotelian claim that an action can be truly imitated through arranging it into a beginning, a middle, and an end is a "sell," a delusion, an aesthetically necessary delusion, perhaps, but a delusion nonetheless. We surely assume that Aristotle more or less had it right: that there will be discernible relationships between the beginning, the middle, and the end of any action, relationships that any ironic reversals will finally affirm. We also assume that a human being will enter a given action uninformed by what that action may teach, that in the course of that action new facts or realities will register upon him, and that at the conclusion of that action he will not be as he was before. It is almost impossible to imagine that a man's first experience in action on the line of battle would not sort itself out into at least this rudimentary shape. Were ever an imitation of a private soldier's action arranged so as to give the lie to myths about the shapeliness of human experience, that arrangement is to be found in *The Red Badge of Courage*.

Consider what we have seen in the case of Private Henry Fleming of the 304th New York Volunteer Infantry Regiment at the battle of Chancellorsville. His desertion from the battle line, an act committed in the presence of hundreds and punishable by the severest rigors of military law, went unpunished because no one noticed it. The wound he received neither debilitated him physically nor educated him about his own mortal condition; instead, it was the most fortuitous thing that could have happened to him and in the end would be the critical link in the chain of experience that would keep him profoundly uneducated about himself and the world. He was led back to the physical security of the 304th New York by a man who perhaps saved his life and certainly shielded his desertion from being discovered, a man who was thus a benefactor of unsurpassed importance in Fleming's life, yet a man whose face he never saw. While Private Fleming was deserting, Private Wilson was standing to his duty, and the result was that Fleming enjoyed a crucial sense of moral superiority over Wilson, which fed significantly into Fleming's superior performance on the battle line the next morning. The emotions and attitudes that led to his panic on the afternoon of May 2 remained essentially unchanged despite the varied, agonized, and potentially educational experiences into which his desertion led him that same evening. The fact that these emotions and attitudes were unchanged then led, directly, to his heroic and appropriately acclaimed conduct on the morning of May 3.

Private Fleming's heroic conduct that morning as the flag bearer of his regiment contributed significantly to the capture of a rebel regiment's flag, but by any cool calculation of battlefield effectiveness, that incident illustrated the reverse of what one would anticipate: it illustrated the supremacy of the rebels' skill and courage. In the course of those two days Private Fleming personally changed in no recognizable way at all, although he became convinced he had become "a man." However much "men" may illustrate their condition by not thinking of themselves as "heroes," Private Fleming had, in the arena of public estimation, become a legitimate hero. He ascended to this radiant success in a battle in which his army stumbled into dismaying failure. The absence of any meaningful shape or meaning in Private Fleming's history was exactly the case in the historical battle of Chancellorsville. The Army of the Potomac began the action with brilliant and unparalleled success, proceeded through the action's middle hours garnering even more successes until it was in an overmastering position, and then found itself at the end of the action retreating in bewildered failure. The rebel army began the action in desperate confusion and proceeded through gravely uncertain middle hours to a conclusion in which its characteristic qualities of tactical skill, battlefield courage, and strategic brilliance achieved a startling victory. But, because its best corps commander in the hour of his triumph was mortally wounded by men of his own army, the rebel army ultimately lost far more in its victory than did the Union army in its defeat.

We have "seen" these things only if we have understood both the general facts of infantry combat in the era of the muzzle-loaded rifled musket, which was the era of "the American Civil War," and the specific facts of the battle of Chancellorsville, which took place on the first days of May 1863, in the eastern theater of "the American Civil War." Not to take these things into account, however loosely, is to miss a good deal of the novel's meaning and to remain unvisited by a very great deal of the intellectual, imaginative, and emotional pleasure to be derived from reading and rereading it. The more deeply a reader trusts that Crane had outfitted himself thoughtfully and appropriately with information about the general realities of infantry combat in a war that ended five years before he was born, and with information about the specific facts of a particular battle that took place eight years before he was born, the more rewarding this great novel becomes.

To return to our initiating query: where then did Crane get such precisely detailed information? The one source that is universally acknowledged, that single issue of the *Century Magazine* with its one map and five articles (two of which are entirely irrelevant to Crane's novel) could hardly have sufficed. Remove (as do the authors of the seminal *Crane Log*) Mrs. Olive Brett Armstrong's loan of the far more valuably replete volumes of *Battles and Leaders of the Civil War* from the list of possible sources, and you must assume that Crane sought out those more replete volumes from a library.[7] Once driven to this assumption, why not follow on from there and ask, Would Crane's eye not have fallen immediately upon the gold letters spelling out "Chancellorsville" on the brown, three-inch-wide spine of volume 25 of series 1 of *War of the Rebellion: Official Records of the Union and Confederate Armies?* The plausibility that Crane found his way to just this source is heightened in particular by certain descriptions in *The Red Badge of Courage*, which are to be found in no other published source (see chapters 1 and 3).

Crane's novel is based, as this study has been at pains to show, upon the realities of combat in the era of the muzzle-loaded rifled musket and upon the strategies and the tactics and the operational details that shaped the battle of Chancellorsville. Readers who do not know something about these things are inevitably limited in their ability to respond knowledgeably to the challenges posed by the novel. Conversely, the more a reader knows about these things, the more fascinating, revealing, and convincing the novel becomes. These realities are right at the heart of the novel. It seems to me that Crane assembled them purposefully, wisely, and from the most authoritative sources his hands could reach and his eyes could survey.

7. Wertheim and Sorrentino, *Crane Log*, xviii–xix.

Bibliography

The editions of *The Red Badge of Courage* to which reference has been made throughout this study are as follows:

Crane, Stephen. *The Red Badge of Courage: An Episode of the American Civil War.* New York: D. Appleton and Company, 1895. Facsimile, with introduction by Joseph Katz. Columbus, Ohio: Charles E. Merrill, 1969.
——. *The Red Badge of Courage: An Episode of the American Civil War.* Restoration and introduction by Henry Binder. New York: Avon, 1983.
——. *Stephen Crane's Novel of the Civil War:* The Red Badge of Courage, *an Historically Annotated Edition.* Edited by Charles J. LaRocca. Fleischmann's, NY: Purple Mountain, 1995.

General Bibliography

Aaron, Daniel. *The Unwritten War: American Writers and the Civil War.* New York: Alfred A. Knopf, 1973.
Adams, Michael C. C. *The Great Adventure: Male Desire and the Coming of World War I.* Bloomington: Indiana University Press, 1990.
Alexander, Edward Porter. *Fighting for the Confederacy: The Personal Recollections of General Edward Porter Alexander.* Edited by Gary Gallagher. Chapel Hill: North Carolina University Press, 1989.
Arnold, Matthew. "The Function of Criticism at the Present Time." In *Four*

Essays on Life and Letters, ed. E. K. Brown. New York: Appleton-Century-Crofts, 1947.

Barnett, Corelli. *Bonaparte*. London: George Allen and Unwin, 1978.

Beckett, Samuel. *Waiting for Godot: A Tragicomedy in Two Acts*. New York: Grove Weidenfeld, 1982.

Beer, Thomas. *Stephen Crane: A Study in American Letters*. New York: Knopf, 1923. Reprint, New York: Octagon Books, 1972.

Benfy, Christopher. *The Double Life of Stephen Crane*. New York: Alfred A. Knopf, 1992.

Bergonzi, Bernard. *Heroes' Twilight: A Study of the Literature of the Great War*. New York: Coward-McCann, 1965.

Berryman, John. "Stephen Crane: *The Red Badge of Courage*." In Crane, *Norton Critical Second Edition*, 276–85. Reprinted from chapter 8 of *The American Novel from James Fenimore Cooper to William Faulkner*, ed. Wallace Stegner, 86–96. New York: Basic Books, 1965.

Bierce, Ambrose. *Phantoms of a Blood-stained Period: The Complete Civil War Writings of Ambrose Bierce*. Edited by Russell Duncan and David J. Klooster. Amherst: Massachusetts University Press, 2002.

Boatner, Mark M., III. *The Civil War Dictionary*. New York: Van Rees, 1959.

Booth, Allyson. *Postcards from the Trenches: Negotiating the Space between Modernism and the First World War*. Oxford: Oxford University Press, 1996.

Brontë, Charlotte. *Jane Eyre*. Toronto: Bantam Books, 1981.

Bryant, Sir Arthur. *The Great Duke; or, The Invincible General*. New York: Morrow, 1972.

Cady, Edwin. *Stephen Crane: Revised Edition*. Boston: Twayne, 1980.

Camus, Albert. *The Plague*. Translated by Stuart Gilbert. New York: Vintage Books, 1972.

———. *The Stranger*. Trans. Matthew Ward. New York: Vintage, 1988.

Catton, Bruce. *Glory Road: The Bloody Route from Fredericksburg to Gettysburg*. Garden City: Doubleday, 1952.

———. *Mr. Lincoln's Army*. Garden City: Doubleday, 1951.

Cazemajou, Jean. "*The Red Badge of Courage*: The 'Religion of Peace' and the War Archetype." In Pizer, *Critical Essays*, 144–51. Reprint from *Stephen Crane in Transition: Centenary Essays*, ed. Joseph Katz, 54–65. DeKalb: Northern Illinois University Press, 1972.

Cecil, Hugh. *The Flower of Battle: How Britain Wrote the Great War*. South Royalton, VT: Steerforth, 1996. Originally *The Flower of Battle: British Fiction Writers of the First World War*. England: Seeker and Warburg, 1995.

Chandler, David. *The Campaigns of Napoleon: The Mind and Method of History's Greatest Soldier.* New York: Macmillan, 1966.

Christie, Agatha. "The Mousetrap." 1958.

——. *The Murder of Roger Ackroyd.* New York: Penguin, 2001.

Clausewitz, Carl von. *On War.* Edited and translated by Michael Howard and Peter Paret. New York: Alfred A. Knopf, 1993.

Coggins, Jack. *Arms and Equipment of the Civil War.* New York: Fairfax, 1983.

Colvert, James. "Crane, Hitchcock, and the Binder Edition." In Pizer, *Critical Essays,* 238–64.

——. *Stephen Crane.* New York: Harcourt Brace, 1984.

——. "Stephen Crane's Magic Mountain." In Crane, *Norton Critical Second Edition,* 301–10. Reprinted from *Stephen Crane: A Collection of Critical Essays,* ed. Maurice Bassan, 95–105. Englewood Cliffs, NJ: Prentice-Hall, 1967.

——. "Structure and Theme in Crane's Fiction." In Crane, *Norton Critical Edition,* 336–41. Reprinted from *Modern Fiction Studies* 5 (1959): 199–208.

Conrad, Joseph. *Heart of Darkness: A Norton Critical Edition, Revised.* Edited by Robert Kimbrough. New York: W. W. Norton, 1971.

Cooper, James Fenimore. *The Spy: A Tale of the Neutral Ground.* New York: Heritage Press, 1963.

Cooperman, Stanley. *World War I and the American Novel.* Baltimore: Johns Hopkins University Press, 1967.

Cox, James. "The Imagery of *The Red Badge of Courage.*" In Crane, *Norton Critical Edition,* 313–22. Reprinted from *Modern Fiction Studies* 5 (1959): 209–19.

——. "On Stephen Crane's *Red Badge of Courage.*" In *Classics of Civil War Fiction,* ed. David Madden and Peggy Bach, 44–62. Jackson: University Press of Mississippi, 1991.

Crane, Stephen. *Maggie: A Girl of the Streets.* In *The Red Badge of Courage and Other Writings,* ed. Richard Chase. Boston: Houghton Mifflin, 1960.

——. *The Red Badge of Courage.* Introduction by J. C. Levenson. Charlottesville: Virginia University Press, 1975.

——. *The Red Badge of Courage: A Norton Critical Edition.* Edited by Sculley Bradley, Richard Croom Beatty, and E. Hudson Long. New York: W. W. Norton, 1962.

——. *The Red Badge of Courage: A Norton Critical Edition; Second Edition.* Edited by Sculley Bradley, Richard Croom Beatty, E. Hudson Long, and revised by Donald Pizer. New York: W. W. Norton, 1976.

——. *The Red Badge of Courage: A Norton Critical Edition; Third Edition.* Edited by Donald Pizer. New York: W. W. Norton, 1994.

——. *The Red Badge of Courage and Other Writings.* Edited by Richard Chase. Boston: Houghton Mifflin, 1960.

Crump, Galbraith. *The Mystical Design of Paradise Lost.* Lewisburg, PA: Bucknell University Press, 1975.

Davis, Linda H. *Badge of Courage: The Life of Stephen Crane.* Boston: Houghton Mifflin, 1998.

Davis, William C. "Foreword." In Edward J. Stackpole, *Chancellorsville: Lee's Greatest Battle.* 2nd ed. Harrisburg: Stackpole, 1988.

DeForest, John William. *Miss Ravenal's Conversion from Secession to Loyalty.* New York: Harper and Brothers, 1867. Facsimile edition with an introduction by Arlin Turner. Columbus, OH: Charles E. Merrill, 1969.

Delbanco, Andrew. "The American Stephen Crane: The Context of *The Red Badge of Courage.*" In *New Essays on the Red Badge of Courage,* ed. Lee Clark Mitchell, 49–76. Cambridge: Cambridge University Press, 1986.

Dickens, Charles. *Great Expectations.* Garden City, NY: Doubleday, n.d.

Dickinson, Emily. *The Complete Poems of Emily Dickinson.* Edited by Thomas H. Johnson. Boston: Little, Brown, 1960.

Dillingham, William. "Insensibility in *The Red Badge of Courage.*" In Crane, *Norton Critical Second Edition,* 264–69. Reprinted from *College English* 25 (1963): 194–98.

Dooley, Patrick K. *The Pluralistic Philosophy of Stephen Crane.* Urbana: Illinois University Press, 1993.

——. *Stephen Crane: An Annotated Bibliography of Secondary Scholarship.* New York: G. K. Hall, 1992.

Dreiser, Thomas. *An American Tragedy.* New York: New American Library, 1963.

——. *Sister Carrie.* New York: Bantam, 1958.

Duffy, Christopher. *Frederick the Great: A Military Life.* London: Routledge and Kegan Paul, 1985.

——. *The Military Experience in the Age of Reason.* New York: Atheneum, 1988.

Dupuy, R. Ernest. *A Compact History of the United States Army.* New York: Hawthorne, 1956.

Eissler, K. R. *Freud as an Expert Witness: The Discussion of War Neuroses between Freud and Wagner-Jauregg.* Translated by Christine Trollope. New York: International Universities Press, c. 1986.

Eliot, George. *Middlemarch.* New York: New American Library, 1964.

Elting, John R. *Swords around a Throne: Napoleon's Grande Armee.* New York: Free Press, 1988.

Esposito, Vincent J., and John R. Elting. *A Military History and Atlas of the Napoleonic Wars*. New York: Frederick A. Praeger, 1964.

Esposito, Vincent J., et al. *The West Point Atlas of American Wars*. Vol. 1, *1689–1900*. New York: Frederick A. Praeger, 1959.

Farrell, James T. *Studs Lonigan: A Trilogy*. New York: Modern Library, 1938.

Faulkner, William. *Absalom, Absalom!* New York: Modern Library, 1936.

———. *The Sound and the Fury*. New York: Random House, 1946.

Fenton, Roger. *Roger Fenton, Photographer of the Crimean War: His Photographs and His Letters from the Crimea*. With an essay on his life and work by Helmut and Alison Gernsheim. London: Secker and Warburg, 1954.

Fischer, David Hackett. *Albion's Seed: Four British Folkways in America*. New York: Oxford University Press, 1989.

Fish, Stanley. *Surprised by Sin: The Reader in "Paradise Lost."* Cambridge: Harvard University Press, 1967.

Fitzgerald, F. Scott. *The Great Gatsby*. New York: Charles Scribner's Sons, 1925.

Foote, Shelby. *The Civil War, a Narrative: Fort Sumter to Perryville*. New York: Random House, 1958.

Fowles, John. *The French Lieutenant's Woman*. New York: New American Library, 1970.

Franklin, Benjamin. *Autobiography and Other Writings*. Edited by Russel B. Nye. Boston: Houghton Mifflin, 1958.

Fraser, John. "Crime and Forgiveness: *The Red Badge* in Time of War." In Crane, *Norton Critical Third Edition*, 211–23. Reprinted from *Criticism* 9 (1967): 243–56.

———. *Violence in the Arts*. Cambridge: Cambridge University Press, 1974.

Frassanito, William A. *Antietam: The Photographic Legacy of America's Bloodiest Day*. New York: Charles Scribner's Sons, 1978.

Fried, Michael. *Realism, Writing, Disfiguration: On Thomas Eakins and Stephen Crane*. Chicago: Chicago University Press, 1987.

Furgurson, Ernest B. *Chancellorsville, 1863: The Souls of the Brave*. New York: Alfred A. Knopf, 1992.

Fussell, Paul. *The Great War and Modern Memory*. New York: Oxford University Press, 1975.

Gaff, Alan D. *Bayonets in the Wilderness: Anthony Wayne's Legion in the Old Northwest*. Norman: Oklahoma University Press, 2004.

Garner, Stanton. *The Civil War World of Herman Melville*. Lawrence: Kansas University Press, 1993.

Gibson, Donald. *The Red Badge of Courage: Redefining the Hero.* Boston: Twayne, 1988.

Glover, Michael. *The Napoleonic Wars: An Illustrated History, 1792–1815.* New York: Hippocrene, 1978.

——. *The Peninsular War, 1807–1814: A Concise Military History.* London: David and Charles, 1974.

Graves, Donald E. *Red Coats and Grey Jackets: The Battle of Chippawa, 5 July 1814.* Toronto: Dundurn Press, 1994.

Greenfield, Stanley B. "The Unmistakable Stephen Crane." In Crane, *Norton Critical Edition,* 299–309. Reprinted from *PMLA* 73 (1958): 562–72.

Griffith, Paddy. *Battle in the Civil War: Generalship and Tactics in America, 1861–1865.* Mansfield, Notts., England: Fieldbooks, 1986.

——. *Battle Tactics of the Civil War.* New Haven: Yale, 1989. A reprint of *Rally Once Again.* United Kingdom: Crowood, 1987.

Habegger, Alfred. "Fighting Words: The Talk of Men at War in *The Red Badge.*" In Pizer, *Critical Essays,* 229–37.

Hagerman, Edward. *The American Civil War and the Origins of Modern Warfare: Ideas, Organization, and Field Command.* Bloomington: Indiana University Press, 1988.

Halliburton, Richard. *The Color of the Sky: A Study of Stephen Crane.* Cambridge: Cambridge University Press, 1989.

Harari, Yuval Noah. "Martial Illusions: War and Disillusionment in Twentieth-century and Renaissance Military Memoirs." *Journal of Military History* 69.1 (2005): 43–72.

Hart, John E. "*The Red Badge of Courage* as Myth and Symbol." In Crane, *Norton Critical Third Edition,* 195–203. Reprinted from *University of Kansas City Review* 19 (1953): 249–56.

Hart, Russell A. *Clash of Arms: How the Allies Won in Normandy.* Boulder, CO: Lynne Reimer, 2001.

Hasek, Jaroslav. *The Good Soldier Schweik.* Translated by Paul Selver. Garden City, NY: Doubleday, Doran and Company, 1930.

Hattaway, Herman, and Archer Jones. *How the North Won: A Military History of the Civil War.* Urbana: Illinois University Press, 1983.

Hawthorne, Nathaniel. "The Birthmark." In *Young Goodman Brown and Other Tales.* Oxford: Oxford University Press, 1987.

——. *The House of the Seven Gables.* New York: Bantam, 1968.

——. *The Scarlet Letter: A Romance.* Oxford: Oxford University Press, 1990.

——. "Young Goodman Brown." In *Young Goodman Brown and Other Tales.* Oxford: Oxford University Press, 1987.

Haythornthwaite, Philip. *Uniforms of the Civil War, 1861–1865.* New York: Macmillan, 1975.

Hemingway, Ernest. *A Farewell to Arms.* 1929. New York: Charles Scribner's Sons, 1969.

——. *Men at War.* Edited with an introduction by Ernest Hemingway. Fifth printing. New York: Berkley, 1971.

Henderson, Harry B. "*The Red Badge of Courage:* The Search for Historical Identity." In Crane, *Norton Critical Third Edition,* 234–43. Reprinted from *Versions of the Past: The Historical Imagination in American Fiction,* 219–31. New York: Oxford University Press, 1974.

Homer. *The Iliad.* Translated by Robert Fagles, with introduction and notes by Bernard Knox. New York: Penguin, 1990.

Horsford, Howard. "'He Was a Man.'" In *New Essays on the Red Badge of Courage,* ed. Lee Clark Mitchell, 109–28. Cambridge: Cambridge University Press, 1986.

Hungerford, Harold R. "'That Was at Chancellorsville': The Factual Framework of *The Red Badge of Courage.*" In Crane, *Norton Critical Third Edition,* 147–56. Reprinted from *American Literature* 34 (1963): 520–31.

Hynes, Samuel. *The Soldier's Tale: Bearing Witness to Modern War.* New York: Viking Penguin, 1998.

——. *A War Imagined: The First World War and English Culture.* New York: Atheneum, 1991.

James, Henry. *The Ambassadors.* Edited with introduction and notes by Leon Edel. Boston: Houghton Mifflin, 1960.

Jaynes, Gregory, and the editors of Time-Life Books. *The Killing Ground: Wilderness to Cold Harbor.* Alexandria, VA: Time-Life Books, 1986.

Jaynes, Julian. *The Origin of Consciousness in the Breakdown of the Bicameral Mind.* Boston: Houghton Mifflin, 1976.

Johnson, Robert U., and Clarence C. Buel, eds. *Battles and Leaders of the Civil War: Being for the Most Part Contributions by Union and Confederate Officers.* Four volumes. New York: Century Company, 1887. Reprinted with a new introduction by Roy F. Nichols. New York: Thomas Yoseloff, 1956.

Joyce, James. *Dubliners.* New York: Penguin, 1992.

——. *Ulysses.* New York: Random House, 1961.

Kafka, Franz. "The Hunger Artist." In *Complete Stories,* ed. Nahum N. Glatzer, with a new foreword by John Updike. New York: Schocken Books, 1983.

Kaplan, Amy. "The Spectacle of War in Crane's Revision of History." In *New Essays on the Red Badge of Courage,* ed. Lee C. Mitchell, 77–108. Cambridge: Cambridge University Press, 1986.

Kaplan, Sidney. "Herman Melville and the American National Sin: The Meaning of 'Benito Cereno.'" In *Critical Essays on Herman Melville's "Benito Cereno,"* ed. Robert E. Burkholder, 25–50. New York: G. K. Hall, 1992. Reprinted from *Journal of Negro History* (1957): 18–57.

Katcher, Philip R. N. *The Army of the Potomac.* London: Osprey, 1975.

Katz, Joseph. "Introduction." In Stephen Crane, *The Red Badge of Courage: An Episode of the American Civil War,* v–xiii. New York: D. Appleton and Company, 1895. Facsimile. Columbus, Ohio: Charles E. Merrill, 1969.

Keegan, John. *The Face of Battle.* New York: Viking, 1976.

Kipling, Rudyard. *Rudyard Kipling's Verse: Inclusive Edition, 1885–1926.* New York: Doubleday, Doran, 1931.

———. *A Kipling Pageant.* New York: Literary Guild, 1935.

Knapp, Bettina L. *Stephen Crane.* New York: Ungar, 1987.

LaFrance, Marston. "Private Fleming: His Various Battles." In Crane, *Norton Critical Second Edition,* 333–49. Reprinted from *A Reading of Stephen Crane,* 89–99, 104–24. New York: Oxford University Press, 1971.

Lalumia, Matthew. *Realism and Politics in Victorian Art of the Crimean War.* Ann Arbor: UMI, 1984.

LaRocca, Charles J. "Stephen Crane's Inspiration." *American Heritage* 42.3 (1991): 108–9.

Leithauser, Brad. "A Nasty Dose of Orthodoxy." *New Yorker,* November 7, 1988, 154–58.

Levenson, J. C. "Introduction." In Stephen Crane, *The Red Badge of Courage.* Charlottesville: Virginia University Press, 1975.

———. "*The Red Badge of Courage* and *McTeague.*" In *The Cambridge Companion to American Realism and Naturalism,* ed. Donald Pizer, 154–77. Cambridge: Cambridge University Press, 1995.

Limon, John. *Writing after War: American War Fiction from Realism to Postmodernism.* New York: Oxford University Press, 1994.

Longacre, Edward G. *The Commanders of Chancellorsville: The Gentleman versus the Rogue.* Nashville: Rutledge Hill Press, 2005.

Luvaas, Jay, and Harold W. Nelson. *The U.S. Army War College Guide to the Battles of Chancellorsville and Fredericksburg.* New York: Harper and Row, 1988.

Malraux, André. *Man's Fate.* Translated by Haakon M. Chevalier. New York: H. Smith and R. Haas, 1934.

Marcus, Mordecai. "The Unity of *The Red Badge of Courage.*" In Crane, *Norton Critical Second Edition,* 233–41. Reprinted from *The Red Badge of Courage:*

Text and Criticism, ed. Richard Lettis et al., 189–95. New York: Harcourt Brace, 1960.

McNeill, William H. *The Pursuit of Power: Technology, Armed Force, and Society since A.D. 1000.* Chicago: Chicago University Press, 1982.

McWhiney, Grady, and Perry D. Jamieson. *Attack and Die: Civil War Military Tactics and the Southern Heritage.* University: Alabama University Press, 1982.

Melville, Herman. *Billy Budd, Sailor, and Other Stories.* Introduction by Frederick Busch. New York: Viking Penguin, 1986.

——. *Moby-Dick, or The Whale.* Edited with an introduction and notes by Tony Tanner. Oxford: Oxford University Press, 1988.

——. "Shiloh. A Requiem." In *The Battle-pieces of Herman Melville*, ed. with introduction by Henning Cohen. New York: Thomas Yoseloff, 1963.

Miller, Wayne Charles. *An Armed America, Its Face in Fiction: A History of the American Military Novel.* New York: New York University Press, 1970.

Milner, John. *Art, War and Revolution in France, 1870–1871: Myth, Reportage and Reality.* New Haven: Yale University Press, 2000.

Monteiro, George. *Stephen Crane's Blue Badge of Courage.* Baton Rouge: Louisiana State University Press, 2000.

Muir, Rory. *Salamanca 1812.* New Haven: Yale University Press, 2001.

——. *Tactics and Experience of Battle in the Age of Napoleon.* New Haven: Yale University Press, 1998.

Musick, Michael P. "The Little Regiment: Civil War Units and Commands." http//archives.gov/publications/prologue.

Myatt, F. *The Illustrated Encyclopedia of Nineteenth-century Firearms: An Illustrated History of the Development of the World's Military Firearms during the Nineteenth Century.* New York: Crescent, 1994. Originally published in 1979 by Salamander.

Nafziger, George. *Imperial Bayonets: Tactics of the Napoleonic Battery, Battalion and Brigade as Found in Contemporary Regulations.* London: Greenhill, 1996.

Nagel, James. *Stephen Crane and Literary Impressionism.* University Park: Pennsylvania State University Press, 1980.

Norris, Frank. *McTeague.* New York: Holt, Rinehart and Winston, 1966.

——. *The Octopus.* New York: New American Library, 1964.

Norris, Margot. *Writing War in the Twentieth Century.* Charlottesville: Virginia University Press, 2000.

Nosworthy, Brent. *The Anatomy of Victory: Battle Tactics, 1689–1763.* New York: Hippocrene, 1990.

———. *The Bloody Crucible of Courage: Fighting Methods and Combat Experience of the Civil War*. New York: Carroll and Graf, 2003.

———. *With Musket, Cannon, and Sword: Battle Tactics of Napoleon and His Enemies*. New York: Sarpedon, 1996.

O'Connor, Flannery. *Three by Flannery O'Connor: Wise Blood; The Violent Bear It Away; Everything that Rises Must Converge*. New York: New American Library, 1983.

Patry, Leonce. *The Reality of War: A Memoir of the Franco-Prussian War and the Paris Commune (1870–1871) by a French Officer*. Translated with foreword and notes by Douglas Fermer. London: Cassell, 2001.

Pizer, Donald. "[Crane and *The Red Badge of Courage*: A Guide to Criticism]." In Crane, *Norton Critical Third Edition*, 120–45. The first portion, "Criticism to 1982," is taken from *Fifteen American Authors before 1900: Bibliographical Essays in Research and Criticism*, ed. Earl N. Harbert and Robert A. Rees, 136–37, 146–56, 160–69. Rev. ed. Madison: Wisconsin University Press, 1984.

———, ed. *Critical Essays on Stephen Crane's* The Red Badge of Courage. Boston: G. K. Hall, 1990.

———. "*The Red Badge of Courage*: Text, Theme, and Form." In Crane, *Norton Critical Third Edition*, 257–68. Reprinted from *South Atlantic Quarterly* 84 (1985): 302–13.

Pleasonton, Alfred. "The Successes and Failures of the Chancellorsville Campaign." *Century Illustrated Magazine*, September 1886, 745 ff.

Pratt, Lyndon U. "A Possible Source of *The Red Badge of Courage*." *American Literature* 11 (1939): 1–10.

Pritchett, V. S. "[Crane's Gift for Raising the Veil]." In Crane, *Norton Critical Edition*, 233–37. Excerpted from *The Living Novel*. London: Chatto and Windus, 1946.

Rathbun, John W. "Structure and Meaning in *The Red Badge of Courage*." In Crane, *Norton Critical Second Edition*, 323–33. Reprinted from *Ball State University Forum* 10 (1969): 8–16.

Rechnitz, Robert. "Depersonalization and Dream in *The Red Badge of Courage*." In Pizer, *Critical Essays*, 152–63. Reprinted from *Studies in the Novel* 6 (1974): 76–87.

Reston, James Jr. *Sherman's March and Vietnam*. New York: Macmillan, 1984.

Reynolds, Michael. *Hemingway's First War: The Making of "A Farewell to Arms."* 1976. New York: Basil Blackwell, 1987.

Rhea, Gordon C. *Carrying the Flag: The Story of Private Charles Whilden, the Confederacy's Most Unlikely Hero*. New York: Basic Books, 2004.

Robertson, James I. Jr., and the editors of Time-Life Books. *Tenting Tonight: The Soldier's Life*. Alexandria, VA: Time-Life Books, 1984.

Rothenberg, Gunther E. *The Art of Warfare in the Age of Napoleon*. Bloomington: Indiana University Press, 1978.

Sartre, Jean-Paul. *Nausea*. Translated by Lloyd Alexander. Norfolk, CT: New Directions, 1948.

———. *No Exit, and Three Other Plays*. New York: Vintage, 1973.

Sears, Stephen W. *Chancellorsville*. New York, Houghton Mifflin, 1996.

Shakespeare, William. *William Shakespeare: The Complete Works*. General editor, Alfred Harbage. New York: Penguin, 1969.

Sherry, Vincent. *The Great War and the Language of Modernism*. Oxford: Oxford University Press, 2003.

Solomon, Eric. "A Definition of the War Novel." In Crane, *Norton Critical Third Edition*, 157–62. Reprinted from *Stephen Crane: From Parody to Realism*, 68–77. Cambridge: Harvard University Press, 1966.

———. "The Structure of *The Red Badge of Courage*." In Crane, *Norton Critical Edition*, 323–36. Reprinted from *Modern Fiction Studies* 5 (1959): 220–34.

Sophocles. "Oedipus the King." Translated by David Grene. In *The Complete Greek Tragedies*, vol. 2. Chicago: University of Chicago Press, 1969.

Stackpole, Edward J. *Chancellorsville: Lee's Greatest Battle, Second Edition*. Foreword by William C. Davis. Harrisburg: Stackpole, 1988.

Stallman, Robert W. "Notes toward an Analysis of *The Red Badge of Courage*." In Crane, *Norton Critical Edition*, 248–54. Reprinted from the introduction to *The Red Badge of Courage*, xxii–xxxvii. Modern Library Edition. New York: Random House, 1951.

———. *Stephen Crane: A Biography*. New York: George Braziller, 1968.

Stephen, Martin. *The Price of Pity: Poetry, History, and Myth in the Great War*. London: Leo Cooper, 1996.

Swift, Jonathan. *Gulliver's Travels and Other Writings*. Edited by Louis A. Landa. Boston: Houghton Mifflin, 1960.

Tate, Allen. *The Fathers*. Baton Rouge: Louisiana State University Press, 1977.

Terraine, John. *The Smoke and the Fire: Myths and Anti-myths of War, 1861– 1945*. London: Sidgwick and Jackson, 1981.

Tolstoy, Leo. *The Sebastopol Sketches*. Translated with introduction and notes by David McDuff. London: Penguin Books, 1986.

Trudeau, Noah Andre. *Bloody Roads South: The Wilderness to Cold Harbor, May– June 1864*. New York: Ballantine, 1989.

Tuchman, Barbara. *The First Salute: A View of the American Revolution*. New York: Ballantine, 1988.

Twain, Mark. *Pudd'nhead Wilson*. With a foreword by Wright Morris. New York: New American Library, 1964.

——. *Selected Shorter Writings of Mark Twain*. Edited by Walter Blair. Boston: Houghton Mifflin, 1962.

U.S. Department of War. *The War of the Rebellion: Official Records of the Union and Confederate Armies*. Series 1, vol. 25, part 1. *Reports: Operations in Northern Virginia, West Virginia, Maryland, and Pennsylvania, Jan. 26–June 3, 1863; Chancellorsville*. Serial no. 30. Washington: GPO, 1889.

Vanderbilt, Kermit, and Daniel Weiss. "From Rifleman to Flagbearer: Henry Fleming's Separate Peace in *The Red Badge of Courage*." In Crane, *Norton Critical Second Edition*, 285–94. Reprinted from *Modern Fiction Studies* 11 (1965–1966): 371–80.

Walcutt, Charles C. "[Stephen Crane, Naturalist]." In Crane, *Norton Critical Third Edition*, 204–21. Reprinted from *American Literary Naturalism: A Divided Stream*, vii–viii, 66–67, 74–82. Minneapolis: Minnesota University Press, 1956.

Walker, Alice. *The Color Purple*. New York: Pocket Books, 1982.

Webster, H. T. "Wilbur F. Hinman's *Corporal Si Klegg* and *The Red Badge of Courage*." *American Literature* 11 (1939): 285–93.

Weller, Jac. *The Peninsular War, 1807–1814*. London: David and Charles, 1974.

——. *Wellington at Waterloo*. New York: Thomas Y. Crowell, 1967.

Wertheim, Stanley. *A Stephen Crane Encyclopedia*. Westport, CT: Greenwood, 1997.

Wertheim, Stanley, and Paul Sorrentino. *The Crane Log: A Documentary Life of Stephen Crane, 1871–1900*. New York: G. K. Hall, 1994.

Wharton, Edith. *The House of Mirth*. New York: New American Library, 1964.

Wheeler, Richard. *Lee's Terrible Swift Sword: From Antietam to Chancellorsville, an Eyewitness History*. New York: HarperCollins, 1992.

Wiley, Bell Irvin. *The Common Soldier in the Civil War*. New York: Grosset and Dunlap, 1952.

Winter, Jay. *Sites of Memory, Sites of Mourning: The Great War in European Cultural History*. Cambridge: Cambridge University Press, 1995.

Woolf, Virginia. *To the Lighthouse*. San Diego: Harcourt Brace Jovanovich, 1955.

Wright, Richard. *Native Son*. New York: Harper and Row, 1966.

Young, R. V. *At War with the Word: Literary Theory and Liberal Education*. Wilmington, DE: ISI Books, 1999.

Secondary Bibliography

This bibliography lists those fictions, including films and plays, that are categorized in the parts of this study seeking to identify dominant patterns in post–World War I fictions. (Works marked with an asterisk do not conform to the general pattern defined in Chapter 5.)

Novels

Aldington, Richard. *Death of a Hero.* New York: Covici-Freide, 1929.

Allen, Hervey. *Toward the Flame: A War Memoir.* New York: Farrar and Rinehart, 1926.

Baxter, Walter. *Look Down in Mercy.* New York: Putnam, 1951. London: Viking, 1957.

Becker, Stephen. *When the War Is Over.* New York: Random House, 1969.

Berger, Thomas. *Little Big Man.* New York: Dial Press, 1964.

Bolesvlavski, Richard, in collaboration with Helen Woodward. *The Way of the Lancer.* New York: The Literary Guild, 1932.

Boyd, Thomas. *Through the Wheat.* New York: Charles Scribner's Sons, 1923.

Boyd, William. *An Ice-cream War.* New York: William Morrow, 1983.

Butler, David. *Lusitania.* London: MacDonald, 1981. New York: Random House, 1982.

Clavell, James. *King Rat.* New York: Little Brown, 1962.

Cloete, Stuart. *How Young They Died.* London: The Book Society, 1969.

Cobb, Humphrey. *Paths of Glory.* 1935. Athens: University of Georgia Press, 1987.

Connery, Tom. *Honour Be Damned.* London: Orion, 1998.

——. *Honour Redeemed.* London: Orion, 1997.

——. *A Shred of Honour.* London: Orion, 1996.

Cornwell, Bernard. *Redcoat.* London: Sphere Books, 1988.

——. *Sharpe's Enemy.* New York: Viking, 1984.

——. *Sharpe's Prey.* New York: HarperCollins, 2002.

Cummings, E. E. *The Enormous Room.* 1922. New York: Liveright, 1978.

De Hartog, Jan. *The Captain.* New York: Avon, 1968.

Deighton, Len. *Bomber.* New York: Harper and Row, 1970.

——. *Goodbye, Mickey Mouse.* New York: Ballantine, 1982.

——. *Winter: A Novel of a Berlin Family.* New York: Knopf, 1987.

DeMille, Nelson. *Word of Honor.* New York: Warner, 1985.

Dos Passos, John. *Three Soldiers.* New York: George H. Doran, 1921.

Eagleton, Clive. *A Falcon for the Hawks.* London: Hodder and Stoughton, 1982.

Fagyas, M. *The Devil's Lieutenant. New York: Putnam, 1970.

Farrell, J. G. The Singapore Grip. New York: Knopf, 1980.

——. Troubles. New York: Knopf, 1971.

Fast, Howard. The Hessian. New York: Morrow, 1972.

Faulkes, Sebastian. Birdsong. London: Vintage, 1993.

Findley, Timothy. The Wars. New York: Delacorte/Seymour Lawrence, 1977.

Ford, Ford Madox. Parade's End. New York: New American Library, 1964.

Forbes, Gordon. Goodbye to Some. 1961. New York: Orion, 1990.

Forester, C. S. The General. 1936. London: Penguin, 1975.

Gann, Ernest K. *The Company of Eagles. New York: Simon and Schuster, 1966.

Goddard, Robert. In Pale Battalions. New York: Poseidon, 1978.

Halpert, Sam. A Real Good War. New York: Anchor, 1998.

Harris, John. Covenant with Death. London: Hutchinson, 1961.

——. The Mustering of the Hawks. London: Hutchinson, 1972.

Heller, Joseph. Catch-22. New York: Simon and Schuster, 1961.

Helprin, Mark. *A Soldier of the Great War. New York: Avon, 1981.

Hersey, John. The War Lover. New York: Knopf, 1959.

Holbrook, David. Flesh Wounds. 1966. London: Buchan and Enright, 1987.

Hooker, John. The Bush Soldiers. New York: Viking, 1984.

Hunter, Evan. Sons. New York: Constable, 1969.

Hunter, Jack D. The Blue Max. London: Frederic Muller, 1965.

——. The Flying Cross. New York: Avon, 1987.

Jeal, Tim. Until the Colors Fade. New York: Dell, 1976.

Jones, James. From Here to Eternity. New York: Charles Scribner's Sons, 1951.

——. The Thin Red Line. New York: Charles Scribner's Sons, 1961.

Kennaway, James. Tunes of Glory. New York: Harper, 1956.

Kenneally, Thomas. Gossip from the Forest. Glasgow: William Collins, 1975.

Longstreet, Stephen. A Few Painted Feathers. New York: Doubleday, 1963.

——. War in the Golden Weather. New York: Doubleday, 1965.

Mailer, Norman. The Naked and the Dead. New York: Signet, 1951.

Manning, Frederic. The Middle Parts of Fortune: Somme and Ancre, 1916: The Unexpurgated Edition of the World War I Novel "Her Privates We." London: Mayflower, 1977.

March, William. Company K. 1933. New York: Hill and Wang, 1957.

Masters, John. By the Green of the Spring. London: Sphere, 1984.

——. Heart of War. London: Sphere, 1981.

——. Now, God Be Thanked. New York: Ballantine, 1979.

——. The Ravi Lancers. New York: Doubleday, 1972.

McDonald, Roger. *1915*. Queensland, Australia: University of Queensland Press, 1988.

McGivern, William P. *Soldiers of '44*. New York: Random House, 1979.

Monserrrat, Nicholas. *The Cruel Sea*. New York: Knopf, 1953.

Myrer, Anton. *Once an Eagle*. New York: Holt, Rinehart and Winston, 1968.

O'Brien, Patrick. *Master and Commander*. 1970. New York: W. W. Norton, 1990.

———. *The Yellow Admiral*. New York: W. W. Norton, 1999.

O'Brien, Tim. *Going after Cacciato*. New York: Random House, 1999.

Patrick, William. *Blood Winter*. New York: Viking, 1990.

Pilpel, Robert. *To the Honor of the Fleet*. New York: Fawcett, 1979.

Pynchon, Thomas. *Gravity's Rainbow*. New York: Viking, 1973.

Remarque, Erich Maria. *All Quiet on the Western Front*. Translated by A. W. Wheen. New York: Grosset and Dunlap, 1929.

———. *A Time to Love and a Time to Die*. Translated by Denver Lindley. New York: Harcourt, Brace, 1954.

Robinson, Derek. *Damned Good Show*. London: Cassell, 2002.

———. *A Good Clean Fight*. London: Cassell, 1992.

———. *Goshawk Squadron*. New York: Pocket Books, 1973.

———. *Hornet's Sting*. London: Harville, 1999.

———. *Piece of Cake*. New York: Knopf, 1984.

———. *War Story*. London: Pan, 1988.

Rock, Phillip. *The Passing Bells*. New York: Seaview, 1978.

Roth, Joseph. *The Radetzky March*. 1932. Translated by Eva Tucker, based on an earlier translation by Geoffrey Dunlop. New York: Overlook, 1974.

Salter, James. *The Hunters*. 1956. New York: Vintage, 2001.

Sassoon, Siegfried. *The Memoirs of George Sherston: Memoirs of a Fox-hunting Man; Memoirs of an Infantry Officer; Sherston's Progress*. New York: Literary Guild, 1937.

Scannell, Vernon. *Argument of Kings: An Autobiography*. London: Robson Books, 1987.

Shaw, Irwin. *The Young Lions*. New York: Random House, 1948.

Shepard, Jim. *Paper Doll*. New York: Dell, 1986.

Sillitoe, Alan. *The Widower's Son*. London: W. H. Allen, 1978.

Smith, Frederick E. *A Killing for the Hawks*. New York: Ace, 1966.

Trumbo, Dalton. *Johnny Got His Gun*. New York: L. Stuart, 1959.

Vonnegut, Kurt. *Slaughterhouse-five or the Children's Crusade: A Duty-dance with Death*. 1969. New York: Laurel, 1991.

Wagner, Geoffrey. *The Killing Time*. New York: Kensington, 1985.

———. *Sands of Valor.* New York: Kensington, 1967.

Watkins, Paul. *Night over Day over Night.* New York: Avon Books, 1988.

Waugh, Evelyn. *Sword of Honour.* London: Chatto and Windus, 1961.

Werfel, Franz. *The Forty Days of Musa Dagh.* Translated by Geoffrey Dunlop. New York: Viking, 1934.

Williamson, Henry. *Patriot's Progress: Being the Vicissitudes of Pte. John Bullock.* London: Sphere, 1930.

Wouk, Herman. *The Caine Mutiny, a Novel of World War II.* Garden City, NY: Doubleday, 1952.

Yeates, V. M. *Winged Victory.* London: Buchan and Enright, 1934.

Zola, Emile. *The Debacle.* Translated by Leonard Tancock. Harmondsworth: Penguin, 1972.

Zweig, Arnold. *The Case of Sergeant Grischa.* Translated by Eric Sutton. New York: Viking, 1928.

———. *Education before Verdun.* Translated by Eric Sutton. New York: Viking, 1936.

Films and Dramatic Works

"All Quiet on the Western Front." 1930. Directed by Lewis Milestone.

*"Anzacs." 1985. Directed by Pino Manta, John Dixon, et al.

"Apocalypse Now." 1979. Directed by Francis Ford Coppola.

"Attack." 1956. Directed by Robert Aldrich.

"Battle of the Bulge." 1965. Directed by Ken Annakin.

"The Blue Max." 1966. Directed by John Guillerman.

"The Boat" [*Das Boot*]. 1981. Directed by Wolfgang Peterson.

"Born on the Fourth of July." 1989. Directed by Oliver Stone.

"Breaker Morant." 1980. Directed by Bruce Beresford.

"The Bridge on the River Kwai." 1957. Directed by David Lean.

"The Brig." 1957. Playwright Kenneth Brown.

"Casualties of War." 1989. Directed by Brian De Palma.

"The Charge of the Light Brigade." 1968. Directed by Tony Richardson.

"Dances with Wolves." 1990. Directed by Kevin Costner.

"The Dawn Patrol." 1938. Directed by Edmund Goulding.

"From Here to Eternity." 1953. Directed by Fred Zinneman.

"Full Metal Jacket." 1987. Directed by Stanley Kubrick.

"Gallipoli." 1981. Directed by Peter Weir.

"Hamburger Hill." 1981. Directed by John Irvin.

"The Hill." 1965. Directed by Stanley Lumet.

"How I Won the War." 1967. Directed by Richard Lester.

"The Jewel in the Crown." 1984. Directed by Christopher Morahan and Jim O'Brien.

"Journey's End." 1928. Playwright R. C. Sherriff.

"King and Country." 1964. Directed by Joseph Losey.

"King of Hearts" [Le Roi de Coeur]. 1966. Directed by Philippe de Broca.

*"The Lighthorsemen." 1987. Directed by Simon Wincer.

"Mister Roberts." 1955. Directed by John Ford.

"Oh! What a Lovely War!" 1969. Directed by Richard Attenborough.

"Paths of Glory." 1957. Directed by Stanley Kubrick.

*"Patton." 1970. Directed by Franklin Schaffner.

"Platoon." 1986. Directed by Oliver Stone.

"Pork Chop Hill." 1959. Directed by Lewis Milestone.

"The Real Inspector Hound." 1968. Playwright Tom Stoppard.

"The Red Badge of Courage." 1951. Directed by John Huston.

"The Red Badge of Courage." 1974. Directed by Lee Philips.

*"Saving Private Ryan." 1998. Directed by Stephen Spielberg.

"Seven Samurai." 1954. Directed by Akira Kurosawa.

"Streamers." 1983. Playwright David Rabe.

"They Came to Cordura." 1959. Directed by Robert Rossen.

"The Thin Red Line." 1964. Directed by Andrew Martin.

"The Thin Red Line." 1998. Directed by Terrence Malick.

"Too Late the Hero." 1970. Directed by Robert Aldrich.

*"Twelve O'Clock High." 1949. Directed by Henry King.

"The War Lover." 1962. Directed by Philip Leacock.

"The Young Lions." 1958. Directed by Edward Dmytryk.

*"Zulu." 1964. Directed by Cy Enfield.

"Zulu Dawn." 1979. Directed by Douglas Hickox.

Index

Note: *RBC* refers to *The Red Badge of Courage*

Aaron, Daniel, 118–19, 139–40, 268, 311
Absalom, Absalom! (Faulkner), 298
Adams, Michael C. C., 268, 280, 311
Adventures of Huckleberry Finn (Twain), 46, 310
Age of Reason, 56, 60, 127
Albright's brigade, 209–12, 215
Alexander, E. P., 202
"All Quiet on the Western Front" (film), 133, 133n29, 273, 284
All Quiet on the Western Front (Remarque): as antiwar novel, 273, 277; artillery in, 135n33; Baumer in, 141, 278, 291; on brutality of modern war, 283n13; as fictional response to World War I, 49, 129; hero's experience of combat in, 290; and historical reality, 49; irony of title of, 133; and myth of malevolent universe, 281n11; and romanticism as misleading, 134n30, 140; stereotypical ideals and preconceptions in, 137n38; and virtues of comradeship, friendship, and love, 278
Ambassadors, The (James), 146, 163, 164, 299
American Tragedy, An (Dreiser), 296
Anderson, Richard H., 46, 47, 80, 206, 229
Animal imagery, 103, 104, 105, 121–24, 193, 195, 216, 222, 224, 256, 295. *See also* Imagery and figurative language
Antietam, battle of, 71–72, 79, 200, 210, 276, 316–17
"Anzacs," 136n35
"Apocalypse Now," 134n30, 135n32, 137n38, 273, 284
Appleton edition (1895) of *The Red Badge of Courage*, 4, 158
Archer, James J., 202
Aristotle, 146, 321
Armstrong, Mrs. Olive Brett, 322–23
Army of Northern Virginia: casualties of, 33, 71, 178, 216; combat leadership of, 45–46; commander of, 10; and flags, 24, 45, 206; at Fredericksburg, Va., 27, 28, 29, 33, 38; uniforms of, 78, 206–7. *See also* Chancellorsville campaign; Lee, R. E.; and specific generals and battles
Army of Tennessee, 72, 113, 201n3
Army of the Potomac: approaches to Chancellorsville by, 28–30; casualties of, 23, 33, 71, 79, 172–74, 205, 216; commander of, 10, 27; at Falmouth, 27, 32–33, 38, 64; size of, 85; tactical situation of, after Hooker's retreat from Wilderness, 7. *See*

DATE DUE
